Ancient Greek France

Ancient Greek France

A. Trevor Hodge

Duckworth

First published in 1998 by
Gerald Duckworth & Co. Ltd.
61 Frith Street, London W1V 5TA

A catalogue record for this book is available
from the British Library

ISBN 0 7156 2796 1

Illustrations: acknowledgements

Figs. 8, 9: Ömer Özygit; Fig. 15: M.E. Aubet; Fig. 16: M. Ponisch; Fig. 27: G. Denizot; Fig. 68: M. Sciallano and P. Sibella; Fig. 76: CNRS / A. Carrié; Fig. 82: A. Rivet; Fig. 90: E. Ripoli Perelló; Figs. 112, 123: J. Bromwich; Fig. 113: J.-P. Clébert; Figs 116,129: R. Ambard.

Typeset by Ray Davies
Printed in Great Britain by
Redwood Books Ltd, Trowbridge

Contents

to
FRED HODGE
et, comme toujours,
à ma
COCO

Preface

Writing a preface one is soon threatened with impalement on the two horns of a dilemma. Traditionally the chief function of a preface is to acknowledge one's indebtedness to all the people who have helped in the creation of the book. This is one horn, for one is embarrassingly mindful of the acceptance speeches at the Oscar awards for films, where the recipient drags out an endless list of people without whom the film could not have been made, forging grimly ahead through scriptwriter, cameraman, gaffer and best boy, while the TV audience wishes he would just get on with it and get it over. To a book such as this, this is a real problem, for the author is all too conscious of the very many people to whom a real debt is owed, for grants, providing photographs, travel assistance, facilitated access to sites and libraries, advice, translation, typing, critiques, and aid of every kind in producing the book. To all of these sources is owed a debt of cheerful gratitude, a debt that is readily and willingly paid. But here comes the dilemma's other horn. If you are going to give coverage as full as that, what happens if you accidentally leave somebody out? This is not a theoretical, academic problem. I myself, in my previous work, have actually done it, and though it is usually greeted with a courteously tactful silence, I do not like the feeling when I become aware of it.

Let me then begin by acknowledging what is easily the greatest financial contribution to the writing of this book. It comes from Carleton University, my employer while I was working on it. I do not here speak of research grants or the like, but of the simple fact that, as a professor, I was paid my regular salary all the time that I was engaged in this way. The book was written, so to speak, 'in the firm's time', which in turn, since, like most universities, Carleton is largely state-supported, means that it was paid for by the Canadian taxpayers. For an academic, of course, there is nothing unusual about this, but, by professors and the general public alike, it is often forgotten; so, as the purchaser digs into his or her pocket to pay for this book, it should be remembered that, were it not for this very large hidden subsidy, the digging would have to go much deeper, if indeed, the book could ever have been published at all.

But I must supplement this general acknowledgment with some more precisely directed animadversions. The Social Sciences and Humanities Research Council of Canada assisted most generously with grants spread over several years, enabling me to travel in the relevant areas in France, and Carleton, in the form of a Research Achievement Award, released me for a year from teaching duties to concentrate on the writing and presentation of my work, a liberality that led the Faculty of Graduate Studies and Research to make various awards covering secretarial assistance.

In France my work has always centred upon the excellent library and other facilities of the Centre Camille Jullian at the Université de Provence, Aix-en-Provence, and I am appropriately grateful to its then Director, M. Maurice Euzennat, and later his successor Pierre Gros, for opening their doors to me. To Dr. A. Tschernia, noted for his work on ancient wine amphorae, I owe a special debt for his interest and understanding as also to many of my 'pro tem' colleagues at the Centre. In the British School at Ankara, where I went in pursuit of material on Massalia's mother city, Phocaea, I was warmly received by the hospitality of its Director, Dr. David French.

At the publishers, Duckworth, it was the sanspareil Colin Haycraft who accepted this work for publication, and after his death the Duckworth staff, notably Deborah Blake, continued the various formalities of production in a spirit of patient and understanding flexibility worthy of Mr. Haycraft himself. To Beverley Hall, formerly Classics Department Administrator of Carleton University in Ottawa, I am indebted for her professional skills at the word-processor for transmuting my (very small) handwriting into a format digestible by the criteria of modern publishing, and to Katherine McKinnon, who successfully wrestled with the production of the bibliography. And my appreciative thanks are particularly offered to the Department of Mechanical Engineering at Monash University, Melbourne, Australia for their ready, courteous and highly efficient assistance in preparing this book, during my time there as a Visiting Professor.

Lastly, there remains the dedication. Normally a dedication is not explained by the author, who leaves it in some enigmatic form such as 'To B.L.J.', but I would wish to make an exception. Author's wives always have a lot to put up with while 'the book' is being written, and I am glad to dedicate this book to mine. The other name is my father. A fine man, but of simple standing and education – after serving in France in 1914-18, he spent the rest of his life as a motor mechanic in a Belfast garage – he was such that I am proud to honour him in any way that I can. He died without ever having seen a book that I had written, and before my marriage. My wife has often said how she wishes she could, just once, have met him. So let them then both share the dedication page of this book. It is the best I can do.

Carleton University   A.T.H.
Ottawa, Canada
  and
Monash University
Melbourne, Australia

1

Introduction

'Massalia: the Oldest City in Western Europe'. Such is the title of a public lecture that I have often given, based more or less on a condensed version of the content of this book. I usually have to apologise for the title, for it invites dispute. What about Syracuse? Rome? Were they not founded before Massalia? By constructive hair-splitting I can usually justify my

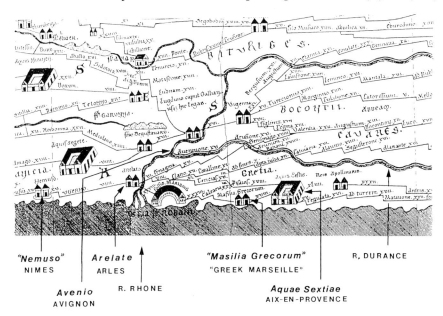

"Nemuso"   *Arelate*   *"Masilia Grecorum"*   R, DURANCE
NIMES   ARLES   "GREEK MARSEILLE"

Avenio   R. RHONE   *Aquae Sextiae*
AVIGNON   AIX-EN-PROVENCE

1. The area around Massalia as shown on the Peutinger Table, a Roman itinerary or road map (twelfth-century copy of a fourth-century AD original). The geographical shape is unrealistic, with north-south distances very compressed and the east-west axis elongated, so that the map could be rolled up on a scroll. The thin lines, mostly horizontal, are roads, and the small zig-zags or jogs are overnight stopping places. The cartographer seems to have had a very exaggerated idea of the importance of Ostium Massiliense ('Port Marseille'), as represented by the imposing semicircular structure at the mouth of the Rhône, in comparison with the minor recognition accorded Massalia itself, a little to the east. The Fossae Marianae (the Rhône Ship Canal, built by Marius) is also shown, running from the Ostium to Arelate, which, moreover, is marked on the wrong side of the river; for the Ostium and the Fossae, see pp. 148-9. The identification as Ancient Greek France is supported by the inscription, just above Massalia, 'Gretia', i.e. Greece.

1

choice. Syracuse after all was in Sicily, an island – does that count as Western Europe? And Rome, though founded long before Massalia (the traditional dates are Rome 753 BC, and Massalia, 600), got off to a very slow start, and was for a long time not a city but a collection of herdsmen's huts at a convenient crossing of the Tiber, while Massalia was a fully-fledged Greek *polis* right from its foundation, with an army, navy, coinage, a constitution, and all the other appurtenances that came with acceptance and recognition in the Hellenic world. And, once founded, Massalia never faltered, continuing in flourishing and unbroken existence right down to today, a chequered history well illustrated by the four names under which the city has, at different times, been known: Massalia (Greek), Massilia (Latin), Marisho (Provençal), and Marseille (French).

Despite this distinction, however, there is much about the ancient city that remains shadowy, problematic, even enigmatic. With this cloud hanging over us, it will be well to begin with a clear statement of our scope and aims which will at least remove misapprehension and mistaken expectations. Greek Massalia began with the foundation of the city in 600 BC, more or less, as an overseas colony of the Greek Ionian state of Phocaea, in Asia Minor, not far from the modern Izmir. It lasted until the conquest by siege (49 BC) by the forces of Julius Caesar in his Civil War with Pompey, a conflict in which the Massaliots, though they tried hard to remain neutral, found themselves eventually driven to declare for Pompey (which, as it turned out, was the wrong side to be on). Our study will be limited by these two dates, making it a survey of Greek Massalia in the days of its independence, excluding (except for a brief note) Roman Massilia, when it had been politically absorbed into the Empire. Because the existence of Massalia was so closely bound up with the life of other Greek cities along the coast of the region, and some of them were actually founded as sub-colonies of Massalia itself, though it is not always sure which, we will enlarge our scope to cover the whole history of Greek colonisation in the South of France, ranging from Monaco and the modern Italian border to Ampurias in Spain. This will, I hope, give us reasonable coverage of what I have termed Ancient Greek France. Moreover, because the interplay, commercial and other, with the Celtic tribes inhabiting the interior, was so vital a feature in the story of Massalia, to that too we will turn our attention; but the reader hoping for a comprehensive account of Celtic Gaul must be warned against a disappointment, for that will concern us only in so far as the Celts impinged upon Massalia and the Greeks. No man is an island, especially not a Greek living in Celtic Gaul, but we must draw the line somewhere.

So what is the enigma? The enigma lies in the evaluation of Massalia. It breaks into two halves. The first half is the modern interpretation. Speak of Massalia to just about any classical scholar (except perhaps a French one) and the reaction is the same: 'Ah, yes, we must never forget the importance of Massalia – the western bastion of Hellenic culture amid barbaric lands, guardian of the access to the Rhône valley, the gateway for

2

classical civilisation to enter the whole of Northern Europe – no, we must never forget Massalia!' The scholar may well accompany this with a slightly guilty start, for in truth, until his memory was jogged, he really *had* forgotten about it. A good deal of lip service is paid to the pre-eminence of Massalia, but one can read the whole narrative of Greek history and never find Massalia appearing in it, or only very rarely. Even its mother city Phocaea is not prominent in any History of Greece, much less its Celtic offspring. And for actual detailed evidence, facts with identifiable names attached to them, one is reduced to the account of the explorer Pytheas (and there is no overestimating *him*) and the insurance fraud of Zeno-themis and Hegestratos (known only because it formed the basis of a forensic oration by Demosthenes,[1] and yet, though a small and isolated case, often adduced as evidence for the extent and practices of Massaliot commerce in general – simply because it is almost the only scrap of written evidence that we have). There is also a series of some five epitaphs of Massaliot citizens who died at Athens. This epigraphical evidence, dating from the third century BC, is not widely referred to or discussed, nor is it easy to form from it any interpretation bearing on our main theme, though it may suggest the presence at Athens of a small colony of Massaliot expatriates, which may, or may not, reflect trading connections.[2] There are also the architectural remains of the fine Treasury of Massalia at Delphi. This represents about the sum total of Massaliot input into Greek history. Its input into Roman, as a naval ally, is rather greater, but there again there is a proviso. Roman history is naturally Rome-centred, so once again we find Massalia playing what seems to us a relatively minor role. The history of Massalia therefore appears to us like the tip of an iceberg protruding above the waves, but, we are confident, only a portion of something much greater – if only we could see it and get at it. We are convinced that it is there, or at least ought to be, but actual access is almost impossible. That is the enigma of Massalia, as seen from the modern viewpoint. Massalia is the forgettable colossus.

Probably as a result of this lacuna, scholarship has concentrated on the few avenues where research into Massalia, and its associate Greek settle-ments along the coast, is actually possible. In simple terms, this means that there has been a great emphasis on archaeology. Even within the archaeological parameters, however, there are further limits and restric-tions. Not too much can be done in architecture since most of the sites lie underneath modern cities, making excavation expensive and difficult – it is unusual to find somewhere right out in the open, like Saint Blaise; somewhere like Antibes, where the modern city is on top of the ancient one, represents the more prevalent pattern. Sculptural findings are rare. The result of this is that there have been very extensive studies of the one thing found in profusion, broken fragments of pots. Massaliot studies are therefore heavily biassed towards exhaustive and complicated analyses of ceramic sherds, a bias that, though reasonable and proper in itself, and one leading to an understanding of ancient economics and trade patterns, yet offers an inhospitable welcome to the reader who is a beginner in the field. This is one reason why ceramics play a relatively small part in this book. Archaeologists who have worked long and productively in the South of France may be disappointed in the following pages, feeling that they pay too little attention to the bulk of current work in the field, but that is the reason why. Instead, I have tried to present as comprehensive an overall picture as possible; with what success, the reader must judge.

The second half of the enigma is the ancient view of Massalia. What did the ancients, Greeks especially, think of it and what sort of reputation did it have? And this also must rank as an enigma because we get very conflicting signals. They reflect not so much its historical or economic standing as its morals. Romans, almost without exception (but led by Cicero) were fulsome in their admiration, praising the Massaliots as a kind of puritan supermen, while speaking of their politics and foreign policy in terminology that tends painfully to remind a modern ear of a right-winger speaking of a friendly banana republic. Greeks had a rather different approach, and tended rather to see Massalia as a kind of 'Naughty Paree, O-la-la!' For one thing, the citizens of Massalia were notoriously effeminate: they wore floor-length tunics, which proved it.[3] Moreover, their morals matched their dress, so that 'going to Massalia' came to be used proverbially as something equivalent to 'going to the dogs'. Suidas, indeed, in his lexicon, quotes such a proverb, which was apparently also current at Alexandria.[4] This reputation evidently spread as far as the Roman comic dramatist Plautus, who refers to it in his play the *Casina* – somewhat atypically for a Roman, but Plautus was early, before the contrary view, endemic in the late Republic, became established.[5]

None of these doubts or variations of the enigma should inhibit our further study of Massalia. It really was a city of first importance, for the economic and social development of the Celtic world if not for its contribution to Greek history. It was through Massalia that Gaul got its first taste of classical civilisation, long before Caesar's legions got anywhere near the place, and when they did we may surely surmise that the onward march of Romanisation often found the way before it already paved by the influence of Massalia. From Massalia the Celts acquired an alphabet, literacy, an exposure to Hellenic ideas, a taste for comfortable living and a taste for wine. It was Rome, with its legacy of the long occupation of Gaul, that irrevocably turned France, in its national attitudes, to face the Mediterranean, and to become in its outlook to a large extent a Mediterranean country (just as it signally did not do so in Britain). But the first turn to that benevolent and beneficent screw was assuredly given by Massalia. This is why Massalia and its history merit our attention.

In view of this it is surprising to find that the Greek colonisation of the South of France is so little studied and known even in France itself. Marseille has its own traditions and stereotypes, and Marius (all Marseillais are called Marius, just as all Scotsmen are called Jock and all Irishmen Paddy) is a familiar figure in French jokes, easily recognisable

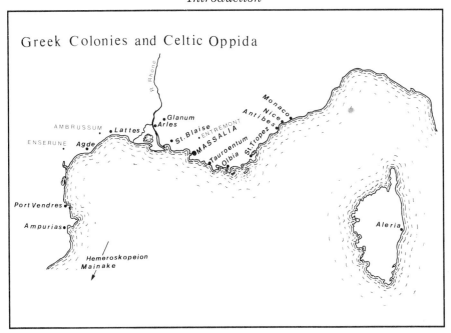

Greek Colonies and Celtic Oppida

2. Greek (mostly Phocaean) colonies in the South of France (detailed account, pp. 138-93) and Celtic centres (pp. 195-208).

from his Texan-like boastful exaggeration,[6] but the early role of Marseille in the introduction of classical civilisation is much less recognised. Indeed, French education usually has accepted only two strands in the early formation of France – Caesar and his legions and 'nos pères, les Gaulois'.[7] The residents of Marseille naturally see it somewhat differently, considering their city's history has been undeservedly neglected, and themselves short-changed, largely through the baneful influence of those faceless aliens who, the French generally agree, are responsible for most of what is wrong in France – 'les Parisiens'. This is not true of French scholars based in the South of France, notably in the Université de Provence and even more in its chief Centre of Archaeological Studies, Aix-en-Provence, whose work has given us almost all that we know about Greek France, but it remains true that the material is scattered through many disparate publications, and is seldom available in any conveniently comprehensive form, such as is attempted in this book.[8] In the nineteenth century the local antiquary Josef Méry indignantly described Marseille as a 'ville antique sans antiquités'. He did not mean it as a compliment, and much of that indifference to its archaeological past that so enraged him has now been dissipated. But in the field of publication there is still leeway to make up, particularly among non-French classical historians. We will make the attempt.

5

We will begin, as the Greek settlers did, in Phocaea, the mother city of Massalia, and then follow their route by sea across the Mediterranean to Provence. We will continue this logical sequence by turning to the land that awaited them, and its topographical characteristics. Thence we will concentrate on their chief foundation, the city of Massalia – what we know of its history, political constitution, economics, and culture. To establish further the regional context, we will then leave it and move along the coast to cover in order the other Greek settlements, moving first to the west towards Spain (including, perhaps illogically, Corsica), then east to the Italian border. We will then advance to look at the Celts of the interior with whom they had commercial and other dealings, with a brief note on relations with Rome. Our conclusion will be the hardest test, for we must then try to give some kind of summary evaluation of Massalia, Greek France, its importance, and its contribution to the march of history. Given the enigma already enunciated, that will not be easy nor can satisfaction be guaranteed, but I can perhaps offer one palliative to the prospective bitterness of the pill: after all the data, such as it is, has been assembled and assimilated, all readers, general and specialists alike, are cordially invited to form their own opinions and conclusions.

2

Phocaea, the Mother City

Phocaea, the mother city that founded the colony of Massalia, was a Greek city on the Aegean coast of modern Turkey. Today known as Foça, it is a small resort and fishing port 70 km north-west of Izmir (ancient Smyrna), boasting as yet but little in the way of classical remains, though this will certainly be changed by continuing excavation. The colonists that founded Phocaea itself were Ionian Greeks, led, so affirmed ancient tradition, by a pair of Athenians, Philogenes and Damon.[1] The site was supposedly given to them by the nearby city of Cyme, on the borders of Ionia proper and Aeolis,[2] and the date, as established by pottery finds, was in the ninth century BC. According to Pausanias the settlers came from the Ionian cities of Teos and Erythrai, whence came also a dynasty of three kings, Deoites, Periclos and Abartos, but the reader must be warned that the history of this early period is very shadowy, and the sources often offer contradictions on points of detail.[3] The main picture is clear, however. The new foundation prospered, and was soon accepted into the Panionion, a local league of prominent Ionian cities.[4] In turn it then founded Lampsacus, on the Hellespont, and Amisos (Samsun), on the Black Sea, and shared with other Ionian Greeks in the foundation of the important trading post of Naucratis in Egypt.[5]

From the beginning, Phocaea was a maritime city, indeed a piratical one, for in the Archaic Age the line between piracy and legitimate commerce was often a thin one, and very blurred. And, far from seeing anything morally wrong with piracy, contemporary society appears often to have respected and admired it as a laudably virile and macho trade, perhaps reminiscent of some modern attitudes towards mercenaries and 'soldiers of fortune'. To this the Phocaeans were probably driven because of the agricultural poverty of their homeland,[6] and when they came to plant colonies overseas they apparently planted this piratical tradition with them, especially at Alalia in Corsica.[7] Accordingly, around the seventh/sixth century BC, from Phocaea came a great wave of western expansion and colonisation that turned the Western Mediterranean into a Phocaean lake (at least as far as the Greeks were concerned, if one forgets the Phoenicians and Etruscans). One may ask why they concentrated so much of their efforts on so distant a region. There were probably two reasons. One is availability. The great period of Greek colonisation came rather earlier than the peak of Phocaean. The earliest Western Greek colony was traditionally Cumae, believed by the Greeks to have been founded, by Euboea, around 1,000 BC, and in reality probably around 750 BC. This was followed by a large number of similar or analogous foundations that dotted Southern Italy and Eastern Sicily – e.g. Syracuse (founded 734 BC), Sybaris (c. 720), Taras (Taranto – c. 700), Megara Hyblaea (c. 750), Zankle (Messina – c. 750), Metaponto (c. 700), Gela (689), Neapolis (Naples – 650). With mainland Greece and Ionia already fully occupied, Cyrenaica (i.e. Libya) under the control of Cyrene (founded c. 630), the Phoenicians holding the Levant, North Africa, Western Sicily, and Southern Spain, the Etruscans entrenched in Northern Italy and as far round the coast as Genoa, while the Egyptians, not unreasonably, occupied Egypt, the Phocaeans really had very little choice in available real estate open to their colonists. The only alternatives to Provence were perhaps the Adriatic, where the Dalmatian coast offered little natural inducement to anyone – despite being just across the sea from Italy it did not become formally part of the Roman Empire until Augustus – and the Euxine (Black Sea) where indeed some colonies were founded, but which was always difficult of access because of the very strong current regularly coming down the Bosphoros. Put simply, therefore, the Phocaeans had to go to the furthest shores of the Mediterranean to plant their colonies because that was all that was left.

The other reason that drew the Phocaeans, like a magnet, to the west, was Tartessos. We will consider this more fully in a later chapter (p. 167ff.), but here may note that it abounded in metals, base and precious alike, in quantities and ready availability to make it a rich prize for any venturesome merchant. The trade route was opened by Colaios of Samos, whose ship was blown by a freak storm from Cyrene the whole way down the Mediterranean to Gibraltar, and out through the Straits to Tartessos.[8] The Phoenicians seem to have installed themselves in the region at an equally early date – hence their occupation of the Balearics and Southern Spain to safeguard the route – but do seem to have made themselves *persona non grata* at Tartessos, judging by the warm welcome there extended to their Greek rivals. It was evidently a triumph of personal diplomacy, for the King of Tartessos, Arganthonios, became a strong philhellene, demonstrating his goodwill by paying for the building of the city walls around Phocaea. From Tartessos, Greek imports were bronze and tin originating either in Tartessos itself or coming through it from further afield, such as Brittany or the Scillies; and, among precious metals, gold and silver, which Tartessos seems to have possessed in abundance[9] – one is struck by the parallel with the enormous cargoes of gold sent home from the Spanish Main by the *conquistadores*. Such, at all events, were the reasons for the string of Phocaean colonies founded in the West. Such were the reasons for the existence of Massalia.

Compared with other classical cities, our knowledge of the history of Massalia is indeed shadowy and fragmentary; that of Phocaea is, if anything, ten times more so. Indeed, we know very little of what happened to it between the foundation of its colonies and its capture in 546 by the Persians under Harpagos.[10] He apparently achieved this by heaping up an enormous siege mound, presumably against the wall provided by Arganthonios, though we do not actually hear of what role it played. The Phocaean population then emigrated overseas to their own colonies, though some of them returned afterwards. Phocaea, however, never regained its former glory and importance. At the battle of Lade (494) it contributed only three ships to a fleet of some 353, though, possibly because of its naval reputation, the command of the entire fleet was given to a Phocaean, Dionysios.[11] The further detailed history of Phocaea need not concern us here. Suffice it to say that it was a minor member of the Delian League, its annual tribune being rated at two talents, and ended up as part of the Seleucid, then of the Attalid, empires. In 132 it might have come to an inglorious end, having joined the revolt against Rome led by Aristonikos, and escaped disaster only because the victorious Romans were talked out of it by their firm friend and Phocaea's loyal daughter – Massalia.

On the economic and cultural front, we may note that Phocaea was famous for its purple dye, and also for its electrum coinage, which was one of the chief currencies of the region until the coming of Alexander the Great.[12] In mainland Greece, the Roman writer Vitruvius tells us that a Phocaean architect, Theodoros, wrote a book on the Tholos at Delphi; from this we may infer, though we cannot be sure, that he designed and built it. The Tholos, of course, still survives, as one of Delphi's most-visited tourist attractions. At Phocaea itself there was a famed sixth-century temple of Athena (the chief deity worshipped there), which, even after it was burned by the Persians, was, in the opinion of Pausanias, 'still wonderful', having been restored afterwards.[13]

Topography and archaeology

The topography[14] of Phocaea is shown in the area plan (Fig. 3). Central to it, both geographically and in importance, is a small peninsula jutting out into the sea, today the location of a secondary school. It is broad and flat on top, with steep sides, making it highly attractive as an acropolis – indeed, if one forgets the surrounding sea, it is hard to look at its surface and not be reminded of the Acropolis at Athens. It is here that was located the Temple of Athena, of which various surviving architectural fragments, including a disc akroterion, are now in the Izmir museum.[15] The peninsula itself must have been an attractive feature, for it offered a natural harbour on each side (that on the north was known as the Lampter, the southern one as the Naustathmos), a situation much prized by early mariners, for it guaranteed that, whatever the direction of the wind, one side or the other always offered a sheltered anchorage.[16] Beyond the peninsula the classical city extended for some distance away from the shore, though only to a maximum of 1 km, and usually only half that. Despite its outstanding

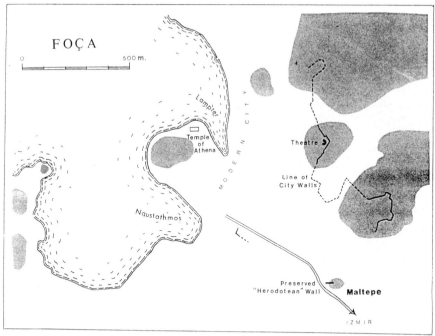

3. Sketch map of modern Foça (ancient Phocaea), showing antiquities. For location of Phocaea, See Fig. 15.

record as a colonising power, Phocaea itself was always relatively small in extent, and hemmed in by hills.[17] Offshore lay a number of small islets that not only offered some shelter from stress of weather, but, some maintain, from their superficial resemblance to seals, gave the city its name,

4. General view of modern Foça taken from Maltepe (Fig. 3), and showing offshore islands (compare with Massalia, Figs. 40, 52).

2. Phocaea, the Mother City

5. Foça: the ancient acropolis (?), viewed from the north, across the Lampter (ancient harbour). The building at the top is a school, near which was presumably located the temple of Athena.

6. The modern citizens of Foça often celebrate their ancestry from ancient 'Fokaia', as in this waterfront café where the menu, working up from a Hamburger and a Cheeseburger, culminates in the attractive proposition of a 'Big Fok'.

Phocaea.[18] They bring up a further point as well, for they recall the Frioul Islands, just off Marseille (p. 98 below), just as the Lakydon there may perhaps be thought to resemble, to some extent, the Lampter at Phocaea. In short, the site of Massalia, quite apart from its other natural advantages, may also have attracted the Phocaean colonists because in some ways it looked like home.[19]

The first serious archaeological study of the site was undertaken in 1913-14 by Félix Sartiaux, a railway engineer with the Chemin de Fer du Nord, who, building on the enthusiasm aroused fifteen years before by the 1899 celebration in Marseille of the 2,500th anniversary of its foundation by Phocaea, successfully promoted the idea that it was high time to have a look at Phocaea itself. Publishing in 1914 a general site-plan, he supplemented this with an account of such antiquities as were still visible. These included a megalithic monument on the road to Izmir and various rock cuttings, some to accommodate votive reliefs, some to provide footings for the city walls, which, being built on bare rock, lacked the foundation courses usual in softer terrain. Indeed, some of these foundation cuttings were mistaken for rock-cut stairways, and so published.[20]

It was not until 1953 that excavation proper was begun, under the auspices of the University of Ankara, and concentrated on the peninsula, the site of the archaic city. Indeed, the question was raised, and not fully settled, whether at that time the site was a peninsula at all and not rather

7. In the South of France the Phocaean memory is kept alive by Les Cars Phocéens, a long-distance bus company (here shown at their Nice office). And the principal overnight express train between Paris and Marseille is named 'Le Phocéen'.

8. The 'Herodotean' wall of ancient Phocaea, at the site of Maltepe (Fig. 3).

an island, separated from the mainland. It was at this period also that were unearthed fragments of an Ionic capital and several column drums from the sixth-century temple,[21] as well as fragments of two other capitals, one 'en forme de champignon et un chapiteau à palmes'.[22]

Further excavations, undertaken from 1988 until the time of writing, expanded their scope to the 'mainland' (i.e. beyond the peninsula) section of the city. A new set of city walls was built, enclosing a much wider area, and a section of this wall has been found, in 1992, at the mound of Maltepe, 500 m out along the Izmir road. This wall, we must clarify, was not the original seventh/sixth century wall built supposedly by contributions from Tartessos to protect the city on the peninsula, but a later structure, encircling the now-enlarged city. It is none the less probably the wall seen and mentioned by Herodotus, and seems to have acquired the accepted title of the 'The Herodotean Wall' in spite of the implicit inaccuracy.[23] The neat and well-trimmed ashlar masonry, built of tufa stone, ranks with the finest Greek work. It dates from 590-580 BC and was probably around 15 m high in its finished state, though it is now preserved to a height of only about 3.5 m. The most striking feature of the wall is that its outer face is not all vertical, its bottom 3 m or so being built on a slope, around 30° from the perpendicular, to act as a kind of continuous buttress,[24] the courses above presenting a vertical face in the usual way. An opening in this wall has been identified as the city gate, a stone ball from a catapult and the presence of a burnt layer attesting to the Persian attack of 546. A theatre

13

9. The 'Herodotean' wall under excavation.

has also (in 1991) been identified and partially cleared, located on the 'colline des Moulins', a hill a short distance inshore from the Lampter harbour, which it shares with a Sanctuary of Cybele; the theatre is dated to 340-330 BC, and hence does not really fall within the scope of this book.

Carthage

To complete our rapid survey of what we may perhaps call the prehistory of Massalia, we turn to the other major power already enjoying a flourishing existence at the time of Massalia's foundation. There arises a question of organisation. It would at this point surely be apposite to turn our attention to the Celts and Ligurians who were already established in Gaul, but because they are also so closely interwoven with the subsequent development of Massalia I have deferred consideration of them to a subsequent chapter (p. 194ff, below). The Etruscans too were a power with which the Massaliot emigrants had to reckon, but here we are excused by *force majeure* from any attempt at analysis – we know so little about them that there is nothing to say. Conventionally described by historians as 'that shadowy people', their influence and dominion was vast – geographically they at one time controlled almost the entire Italian peninsula from Genoa down to Naples, and occupied Rome itself. From them the Romans did inherit various cultural institutions (notably gladiatorial games) and influences (notably in religion), but as Etruria came to be submerged in the expanding spread of the Roman Empire so did any knowledge of its history and civilisation.[25]

However, one thing seems reasonably sure. Unlike the Romans, the Etruscans were interested in trade (and, by a natural extension, piracy), and so would come into contact with the Massaliot merchants. The individual Etruscan city with which contact, or conflict, was commonest seems to have been Caere, the modern Cerveteri,[26] which took part in fighting the Greek colonists at the naval Battle of Alalia, around 535 BC.

We now turn to Carthage. The Carthaginian 'empire' in the Central and Western Mediterranean came well before the Phocaean colonisation, and Carthage itself was founded, traditionally in 814, as the result of some kind of political upheaval in its mother city, Tyre. The region was already well known to Phoenician traders, and Phoenician (i.e. Carthaginian) sub-colonies were founded in large numbers, presumably to reinforce the Phoenician grip on the Western Mediterranean and, in particular, the trade-route through the Straits to Tartessos. These included Solunto, Panormo (modern Palermo), and Motya (near Marsala), in Sicily; Tharros, Sulcis, and Caralis (Cagliari) in Sardinia; Utica and Hippo in Tunisia; Malta and Ebusus (Ibiza, Balearics); Malaka (Malaga), Sexi (Almuñécar) and Abdera, on the South coast of Spain; Lixus, in Mauretania; and Gadir (Gades, Cadiz) in Tartessos.[27] Presumably also even before the formal founding of these cities, there were many Phoenician traders operating in the area (as also did the Phocaeans before the founding of their own colonies), and there are few sites at which pottery and the like does not attest at least a passing Phoenician presence.

Carthage was built on a peninsula projecting into the Gulf of Tunis, close to the modern city of that name. Its most prominent features were Byrsa, a hill serving as acropolis, and the harbours. There were two of these, evidently excavated artificially, a large oblong one for commercial traffic, and a circular inner one with a round island at its centre; this one was the naval base. Remains of both these harbours still survive, in the form of extensive lagoons.[28]

Tyre was a monarchy, and so was its colony Carthage, the first Carthaginian monarch being by tradition the queen Elissa, who, under the rather better known name of Dido, achieved posthumous fame in the pages of Virgil's *Aeneid*. Her husband being slain by his brother-in-law Pygmalion over a disputed succession, the widowed Elissa sailed with a group of surviving loyalists to Carthage, where, being cordially received both by the native Libyans and the Phoenicians of Utica (which already existed), she founded the new city and capital of the Phoenician West.[29] Ruled by the emigrant aristocracy who accompanied Elissa, Carthage was in every sense a full-fledged Phoenician (or Tyrian?) city. At the same time, as Aubet puts it, 'Carthage from the outset developed its own, almost "Punic" socio-cultural dynamic.' It became an expansionist, militaristic power in a way that Tyre had never been, a status recognised by a 509 BC treaty with Rome carving up the Western Mediterranean into spheres of influence, to say nothing of the Battle of Alalia against a Phocaean fleet.[30] At home, Carthage flourished as an agricultural state, the rural nobles enjoying large slave-worked estates rather like the Roman *latifundiae*, which were highly productive of grain, vines, and, in particular, olives (an important export). Livestock was reared by native Libyans, who retained ownership of their land and paid a heavy tax for the privilege. Such indeed was the agricultural expertise of the Carthaginians that they wrote treatises on agronomy, which were so highly thought of that the Roman senate voted to translate them into Greek and Latin, to make them readily available.[31]

In religion, the Phoenicians worshipped a fairly restricted number of gods (often only two per city), in comparison with the widespread polytheism of the Greeks and Romans. The most widely accepted was perhaps Melkaart (sometimes hopefully equated to Herakles), to whose temple in Tyre the Carthaginians supposedly sent an annual tribute of one-tenth of their public treasury.[32] Other prominent deities were Tanit, Baal, and Astarte. Melkaart was particularly associated with the reigning monarch, many of whom identified themselves with an incarnation of the god, somewhat like the later practice of deifying Roman emperors, while the others were closely connected with leading families in the aristocracy. But the chief and best-known manifestation of Phoenician religion was indeed a very human one. It was human sacrifice.

Human sacrifice was practiced by pretty well all Mediterranean peoples, but by the classical era most had given it up. Memories remained embedded in Greek myths such as that of Iphigeneia or Theseus and the Minotaur,[33] but it was among the Semitic peoples that it was most widespread. The best-known occurrence is of course the intended sacrifice of Isaac by Abraham (Genesis 22, 2), to which we may add the self-sacrifice of Elissa, who in the legend burned herself alive on a funeral pyre, and that of the Carthaginian general Hamilcar, who, this time as a matter of attested history, did the same thing. But a much more widespread, striking, and characteristically Carthaginian manifestation of it was the Tophet. Tophet is the name of a sacred precinct attached to the city of Carthage (and to other Phoenician cities in the West also), devoted to the ritual sacrifice of babies by burning them alive. It should be noted that there is no doubting the reality of this. It is not a question of myth or tradition. The actual site has been excavated, yielding more than 20,000 cinerary urns containing the cremated remains of newborn babies and young (2-3 year old) infants, and from the dating it is plain that the practice continued uninterrupted from around 700 BC to the fall of Carthage in 146. The purpose of these sacrifices remains uncertain, whether it was a regular fate awaiting all firstborn, or a recourse invoked in times of national or other emergency. Sometimes animals were apparently substituted, but the practice, not surprisingly, gave the Phoenicians a very bad reputation among the Greeks and Romans, all of whom knew about it. And I doubt if modern readers will think highly of it either.[34] Such at all events, were the Carthaginians, and such was the Carthaginian civilisation with which the Massaliots perforce had to deal.

3

The Seaways to Massalia

Most Greek colonies maintained close relations with the mother city that had founded them, even if those relations were not always amicable. Massalia seems to have remained emotionally close to its founding city, Phocaea, to a remarkable extent, and one wonders whether Massaliots – though there is no actual evidence for it – may not have indulged in nostalgic reminiscence for 'the old country' in the way that is often attributed to Irishmen overseas. Thus, given that Phocaea was at one end of the Mediterranean and Massalia (as also the other Phocaean colonies in Provence) at the other, it follows that for Massaliots the sea routes to the East were of particular importance, quite apart from Massalia being, in general terms, a trading state. It was not just commerce that drove Massalia out on to the sea, but also a clinging to the source of her national Hellenic identity. This was of course to some extent true of all Greek colonies overseas. Greeks never forgot that they were Greeks. But Massalia ought to have been influenced by this psychological effect more than most, because of both its importance and its remoteness. To a Massaliot, therefore, sailing conditions must always have been of prime importance, and not just local conditions in the West: of equal consequence would be conditions throughout the whole length of the Mediterranean, because along it ran that psychological lifeline to Phocaea (as least, while the mother city still existed as an independent state; afterwards, of course, it was still a vital link to Greece as a whole).

Ships and navigation

Studies of the ancient world have seldom gone into any great detail on sea routes and weather conditions, certainly not as compared with land topography.[1] The cause of this is, I feel, partly a misapprehension by those who are not themselves mariners. To the landsman, Homer's 'trackless sea' seems exactly that, an endless, uniform, flat, blue plain, devoid of any equivalent to the hills, rivers and valleys that give shape to the terrestrial landscape. He may be aware, but only in an abstract way, that such things as currents and hidden reefs exist; he cannot see them. From this comes a further misapprehension. It is that the sea route from departure to destination, or between the choke points (such as Cape Malea or the Straits of Messina), is a straight line. Unlike the circuitous routes by land, by sea

18

one travels direct, and scholars, one suspects, have often laid out sea routes simply by drawing straight lines on a map, something nobody would ever dream of doing for routes by land. This is an insidious error, for the technique, broadly speaking, will actually work in the modern world of powered vessels. In a steamship or a motor boat one can point her bows straight at the destination and simply go there. But under sail things are quite different, whether for a modern yacht or an ancient square-rigged freighter. It is not just that the course may involve extensive zigzags as the vessel tracks into the wind. That is the smallest of the complications. More serious are the delays imposed by contrary winds, making journey time quite unpredictable, and above all the necessity for setting a course governed by the prevailing wind patterns. This often involved very considerable detours from the direct course, but was much quicker and more reliable in the end.[2] However, no sooner is this point made than it must again be modified. For ancient rowed galleys were indeed something like powered craft, and presumably could, to some extent, hold a direct course under oar power independently of the winds. And while this would be irrelevant for shipping between the ordinary run of Greek colonies and mainland Greece, where communications were normally in the hands of freighters under sail, the Phocaea-Massalia run was an exception: we are specifically told that the Phocaeans regularly used pentekonters for their long-range voyages, unlike all other cities.[3]

The pentekonter was a fifty-oared galley (25 oars each side), the predecessor of the more sophisticated trireme, the standard warship of classical Greece. Although a good deal is now known about the sailing and handling characteristics of the trireme, especially since the building of a replica, the *Olympias*, we have no similar data on the pentekonter. Of course, since it was also an oar-driven vessel with a single square mainsail, one can extrapolate from what we know about triremes.[4] Essentially, therefore, it sailed best running before the wind, with the wind either astern or on the quarter. By bracing round the sail to turn it, in effect, into something like a fore-and-aft rig,[5] the ship could still make headway with a wind on, or even forward of, the beam, but it would be slow going, and, without a proper deep keel to bite into the water and hold the ship on course, there would be considerable sideslip down to leeward, resulting in a sort of crabwise progress. Under oar power the pentekonter could in theory hold any course independent of the wind, though again that would surely required modification in practice. A strong wind on the beam would tend to push the vessel sideways, and in any case might make ship-handling difficult if it caused heavy seas to build up.[6] But, as with triremes, the ideal was to run under both sail and oar-power together. Although this would presumably give the fastest speeds, it would not necessarily be common practice, for rowing is an exhausting activity, and, since we are speaking of commercial voyages where, unlike naval manoeuvres, there is no particular need to hurry, the crew would no doubt welcome the chance to rest while letting the wind do all the work. We may note, for purposes of comparison, that under oar power a trireme could attain speeds of up to nine knots, but only in short spurts; over long distances the speed was more likely to be around five.

But there were other characteristics of the pentekonter, as opposed to the orthodox freighter, which deserve our attention. First, it had a much larger crew. There were fifty men on the oars alone, as well as the helmsman and a few deckhands, while a freighter would very likely have a crew of no more than five or six, being entirely sail-powered. From this come various results. First, having so large a crew the ship would be able to offer a stout resistance to pirates. This assumes that the oarsmen could also fight, unlike the oarsmen of the classical trireme, but like the heroes manning the Homeric galleys, and the later long ships of the Vikings. In a piratical attack, numbers were always decisive, rather than the size or fittings of the pirate ship, just as in the seventeenth and eighteenth centuries privateers always carried a large crew with which to overwhelm their victims.[7] This may therefore be the reason why the Phocaeans chose to use pentekonters for their voyages to the Western Mediterranean in the sixth century. It is not known whether at this period the Western Mediterranean was particularly infested with pirates but it was certainly infested with Carthaginians and Etruscans, and Massaliots seem to have regarded Etruscans and pirates as being much the same thing, a sentiment that the Etruscans no doubt reciprocated.

Second, from the large crew sprang other results. First, the pentekonter was suited to the transport of large numbers of people, as with the Homeric heroes, but not as emigrants.[8] The ship could not deposit fifty or so men on to the shores of Massalia, there to remain as settlers, leaving nobody to man the oars for the return trip (unless the ship was to stay there, as part of the new colony's resources). For the foundation of the city, therefore, as for any subsequent reinforcement, we should probably assume that the colonists travelled in ordinary freighters rather than the pentekonters specified by Herodotus, though there may have been a pentekonter escort. Second, the pentekonter was, like the trireme, essentially a short-range craft. Not only did it have no sleeping accommodation, but, being an open boat, did not even have a deck where one could lie down. At night, therefore, the ship would remain at sea only in exceptional circumstances, for normally sunset would see it anchored close inshore while the crew bivouacked on the beach. Any long voyage would thus become a series of short hops, hugging the coast and avoiding voyages across the open sea whenever possible.[9] Third, there is the question of supplies. An appropriately large amount of sustenance had to be carried for the large crew, and a pentekonter had much less space to carry it in than a freighter. It is not a question of food, but water. Quite an amount of concentrated food such as dried figs could be stored under the thwarts; water, whether carried in amphorae or even wineskins, is much more bulky, and the crew, sweating and dehydrated by toiling all day at the oars under a blazing Mediterranean sun, would need a great deal of it.[10]

Frequent refills would again limit the range of a pentekonter, and must often have proved a governing factor. Scarcely anyone has ever tried to estimate the actual water consumption of a pentekonter crew,[11] but the picture painted is surely again one of short hops, while a freighter would have much greater endurance for sailing long distances non-stop. Perhaps, however, we may note a further factor. One of the advantages of a pentekonter was that, thanks to oar-power, it could not be becalmed, like a freighter. And a freighter, lying becalmed for any length of time, would not simply lose time: all this time it would also be consuming fresh water, and might even run short of it.[12]

Apart from all these strengths and weaknesses peculiar to pentekonters, there remain all the further and familiar qualifications affecting ancient navigation in general. The sailing season lasted only from May till October,[13] and though ships may sometimes have sailed in the winter, any regular voyages between Massalia and Greece or Phocaea were out of the question. It was not just that the weather was bad – in the Mediterranean you can get gales of impressive intensity in August – but also the reduction in visibility coming from longer nights and fog by day. To a world lacking the mariner's compass this was a vital matter, for navigation, while it may sometimes have used the stars, depended chiefly on getting a visual fix on some landmark ashore (Fig. 15).

This depended not only on distance from the land but also on whether the land was low-lying or mountainous, for while a rock 10 metres above sea level becomes invisible at 13 km, a mountain 2,500 m high can be seen 200 km away.[14] As the figure shows, the coasts that were most lacking in such mountainous landmarks were Libya and Egypt, while (by hugging just Southern Turkey, then Cape Malea (Greece),[15] Sicily, and Algeria) it was in theory possible to sail the entire length of the Mediterranean, from the Levant to Gibraltar, without ever being out of sight of land.[16] But all of this depended on daylight, and good visibility, where one could get a fix on the landmarks. If one could not do this one might get lost, but of course that was a small matter compared with the very real danger of running on to the rocks and sinking. This was especially true of the Aegean, studded with its countless islands. One often hears this praised as a natural nursery for primitive sailors, where you are never out of sight of land, but in a modern mariner's handbook it looks more like a slaughterhouse, where, driving along under the press of heavy weather, you only see an island when it is already too late to dodge it.[17] On a similar basis, sailing by night, which freighters often did, may well have been slower than sailing the same route by day; in the darkness one could not see squalls or bad weather approaching, so a prudent captain might choose to proceed under shortened sail, as a precaution in case he got caught unexpectedly.[18] And there were no maps or charts, though the captain might have a '*periplous*', or written itinerary listing in sequence the various harbours and anchorages along the coast. Navigational instruments were limited to the sounding lead, its base, like that of its modern counterpart, hollowed

21

out so that it could be armed with a plug of wax or tallow so as to bring up, adhering to it, a sample of the sea bed – gravel, sand, mud, or whatever. Latitude could be, in theory, determined by a portable gnomon (a type of sundial) – Pytheas had one – but it would be hard to get a reliable shadow line on a pitching deck, and in any case I am sure few captains could or did operate on so sophisticated a level.

Such, then, was the equipment with which the Phocaeans and the Massaliots ventured forth on to the seaways connecting their two cities. But the vital factor is the weather they encountered en route. That must be our next consideration.

Mediterranean weather

It would be improper in this book to engage in a detailed study of the whole range of Mediterranean weather, but a brief account of the principal winds and currents is appropriate.[19]

Currents

We begin with currents. The overall picture is shown in Fig. 10.[20] The Mediterranean, being in a relatively hot climate, has a high rate of evaporation that leaves it high in salinity. To replace the water evaporated, a steady current enters it at Gibraltar and another by the Bosphoros, the rate of both depending on the local winds and, at Gibraltar, the tides in the Atlantic.[21] Within the Mediterranean there are two general patterns. One is the overall pattern: currents circle the Mediterranean basin, rotating anti-clockwise and staying close to the shore. Second, the Mediterranean is broken up by land masses into a number of semi-enclosed stretches of water, conventionally called 'seas' – the Ligurian, Tyrrhenian, Adriatic, Ionian, Aegean, and – no particular name – the sea around Cyprus and the Levant. In each of these six areas the currents also

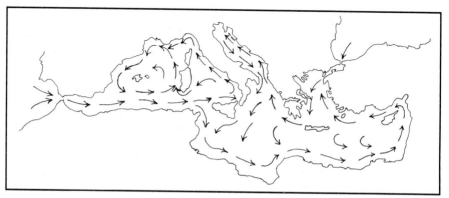

10. Currents in the Mediterranean. The general picture is one of anti-clockwise rotation, with a single straight west-east current along the North African coast.

rotate anti-clockwise. What this comes to is that one long current enters at Gibraltar and goes swirling along the whole length of the North African coast and then curving north up the Levant; while above this is a series of six rotaries, all independently turning anti-clockwise. Essentially, this means that along the coast of North Africa there is a· current setting eastward, while along southern Europe there is one, though not continuous, setting westward. In general, these currents extend outwards from the shore for some 4-5 nautical miles, and flow at rather less than one knot, often showing a temporary acceleration up to two knots as they squeeze past some projecting headland.[22] Moreover, they are often retarded or even arrested by contrary winds, which indeed can even create a current in areas normally devoid of one – it is a saying of fishermen in the Gulf of Genoa that 'le vent fait le courant'.

Currents therefore have much less effect on Mediterranean navigation than the winds (which can get up to 20 or 30 knots without even being classified as strong), but neither are they negligible. Where two currents meet, the product can be a sea rough enough to be avoided if possible, and if there is no wind, a current that will carry a ship and its cargo a mile every hour, with no effort on anybody's part, is something not to be despised.

Winds

Winds in the Mediterranean are governed largely by depressions.[23] Some of these enter it from the outside, already formed; they come in from the Atlantic, some through the Straits of Gibraltar, some from the Bay of Biscay across the 'isthmus' joining France and Spain (the 'Garonne – Carcassonne route'), and some via Morocco and the Sahara (where they are also formed) swinging north to enter the Mediterranean over Algeria. But the great majority (69%, or about 52 per year) are born in the Mediterranean itself,[24] in the Gulf of Genoa, from which they are often referred to as Genoa depressions, and this is where they are at their strongest. Thence they move east, weakening as they go. Sometimes they even die out completely, but sometimes revive in vigour so that they often look like a second set of depressions, newly born around Crete. It is, of course, quite possible to have two depressions in the Mediterranean at once, one newly formed off Genoa while its predecessor has not yet cleared the eastern end.

Our next task will be to study the pattern of prevailing winds and gales generated by this system, as well as the local phenomenon of land-sea breezes.[25] This is best illustrated by the four maps, Figs. 11-14. The first two show the general direction of prevailing regional winds and gales, while the second pair show how often such winds and gales occur. Being based on the work of the Meteorological Office, the picture is of year-round weather, but is of course also valid for the ancient sailing season. The reader must also remember that weather is so interdependent and con-

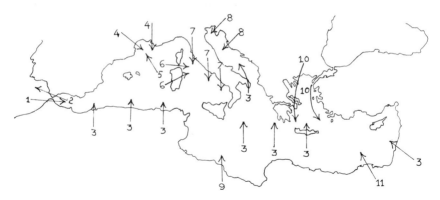

11. Prevailing winds in the Mediterranean. Their local names are: (1) Vendeval; (2) Levanter; (3) Scirocco; (4) Mistral; (5) Marin; (6) Libeccio; (7) Tramontana; (8) Bora; (9) Ghibli; (10) Meltemi (summer only); (11) Khamsin.

stantly changing a phenomenon that a map cannot give a definitive picture but only a general (and simplified) synopsis of the ingredients most commonly present.

Fig. 11 shows the prevailing regional winds. The first thing that strikes the eye is that just about all regular winds blow into the Mediterranean and none out of it.[26] Many of them have local names, and four stand out in importance. First must come the Mistral, the strongest of them all and the wind *par excellence* of Marseille; it will be considered in detail later (p. 31f. below). Second, the Bora (Gk. Boreas), an eastern version of the Mistral that comes in round the other side of the Alps and reaches the Adriatic at Trieste. Third, the Meltemi (in antiquity the Etesian winds), a summer seasonal wind sweeping down the Aegean from the Dardanelles.[27] All three of these come from the north; they are complemented by the Scirocco, a southerly from the Sahara, found along the whole length of the North African coastline. This too is a strong wind, blowing right across to the Ligurian coast if there is no Mistral to stop it, and with such force that the sea level at Genoa and Marseille begins to rise, as much as 24 hours before the arrival of the wind.[28]

Our next step is to identify which of these winds blow the strongest, and how often. This is shown in the next map, Fig. 12. In some areas this is the same as Fig. 11, in others markedly different; that is, there are areas where often the prevailing wind strengthens to gale force, and others where, when a gale does come, it comes from quite a different direction. Thus in the Aegean the Meltemi often strengthens to a gale in the same direction (northerly), and likewise the Tramontana on the West coast of Italy, and the Bora at Trieste; while along the coast of North Africa, where the Scirocco normally blows off-shore, if a gale springs up it will probably be a nor'wester, blowing on-shore. The strong influence of the Mistral is also plain , sweeping down and along the whole length of the Mediterranean. The heavy arrows, marking areas of particular frequency, also tell

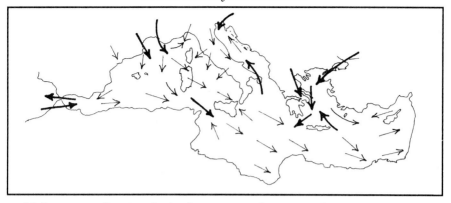

12. Mediterranean: direction of gales (heavy arrows show greater frequency).

their own story. That Gibraltar is a trouble spot comes as no surprise, but we must also note the heavy arrows, indicating frequent gales, in the Gulf of Lions and the Aegean.

For more precise information we move on to Fig. 13, on which are recorded, after the fashion of isobars, the percentage of observations that over a period of years, recorded a strong wind (Beaufort 6 and above), direction unspecified. Three areas stand out – once more, the Aegean, the Gulf of Lions, and Trieste, all with a 16% observation rate: that is, winds of Force 6 and over occur there on more than 58 days of the year, as compared with only 32 days (9%) at Gibraltar, and only 25 days (7%) at the Syrtes of North Africa, so often mentioned by classical authors in tones of dread. Horace's 'raucus Hadria',[29] on the other hand, lives up to its reputation, particularly at the north end. The windiest parts of the Medi-

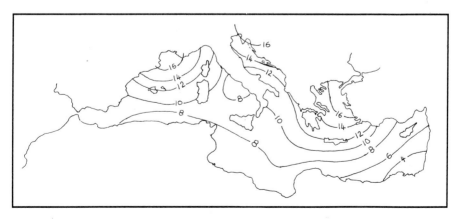

13. Mediterranean: mean annual percentage frequency of observation of strong winds (Beaufort 6 and above). It will be noted that the calmest part of the Mediterranean is off the Nile delta.

25

terranean, in short, are its three top corners, the Aegean, the Adriatic, and the Gulf of Lions (i.e. Marseille/Genoa).

So much for strong winds. For gales we now turn to Fig. 14. Again there is a significant difference from the previous map. The windiest locations (including gales) we noted, but there was no way of telling whether gales were more frequent in one rather than another. It is this lacuna that is filled by Fig. 14, showing, on the same principle as Fig. 13, the percentage of gales recorded in all observations. It needs no comment, for the contours come so thick and fast in the Gulf of Lions that I had not space to write in upon the close-packed lines the relevant figures. The concentration is massive, and the observed frequency of 6.8%, some 45 km or so out in the Gulf, is almost three times as high as anything in the Aegean. It also is local, and does not extend very far. This is the birthplace of the Genoa depressions and the gales concerned are, of course, the Mistral. The rest of the Mediterranean looks uniform by comparison, though the Aegean still manages to register five times as many gales as the calm waters off the coast of Egypt.

However, we must here make an important point. To a sailor, not all gales are equally dangerous, and some are not dangerous at all. A perfectly ferocious gale can be raging without endangering any sailor of even the most modest competence, because no competent sailor will be at sea in such conditions. Given adequate local knowledge, storms can usually be predicted in time to take shelter, and the sailing handbooks, when discussing 'what to do if caught in a gale' usually begin with the bleak comment that you had no business getting caught in the first place, not if you know your trade. In antiquity the skill most important for a sailor was the

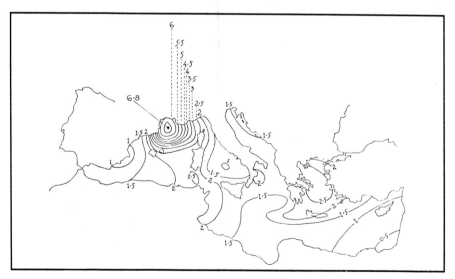

14. Mean annual percentage frequency of gales (Beaufort 8 and above). The very heavy concentration at sea off Marseille is to be noted.

3. The Seaways to Massalia

patience to sit quietly in harbour waiting for the right weather; a cautious skipper was better than a good one.[30] What this means is that the seas off Massalia (and indeed in the Aegean) were not particularly dangerous, but you did have to know what you were doing, and have the self-discipline to stick to it. Of course, a ship may be caught in the open sea, with no shelter at hand,[31] but even that is not as bad as it might seem, for you can always ride out the gale by streaming a sea anchor, or just run before it under bare poles until it blows itself out. But you must really be in open sea, with plenty of sea room to run in, for the real danger is not that the vessel will founder in deep water, but that it will be driven on to the rocks of a lee shore. Once the storm gets going, land is to be avoided at all costs. And off Massalia, the Mistral, the gale *par excellence*, blows straight out to sea (Fig. 12) with no land before it until Sardinia, or sometimes even North Africa, giving a storm-driven ship a long and clear run.

Sea-routes from Massalia: long distance

We now consider what effect this pattern of weather had on shipping. The commonest long voyage undertaken by Massaliot skippers was of course the run to Ionia or Greece, and Figs. 11-12 give a clear and simple picture. If the Mistral was blowing, it would give a good start in the right direction. If it was blowing strong, then it and the eastbound North African current between them would carry the ship two-thirds of the way there, almost automatically, leaving the captain with no problem in seamanship more profound than managing to dodge Sardinia and Sicily. Strong Mistrals are not a thing Marseille was, or is, short of, and it probably meant that quite

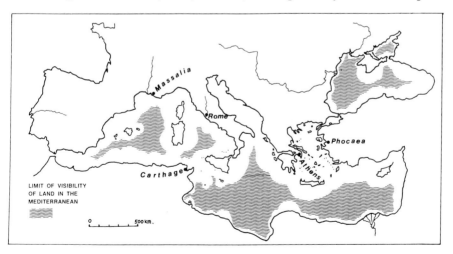

15. The shaded areas represent the areas at sea that, in good conditions, are out of sight of the land. There is no fixed distance for this, for it depends on how high the land rises. The coast of Libya and Egypt, as also Roumania, is so low-lying that it comes into sight only when a ship is quite close inshore.

27

a few Massaliot ships were blown most of the way to Greece (at least as far as Crete) willy-nilly, no matter where they were bound for.[32]

This, of course, is not what one expects. One expects the ship to follow what on the map is the shortest course, via the west coast of Italy and Messina, where Rhegion, Velia, and Aleria are often mentioned as useful way stations. But the winds are unhelpful or indecisive. A strong Mistral can carry a ship over to the Italian coast, even reversing the normal currents and generating a strong two-knot current flowing from Cap Corse eastward to Elba, but there is nothing to compare with the route via the Malta Channel. Meteorologically, the Malta Channel is much superior, and the French sailing directions are quite categoric: in summer, sailing vessels are specifically warned off the route via Bonifacio and Messina and recommended to steer south of Sardinia and Sicily, while cautiously keeping clear of the coast of Africa.[33] For an eastbound voyage, this route is clearly to be preferred, but only if we limit our consideration to the weather. Lacking a compass, an ancient skipper might have preferred to follow the coast, even if it took longer, and in any case the Malta channel came close to Carthage and was presumably under her control – given her uncooperative attitude at Gibraltar, would she have permitted passage? Sometimes the question must have been academic, when a strong nor'wester blew a Massalia-Greece bound ship into the Malta channel in weather so stormy that the Carthaginians could not do much to stop it.[34]

Conditions for the westbound trip, Greece to Massalia, are quite different. The head-on Mistral is something to be avoided, and the best way of avoiding it is to take the inside passage, via Messina and the Italian coast. Currents are in general helpful, though weak, and once in the Gulf of Genoa four to six nautical miles a day could be logged using the current alone. Progress along this route would be reasonable but unspectacular, involving a good deal of hanging around waiting for a favourable wind for the next hop. One thinks of the analogous situation of the Alexandria grain clippers, which stormed down straight from Puteoli to Alexandria, and then dodged slowly around the coasts on the way back. Surprisingly, the Straits of Bonifacio, between Corsica and Sardinia, are to be avoided, not because of bad weather but because one can be becalmed; the route from Elba (a conveniently sheltered point to await the right wind) up to Cap Corse, and thence across to Nice, is recommended as the preferred route for summer-time traffic from the Eastern Mediterranean to Toulon and Marseille.[35]

The evidence of meteorology for the trade route between Massalia and Greece is thus clear. Westbound, it runs up the coast of Italy, making calls at Velia, Aleria, and other such ports; eastbound, it runs direct and almost non-stop across to North Africa, and then along to Cyrenaica and Crete. Velia, Aleria and the like thus become in effect one-way ports, handling (as far as Massalia is concerned) only traffic from Greece, not to it. Naturally, this does not affect ships sailing from Massalia specifically to these ports with cargoes to be landed there; there must have been a certain amount of return freight carried to Magna Graecia to balance Massalia's import of Campanian wine. But, trade apart, on the basis of sailing conditions alone the position is clear.

The other principal trade-route extended westward from Massalia towards Ampurias and Gibraltar, and could be used both by coasting traffic along the Iberian littoral and by traffic coming direct from Magna Graecia and bypassing Massalia altogether.[36] This is also the route for Massaliot traffic to the Atlantic, but there we are faced with a difficulty. Massalia was plainly interested in the world beyond the Straits of Gibraltar; of that, the exploratory voyages of Euthymenes and Pytheas (p. 130f. below) would by themselves be sufficient proof. The difficulty, as so often, was the Carthaginians. Orthodox doctrine has it that Carthage, until its conquest by Rome, maintained over the Straits a monopolistic control both rigorous and vigorous, effectively barring passage. It is not clear either that they did, or could, blockade the Straits by naval force. We are told that they used to drown anyone sailing past their land to get to Gibraltar, but that is not the same thing as patrolling the Straits themselves. What we do hear, repeatedly, is that navigation of the Straits was very difficult, and that the Carthaginians, who knew how to do it, guarded the secret jealously, adding in for good measure all sorts of horror stories about the Atlantic (which they represented as a kind of nautical jungle, full of sea monsters), designed to scare away all comers.[37] In this they were successful, for, so far as we can see, shipping of all the other Mediterranean countries remained bottled up in the Mediterranean, while the Phoenicians regularly sailed out into the Atlantic, even, on at least one occasion, circumnavigating the entire continent of Africa.[38] Moreover, the geographical pattern of foundation of the earliest Phoenician colonies clearly reflects an interest in trading out into the high seas of the Atlantic. The earliest, founded some four centuries before the arrival of the Phocaeans in the Western Mediterranean, before even the foundation of Carthage itself (the Phoenicians involved came from around Tyre and Byblos, in the Levant), were Lixus, Gadir and Utica. Of these the first two were just outside the Straits of Gibraltar, one in Europe and one in Africa, while the third, near what was later to become Carthage, was a valuable way-station on the route. Taken together they attest a very early Phoenician interest in the Atlantic.[39]

This general picture of Carthaginian obstruction, however, calls for closer inspection. For example, it has been suggested that the Carthaginians must have facilitated the passage of Pytheas and Euthymenes, permitting them to top up with water and victuals, and guiding them through the tricky waters of the Straits.[40] Certainly navigating the Straits was, and is, no walkover, and I suspect that this was a much more serious objection than a Carthaginian blockade. Winds are not so great an obstacle, for in this region they always blow from either the east or the west (northerlies and southerlies being almost unheard-of), so it is a question of waiting until the right one is blowing. This may call for considerable

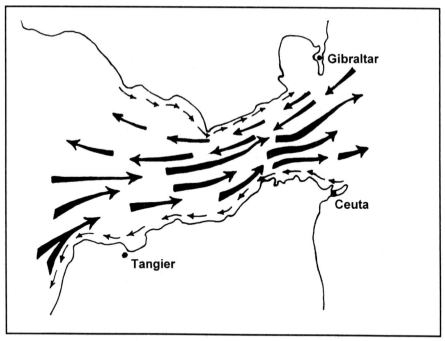

16. Currents through the Straits of Gibraltar. It will be seen that the secret of sailing out into the Atlantic is to steer fairly close inshore to Gibraltar and so pick up the outgoing current.

patience (up to two months, in fact), but trying to get through in the teeth of a contrary wind is inadvisable, for they can be very violent.[41] But it was probably the currents that were the crucial factor. They are shown in Fig. 16, and there are four separate streams. The main one, running eastward, occupies most of the width of the Straits, but there is another counter-current, flowing outward, or to the West, immediately to the north of it, on the Spanish side. This is the one you want to aim at to get out into the Atlantic. To confuse matters further, there is also a small and narrow current, running close along each shore and in opposite directions to each other – inward along the Spanish shore, outward along the African. The secret of passing the Straits, therefore, was to make an approach on the Spanish side, but not too close inshore, from the general direction of the Balearics, and then, with an easterly wind, to aim at a point about three-quarters of the way across (i.e. from left to right, as the captain would view it from the Mediterranean). Of course, once one was out into the Atlantic, getting back was easy. All one had to do was aim at mid-channel and, with a favourable wind, ride the flood of the mainstream through the Straits. The strength of these currents is considerable for, when assisted by the state of the tides in the Atlantic, they can run up to 5-6 knots and are perceptible up to 20 km out in the Ocean. The interplay of tides, currents and winds can also produce, without warning, some very rough seas, and sailing across the Straits, from Spain to Africa or vice versa, can be even more taxing than going through them, involving, dependent on current conditions, a good deal of tacking and zigzagging. Even today this can be a dangerous business, and it is not unknown for even a large modern steamer to sink while on passage.[42] Indeed, these nautical hazards were enough to induce merchants bound for Tartessos sometimes to avoid the Straits altogether, by putting in at Malaga, unloading, and going forward overland: that took only five days, while waiting for the right wind to get past Gibraltar could take weeks.[43]

I have never been quite convinced by the proposition that Carthaginian opposition and difficult navigation together were enough to bar Greek traders from the Straits. Certainly it would have taken more than tricky currents to stop the archetypal Greek mariner, Odysseus, he of the many wiles, and it should not have been impossible to find friendly local guides – until its destruction, at least (p. 167 below), Mainake was a Greek colony not far from the Straits, and its inhabitants must have known the secret of the currents. And as for Carthaginian naval force, the Massaliots do not seem to have stood in great awe of it. They had defeated them several times,[44] and it is hard to believe that if the Massaliots had really wanted to sail out into the Atlantic, they would have let the Carthaginians stop them. There was, I think, a much stronger reason. Why, after all, would they, or the Greeks in general, have wanted to trade along the Atlantic shore on a regular basis? Tartessos, it is true, had rich pickings to offer, but, as we have noted, they could just as easily be sent overland and shipped out through Mainake or some equivalent port, and at a considerable saving in time. The real prize was tin from Brittany, Cornwall, and the Scillies, but, we are told (Diodorus 5.22.4) that a lot of that was sent overland across France on pack-horses and down the Rhône. That was a simple and rapid route, which took only 30 days. By comparison, the sea route from Massalia to Cornwall, via Gibraltar and the Bay of Biscay, is over three and a half times as long, and through two regions – the Straits and Biscay – renowned for bad sailing weather.[45] Why then would Massaliot sailors, or other Greeks, have wanted access to the Atlantic? The Carthaginians, of course, had no choice. To take advantage of the Rhône route they would have to face quite a long voyage across to Massalia, and no great guarantee of a cordial reception when they got there. So, given the geographic realities, it made good sense for the Carthaginians to sail the Atlantic, but not the Greeks. Put this way, the Carthaginian monopoly of the Straits appears in a striking new light: they were left with a monopoly of the Greeks' leftovers that nobody else wanted.[46]

Sea routes from Massalia: local

Sailing, like everything else at Massalia, was dominated by the Mistral, the '*maître-vent*',[47] to which the climates of Greece and Italy can offer no counterpart. It originates in the North Atlantic, and reaches the Mediter-

31

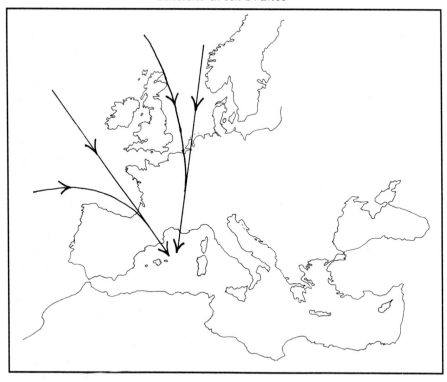

17. The two chief sources and paths of the Mistral. Their meeting in the Golfe du Lion is largely responsible for its very stormy nature (Fig. 14).

ranean in two streams (Fig. 17). One sweeps down from Iceland over the North Sea and along the valley of the Rhône, reaching the sea at the Camargue and Marseille, its influence being felt eastward along the coast as far as Fréjus and the Esterel (though much diminished; the Côte d'Azur proper (Antibes – Nice – Monaco) is sheltered from it by the Alps). The second stream comes in via the Bay of Biscay and the valley of the Garonne, reaching the sea around Perpignan/Béziers; the two streams meet at a point out at sea, half way between Marseille and the Balearics, making this the real storm centre of the Mediterranean (see Fig. 14). In strength, a 'strong Mistral' at Marseille rates around Beaufort Scale 6 (21 knots). It usually blows in a series of three or four days at a time,[48] but is essentially a daily phenomenon in that, while it is blowing, it is every day moderated by the sea breezes as they build up during the afternoon, so that, typically, it begins with dawn or before, reaches its peak around mid-day, and subsides around 5 pm, to be followed by a relatively calm night.[49]

Though nothing like as common or as violent as the Mistral, there are of course other winds that blow from time to time. A south wind, the Marin, or northward extension of the Scirocco, can cause heavy seas and swell to which quite a few ports, especially along the Maures and Esterel (i.e. from Hyères to Nice and Monaco), would, in the days before modern breakwaters, be exposed; and in the narrow calanques (p. 47 below) a sea coming in from the south is often funnelled into forming very heavy breakers. St. Tropez (ancient Athenopolis?), with a harbour very unusually facing north, is even exposed to the Mistral, which can also be felt in the great roadstead of Toulon. But in general the prevalence of the northerly Mistral and the predominance of ports facing southwards that are backed by mountains to give shelter from it does mean that good harbours abound along this coast.[50] There are other winds too. Bourdeaux advises the yachtsman that the east wind can be very strong even in summer, causing heavy seas to build up. The wind recommended for local sailing is *Le Poulain,* which is common in periods of good weather; it arises from the north-east in the morning, and, as its strength increases, veers around by mid-day to the south-west; by evening it has gone right round to the west and slowly dies out. By night there is relative calm, with a gentle land breeze then arising, blowing lightly off-shore. This last would be ideal for ancient freighters, for it would give the vessel an easy passage out of the port of Massalia (which is very difficult, even for modern steamers, if there is a strong Mistral; the entrance channel into the Lakydon, the harbour of Massalia, faces north-west, so, with a Mistral, it is hard to leave and easy to enter) and well into deep water before the Mistral got going in the morning, to give Greece-bound traffic a clear run right down to the south of Sardinia. One suspects that this must have formed a common pattern of Massaliot navigation, for the whole principle of navigation in this area is formed on sailing *with* the wind. Moreover, it is best to leave at night (though that means dodging the Frioul Islands in the dark) or early morning, for if the wind freshens uncomfortably during the day, as it often does, then you will either be able to take shelter knowing that you have already made good progress, or you will be far out, with plenty of sea-room to manoeuvre in and deal with the press of weather.[51]

We may conclude by noting the actual frequency of winds from different directions, as registered over a period of years at Marseille. This is shown graphically in Fig. 18, in which they are represented as a polar diagram, and here below in tabulated form (in days per year). Wind strength is neglected. Two things become apparent. One is the immense preponderance of the Mistral (NW), 136 days of the year (= 37.3%); the next commonest is its opposite, the SE wind (49 days); E and SE are relatively common, and S is the rarest of all. The second point is how uniform in direction the Mistral is, being concentrated entirely on one compass heading: Mistral is NW and nothing else, and something as close to it as northerlies are not particularly common.

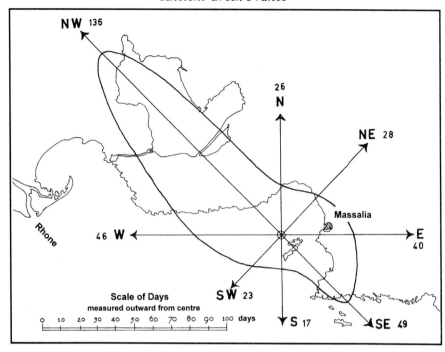

18. Polar diagram of relative frequency of winds blowing in Provence, based on readings at Marseille, Aigues Mortes, Sète and Port Vendres. The very heavy preponderance of the Mistral (from the north-west, on 136 days of the year) is striking.

Mean frequency of winds in Provence (Fig. 18)

Direction	Days per year	% of total
NW (Mistral)	136	37.3
N	26	7.1
NE	28	7.7
E	40	10.9
SE	49	13.4
S	17	4.7
SW	23	6.3
W	46	12.6

Our last point must be Bourdeaux's advice to yachtsmen on the various months of the sailing season. For him, it begins in June, and ends in October – five months of the year. In summary, June is the best month, October suprisingly good, and August, at the height of the summer, surprisingly bad.[52] Within these limits, sailing to and from Massalia presented no great difficulty despite its storms, provided two conditions were met. First, you had to know what you were doing, and what weather was required. Second, you had to have the patience to wait for it.[53]

With that established, we may now follow the Phocaean colonists ashore and see what kind of land awaited them there.

4

The Topography of the Region

When the Greeks – whether Phocaean colonists or ordinary traders – made their landfall at the end of their voyage, what kind of terrain, what country, what topography did they find awaiting them? Today, the South of France is so famous as a resort centre that any description might seen unnecessary, but I do not think that is so. Fame does not always bring familiarity, and the exotic glamour of the Côte d'Azur is enough to put some people off; and in any case readers with classical interests are more likely to have travelled to Greece, even if it is farther to go. So, what did the Greeks find?[1]

The area relevant to Greek colonisation is simple to visualise. It looks like an inverted letter T. Moreover, each section of this schema is topographically distinct from the others and internally uniform. The vertical line of the inverted T is the valley of the Rhône, running straight north from the Mediterranean and giving easy access to North and Central Europe. At its southern extremity, the junction point of the T, where the Rhône enters the sea, lies the Rhône delta, the flat and marshy world of the Camargue. On either side of this point, Greek colonies stretched in a long line along the coast, east along the Côte d'Azur until, around the modern frontier with Italy, they ran up against the power of Etruria; west, they extended to the Pyrenees (which were no obstacle since their communications were sea-borne) and down the coast of Spain, tailing off in numbers as the distance from Greece increased and so did resistance from Carthage, which occupied Southern Spain. The two halves of this littoral, east and west of the Rhône, are in appearance completely different. The eastern half, including Marseille, Toulon, Nice and Monaco, is rocky and mountainous, while the western half, including Montpellier, Narbonne, Béziers and Perpignan, is flat and sandy. There are of course exceptions. Beaches, such as that around Fréjus, do exist in the Côte d'Azur, and in Languedoc (what I have called the western half of the T)[2] there are occasional rocky promontories, such as that occupied by Sète (and once over the Pyrenees and past the Spanish frontier the distinction largely breaks down); but in general what I have said stands, and Figs. 23 and 24 can be taken as representative.

To get out of this region by land is easy to the west, very difficult to the east. A short distance in from the sea the Pyrenees are pierced by the col de Perthus, a low pass giving easy access to Catalonia and Spain. At the

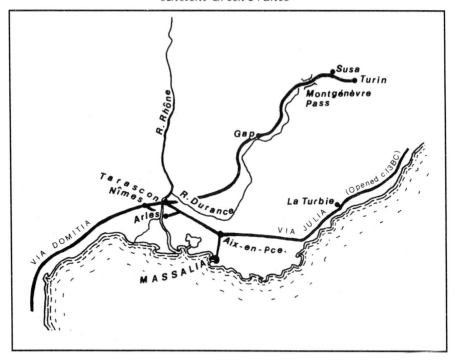

19. Roman roads in Provence. Though in appearance more circuitous, the Montgénèvre route was by far the easiest, while the coastal Via Julia was only opened by Augustus. Massalia clearly owes its importance to sea traffic – no major Roman road goes through it, and it is served only by a dead-end branch.

other end, there is no equivalent for traffic bound for Italy. A rough, rocky track around the coast existed, known to the ancients as the Via Heraclensis (because Heracles was supposed to have passed that way on his return from his labours in the West), but did not become passable for serious transport until the Roman road was put through by Augustus. Until then, overland traffic between the South of France and Italy had to detour far inland (See Fig. 19), up the valley of the Durance and thence over the Alps by the cols of Montgénèvre or Larche, descending on Turin and Cuneo in the basin of the Po (as Hannibal supposedly did on his invasion of Italy). At both ends, these coastal mountains could readily be bypassed by sea, and sea-borne traffic round the Pyrenees to Spain was common (and easier even than by land). In the Côte d'Azur, the same solution was theoretically possible, but Northern Italy being in the usually hostile hands of the Etruscans, there was not much reason for the Greek colonists to go there or expectation of a welcome if they did.[3]

To the south this territory is limited by the sea, but there are northern limits too and it does not extend on indefinitely into the French interior. The northern limits are the mountains. On the Côte d'Azur the Alpes

20. Arles (ancient Arelate): the theatre (bottom left) and amphitheatre (now used for bullfights) are both of Roman date. The Roman road to Spain crossed the Rhône on a floating pontoon bridge just downstream (i.e. nearer the camera) from the two modern piers standing in the water close to the riverbank.

21. Excavations off the Bd. des Lices, Arles. Not everyone eulogises Roman roads, and the sign warns pedestrians: 'Roman Paving, Hard Going'. A public footpath led through the site, hence the sign (which disappeared a week after the photograph was taken).

22. The summit of the Montgénèvre Pass, looking toward Italy. On the French side it is reached by a gentle rise, leading, on the Italian side, into a steep gorge.

23. The beach between Agde and Sète. The formation, a long sandbar forming the beach and, on the landward side, enclosing an extensive lagoon, is typical of the Languedoc coast.

24. Typical coastline of the Côte d'Azur: the cliffs near Cassis.

Maritimes sweep down to sea with a precipitous abruptness that leaves only the narrowest of coastal strips free for settlement and often not even that. In any serious sense, lateral communications are not easy and inland ones very difficult; even in these days of modern technology, the *trains grande vitesse* (TGV) from Paris to Nice run straight down the Rhône valley to Marseille, and then east along the coast, instead of cutting across the third side of the triangle. And in Languedoc, the western half of our area, the situation, though less extreme, is essentially the same. The mountains, namely the Massif Central and the Cevennes, are nothing like the Alps in scale and are in any case much further in from the coast, leaving a coastal plain some 40 km or so wide, but they rise high[4] and again form a natural boundary to our area.

A further point arises when one looks at a map of the rivers of France (Fig. 25). With the exception of the Rhône and the Seine, they all rise in the South. The Loire in particular, which one always thinks of as an Atlantic river, entering the sea at Nantes, actually rises in the Ardèche, and it is not the only one. In one small area a little east of Mende (Lozère), are the sources of the Loire,[5] the Allier, the Tarn, the Lot, the Hérault, the Gard, and the Ardèche, which flow outward from it in all directions. What this means is that this area is the watershed of France, and, since it is so very far south, this means in turn that the land slopes down from it much more steeply on the side facing the Mediterranean than on the north. The Cevennes/Massif Central block is thus shown to be not a ridge or a chain of peaks, but rather an escarpment, with one side rising quite gently to the

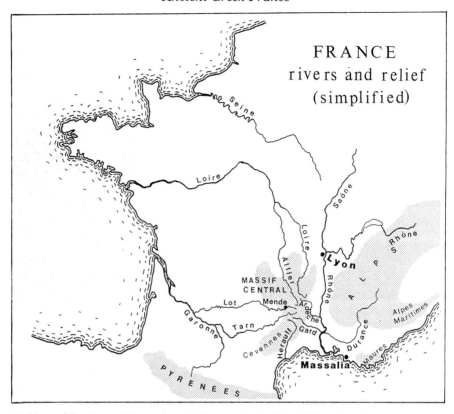

FRANCE
rivers and relief
(simplified)

25. Many of the rivers of France have their source in the Massif Central, in the region around Mende, possibly facilitating transfer of waterborne freight (i.e. on rafts). The 'Gateway of the Rhône' to Northern Europe is also prominent.

crest, and the other dropping away much more sharply. And it was the steep slope that was facing the Greek colonists, thereby accentuating its function as an isolating factor. Of course, Greek colonisation normally did take the form of strip development, represented by a string of cities and trading posts stretching along some suitable littoral, with no attempt to extend political control far inland, so it would probably have taken that form along the Provence coastline anyway; but we should note that, independently, the area was hemmed in by natural features to form the long strip noted above.

The Rhône

We will now consider in greater detail the characteristics of these areas that we have defined. First comes the Rhône.[6] A broad river, fed by the melting snows of Switzerland, it is the only natural gateway from the Mediterranean into the interior of Europe, a distinction from which its

40

26. The Rhône near its mouth. The photograph was taken from the west bank, and the town visible on the far side is Port St. Louis.

only competitor, the Danube, is eliminated by its circuitous course and the need to negotiate the Dardanelles and the Bosphoros before one even got to the start. Naturally this does not mean that the Rhône was the only route of access. There were Alpine passes, cattle drifts, mule tracks; indeed, before the coming of the Greeks and Romans, the whole of Europe was criss-crossed by a network of these unsophisticated but effective routes that, as well as serving local needs, carried an extensive long-distance traffic in such necessaries as salt and tin.[7] But the Rhône formed the main highway. Land traffic could follow its valley with relative ease, for the valley is wide enough to permit easy passage, and there are no gorges or marshes to be negotiated. Water traffic had to contend with a strong current, but no other difficulties. And once one got as far north as Lyon, then routes fanned out in all directions as the country flattened out – on along the Rhône into Switzerland, up the Saône to the headwaters of the Seine, or across to the valley of the Loire and thence Brittany.[8] We must also remember that water transport in the ancient world was much more extensive and hence more important than we often think, and that many small or shallow rivers that we would dismiss out of hand as being hopelessly un-navigable were in fact widely used, not by boats but by rafts and inflated bladders (*utri*). These did not even require to have the boatman ride on board. He could tow his craft from the river-bank, or, in shallow water, control it by wading alongside. This meant that even the merest stream with a foot or two of water in it could be pressed into service,

41

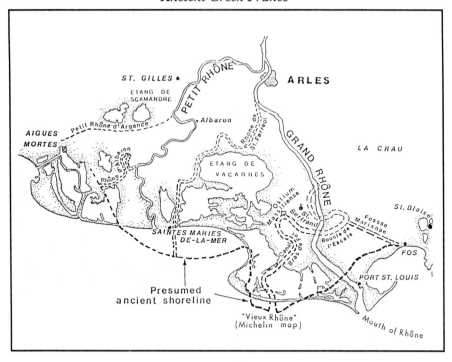

27. The Camargue, ancient and modern. The coastline has changed considerably, as have the number of mouths of the Rhône and its course.

and if the technology sounds inappropriately primitive, it was effective: it did not require a technical genius to realise that a load was more easily transported by floating it along a raft than by carrying it on your back. This of course does not mean that boats proper were not used on the Rhône itself, merely that through rafting it provided a series of water-borne connections to areas we would not think of. Even in Roman days rafting was a sufficiently important occupation at Arelate (Arles) for its practitioners (*utricularii*) to have formed a guild; some of the best seats in the Nîmes amphitheatre were marked off as reserved for them.[9]

The Camargue

The Camargue, loosely speaking, is the delta of the Rhône. Upstream, the head of the triangle is at Arles, where the Roman Via Julia/Domitia crossed the river on a floating bridge (to accommodate variations in level caused by floodwaters); today, Arles remains the lowest crossing point of the Rhône.[10] Here also the Rhône splits up into its two main arms, forming the sides of the triangular delta, the Grand Rhône entering the sea near Fos, and the Petit Rhône at Saintes-Maries-de-la-Mer. It also splits into several subsidiary streams, and throughout history has often changed

42

28. The Camargue: a typical view, near SS Maries de la Mer.

course. Even the number of mouths has been subject to change, varying between two and five. On all of them navigation was difficult because of silting, and the low-lying coastline, screened by endless sandbars, made it hard for ships approaching from the sea to find the way in, even from close inshore; the Massaliots sought to rectify matters by erecting towers at the principal mouth as markers, but it always remained a problem.[11] An attempt was made to by-pass it by Marius, who dug a ship canal, the Fossae Marianae, from somewhere around Fos (which inherits the name) to the Grand Rhône further upstream. Now completely obliterated, not least by the development of Fos as a modern Europort for supertankers, its course has been much disputed (some studies carrying it all the way upriver to Arles), but its most probable course seems to have been from the Étang Galéjon (no longer existing), which communicated with the sea, round the Ile de Lansac and into the Rhône at the formerly-existing Boucle de l'Escale, a total length of 7 km (Fig. 27).[12]

By land, the Camargue is deceptive in two ways. The first I have already hinted at by describing it as a delta, 'loosely speaking'. Strictly speaking, the picture is more complicated. A delta is formed when a river carrying a lot of sediment in suspension in its waters meets a sea that is more or less stationary, with not enough tides or currents to scour the sediment away. The braking effect on the river water causes it to deposit its sediment, building up a delta, as in the Nile. A first glance at the map suggests that the Rhône does this too, but this is not wholly so. In the sea there is a strong offshore current (2 knots) running from east to west. The mouths

43

29. The Camargue: sunset over the Étang de Vacarrès.

of the Rhône facing south-east encounter this head-on, so that the braking effect and subsequent build-up of a delta do in fact occur. But on the other side, the story is different. The mouths of the Rhône facing south-west discharge their waters into the sea current that is moving the same way, so the sediment remains in suspension and there is no delta-like build-up. Except for the south-east corner, therefore, where the coastline has advanced, there has been no silting. Conversely, at the south-west corner the coastline has been receding and Saintes-Maries-de-la-Mer, which in mediaeval times was several kilometres inland, now is not only a coastal resort but has to be protected by massive sea walls against further erosion. The present topography of the Camargue is therefore very different from that of antiquity – indeed, it has changed more extensively than any other part of the area we are considering – but the change is not of the progressive and uniform sort that we expect from a delta.[13] The second potential deception awaits anyone who visits the Camargue and, looking at its endless vistas of marshy pools where land and water intermingle, extrapolates from this into ancient times. In Greco-Roman times there was a great deal more firm ground than there is now. There was more arable land, even some forest, and in all parts of it except in the south-east corner mentioned above, excavation regularly turns up coins, potsherds and other evidence of ancient habitation. Grain was produced, and iron ore, in transit from mines in the Cevennes, sometimes smelted there. The picture, in short, is one of much greater prosperity than one would nowadays suspect.[14]

30. La Crau: the side of the dug trench clearly shows the stony nature of the ground.

31. La Crau: high windbreaks (left) commonly shelter the fields from the blast of the Mistral.

On the other hand, if one is looking for a poor and desolate area, one has not far to go. Immediately to the west of the Camargue is the stony plain of La Crau, lying between Arles and Salon, and stretching south to the sea at Fos. Swept by the often ferocious blasts of the Mistral, a certain amount of it has today been rendered cultivable by surrounding all the fields with windbreaks of cypresses and other tall plants, but nothing can be done about the millions of stones that litter its surface and topsoil, giving it its ancient name of 'Stony' (Fig. 30, 31). Greek legend accounted for them by telling how Heracles fought the Ligurians there, assisted by these missiles; the result was an inhospitable desert that, unlike the Camargue, was evidently never settled; excavation regularly draws a blank.[15]

The Côte d'Azur

The modern celebrity of the Côte d'Azur was late in coming. The difficulty of coastwise (and other) communications and the general absence of arable land for long condemned the area to relative poverty. Monaco itself has a history going back to the sixth century BC – it is mentioned in Hecataios – but its prosperity dates only from the coming of the coastal railway that made it accessible. Sometimes the coastal mountains can be by-passed by inland valleys, notably the 100 km long one that gives wide and easy access from Aix-en-Provence all the way to Fréjus (and in antiquity carried the Roman Via Julia), but all the Greek colonies were, like Greek colonies everywhere, located along the coast, and apparently did not penetrate far enough inland to exploit such communications for their immediate needs. The coastal picture was thus largely the same as that presented in mainland Greece by the Isthmus of Corinth, celebrated in Greek legend by its unflattering sobriquet, Kake Skala, 'The Bad Stairway', and a notorious bane to travellers in every age. To this general rule Massalia was something of an exception, for though it was to some extent hemmed in by the twin chains of the Étoile and the Estaque (and still is), it did have access to the more fertile lands around Aix (which is probably as far as its direct political control went, if that far), and above all was well placed to control the vital Rhône valley access. This it could do because, given the difficulties of silting and sandbars, evidently nobody could build a city at the mouth of the Rhône itself – nobody even tried – while the Massaliots were within easy maritime striking distance and firmly based on one of the best natural harbours on the whole coast.[16]

This brings up a further characteristic of the Côte d'Azur, or the area east of the Rhône. Its rocky, mountainous coasts offered abundant good harbours, and of the type that the Greeks particularly liked. To a landsman, rocks are something to be feared and avoided; he instinctively prefers a sandy beach. To a sailor, who knows where the rocks are and how to avoid them, they can be a friend in need because they can form a natural breakwater against heavy seas and, if they rise high enough, can also offer shelter from the wind. A long, straight beach, on the other hand, offers shelter from nothing. One thinks, for example, of the Adriatic coast of Italy, with mile after endless mile of beaches and no real port anywhere between Ancona and Bari, and even the south of Italy, from Taranto round to about Locri, is not all that much different. The rocky inlets of Greece and Asia Minor are a very different story, and the Côte d'Azur offered Greek mariners abundant sheltered harbours of the type they were accustomed to.[17] Around Marseille are a number of calanques (a calanque is a kind of miniature fjord;[18] see Figs. 32-4) that must have been welcomed by Greek seamen, as they are by modern yachtsmen. They do not seem to figure at all in ancient history though they must have been in use. I expect the explanation is that they offered altogether too good a harbour, ringed around with steep cliffs that barred all landward access, and so offered nothing else. What the Greeks liked was a sheltered harbour, or preferably two of them side by side, with the harbour city located on a peninsula in between, thus guaranteeing that, whatever the weather and wind direction, one of the two sides was always sheltered. The best known examples of this are the Peiraeus, with its ports on both sides of the central peninsula, and perhaps Cyzicus, but the specification also includes Phocaia itself, built on a promontory between two harbours, and may have (depending on whether the creek of la Joliette was in use) also included Massalia.

However, whether of single or double configuration, one thing is clear. The Côte d'Azur offered plenty of such natural harbours, and they nearly all had one further advantage. Because they mostly faced south, on to the

32. A typical calanque, the Calanque d'En-Vau, near Cassis.

33. The Calanque Port-Miou, Cassis.

sea, they were sheltered from the north-west blasts of the Mistral. The chief exception here is the enormous land-locked anchorage of Toulon, which is so big that the coastal mountains can effectively shelter only the inshore half of it. This may be why this, the finest natural port on the whole coastline and traditionally the great Mediterranean base of the French navy, plays no part in antiquity.[19]

But, to be properly useful, a good harbour needs something else, a requirement often overlooked by modern commentators. It has to have some reason for people to go there, other than the fact that it is easy to do so. What this boils down to is that there can be two such reasons. One is that the harbour is required for purely seafaring needs. It is necessary for the coasting trade, offering a stopover where supplies can be replenished, water casks refilled, or perhaps a secure shelter in case of bad weather. That is, ships do not go there for reasons of cargo or traffic, but because it is a necessary or convenient step in their progress towards their real destination, in much the way that, in the nineteenth century, steamships were dependent on the existence of a world network of coaling stations, since their inefficient engines used a great deal of it and they could not go very far without refuelling. The distance that ancient freighters regularly covered non-stop is subject to some dispute,[20] but no doubt there were quite a number of small inlets along the Côte d'Azur that grew up chiefly to fill this need. Many of them may be referred to as 'comptoirs', trading posts, but probably they really existed as marine service stations rather than because of any trade that they generated.

34. Calanque, near Cassis.

The second reason for establishing an important harbour is that there has to be a source of trade. This sounds so obvious a truism that one hesitates to mention it, but it is often overlooked and one sees statements that a city become great and famous because it had a good harbour, as if

49

nothing else were needed. Less obvious but equally true is the converse. Trading opportunities may be so great that a port develops and prospers even if its harbour is a bad one. The greatest and most famous port in the whole of the ancient Mediterranean, Alexandria, was not particularly good for sailors, and the same thing was true of Gadès, Puteoli, and Narbonne. The excellence of the harbours at Peiraeus and Syracuse was almost the exception rather than the rule, and is liable to give us a wrong impression.[21] Even Massalia, as we saw (p. 33 above), was not wholly satisfactory. The desolate, mountainous terrain of the Côte d'Azur, devoid alike of productive arable plains and the access to a rich hinterland exemplified by the Rhône valley, must have meant that most of the Massaliot colonies along it were essentially way-stations for coastwise shipping. In Languedoc, the situation was very different.

Languedoc

The sea current prevailing off the mouths of the Rhône, as we have seen, caused an asymmetrical build-up of the delta. On the eastern side, it did build up, while on the western side the sediment brought down by the river was not deposited, but wafted away by the current. Eventually, however, the current did deposit it, along the Languedoc coast, building up a series of spits and sandbars that often isolated existing bays as lagoons cut off from the sea, creating today what is known to geographers as a 'lido' topography. These spits, often no more than 2 m high but up to 20 km long, today in use as beaches and holiday resorts, effectively cut off what was in any case a low-lying mainland not rich in natural harbours (Fig. 23). Overland lateral communications were easy, for the land was flat (a great contrast with the Côte d'Azur), but the route ran parallel to the coast and some distance inland. The point is clearly illustrated by the patterns of modern urbanisation. In the Côte d'Azur, the cities – Marseille, Toulon, Cannes, Antibes, Nice, Monaco – are all on the coast, even if they are not great ports. In Languedoc – Montpellier, Béziers, Narbonne, Perpignan – they are all some 10-15 km inland, often served by some separate coastal centre (much as Athens was by the Peiraeus) whether for needs of trade or, more commonly nowadays, recreation.

This does not make for good harbours. The area has two good-sized rivers, the Aude and the Hérault, but the Aude (the ancient Atax of Pomponius Mela) is almost a non-starter. Its mouth beset by shifting sands, it has radically changed course since classical times. Then it had two arms (like a delta), one running due east and forming the existing river; the other ran south and had the city of Narbo built on it (where the Via Domitia crossed it by a Roman bridge still forming part of the downtown core of Narbonne), entering the sea at Ste. Lucie, where the ancient harbour was located on the Étang Bages, 5 km from Narbo. Course changes have now isolated this section so that it is no longer part of the Aude at all, but a separate stream, the Robine. The Hérault is more promising. On it was built Agde (Gk. *Agathe Tyche*, 'Good Luck City'), with deep water river access to the sea. The city was built some 5 km upriver and provides almost the only example in the whole area of what we would call an estuary port. These advantages did not, however, permit it to develop into a major centre, and the area enveloped by its walls[22] remained quite small, about 200 m in diameter. What all of this emphasises, of course, is that the existence of good harbours is not the only requisite for commercial development (otherwise the only good natural harbour in the whole Languedoc coast, Sète, would show some signs of significant ancient settlement, which in fact is signally absent). What was important about Languedoc was the existence of a good, arable coastal plain.

We have considered the question of harbours and access by sea. We now move to the land and its products. For some of this material we will perforce be relying on evidence from the Roman period, so it may not be strictly relevant to the colonisation of the Greeks, and what they found when they landed: its relevance will lie in the light it throws on the sort of land that awaited them, and its potential.[23] For this it will be convenient to abandon our topographical breakdown and deal with the area as a whole – roughly speaking, the modern Provence.

Provence – agriculture and other products

On the farmland of Languedoc and, presumably, what there was of it on the Côte d'Azur, the usual grain and vegetable crops would be raised. As well as that, there were two crops that the Greeks themselves always regarded as peculiarly characteristic of their civilisation, olives and the vine. When, in Homer, Odysseus lands in a strange country, one of the things he automatically notes, along with other more relevant points (such as its harbours), is whether it would be good for growing them.[24]

Olives

Olives were a vital part of the classical economy. They were eaten, and olive oil was used as a seasoning for salads, as a cooking oil (for frying and so forth), for lamps, and as a substitute for soap. In trade, olives could be transported as freight, but it was much more usual to press them locally and then ship out the oil in amphorae. Like wine, olive oil existed in a large number of different qualities, depending on how many pressings the olives had already been through, and on the region of origin. In our area, olives are grown without trouble all along the coastal plain, but the climate becomes too cold for them north of Avignon (Fig. 35). Olives freeze at around $-6°C$, and temperatures as low as this are registered in Marseille, roughly speaking, about once in ten years: 'gel des oliviers' is officially recorded as an indication of a particularly severe winter.[25]

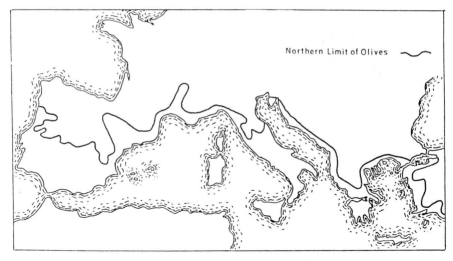

Northern Limit of Olives

35. Limits of olive cultivation in Southern Europe.

Wine

The other great contribution of the Greek colonists to the agriculture of Gaul was the vine, and its end-product, wine. Massaliot wine we will consider more closely when we are studying Massalia (p. 117f. below), but we may here reasonably turn to wine and the role it played in Greek and Celtic France as a whole. For wine was a Greek invention. It was not the only alcoholic drink known. The East, the Egyptians and other Orientals, had for long drunk beer, and to the West so did the Gauls and Germans. But when the Greeks colonised, they brought wine with them, and seldom did the gift go unappreciated. Wild vines already existed (the lambrusque) around much of the Mediterranean coastline. The difference was that the Greeks had learned how to cultivate the vine, and how to make wine from it. They also imported vines from Greece, this being quicker than domesticating the wild local vines.[26] The overseas origin of viticulture was always recognised in France, and so celebrated in a fourteenth-century poem written in Provençal:

> Sains Bacus selon l'ystoire
> D'oultre mer vint, c'est chose croire.[27]

However, although the land was certainly suitable for growing vines, and although vines were grown and wine made by the Greek colonists, we must not overestimate its importance. Wine was indeed traded and consumed in large quantities, but throughout our period it was largely imported wine, from the vintners of Campania and Apulia. It is only with the era of Augustus that this trade tapers off, and is replaced by wine now produced in large quantities in Provence and elsewhere in Gaul. Until then, local production seems to have been much more limited (perhaps just enough for the Greek settlers themselves), though the subsequent boom in exploitation proves that the land was suitable for it.[28] It must also be made clear that a somewhat divergent view has been held, and that one of the motives in the choice of sites for Greek colonies, it is suggested, is wine-based – they wanted to lay down vineyards in locations convenient to a large potential barbarian market, to which they could sell wine in large quantities.[29] But it does also remain true that a great deal of this wine, during the period of Massaliot independence, was imported. Perhaps Massalia simply could not produce enough.

Herbs

We are liable to underestimate the economic importance of herbs in antiquity. Some cities could just about live on their production and export of herbs: Cyrene made its fortune out of silphium, and recognised the fact by putting a picture of it on its coinage, while Selinus, in Sicily, was named after the wild celery which grew locally. Herbs were used in cookery and flavouring drinks, and, of course, were almost the only kind of medicine that existed. Provence is still famous for its herbs, especially lavender, to the raising of which whole farms are devoted. In antiquity it was known as *stoechas*, from the Stoechades Islands (now the Porquerolles archipelago, off the coast of Hyères), while Massalia was also celebrated internationally for its hellebore. The Gauls dipped their hunting arrows in it, with the object of tiring out the animal thus wounded, something like a modern tranquilising gun. *Seseli* ('sil Massilieuse'), variously identified as saxifrage, hartwort, or fennel, seems to have been a kind of aniseed, and was used in alcoholic drinks; it has accordingly been identified as the ancestor of both Greek ouzo and the pastis that is still the hallmark drink of Marseille. *Apsinthion* (wormwood), growing on the slopes of the Alps and traditionally known as a 'puissant sudorifique' has been claimed as the origin of absinthe, and Celtic nard (*saliunca*) enjoyed as high a reputation as the Indian.[30] We may also, in closing, note among the vegetable resources of the area a profusion of wood. It was not something the colonists particularly needed or were attracted by, but it was there.[31]

Salt

One of the most important products was salt.[32] Because we normally see and use salt only in pinches, we underrate its importance. It was early recognised as an essential in the human diet, and vital in preserving fish and pork. 'Salt roads', dating back to prehistoric times, testify to how far and wide it was sought – the Via Salaria running up the Tiber valley from Rome is only one of such. Salt comes from two sources. One is rock salt, which is mined like any other mineral. The other is salt pans, flat, shallow pools, either natural or artificial, in which salt is formed from sea water by evaporation. This sounds simple enough, but in fact it was quite rare to find the requisite combination of conditions. The Atlantic coast of Gaul, for example, was unsuitable – winds from the Ocean were humid, and there was not usually enough sun to evaporate the brine – the Scilly Islands, in the middle of a salty ocean, actually had to import salt, bartering tin for it. The Mediterranean coast, however, particularly Languedoc, was exceptionally well suited: it had shallow lagoons, and hot sun and strong winds to assist the evaporation, and consequently produced a great deal of salt; and, because of its more limited expanse and higher evaporation from hot weather, the Mediterranean water is more saline than the Ocean to start with. To an unaccustomed eye, the mountains of salt produced in a modern plant must impress by their sheer scale, but they must also remind us that in antiquity too this product doubtless accounted for a greater volume of trade than we normally think. In 1952, salt production in the South of France was 620,000 tons, and the Camargue accounted for more than half (Figs. 36, 37). Of course, salt pans also existed elsewhere in antiquity – the Euxine, Lemnos, Euboea, Larnaca (Cyprus), Taranto and South Tunisia; also alongside the Phocaean colony Alalia, in Corsica, which may have influenced its location – but Languedoc and the Camargue remained one of the biggest producers.[33]

Salt production might be a reason for founding settlements – indeed, given that salt had to be produced, settlements there had to be – but, unless combined with other activities, they were subject to certain limita-

36. Salt pans near Fos, for the production of salt by the evaporation of sea water.

37. A veritable mountain of salt, at Salin de Giraud, in the Camargue.

tions. One was location. The settlements had to be wherever the salt pans were, irrespective of harbours, military considerations, or supporting a population. The work does not seem to have been labour-intensive, so, without any other economic support, only a small community would be viable. But the merchants based there would be no mere local 'general traders' or peddlars; they would be interested in long-distance markets.[34] And, unlike the wine trade, salt manufacture was presumably established in Gaul before the arrival of the Greeks, so that what happened, since the Greek colonies occupied the coastal strip and that is where the salt was produced, is that the Greeks took over an existing local industry and then sold to the Celts what they had previously produced for themselves. One would expect this to have been a source of contention, but we do not hear of anything. Perhaps, at this early stage, the Celts were not sufficiently organised or united to object.[35]

Fish

As in all Mediterranean coasts, fish were an abundant resource sometimes eaten fresh, sometimes salted and exported. In Provence there was an added feature, the shallow étangs and lagoons, where the fishing was better than in the deep waters off the Côte d'Azur. The shallow water encouraged the use of the harpoon and trident, which were especially effective in windy weather that stirred up the bottom mud: in such weather, we are told, the inhabitants simply go out and harpoon all the fish they want, to the extent of the Gauls even feeding their horses and oxen on them.[36]

The mullet (Lat. *mullus*), still a common fish at Marseille, was sufficiently celebrated for Milo in his letter to Cicero to make a joke about relieving his exile in Massalia by eating them; oysters were plentiful (the Étang de Berre was famous for them and there were even oyster beds in the Lacydon itself, the harbour of Massalia), and so were tunny. The tunny is, strictly speaking, an Atlantic fish, but shoals of them come in through the Straits of Gibraltar. This means that tunny fishing is best in the Western Mediterranean (as opposed to, say, the Aegean), and Massalia was famous for it, as was Antipolis.[37]

Metals

Gold was a metal in which Gaul was traditionally rich. Gallic society was seldom sufficiently developed to use it as currency and a lot of it seems to have been dedicated in temples or worn in the form of neck-torques or other adornments. This has sometimes prompted remarks that the Gauls had more gold than they knew what to do with, though this probably underestimates the common practice, among primitive peoples, of carrying their wealth around in the form of ornaments as a recognised way of both impressing others and keeping safe their capital. Not much gold was to be found in Provence itself, but it was mined in the Cevennes and the Pyrenees and so was readily available by trade. Further inland, it was also to be found by panning in rivers such as the Rhône, the Gardon, the Ardèche and the Hérault. Silver and lead (the two are often found together in the same ore, *galena*) were available in reasonable abundance in the Maures, the long range of coastal mountains stretching from Toulon to Fréjus, possibly doing something to compensate for their agricultural infertility. Copper and iron deposits are also recorded in the same general area. The export of minerals from this arrière-pays may also have been a supplementary reason for the foundation here of a string of small Greek ports (such as Caccabaria, Olbia, Pergantion, and Athenopolis), complementing their value as service stations for coastal navigation.[38]

But by far and away the most important metal was tin, and that in spite of the fact that there were no tin deposits whatever in the area. Its importance was a product of two factors. First, tin is an essential ingredient in the manufacture of bronze, this being an alloy of tin and copper. Copper was abundant in the Mediterranean basin (notably in Cyprus, which gave its name to it), but tin was not. Second, the chief source of tin was Brittany, Cornwall, and the Scilly Islands. From there, unless it went by sea all the way round by the Straits of Gibraltar, it simply had to come down the Rhône to reach the Mediterranean around Massalia, which thus occupied a strategic position (in modern parlance, a 'choke point') controlling this vital and valuable traffic.[39]

The value of tin in the ancient world is easily forgotten. Modern

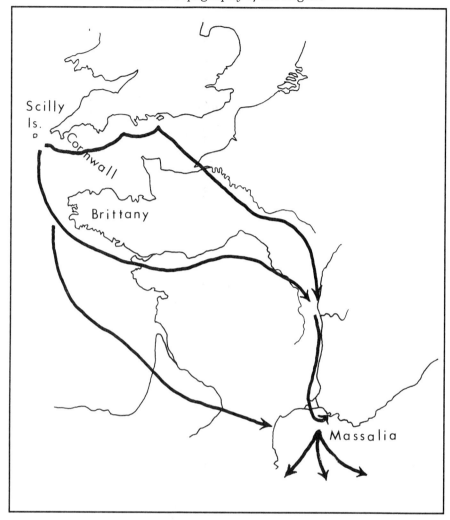

38. Routes for the transport of tin across France.

associations – tin soldiers, tin cans – are all pejorative, suggesting something as flimsy as it is cheap and common. Bronze is a different matter. Yet without tin you cannot have it, and the whole Bronze Age was carried on the back of the tin trade. Not only did the addition of the tin to the copper give an alloy that was harder and tougher, but in its molten state it was also less viscous, facilitating delicate casting: in a complex mould, molten bronze will get into all the corners and crannies, while molten copper may not. And the tin, upon which all of this bronze depended, came from the ends of the earth. The situation may strike a familiar chord with readers living in one of the modern Western countries so dependent on oil from the Middle East. Indeed, to have the whole of early Mediterranean civilisation depending for centuries upon this incredibly tenuous and attenuated link seems so improbable that attempts have been made to identify other sources of supply, in Iran, Turkey, Bohemia and elsewhere (see n. 39). Certainly we shall be safe in sticking with Cornwall and Brittany as the major source, and, for our purposes, the only one that counts. This ought to have left the Bretons and the Cornishmen in a fine position to exercise an economic stranglehold on the whole of Greek civilisation, to say nothing of the rest of the Mediterranean, but they seem to have lived in much too primitive and disorganised a state to recognise their good fortune, much less to take advantage of it. Instead, as the tin caravans made their way south down the Rhône, Massalia (once it was founded) was the first place they came to that was sufficiently developed to exploit financially this vital traffic as it passed through. It was also the last, for once on board ship the tin could follow any route to any part of the Mediterranean without being obliged to pass by any particular strait or other point where tolls could be levied. The tin routes from Brittany to Greece were thus something like a letter X, converging as they crossed France and diverging again once they put to sea, with site of Massalia at the midpoint, the point of intersection.[40] It was the one place that could not be dodged, and tin was the one thing that everybody had to have. Thus, although tin was purely a transit traffic rather than a locally indigenous export, one of the great advantages inherent in the location of Massalia was that it was ideally positioned to get rich from it. Whether or not the Phocaeans realised this when they picked the site for their colony we can hardly say, but since the trade had, by definition, been going on all through the Bronze Age, that is for several millennia previously, the Phocaeans had at least had plenty of time to note and observe it. So, of course, had everybody else, but when it came to planting a colony there the fact remains that it was the Phocaeans that did it.

Miscellaneous

We may finish by listing other Celtic products of lesser importance that were available at or through Massalia and Provence. Henri Ternaux, writing in 1826, is scarcely an up-to-date authority, but for conciseness his list of Celtic exports could hardly be bettered – 'metals, honey, cheese, grain, wool, hides, leather, cattle, dogs, slaves, and lots of things like that' (*permulta hujusmodi*).[41] One can only comment that at least they had a diversified economy. For our purposes, this list is not wholly relevant. Celtic grain was not important for the economy of Greek Provence, and slaves so important that we will consider them as a separate item below, in the section on Massalia. They are passed over here because they were, in a way, a resource available to Greek colonists anywhere that they chose to avail themselves of it, and not inherent in the topography.

Basalt, on the other hand, was. The value of this hard, rough, black rock lies in the fact that it was used for millstones. There were two sources of it in Provence, at Agde and Ollioules, a little north-west of Toulon, and millstones made from it and exported have been found over a wide area. Coral was to be found in the Stoechades Islands (off Hyères), and was mentioned by Pliny.[42] It is also possible that from one of the Stoechades came supplies of murex, the well-known source of purple dye, but this seems to be based on nothing more solid than the island in question being named Phoinike, i.e. 'Scarlet'. Garnet was a different matter. The garnet is a semi-precious stone, deriving its Greek name, *anthrax*, 'coal', from the way it glows bright red under strong light, and is often found in association with iron ore. Some of it was produced high up on the Alpine passes, notably the Simplon, the St. Gotthard, and the Tende (between Cuneo and Ventimiglia), also in Elba and Corsica, but the two major sources were in the western coastal ranges of the Côte d'Azur, namely, the Maures (Toulon-Fréjus) and the Esterel (Fréjus-Cannes). In Roman times, and hence possibly also in Greek, the stone was evidently worked locally, and then exported, principally through Massalia though some of the small ports in the immediate area may also have benefited from this trade, as we have suggested above that they did from metals. Some was doubtless used to decorate native Celtic jewellery, as it certainly did in the Late Empire.[43]

It remains only to mention one prominent but ambiguous asset of the region. It was full of rabbits. Rabbits have long been accepted as the poor man's game, and are a welcome enough supplement to the cooking pot for them often to be raised commercially in modern Greece on rabbit farms. To the ancients they were a pest, pure and simple. They were not uniformly spread though the Mediterranean, and until they moved West, mainland Greeks had evidently never heard of them at all, and, having no word in their language for them, called them 'earth-digging hares'.[44]

This brings us to the end of our summary of ancient Provence and its natural resources, both those locally present and those available by import from Gaul. Some are more important than others and we may here anticipate and declare that, as things eventually worked out during the Greek colonisation, the economy came to be based on an exchange of wine and metal goods for slaves and tin. This will be studied further when we come to consider Massalia and its trade. Considered regionally, Languedoc was fertile and provided abundant grain to support the colonists (with even greater supplies close at hand in Aquitania), while the Côte d'Azur was mountainous, poor, but with some minerals. Massalia was located between the two and also enjoyed, by the Rhône valley, a high road of access to Central Gaul and Northern Europe. What, then, was all this worth? In colonial terms, was this a good area to colonise?

Appraisal

The question 'How good was this region?' is best answered with another: 'What did the ancients think of it?' But this is no great help, because the ancient texts described Provence both as very good and very bad – nobody seems to opt for anything in between. Thus to Diodorus, Provence (or at least Liguria, i.e. the Côte d'Azur) is 'stony and altogether wretched' with its inhabitants leading a toilsome and degraded existence. Cicero, in spite of his high opinion of Massalia itself, thought the same about the hinterland: making anything grow there was an endless struggle, and the people were consequently a gang of rough and tough hillbillies. Strabo joins the chorus, insisting on the unsuitability of the ground for growing grain, though he admits that it is all right for olives and vines.[45] Justin, on the other hand, tells a story that, if it is true, cannot but be strong evidence on the other side. The Phocaeans, he says, went right as far as Gibraltar in their search for a good site for a colony, and when they got to Provence ('around the mouth of the Rhône' is how he puts it) they were so impressed with what seemed to them a veritable paradise that they rushed straight home to Phocaea to spread the good news to all their friends. This 'Come and see what we've found!' reaction would be even more convincing if Justin did not qualify it by saying that the Phocaeans were driven to colonise abroad by the aridity of the cramped corner of land that they called home, on which almost anything at all would seem an improvement. It would also help if Justin himself were a more reliable witness. In fact he has been lambasted by practically every modern historian as an undiscriminating scribbler, but even a bad historian can sometimes get things right by accident, and an unreliable author can be perfectly sound if he happens to be repeating material from a reliable source. For what it is worth, the very much later writer Gregory of Tours, speaking of the Provence of the sixth century AD, describes it as 'a delightful spot', a verdict with which most modern visitors would concur.[46]

Comparing these references one would almost think they were talking about two different countries, and this may indeed be the truth. We have already noted how our area is split into two vastly different sections, the rocky and mountainous Côte d'Azur and the dunes and lagoons of Languedoc. It may be that our sources are in fact describing the two separate halves, and hence come up with two different descriptions. The unflattering comments of Cicero and Diodorus could well be aimed at the Côte d'Azur – it was closer to Italy so Romans perhaps might be more familiar with it, and in any case Cicero and Diodorus are both specifically referring to Liguria and the Ligurians, which rules out most of Western Provence. The Phocaeans, on the other hand, were initially attracted by Massalia, which is not quite the same thing, and is only marginally, if at all, to be considered part of Liguria. We must also remember that while it is true that all Greek colonies depended first and foremost on agriculture for their own needs, the Phocaeans by all accounts placed more importance than most on commerce and seafaring, being driven to it by the poverty of their homeland.[47] They thus might well be willing to accept land that would be disdained by Romans, accustomed to the relatively lush pastures of Italy, particularly if it had plenty of harbours, a resource that the land-bound

Romans would in turn be liable to underrate. The Côte d'Azur, after all, is not notably rougher or more agriculturally intractable than mainland Greece itself, to say nothing of Ionia. None of this is too helpful in answering our questions, How good was this region for colonies? What it comes to is, it depends on which part of the region one is considering, and who are the prospective colonists considering it – what are their aims, their priorities, their criteria, and what are they used to? By absolute standards, the reputation Provence has established over countless centuries speaks for itself. As colonies go, this was prime territory. But what did the colonists themselves make of it, and how did they get on there? That will be our next concern, and that of our next chapters.

5

The City of Massalia

In the story of the Phocaean colonisation of the Western Mediterranean, Massalia and Alalia (Corsica) might almost be considered together, as a pair. Their dates of foundation do not coincide – Massalia came first, being founded about 600 BC and Alalia around 565 – but, relatively speaking, they are not far apart, and fit into the same chronological context of Phocaean penetration of the region, forming as it were a common response to the same impulse. Unlike other subsequent colonies that often seem to have been founded as sub-colonies of Massalia, Alalia was founded independently of it, and the two states existed in parallel, enjoying close and friendly ties with each other in a region otherwise unwelcoming: relations with the Etruscans were uniformly hostile, and with the Phoenicians at the best ambivalent, though, given the Phocaean colonists' fondness for large-scale piracy, nothing else was really to be expected. To Phocaeans in the mother city they no doubt represented twin beacons of their own civilisation firmly planted at the ends of the earth, much as Englishmen in the great days of the British Empire thought of Australia and New Zealand. Other Greeks, whose own colonies were closer to home, doubtless thought of them rather as being at the back of beyond.[1]

All of this would seem to make a good case for considering the two cities together. However, when one considers the immediate circumstances of their foundation, particularly the geographical, they could hardly be more unlike. One's first thought on visiting the two sites might well be that they could not possibly have been founded by the same people (as, of course, they were). We will examine both cities in detail later on, but we may here note some of the obvious differences. The most obvious is the harbour. Massalia was plainly chosen above all for the excellence of its harbour, the Lakydon.[2] This is no surprise, for it is what we would expect of a seafaring people. The surprise comes when we look at Alalia. At present it has no harbour at all, only a long, straight exposed beach exactly like those in Languedoc, that we have above criticised as being unsuitable for sailors. In antiquity there was of course a port – that is beyond question – but where was it? The prevailing opinion is that merchant shipping docked along the banks of the nearby River Tavignano, while the equally nearby pool *L'étang de Diana* served as a naval base. There is next to no evidence for this, and the identification is based on little more than the meanings of preserved place names,[3] and the not unreasonable argument 'Well,

62

39. The statue outside the Gare St. Charles, the main railway station at Marseille, shows a presumably Hellenic lady arriving on the bows of a ship, and reminds us that this is 'Marseille, Colonie Grecque'.

where else could the harbour have been?' Where, indeed? But this is a far cry from the Lakydon, and it was not for want of opportunity. In a land as mountainous and rugged as Corsica, good harbours, of the rock-sheltered type, are to be found at every turn, and the founding fathers of Alalia deliberately passed them all by, choosing a site on the only extensive flat and straight length of coastline in the entire island. Indeed, if one is looking for a parallel to Massalia, it would surely be hard to overlook Bonifacio as a possible site for a maritime colony. Not only does it have a superb land-locked harbour very much on the model and proportions of the Lakydon, but boasts also an almost impregnable acropolis, surrounded on three sides by cliffs falling sheer for 60 m down to the sea below; and it commands the vital trade route passing through the narrows between Corsica and Sardinia. Yet this spectacularly strategic site plays little part in classical history and seems to have been completely ignored by the Phocaeans.[4]

When we look landwards, it is the same story. The founders of Massalia seem to have had their eyes on trade, not agriculture. The city is hemmed in by the mountains, which come right down to the sea on both sides of it and arable land is at a premium. Alalia, on the other hand, is in a good-sized plain, the only one in Corsica, and the city itself is on a low plateau some 3 km inland from the coast (unlike the Massaliots, who lived right on top of their harbour). There is, of course, nothing wrong about settling a colony on good agricultural land, but it does seem to indicate a different set of priorities. We would at first sign surely be tempted to declare that Alalia was obviously founded by farmers and Massalia by traders,[5] did we not know that both sprang from the same mother city, Phocaea.

The foundation of Massalia

Massalia was founded around 600 BC by Phocaea. Both facts, the date and the Phocaean connection, seem wholly certain. That Massalia was a Phocaean foundation is clearly stated by all our ancient sources, led by the weighty authority of Thucydides and followed by Strabo, Pausanias, Livy, and others.[6] The proposition might also be deemed self-evident since this end of the Mediterranean was extensively penetrated and settled by the Phocaeans and nobody much else seems to have gone there. The date is a different matter.

Though none of our ancient sources gives an actual year for the foundation, they are split between two rough datings fifty years or so apart, one group opting for a date around 600 BC,[7] the other for around 545. The 545 date is usually, it seems, the product of a common mistake. Around 545 Phocaea was attacked and taken by Harpagos, a general of Cyrus the Great, king of Persia. A large part if not all of the Phocaean population immediately emigrated as refugees and were taken in by their own colony of Alalia, which had been founded perhaps some twenty years before. The mistake arises out of the belief that it was on this occasion that they also founded Massalia, which can thus be dated by the fall of Phocaea. This erroneous idea is shared by Pausanias, Timagenes and Hyginus.[8] Of the two rival datings, 600 and 545, the first is known to be the correct one, because it is confirmed by the archaeological evidence of potsherds.[9] Other sources are simply less explicit. Thucydides relates the founding of Massalia to the Battle of Alalia (536/5), which links it to the lower date without specifically saying so, while Herodotus, giving a full account of the Phocaeans fleeing the incursions of Harpagos, simply sends them to Alalia and never mentions Massalia at all. But all of this may be briefly summarised. Despite the authority and reliability of Herodotus and Thucydides, this time they are both wrong, and 600 is to be definitively accepted as the foundation date of Massalia.[10]

For the expedition itself we are dependent on ancient sources of varying reliability. Strabo graphically describes the sailing of the expedition from Phocaea, under the divine guidance of the goddess Artemis of Ephesos and her human representative, the priestess Aristarche. The arrival at Massalia is recounted by Justin. In his account the expedition is under the command of a Phocaean named Protis, and on arrival the Greeks were not only hospitably received by the local Celtic chieftain, Nannos, but invited by him to the betrothal ceremony of his daughter, Gyptis. At the feast, Gyptis asked to choose her own husband, turned away from all the Celtic suitors and picked Protis. Her father, honouring her choice, made over as a gift to the new colonists a tract of land from his realm, on which they built the city of Massalia – and, one is tempted to add, lived happily ever after. This, of course, is pure romance and not to be taken seriously. Most Greek colonies equipped themselves with a foundation myth and some sort of legendary founder to be appropriately honoured in tradition.[11] And the story itself is a common one, in folk tales, the princess who falls in love with the romantic and handsome stranger from the sea – one cannot but be reminded of Odysseus and Nausicaa in Homer's *Odyssey*. Nevertheless, it does probably preserve, in legend form, an actual historical truth: that the emigrant Phocaeans were kindly received, and founded their colony by peaceful agreement with the natives, not by conquest.[12] We may imagine, then, if we are romantically inclined, the Phocaean emigration fleet arriving off the Lakydon one day in June, the crews sitting back on their benches and cheerfully hailing it as a good omen that after the long, hard pull from Phocaea the pentekonters were wafted effortlessly in on a favourable breeze; while on the beach clustered a welcoming throng of native Celts and, lining the deck, smiling migrants told each other this was indeed a good land, just like home as they had been promised.[13] Purple prose aside, what met their eyes as the ships entered harbour? One thing we may be fairly sure of. To some of those on board it was familiar territory. There can be no question of the fleet sailing along the coast and picking Massalia simply because it looked like a good place to stop. There had already been extensive Phocaean penetration of the region by traders and the geography of the Western Mediterranean was no secret on the Phocaean waterfront. Even if we are disinclined to believe Justin's account[14] of Phocaean seafarers hurrying home full of the praises of Massalia as a site for a colony, on the general principle that Justin cannot be trusted, still his account does fit it in well with what we know to have happened, and there is nothing inherently improbable about it.

We may take it, then, that the Phocaean fleet was specifically bound for Massalia, knew where it was going, and how to get there. We may also take it that it carried on board a number of traders and skippers who had been there before and were prepared to act as pilots and beachmasters.

It is less certain but still, I think, probable that the Celts knew they were coming. There had already been extensive commercial contact between Celts and Phocaeans. The Phocaean expedition was a well-planned enterprise, unlike the rushed emergency evacuation in 545, and in the civic debate preceding the sailing, traders returning from the West must have been asked pointed questions about not only the geography and economic conditions of the region but also on the potential and probable reaction of the native tribes. Given that these issues were probably being aired for two or three years before the actual colonisation, it is reasonable that on their various trips west the Greek traders would then sound out the local Celts, who would therefore either be able to make a good guess at what was coming, or, more probably, would come to an actual firm agreement. Why not, after all? It would manifestly be comforting for the Phocaean colonists to know in advance that they were not going to be refused admission on arrival and have to fight their way in, and from their subsequent behaviour it does not look as if the Celts were against the idea. So we may hypothesise that a deal was done beforehand. It would be interesting to know whether this was common practice in founding colonies, but it is an aspect of Greek colonisation on which our information seems to be decidedly scanty.

If the Celts did have a previously agreed understanding with the Phocaeans and so were expecting their arrival (or even if they hadn't and weren't), they were still probably standing on the beach when they pentekonters sailed in. The fleet would approach Massalia by coasting along the shore, probably from the east, having made the crossing from Corsica to somewhere around Nice or Antibes. It is perhaps possible that they came in rather from the west after making landfall at the mouth of the Rhône or even further west. What is almost certain is that they did not come straight in from the open sea, given the difficulty of accurately navigating or even knowing what the course should be. The speed of the fleet was probably no more than 2.5 knots – fleets (especially one heavily laden with emigrants and all their paraphernalia) were notoriously slower than single ships – covering perhaps 40 km per ten-hour day. This means that when the fleet arrived at Massalia, it had spent the night before anchored no further away than La Ciotat, more likely at Cassis. A message coming by land, reporting the approach along the coast of a large fleet, would have travelled much faster – particularly since the messenger would not have to stop when it got dark, as the fleet did –, so Nannos, or whoever was chief of the Celts locally, ought to have had warning of the Greeks' coming. He ought to have known at least half a day before their arrival, probably much more, particularly if they were expected; in any case, ample time for everybody to get down to the shore and see what was happening. Even if the Greeks had wanted to surprise the Celts, their slow, highly visible approach along the coast would have made it impossible.

The topography of Massalia

When it comes to ancient descriptions, probably the most familiar is that the place looked as if it were in a hollow, in the shape of a theatre. Though sometimes applied to Massalia itself, the original text – the words are Strabo's – actually describes not the city but its harbour, the Lakydon. To a modern visitor it looks apt, because the Vieux Port, the nerve centre of the modern city, is ringed around by it, like the *cavea* of an ancient theatre. The simile seems all the more apt because there is high ground on all three sides (the fourth being open to the sea), particularly to the south, where it rises to a peak carrying the most famous monument of Marseille, the church of Notre Dame de la Garde.

The description by Julius Caesar was very different. 'Massalia', he wrote, 'is washed by the sea on just about three sides of the town; that leaves the fourth side, which is an approach by land.' This describes a situation the complete opposite of Strabo's, the difference between a city ringing around a bay, and one on a projecting peninsula; it is the difference between the concave and the convex.[15] Which is right? In fact both descriptions are justifiable, but Caesar's is the better. The ancient city, built by the Greek colonists, was located entirely on the north shore of the Lakydon, on the Butte St. Laurent and Butte des Moulins, and probably the Butte des Carmes as well (Fig. 42). The harbour may indeed have looked like a theatre, encircled by high ground, but (unlike today) the city was only on one side of it. On the other hand, it really was built on a peninsula. This is not obvious today because the ancient shoreline north of the harbour entrance has now been completely obliterated, partly by natural causes but particularly by the construction of the New Harbours (notably Le Bassin de la Grande Joliette), begun in 1845, to accommodate increased traffic to colonise French North Africa and the Suez Canal. In particular, the creek of La Joliette, which now hardly exists at all, went far back into the land, forming a considerable bay (though it is not certain how far it extended). This, as Fig. 42 shows, lent the ancient terrain that peninsula aspect noted by Caesar and for which the eye today seeks in vain. Indeed, appearances are doubly deceptive, for not only has the extent of the modern city spread to envelop the Vieux Port, but its business area has moved east as well, moving the essential town centre from the old site on

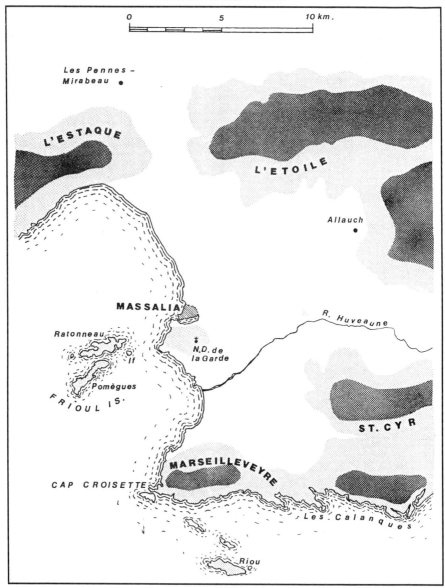

40. The environs of Massalia, encircled by hills.

the peninsula down to the lower end of the Canebière, thus emphasising the mental image of Marseille as a horseshoe-shaped city surrounding the harbour; or, as Clerc put it, the relationship of town and harbour is a 'sorte de cuvette dont il est le fond'.[16]

The Lakydon (Figs. 43, 51) evidently deriving its name from a spring

41. R. Huveaune, at La Penne-sur-Huveaune.

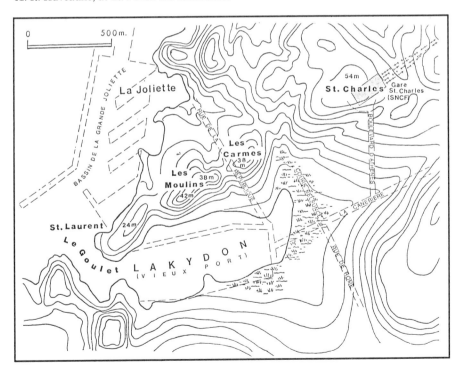

42. Topography of Massalia. It will be noted that in antiquity the Lakydon extended further inland than the Vieux Port does now.

43. The Vieux Port and Le Goulet, looking east from the Pharo Park.

44. The Vieux Port (Lakydon), with Notre Dame de la Garde on the hill in the background.

45. Marseille, from the terrace of Notre Dame de la Garde.

46. The east end of the Vieux Port, now largely a pleasure harbour with some fish traffic.

47. Set into the paving of the quay of the Vieux Port (almost opposite the lower end of La Canebière), a bronze plaque commemorates the arrival of the Greeks.

48. 'On this very spot (*ICI*) around 600 there landed Greek sailors from Phocaea, a Greek city of Asia Minor. They founded Marseille, and from there Civilisation spread through the West.'

flowing into its 'Horn', was perhaps the finest natural harbour between Italy and Spain.[17] It was considerably larger than the Vieux Port is now, curving round at its eastern end to bite deep into the land and form what the excavators have come to refer to as the 'horn of the harbour', *la corne du port*; it was also deeper.[18] Along the southern shore and in the 'Horn' a lot of the land was marshy and unsuitable for either building or docking ship. The same was true of the eastern end, where a very high water table has, even in the early 1900s, required modern structures, such as the Bourse and Chamber of Commerce, to be built on piles.[19] The southern shore, otherwise unoccupied, was therefore used as the cemetery of Massalia,[20] it being a standard rule of Greeks and Romans alike that burials could not take place within city limits. Fortunately, the northern shore of the Lakydon had a good beach where ships could run ashore and be unloaded over the stern (which was normal Greek docking practice), and this became the commercial waterfront of early Massalia. Remains of wooden piling and planking seem to indicate the presence of jetties, floating pontoons to facilitate unloading, and slipways for hauling ships up and out of the water, but nothing more elaborate or permanent – not, at least, at this early date. The actual waterfront was perhaps 50-100 m north of the existing quayside, and both traces and reconstructions *in situ* are to be found inside the Musée des Docks Romains, installed in the ground floor of a modern office building at the Place Vivaux. At a later date, in the Hellenistic era, the 'horn' was developed as a port, with masonry quays. The development proceeded slowly, reaching full fruition only in the Roman era. Until then, the North side of the Lakydon carried the bulk of Massalia's marine traffic (apparently in amicable co-existence with extensive oyster beds on the same location). This can be easily misunderstood, because today all the most impressive archaeological remains are to be seen at the 'horn', and one can easily forget that, being of Hellenistic or Roman date, they do not reflect the situation in the classical age of Greece; while literary sources, such as Strabo or Avienus, are of late date also.[21] We may note, moreover, that the harbour, effectively stretching along this northern shore of the Lakydon, must itself have been subdivided to cater for the various needs it served. Clerc distinguishes three. There ought to have been a fishermen's wharf, a deep-sea port, and a naval base, this last served in turn by ship-sheds (like those at Zea, in the Peiraeus), a chandler's store for rigging (like Philo's Arsenal at Athens) and armoury (possibly shared with the army), and a shipyard, for new construction. The commercial harbour would also need sheds or warehouses where cargoes could be temporarily stored until shipped out or disposed of. And alongside the fishing harbour there no doubt grew up a quayside fish market, unless the agora was close enough for the fish to go there directly. I am not, of course, suggesting that all these elaborations were installed by the colonists as soon as they landed, but it seems reasonable to assume that they grew up over the years.[22] There remains yet a further possibility to examine. What about La Joliette? Was it also in use as a harbour? There certainly was a bay at that location, with a stream running down into it from the low col between the Butte des Carmes and the Butte des Moulins. How extensive it was remains a problem, but it would, in a small way, have provided an alternative to the Lakydon, and in general the Greeks liked sites that offered a double harbour, two anchorages facing in opposite directions, so that, depending on wind direction, one was always sheltered. One thinks of the Peiraeus, and even Phocaea itself (Fig. 3), which both answered to this prescription. This was perhaps less applicable to Massalia than other cities, because the Lakydon was so sheltered on all sides (getting in or out of it through the Goulet might be a different story). Nevertheless, La Joliette was there, and could be used if needed. In 1153 AD it was still an operational port, in 1773 just a sandy beach.[23] In the Lakydon, the water level was almost the same as it is today. Maurice Euzennat, the original excavator of the 'horn' site, has noted that in antiquity the water was 20-30 cm lower, on the evidence both of the barnacle line on the Roman quay and of the fact that certain of the older drains otherwise would not have been able to discharge their contents into the sea. A more recent study, based on Antibes, has found that up to 750 BC the sea was 1-1.5 m below today's level, 0.5-1 m above it by 500, and 1-1.5 m above it by 300; it then subsided to reach the present level around 100 BC and 1.5 m below it around 1 AD, at which point it started rising again.[24] The reader should note that although we are here speaking of changes in the level (as do almost all publications), what is really meant is a change in the relative levels of land and water. It is not necessarily the water that has changed, and a lower sea level may just as well be caused by the land rising as the sea sinking. The chief difference is that while variations in level of the water must, within limits, be uniform overall, since water finds its own level, land movements on the other hand can be local. On the whole, variations in the 'sea level' in the ancient Mediterranean seem to have been caused by land-changes rather than sea-changes.[25]

We close our consideration of the Lakydon by turning to winds. The harbour itself is well enough sheltered, but a glance at the map will show that the Goulet is a problem. It is narrow (only 100 m wide), twisty, and it faces the north-west. The north-west is the direction from which comes the Mistral, which, at Marseille, blows on an average of 136 days in the year, or more than a third of the time. When a Mistral is blowing, therefore, it is very easy to enter the Goulet, for the wind is dead astern, but very hard to leave harbour, with a strong wind dead ahead, no room to manoeuvre, and rocks close on either side. Indeed, *Instructions Nautiques*, the nautical pilotage publication of the French government, emphasises that with a strong north-west wind (i.e. a Mistral), getting out of Marseille is dangerous even for a large steamer; the recommended procedure is to rush it, full steam ahead.[26] For an ancient square-rigger it must have been very different indeed, and the Massaliots must often have been grateful if they had inherited the Phocaean preference for pentekonters, which could go out under oar power alone if the wind proved contrary; though I would doubt if even that would rank as easy sailing. In fact, there were two solutions to the problem. One was simply to wait till the wind changed, which on an average shouldn't have meant more than a day or two, and was a strategy very familiar to ancient mariners. The other was to leave port on the land breeze. This was, and is, quite regular. The different rates of heating and cooling of land and water can result in an alternation of breezes blowing from sea to land by day (Beaufort scale 4) and the reverse by night (Beaufort 2-3).[27] The effect is local, being seldom felt more than 10-15 km from the coast, but they are often helpful to shipping entering or leaving port. Like its better know but milder Aegean counterpart, the meltemi, the Mistral is also a day-time wind, rising at down, reaching its peak around 10 am (12 in winter), and dying down to a calm at night fall.[28] One would therefore expect the Lakydon to have seen a regular pattern of ships arriving by day with the wind behind them (and daylight to help them, running in on to a lee shore and making the difficult landfall of the Goulet), and leaving by night, on the land breeze, to pick up the Mistral out at sea in the morning. I know of no evidence that this pattern existed, but it sounds reasonable.

The ancient city

The ancient city of Massalia probably owed its name to a Hellenic corruption of some native Ligurian toponym, which – it is always possible – may not have meant very much even to the Ligurians. The origin is probably by now beyond recovery, and though half-hearted attempts have been made from time to time to reconstruct from 'Massalia' some form of words that would actually mean something in some known (or unknown, which makes it much easier) language,[29] it is not a problem that we have much chance of resolving, nor one that need here trouble us greatly.

The Greek city was built, as we have noted, along the north shore of the Lakydon. Originally it was no doubt little more than a few rows of houses parallel to the beach, but gradually it spread to cover most of the peninsula. Up the middle of the peninsula runs a ridge of hills like a spine, getting higher as they go inland. There are four peaks, the *Buttes* of St. Laurent, Les Moulins, Les Carmes, and St. Charles. It was always accepted that St. Laurent and Les Moulins were within the circuit of the city walls and St. Charles outside it. The only problem was Les Carmes, was it inside the wall or outside? This question has now been answered, by a series of small excavations. Les Carmes was inside, and, for classical Massalia, the city walls followed the dotted line marked on Fig. 51, starting at the 'horn' of the harbour, enclosing Les Carmes; and then swinging west (along the alignment of the modern Boulevard des Dames) to meet the coast a little south of La Joliette, which probably was not included in the circuit.[30] It will be convenient now to consider the city that lay within that circuit, leaving temporarily aside the excavated site of the

49. Lithograph of the north side of the Vieux Port, near the Fort St. Jean, in the seventeenth century.

50. Lithograph of a distant view of Marseille, in the fifteenth century. It clearly shows the perspective of the city as 'sea-girt', located on a peninsula.

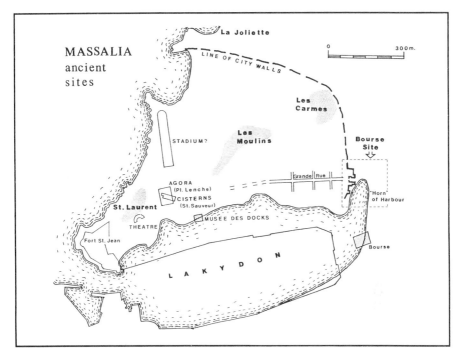

51. Ancient sites in Massalia.

52. Air view of Marseille, showing offshore islands: the very small one is the Chateau d'If. The Bourse site (excavations of the ancient port and walls) is the flat ground immediately behind the three high-rise buildings at the very bottom, centre-right, of the picture.

77

'horn' of the harbour, or, as it is more usually known, the excavation behind the Bourse.

It can be conjectured that the city was walled on all three sides.[31] On the two seaward sides no trace of walls has been found, so one can only argue that they would not have been left unprotected. On the landward side a fragment of circuit wall has been found on the slopes of the Butte des Carmes, showing that, in the Hellenistic era, at least, Les Carmes formed part of the enclosed city. It is, however, possible that this represents a later enlargement, and that the original, archaic wall passed on the other side of the hill, thus excluding it.[32] Gates would be provided at appropriate locations. There must have been at least three: one somewhere to the north, around La Joliette, one to the south, a watergate giving access to the docks along the north shore of the Lakydon, and the main gate to the east, giving access to overland communications towards Aix and Toulon. This last has been uncovered and forms part of the Bourse excavations at the 'horn' of the harbour, which we will consider in detail as a separate topic later on (p. 80 below).

Within this walled circuit (the Hellenistic one, at least) lay a city covering an area of over 50 ha, with an estimated population of around 30-50,000.[33] We know very little of it. A certain amount of destruction was caused during the siege by Caesar's forces in 49 BC, and much more of Greek Massalia was lost during the general reconstruction of the city under Nero. In the intervening centuries, investigation was hindered by continuous occupation of the site. In 1943 the occupying German forces blew up a large part of the town, 'pour mieux tenir en main une population indocile'; the area affected was the north waterfront of the Vieux Port, which was then hurriedly rebuilt in the post-war years with little attempt at archaeological excavation. All of this, it will be realised, was inauspicious for historical study of the Greek city.[34] However, it has been established that the street plan was on the grid pattern, with the major axis running NE-SW, on roughly the same orientation as the Buttes des Moulins – St. Laurent. The main street running from the Agora to the east gate, existed as far back as the sixth century BC, as has been confirmed by excavation, and secondary streets no doubt ran at right angles to it.[35] On the plan and design of private houses we can say very little. Traces have been found in various excavations, but these have usually been rescue operations, of limited scope and executed in haste. Fragments of houses have been located but not enough to form any coherent picture. A potters' quarter has been identified on the Butte des Carmes (and, from the pottery found, was apparently in operation from the foundation of the city in the sixth century, at which time it would have been outside the walls), but that is about all. Houses are thought to have been generally of the type exemplified by Olynthus,[36] but this is, and has to be, pure guesswork. Vitruvius was much struck by the fact that their houses had thatched roofs, which he evidently took as a sign of unsophisticated barbarism, but as roof tiles have in fact been found, presumably all that this means is that some roofs were tiled and some thatched, and it was the thatched ones that, still existing in the Augustan era, made an impression on Vitruvius.[37]

Public monuments

By now the reader may well be wondering whether from this mish-mash it will be possible to resurrect a coherent picture of the ancient city. The answer is, only partly. As well as the great amorphous mass of private dwellings, there were certain standard features common to all Greek cities – theatre, stadium, agora, acropolis, temples. Massalia certainly had them, and usually the location at least can be tied down, thus giving us an outline city plan, even though surviving fragments may be very rare.

The theatre is deceptive, for if one goes to the rue des Martégales, near the Butte St. Laurent, one can find there incorporated into the modern architecture of a school scattered remains of what is locally identified as the 'Théâtre Grec'. A few stone blocks from four rows of the cavea are preserved, but the stone theatre was actually of Roman date, though a Greek original with wooden seating, now long gone, probably existed on the same site. This site is thus pinpointed with reasonable probability, though no Greek remains survive.[38] The acropolis was presumably on the Butte des Moulins. Les Carmes having been outside the walls, in the Archaic era at least, there is really no other possibility except St. Laurent, which is lower. Nothing further is known of it. The stadium must have been located somewhere that was flat and about 180 m long. If it was inside the city walls, then that means that it must have been in the location shown in Fig. 51, since that is the only one that is topographically suitable. After that it comes as a coincidence almost too good to be true that on this very site was found a fragment of a Greek inscription reading 'The Stadium'. The stone block was re-used as part of a tomb in Roman days, and discovered in 1852 during the building of the La Major cathedral: it is a striking confirmation of the position of the stadium, although Clerc puts it outside the walls, aligned pretty well along the route of the present day Canebière.[39] As for the agora, that has always been placed on the Place de Lenche, on the low saddle between St. Laurent and Les Moulins. It means that, unlike most agoras, it did not enjoy a central position, but perhaps formed a link between the acropolis on Les Moulins and the fish market and other commercial enterprises flourishing along the Lakydon waterfront. Nothing whatever is known about its shape or form.[40]

That brings us to the temples. Strabo mentions two, on the heights of the acropolis and dedicated to the Delphic Apollo and the Artemis of Ephesos. The Ephesian Artemis, much venerated at Phocaea, was credited as the guiding spirit behind the Phocaean emigration to Massalia, and, says Strabo, was worshipped as the principal deity in Massalia and other colonies. The Apollo connection is corroborated by the building of a treasury of Massalia at Delphi. Athena sometimes appeared on Massaliot coinage, and the city may well have had a third prestigious temple, dedicated to her.[41] From one of these temples is preserved a single Ionic capital, highly archaic in style. In view of the key role of Artemis in the colonisation, her temple was undoubtedly one of the first things the newly-arrived Massaliots built, and so the capital may reasonably be attributed to it – hence its archaism. It remains the most impressive relic extant of Massaliot monumental architecture – always excluding the Bourse site (below).[42]

Before we turn to the Bourse, however, two more structures remain to be mentioned. The first is the Docks. The location of this complex (Fig. 51) has already been described, as well as some of its constituents. In the Musée des Docks we see a number of great storage jars, *pithoi*, still *in situ* and cemented into place; they are of Roman date. The rest of the museum is given over to a display of cargo amphorae, anchors, sounding leads, and other maritime artefacts, including the carbonised ribs and planking of a small section of a merchant ship.[43] More recently, a further section of the ancient waterfront has been uncovered by an extensive excavation under the Place Jules Verne, just behind the Mairie and alongside the museum. This has uncovered several warehouses, complete with *pithoi* (or *dolia*, the Latin term), and remains of the wooding piling that formed the various wharves, jettys, and slipways; also discovered were the remains of three cargo ships (second-fourth century AD) that had been deliberately scuttled, heavily ballasted with stones, to form a foundation for further dock construction.[44] The other structure is the cisterns of St. Sauveur. The convent of St. Sauveur, at the Place de Lenche (the ancient agora) was built on top of a series of what a 1696 publication called 'neuf grottes souterraines'. Largely destroyed in the post-war reconstruction, the remains have now been re-studied and identified as a group of cisterns, dated to the second century BC, and intended to augment the water supplies of the Greek city. A series of seven chambers, each 5 x 10.4 m, is arranged side by side, with a long gallery running along the back of them. The whole complex measures about 50 x 15.7 m and is roofed by a series of barrel vaults in cut stone, the workmanship of which corresponds to the Hellenistic walling in the Bourse site. The purpose of the installation was perhaps to provide reserve supplies of water in time of siege, but it is not plain where the water came from. The most likely source seems to be the surface run-off from the agora itself, which is paved.[45]

The Bourse site ('horn of the harbour')

The Bourse, that is, the Marseille Stock Exchange, is a large building on the north side of the Canebière, just before it reaches the Vieux Port. In antiquity this end of the Lakydon curved round to form a 'horn', or *Corne du Port*, the horn itself being behind the present Bourse. In 1967 this area was scheduled for redevelopment, the chief attractions being a shopping centre and a multi-storey parking garage. During the clearance opera-

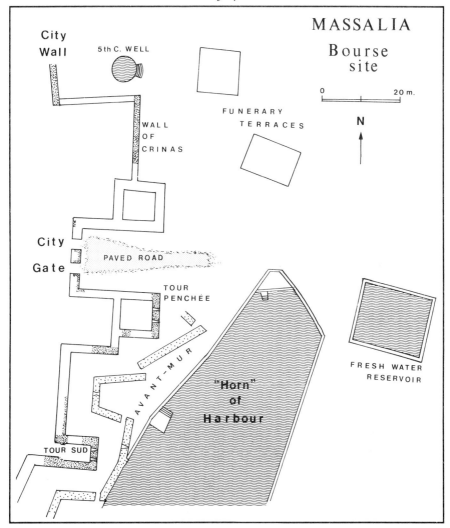

MASSALIA

Bourse
site

City
Wall

5th C. WELL

FUNERARY
TERRACES

N

0   20 m.

WALL
OF
CRINAS

City

Gate

PAVED ROAD

TOUR
PENCHÉE

AVANT-MUR

"Horn"
of
Harbour

FRESH WATER
RESERVOIR

TOUR SUD

53. Plan of the excavations on the Bourse site. The ancient city was to the left, inside the City Gate.

tions, antiquities so spectacular began to come to light that the entire redevelopment had to be first put on hold and then redesigned so as to preserve as much of the antiquities as possible. This was done, and the shopping centre now incorporates a museum overlooking the site, which has itself been landscaped into a park, the Jardin des Vestiges. This site is by far the most important archaeological centre of Ancient Massalia, and will be considered in detail. However, I must warn the reader of an inconsistency, and one of my own making. The question is one of chronology. Not all of the antiquities on the Bourse site date from the period of

Greek Massalia, with which this book is concerned. Some are Roman. I shall, however, describe the whole complex, noting dates where necessary and applicable, for I think it better to do this than to present the reader with a picture from which the non-Hellenic elements have been expunged: this might well lead to confusion, when it was compared with the publications, which print plans of the entire complex, in which Roman-date elements are prominent.

Unlike all the material we have considered so far, this excavation and its contents lie outside of the city. Down its western side runs a section of the city wall, dated to the second century BC. It is built of pinkish limestone from the La Couronne quarries, the blocks fitted together without cement or metal clamps, their exposed outer faces treated with decorative herringbone striations; this treatment also occurs on the walls of Saint Blaise (Fig. 78 below) and is characteristic of Greek work in this region. The wall is of the *emplekton* technique and 3 m thick. It seems to have been built on top of an earlier (fourth century?) wall following the same alignment. Presumably we are to imagine a wall like this running along the whole length of the landward side of the city, the dotted line on my Fig. 51, and perhaps along the two seaward sides as well. A very well preserved section, some 16 m long and six courses high, and conventionally known as the 'wall of Crinas'[46] is one of the most imposing features of the Bourse excavation. Just south of it, the city wall was pierced by a gate, a 'dipylon' of two passageways, through which ran the main road from Massalia to the east

54. Bourse site: the Wall of Crinas, shortly after excavation.

55. Bourse site: general view, shortly after excavation; the prolific weeds have since been cleared away.

56. Bourse site: tower north of paved entrance, with Wall of Crinas in the background.

57. Bourse site: paved roadway entering the City Gate.

and, eventually, Rome (to which, however, the sea would offer the normal route for most travellers). The roadway passing through the gate was aligned with the modern Grand Rue (*sic*) within the city, itself on the orientation of the chief thoroughfare in antiquity; the roadway, at the gate at least, was paved with large flat pavers (of Roman date), with transverse striations to give a better grip to the feet of animals in passage. The gate was flanked by a pair of large, square towers. The north tower exists only in its foundations, but its companion across, the roadway, the 'Tour Penchée' is better preserved, with arrow-slits in its ground floor walls: upper stories presumably accommodated machine-bows and torsion artillery.[47] A third, slightly smaller tower ('Tour Sud') is partly preserved, a short distance to the south. It was these imposing walls which confronted Caesar's forces in the siege of 49 BC. The Roman assault on the city came from the landward side, and the Roman camp was probably on the Butte St. Charles, more or less on the site now occupied by the SNCF main-line station, the Gare St. Charles. This coincidence effectively prevents confirmation by excavation. Before leaving the city walls, we may also note that at a much later date (probably fourth century AD) there was added a second, roughly built and irregularly aligned, wall (the 'avant-mur'), outside the principal one. This plainly formed an outer line of defence but, being so late in date, need not concern us in this book (though the reader will not be able to escape its aggressive prominence either on a site visit or in the published plans, including my own).

A short distance in front of the wall (i.e. to the east) is the other most distinctive feature of the site, the dock and quays forming the 'horn' of the Harbour (*Corne du Port*). Originally, at the time of the Greek foundation, this was a marshy area, which the main road out of the city crossed on a causeway (possibly as early as fifth century BC). Into it ran the Lakydon stream, which gave its name to the whole harbour, but this was insufficient to keep the 'horn' clear, and silting remained a perpetual and permanent problem. This muddy and possibly malarial swamp had little attraction for mariners (or, one suspects, anyone else), and ships continued to berth alongside the main docks, on the north side of the Lakydon proper. Eventually efforts were made to develop the 'horn', possibly as an auxiliary dock to accommodate traffic overflowing from the main harbour in a time of prosperity. The water in it seems never to have been much deeper than 2.7 m and though in the Roman period it was endowed with the fine set of masonry quays that make it so impressive today, it seems never to have been more than a backwater of the main Port of Massalia, and ended its life in the fourth century AD decaying to the inglorious status of a ships' graveyard, with the marsh slowly reclaiming the harbour and the abandoned hulks lying on its mudbanks, their decks awash.[48]

The masonry quays gave a firm and definite form, that of a truncated V, to a 'horn' that otherwise must often have trailed off amorphously into an ill-defined muddy marsh. The walls of the quay are 4.4 m high, and their most interesting feature is the mark of the ancient sea level, imprinted on the masonry by the erosion of the waves and marine organisms. As noted, it is about 20 cm below the present sea level. There is little else in the way of harbour installations – no bollards, for example, or pierced stones for mooring ships – but there is a set of steps leading down to the water to give easier access to small boats, and a second set was provided from a small wall cutting off the northern tip of the dock at an angle. The steps are late, from around the third-fourth centuries AD, but the main quays are dated to 75-80 AD.[49] A short distance beyond the tip of the harbour is a large (17.5 x 15 m) oblong tank or reservoir, filled with fresh water from a local spring. Perhaps its most striking characteristic is its proportions – by normal standards it seems excessively wide and shallow, and to modern eyes looks more like a swimming pool than anything else.[50] Dating from the early second century AD, but possibly with an earlier predecessor, it may have had a double function. First, it may have been designed as a settling tank to stop the spring carrying sediment into the harbour and clogging it up – an aim in which, if that is true, it was manifestly unsuccessful. Its second purpose may have been to supply fresh water for ships in the harbour. With a capacity of over 400 m³, the provision seems excessive, but there is possible evidence for a wooden water-lifting wheel associated with it, which would suggest that the water was drawn off for use.[51] It is always possible that dwellers at this end of the city found it convenient to go there for their water supplies, for it is not far outside the city gate. If so, they were of course relying on a resource that was militarily vulnerable: they could be cut off from it by a besieging

58. Bourse site: the Fresh Water Reservoir.

enemy, as indeed happened during the siege by Caesar. The reliance, however, would certainly not be very great. Most cities had plenty of cisterns and wells within the walls, and even aqueducts were a luxury rather than a necessity. There was no doubt an abundance of water sources in the city proper, and indeed a section of aqueduct dating from the Archaic age and perhaps from the foundation of the city has been discovered on the north slope of the Butte St. Laurent, near the Cathedral. From this period also comes a large, monumental well on the Bourse site near the Mur de Crinas (and hence outside the city walls). It is 6 m across and the access stairway has been dated by pottery to at least the fifth century BC; it may well be earlier.[52] Other features and objects also were uncovered in the Bourse excavations, but the survey above will suffice for the purposes of this book. The visitor to the site should also be advised that he will find it somewhat modified. Landscaping has transformed the excavation into a Jardin des Vestiges. In particular, the 'horn' of the Harbour has been filled in and a grassy lawn now replaces the water of the dock, enfolded between the arms of the two masonry quays and set at the ancient sea level. To the east, the shopping centre was eventually built, redesigned to encroach as little as possible on the ancient site, and now incorporating a museum, in which one may examine the various artefacts while at the same time viewing through large picture windows the site from which they came.

59. Bourse site, now transformed into parkland. The figures are entering the ancient city by the paved road to the City Gate.

60. Bourse site: the 'Horn of Harbour', now transformed into a lawn. The grass reproduces the ancient water level.

61. Bourse site: This has now been 'amenagé', adapted as a park, the 'Jardin des Vestiges'. The building in the background is the new museum (Musée d'Histoire de Marseille).

Chronological summary

The various stages in the urban development of Massalia have been well summarised by L.F. Gantès.[53] They are:

1. 600-580 BC: first settlement, extending from St. Laurent to Place Vivaux (Musée des Docks), on a site evidently devoid of any previous occupation. Architecture in stone, mud-brick, wood; orientation NS/EW.

2. 580-540: archaic city, now expanded northwards to present site of Cathedral de la Major.

3. 540-520: realignment of buildings and remodelling of street plan. Start manufacture of local Massaliot wine amphorae.

4. 520-480: archaic city expanded to cover whole length of north shore of Lakydon, Buttes St. Laurent, Moulins, Carmes. Some traces on Bourse site.

5. 480-320: the classical city. Urban development of west slope of Butte des Carmes (175-140 BC). Caves St. Sauveur.

The La Couronne quarries

There remains one point to consider before we leave the architectural remains of Massalia. Where did it all come from? A lot of the buildings, probably most, were doubtless constructed of wattle-and-daub or sun-

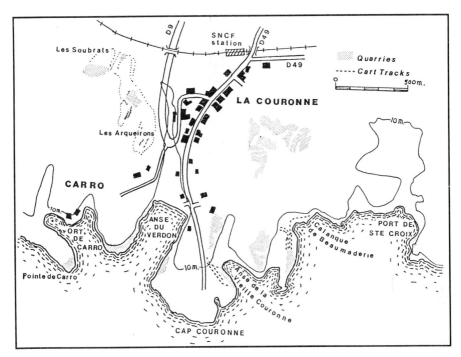

62. La Couronne, the site of the quarries from which much of the stone for building Massalia was extracted.

63. La Couronne: wheel ruts for carts carrying quarried stone at the Calanque de Beaumaderie: 'double track main line' to left, and 'single track branch' to right.

89

64. La Couronne: loading area at Calanque de Beaumaderie. The ships to be loaded docked just to the right out of the picture. The multiple tracks are not necessarily of the same date, nor all in use together.

dried brick, locally made, but what of the masonry structures, such as the walls? The stone, as it happens, came almost all from one clearly identified source from which most of Massalia, Massilia, and a good deal of Marseille, was built. This source is the quarries of La Couronne, which accordingly deserve inclusion in any account of the city.

La Couronne is on the coast (by Cap Couronne), 40 km west of Marseille, at the south-west extremity of the mountainous Chaine de l'Estaque.[54] Below the village lies the Anse du Verdon, and, about 500 m to the east, the Anse de Ste. Croix. Between the two a square, flat plateau projects into the sea. The ancient quarries are scattered around on top of this plateau, and in the heights overlooking the Anse de Ste. Croix; some are also to be found along the coastline at Carro, just west of La Couronne (Fig. 62). The top stratum was often of friable rock, which had to be removed and stacked to one side in heaps of spoil, before the quarrymen could get at the good-quality building stone below. From the quarry, the stone was carted down to the shore and transported to Massalia by sea, in flat-bottomed barges.[55] The most interesting feature, however, is the transport from the quarry to the shore. This was by carts, and the carts ran with their wheels in grooves cut in the rock surface, like an ancient railway. It must be clearly stated that we are here dealing with grooves sharply delineated and carefully cut to facilitate passage and to keep the carts straight on crossing bumpy sections of rocks; they are not ruts naturally worn by the

90

wheels.[56] This is not uncommon, but no other ancient quarry that I know of has these tracks preserved in such profusion. Some are to be found on the east side, alongside the Anse de Ste. Croix. One may almost describe it in railway terms. The carts arrive from the quarry on a double track main line, with a junction serving a single track branch that follows round the edge of the Anse. Traffic from both lines then arrives at the dockside and is received in a (Figs. 63, 64) marshalling yard of some dozen or so tracks abreast, on a flattened-out area of the rock surface. Boats can come close alongside and load directly from the nearest track. However, we must here regretfully enter a caveat. This track network is not so sophisticated or extensive as it appears at first sight. The La Couronne quarries were still being worked all through the history of Marseille, right up to the nineteenth century,[57] and much of the complexity is caused by the super-imposition of tracks in use at different periods. Plainly the tracks themselves cannot be dated – how can one date a groove cut in a piece of rock? – but there is clear evidence that all were not in use at once. Sometimes they overlap (particularly in the 'marshalling yard'), and close examination shows that sometimes the tracks are of different gauges (i.e. the two grooves are cut a different distance apart, so that the wheels of the same cart could not have fitted both).[58]

The Treasury of Massalia at Delphi

Leaving Massalia geographically but not culturally, we may close this chapter with a note on what has to be the best preserved example of Massaliot architecture anywhere. This is the Massaliot Treasury at Delphi, in Greece. Its presence there testifies not only to the depth of Massaliot feeling for the Delphic Apollo (who had a temple also in Massalia itself, close to that of Artemis) but to Massaliot wealth and, presumably, influence at Delphi. At both Olympia and Delphi the number of national treasuries was quite small, not more than seven or eight, and quite a lot of wealthy and famous cities never had one at all. Thus, though we do not know what were the required conditions for building a treasury at Delphi they cannot have been easily met (or everyone would have had one), and the mere fact that Massalia managed to achieve it must stand as a signal mark of distinction. That said, it must come as an anti-climax to admit that at Delphi we are not sure which building it is.

Certainly there is a building of treasury-type on the Marmaria site at Delphi that has always been known as the Treasury of Massalia. The building (6.14 x 8.4 m), of Parian marble, is distyle-*in-antis* with capitals formed by a spreading leaf pattern that is generally described as Aeolic, and seen as appropriate in view of Massalia's Phocaean origins.[59] Around the outside of the wall base it also carries a very large and bulbous bead-and-reel moulding of markedly archaic appearance: the building is dated to around 540 BC, which puts it just after the Battle of Alalia, when Massalia may have enjoyed a particular spurt of prosperity brought on by

65. Treasury of Massalia at Delphi.

66. Treasury of Massalia at Delphi, north-east corner of back wall, showing the bead-and-reel moulding which, by its archaic form, suggests a date of between 540 and 500 BC.

the elimination of Alalia, as possible commercial rival. The problem is, is this the Treasury of Massalia?

There is no doubt at all that Massalia did have a treasury at Delphi. Among other indications, there is the clear statement of Diodorus that in 396 the Romans marked their victory over Veii by sending to Delphi a gold krater and deposited it 'in the Treasury of the Massaliots', not having a treasury of their own.[60] But where is this treasury? And is it the one in Marmaria that is commonly so identified?

The Marmaria identification comes from Pausanias, the Roman travel writer, who says that as you come into Delphi you meet a row of temples, and in the fourth and last one there is a Massaliot offering. This raises two problems. One is that Pausanias does not actually say that the building is a Treasury of Massalia, only that there is a Massaliot offering in it (he calls it a Temple of Athena). But much worse is the fact that the row of remains, as preserved today, consists of not four but five buildings. So which one is Pausanias leaving out? And does this throw his counting out of sequence? Come to that, can we even be sure which end he is counting from? All of this is enough for the French now to list the building in their site guide book as the Tresor éolique 'de Marseille', leaving the inverted commas to alert the wary.[61]

6

The History of Massalia

Massalia, as we have seen, was founded about 600 BC, apparently with the acquiescence of the local inhabitants, in particular the Segobriges, who were the Ligurian tribe already on the spot and in occupation. The honeymoon did not last long. We know little in detail, but Justin (our only source for this period) recounts how after the death of Nannos, the Segobrigan chieftain at the time of the foundation, his son, Comanus, mounted an attack on the city in attempt to regain the territory previously lost. The plan was for a small commando force to penetrate the city by stealth, taking advantage of a regular floral festival which permitted uncontrolled access with no checkpoints on the gates. The following night this force was to open the gates to Comanus and the main army, lurking in convenient concealment outside.[1] However, security was breached. The Massaliot authorities were warned, and staged a counter-ambush against the attackers, in which Comanus and seven thousand of his men died. From then on, as Justin puts it, the Massaliots 'fought great wars with the Ligurians and with the Gauls'.[2]

After this inauspicious beginning (or auspicious, depending on one's point of view), the history of Greek Massalia becomes a thing of insubstantial shadows. The earliest literary references all date to after 350 BC, and are few and far apart. We have no history of the city written by a Massaliot (or indeed any Massaliot literary writing at all), nor any coherent history of Massalia written by anyone else. This does not mean that our knowledge of Massaliot history is a blank. History is of two kinds. There is what we may call the historical narrative. This is the sequential record of important events, battles, legislation, rulers, and the like. It is a diet of dates, and – though often condemned and contemned for it – necessarily so. That is exactly the sort of record that we do not have for Massalia.[3] I do not mean that we know nothing about this at all, only that our knowledge is very spotty. What happens is that we hear of Massalia only when it somehow impinges upon the history of another, better-documented society, such as Greece, or, more often, Rome. This momentary congruence past, Massalia sinks back into the mists of history from which it emerges only briefly and fitfully. Sometimes the events concerned are of major importance, such as Massalia's role vis-à-vis Hannibal in the Second Punic War. Sometimes it is nothing more than a pair of swindling Massaliot grain dealers turning up in an Athenian court.[4] From this meagre collage of isolated high spots and chance references we can try to create an outline of Massaliot history, but plainly we should not expect too much of it.

The second kind of history is more general, wider in its scope. It is a history not of narrative, but of trends. What was the extent of Massaliot trade? What was the economic base of the city, the closeness of its relationship with its mother city, the political power of its oligarchs? How far did its political and commercial influence extend through Provence, and how deeply? Was its navy really powerful enough to count? Questions such as these may be answered, with varying degrees of confidence and reliability, on the basis of comments in our literary sources (often non-historical ones, such as the speeches of Cicero) and on the evidence of archaeology: by far the most important and widespread source being amphorae, the jars in which wine and other frequently-traded products were shipped. Such material will rarely give us the dates for historical events (though coins are a notable exception to this rule) but will help us to form a picture that will set in context and sometimes answer questions such as those I have listed above. We will now try to combine these two approaches so as to produce a History of Massalia, though the reader will need no further warnings on its inadequacy.

The sea battle of Alalia has already been mentioned. Its date of 536/5 provides a much-needed chronological anchor for early Massaliot history,[5] though it is not clear that Massalia was actively involved. What is clear is that there was a clash between the Phocaeans of Corsica, operating out of their base at Alalia, and a joint Carthaginian and Etruscan force. The result was a Pyrrhic victory for the Phocaeans, who abandoned Alalia and with it all claim to Corsica, and moved to South Italy, eventually ending up at Velia, just south of Paestum. Though dignified by the name of a battle, one is tempted to see it in nothing more than a piratical scuffle between rival gangs of freebooters. Yet the fleets involved were large, if we are to trust our ancient sources,[6] and the consequences vital for Massalia. The Massaliots may even have sent ships to help their brother Phocaeans, and such an unrecorded addition to their strength might help to explain how the Alalians, apparently outnumbered two-to-one, could end up with something they could claim as a victory, even a Pyrrhic one; against odds like this one might have expected them simply to have been wiped out. As to consequences, it is impossible for a major centre of Phocaean, indeed, Hellenic power in the area to have been removed without Massalia being affected. It is harder to say in just what way. Alalia was probably a convenient, if not an actually vital, way station on the route to Phocaea and the Aegean, and its elimination would make even harder a voyage that was already long and difficult. On the other hand, it essentially freed Massalia from all competition in the area, commercial and otherwise, and set her firmly on the course she was to maintain for the next four centuries as the unchallenged champion of Hellenic culture in the Western Mediterranean and the undisputed centre of its trade. For Massalia, the Battle of Alalia marks her coming of age.

Back at Massalia, an unstable relationship with the Ligurians came to a head with a Ligurian attack – date unknown. The attack was led by a Ligurian chieftain named Catumandus, but fizzled out in suspicious but shadowy circumstances. All we know is that the Ligurians, after besieging the city, apparently suddenly lifted the siege and went home, for no known reason. The most likely explanation is that they had been bought off by the Massaliot treasury. This early precursor of the Danegeld so familiar in early England is not without ancient parallels. In 390 BC the Gauls captured Rome itself and only left when a substantial national ransom had been paid. Very likely the same explanation lies behind the Ligurian withdrawal from Massalia, for modern historians, more sceptical than their ancient counterparts, usually discount the version generally accepted in antiquity (and at Massalia in particular), namely that Catumandus recoiled in terror after being visited in his sleep by a celestial vision of the goddess Athena, who explained just what she would do to him if he persisted in his assault on a city that enjoyed her personal favour and protection. On leaving he supposedly congratulated the Massaliots on the power and efficiency of their divine patroness, and sealed the bargain by going to her shrine in the city as a worshipping suppliant.[7] Indeed, as we leave this topic there is a further point to be noted. It is recorded by Justin (though by nobody else) that when the Gauls were paid their ransom to leave Rome, Massalia made a cash contribution to help pay the Romans' bill. If so, it would confirm that the tactic of buying one's way out of trouble was already familiar to fourth-century Massalia.[8] Moreover this well marks what was to develop as the keystone of Massalia's foreign policy, a close and enduring alliance with Rome, and it is almost irrelevant whether the story is true or false: it is so closely indicative of the reality that, if it is not true, then it ought to be. We may also note, among other Massaliot incursions onto the world stage, that close relations were established with the oracle of Delphi. The victory over the Carthaginians (presumably the battle of Alalia) was commemorated there by an offering, and a Treasury was built on the Marmaria site, below the sacred precinct, stylistically linked to Asiatic art and motifs, a deliberate echo of the Phocaean mother city.[9] Significantly, this treasury was also used by the Romans, who did not have a treasury of their own, for the deposit of various rich offerings.[10] Finally, we may close by noting that Massalia seems to have been represented on an embassy sent to Alexander the Great, no doubt again reflecting its oriental interests.[11]

The *chora*

While the above events were taking place, the Massaliots were settling into their new home and establishing control over the surrounding territory. This brings up one of the two most widely debated aspects of ancient

Massaliot history, the *chora* (the other aspect is the Phocaean exploration of the Western Mediterranean leading up to the foundation of Massalia). The word, used by various sources means 'land' or 'territory'. The problem is, what was it? Just what was 'the territory of Massalia'? The problem is exacerbated by two factors. One is chronological – as with other facets of Massalia, or indeed any city, what the territory of Massalia was will depend on what time we are talking about. The other factor is, what do we mean by the word *chora*, 'territory', itself. Are we speaking of the political borders surrounding the city, beyond which the Massaliot writ did not run, or do we mean something wider and more amorphous, perhaps better translated as 'sphere of influence', commercial, cultural, or whatever? The actual work *chora* in Greek is normally translated 'land', and appears in various ancient sources – Aristotle, for example, says that the Étang de Vaccarès is in the Massaliot *chora*. The term has caught on in modern studies, but there has been one unfortunate result: often, instead of concentrating on the factual evidence, they tend to get mired down in semantics – 'Just what do we mean by "territory"?'[12] It will therefore, I think, be most convenient for us to leave the terminology aside and consider only the factual evidence as it bears on the history of Massalia. This can be grouped under three categories. One is the land actually possessed and legally owned by Massaliot settlers, who enjoyed Massaliot citizenship and lived either on their land, as homesteaders, or in the city itself. The second category embraces all those colonies and trading posts along the coast of Provence that were either in close contact with Massalia or were even themselves founded by it, as sub-colonies, and which collectively formed the centre, the vehicle, for Hellenic culture and commerce. The third category is the Celtic/Gallic tribes that were so penetrated and permeated by Massaliot commerce that they effectively became part of Massalia's sphere of influence. These three categories essentially represent three different things, and they will be considered separately. The second, Greek colonies, will fall under our Chapters 9 and 10; the third, relations with the local tribes, Chapter 11; and we now turn our present attention to the first. As a modern politican or diplomat would put it, where were the actual borders of the State of Massalia? 'Borders', of course, is a somewhat modern concept which, though it clearly and usefully describes what we are considering, must not be taken too literally. The ancient world was well accustomed to the idea of national sovereignty and national territory, but actual borders, frontiers, were often somewhat more amorphous, particularly when we are dealing with those between a Greek colony and the native population of the hinterland. The extent of Massaliot political control inland is in any case of questionable importance, for it never went very far. Greek colonies in general were content to control the harbours and points where overland trade routes debouched upon the coastline, with the reservation that sometimes they also included within their boundaries enough arable land to feed the colonists on a subsistence basis, or even to produce a surplus for export.[13] Massalia followed this rule and her political domination did not extend far into the interior.

In a more detailed study, we may turn first to the offshore Frioul Islands (Fig. 40). There are two of them, Ratonneau and Pomègues, as well as the tiny but much more celebrated Île d'If, of Edmond Dantès fame in the Dumas novel. These islands, to-day little more than bare rock, were heavily wooded until the nineteenth-century and pastured herds of goats. In antiquity they may well not only have been inhabited, but possibly were settled even before Massalia itself. The Greeks, did at this period, often settle on offshore islands either as a first step towards mainland colonisation or to complement it. Thus the Lerins, off the cost at Cannes, bear traces of Greek settlement, and at Ampurias the original Greek settlement was on an island facing the site of the later historical city. At Phocaea, where there were also offshore islands, the citizens were all aware of their strategic and commercial importance, stoutly resisting all attempts to place them under foreign control. So the Frioul Islands were probably an integral part of the *polis* of Massalia, and may even have been the first part of it to receive Greek settlers.[14]

On land, the area available for possession and development was very circumscribed. To both north and south, ribbon development along the coast was blocked off within a few kilometres of Massalia. To the north it was limited by the ridge of L'Estaque, which extends westward right to Martigues (Fig. 40), and effectivly prevents coastwise settlement or communication. To the south, the coast road peters out before the massif of Marseilleveyre, which lines the whole coast eastward as far as Cassis, dropping sheer to the water like a great wall, pierced only by the calanques, miniature fjords that are fine natural harbours but have no land access at all. Indeed, all this coast, from Cap Croisette east, is today still accessible only by sea or on foot. From Massalia inland there is an arable plain of limited dimensions, also hemmed in by mountains. At this early date any expansion there was probably was centred in the valley of the Huveaune. This is the only route out of Massalia that does not involve hill-climbing. It is level as far as Aubagne, and beyond. The trouble is that it does not lead to anywhere one would want to go. The Rhône valley is in the other direction altogether, and even travellers to the east, towards Italy (who would in any case go by sea) would begin by heading north, up the Valley of the Durance and over the Col de Montgénèvre, the coastal road not having yet been opened. But for settling in the Huveaune valley, the terrain was probably the best option open. The river (Fig. 41), though small, runs fast and so carries a large volume of water, facilitating irrigation. This was probably the first area of Massaliot overland expansion.

To the north, betwen L'Estaque and L'Étoile, a broad, low saddle provides, then and now, the principal route of overland egress from the Massaliot plain, via Les Pennes – Mirabeau. Though not itself of any particular attraction agriculturally, it gives easy access to the Étang de

Berre, Aix-en-Provence, and the Celtic tribes who lived there. The Celts lived in settlements traditionally referred to as *oppida*, and though one or two have been found actually in the area we have just described as 'the plain of Massalia',[15] most are to be found outside it. Effectively, the *oppida* begin at Les Pennes; the nearest is Baou Roux, near Bouc-Bel-Air, 4 km north of Les Pennes; the biggest and most important is at Entremont, just outside Aix-en-Provence. Most of the *oppida* in this area, and around the Étang de Berre, were certainly subject to Massaliot economic influence from a very early date, but established political control is a different matter. Where did the borders run? We are surely safe in assuming some expansion in succeeding centuries from the limited sixth-century occupation of the Massaliot plain, but greater precision than that is almost certainly illusory. Hemmed in by the mountains, Massalia had few natural avenues for territorial expansion. The easiest would certainly have been up the Huveaune to Aubagne. In fact, Massalia's trading interests seem to have attracted her instead towards the Rhône, and the enigmatic site of Saint Blaise attests to her territorial interests, if not actual occupation. Saint Blaise (see p. 143 below) is a Greek fortified site of obvious importance on the west side of the Étang de Berre. The problem is that we do not really know its status – a trading-post or *comptoir*, an outlying bastion of Massaliot power, an independent foundation, or even a *polis*? The Fossae Marianae, dug by Marius' men and presented to Massalia by a grateful Rome, entered the sea at Fos, not far away, and so presumably this area was under Massaliot political control at the time. The same applies to the Ostium Massiliense, the Port of Massalia built on the Rhône itself. Both of these are of little immediate relevance to us at they belong to a much later period, but they do show the direction in which Massaliot interest lay, and this was therefore the presumable direction of any territorial expansion that occurred.

The Punic Wars

While Massalia was in this way extending its power by land, even if only to a limited extent, it continued warring with its neighbours. The warfare was not doubt sporadic and we have little precise record of it. The Ligurians were the usual enemy, though Massaliot maritime interests also ensured a series of clashes with the Etruscans and the Carthaginians. Justin remarks that 'they often routed the Carthaginians, and spared them in their defeat', while Strabo observes that in his day the city was crammed with war memorials from past naval victories 'over those unjustly disputing command of the high seas'. One does not have to be a cynic to see in these naval triumphs a series of piratical scuffles and brigands' brawls rather than anything on the level of Salamis or Actium, particularly in view of the Phocaeans' national heritage as freebooters and buccaneers.[16]

One thing, however, clearly grew to reality in this period, and that was a strong working partnership between Massalia and Rome. As early as the Gallic invasion of 390, this was enshrined in a formal treaty granting Massaliots *aequum ius*, 'equal rights' at Rome, as well as immunity from taxation, reserved seats in the theatre, and other marks of significant if symbolic recognition. What the Massaliots actually did for the Romans in these two centuries leading up to the Punic Wars is harder to tie down. Roman writers of later years repeatedly speak of Massalia as their staunch ally whose valour and fidelity was tested on countless fields, but without saying where and when. Cicero, a well known, even notorious, Massaliophile, always speaks in glowing terms of this city which he never actually went to, heaping on it praises for past services largely unspecified, and it was left for a modern Marseillais scholar, Michel Clerc, to bring us down to earth: 'Si l'on veut entrer dans le détail, et spécifier quels ont été les services rendus par Marseille à Rome, lors des guerres soutenues contre les Gaulois, on se trouve fort embarassé.'[17] For the first time, but assuredly not the last, we may discern in our accounts of Massalia a certain spirit of inflation. It is perhaps unfortunate that in modern France the stereotype Marseillais is also characterised by an exaggerated boasting that more or less resembles that popularly attributed in the USA to Texans.[18] However, we too may generalise. We can probably identify areas in which Massalia did in fact assist Rome. First, she provided a navy upon which Rome would call if necessary. The Massaliot land army does not seem to have amounted to very much, and indeed we never hear of it. That did not matter. Rome had plenty of soldiers, but relied on her allies for ships. There Massalia could and did help, though her navy in later years, as we shall see (p. 105f. below), suffered a severe decline. Second, her very presence kept open the road to Spain. Till the building of the coastal Via Julia, overland communications did not pass through Massaliot territory but some distance to the north (as indeed did Hannibal), but Massalia was plainly close enough to the route to have some influence and control over it. Third, it gave Rome a window on Gaul. Since the Gallic invasion and occupation of Rome, warfare between the Gauls and Rome had been continuous if intermittent, and was to remain so until Caesar settled things by conquering and annexing Transalpine Gaul. Moreover, the Gauls' occupation of Rome had left a particularly deep mark on the Roman, and indeed the Italian, psyche. The Gauls were feared, and one of the reasons that Hannibal did not attract more local support in Italy was that the presence of Gauls in his army awoke old memories. Even if you were not at the moment fighting the Gauls, you needed to keep an eye on them, and Massalia was an ideal centre for gathering intelligence, more or less in the way Berlin was in the old days of the Cold War.

When we come to the Second Punic War, Massaliot participation again seems somewhat limited. There is no doubt where their sympathies lay. Rome was their traditional friend, a kind of Big Brother, and though Hannibal himself might leave them cold, the Gallic allies in his army were their long-standing natural enemies; and the Ligurians had already at various times served with the Carthaginians.[19] They could hardly dodge the conflict even if they wanted to, since Massalia lay on Hannibal's route, though as noted it did not actually pass through Massalia itself. In fact, Hannibal probably crossed the Rhône at Tarascon, between Avignon and Arles, and for his crossing he used shipping (even dugout canoes) locally available. One would have thought that it would have been possible for Massalia at least to make the crossing more difficult by removing all boats from the Rhône. It wouldn't have needed an army for that, and if Tarascon was not under Massaliot political control, at least the river ought to have been covered by their general sphere of influence. At all events, Hannibal got through, without being seriously impeded by Rome's chief ally in the region.[20] Apart from all this, Massalia's chief act of assistance during the war was to pass on to Rome a warning that Hasdrubal's relief expedition was coming; otherwise all that is recorded is the usual general aid and support in vague terms.[21]

In the century after the Second Punic War, the history of Massalia reverts to being a spotty and ill-documented series of skirmishes and affrays with the Ligurians, from each of which the city is rescued by the military intervention of the Romans. Immediately after the war, says Livy, Massalia was repeatedly harassed 'by land and by sea' by Gallic tribes that objected to the Massaliots' pro-Roman sympathies, as demonstrated during Hannibal's invasion. Naturally, one's mind boggles at Massalia, the Queen of the Western Wave, being harassed *by sea* by a rag-tag assortment of Gauls – of all people – but of course they may have had assistance from other sources.[22] In 154 BC the Oxybii and the Deciati, two Ligurian tribes, attacked and besieged Massalia, Nicaea (Nice) and Antipolis. Roman intervention again saved the day, and awarded a tract of their land to Massalia in settlement. It would be nice to know if this had any effect on the spread of the Massaliot *chora*, but this remains uncertain.[23] The next round was in 128 BC, when the Salyii, the Celtic tribe controlling the territory around Aix, 'erupted against Massalia', devastating the *chora*. Again the Romans, this time under M. Fulvius Flaccus, obligingly chased them away.[24] By now, however, it was painfully clear that no one could realistically entertain hopes of the Massaliots actually protecting their own land, and Rome turned to a more effective and permanent solution. It is hard to say whether this was inspired by gratitude towards a loyal ally or pure expediency. Certainly Rome needed to keep open the road to Spain, and that was done, quite possibly from a blending of the two motives. The chosen means was the establishment of Narbonese Gaul as a province,[25] though that was not necessarily an intention coherently planned from the start. In 122, then, there was founded the Roman military *colonia* of Aquae Sextiae, the modern Aix-en-Provence. This forcibly replaced the Celtic *oppidum* of Entremont, on a hill-top in the suburbs of the modern city, and established a permanent Roman military presence within easy striking distance (and protecting distance) of Massalia.[26]

The newly established Roman presence was soon put to the test. A complicated and convulsive series of raids, migrations and invasions on the part of various Germanic tribes, supposedly set in motion by some of their traditional homelands in Jutland suffering inundation by the sea, culminated in a mass incursion into Narbonese Gaul, apparently as a preliminary stage in a campaign aimed at the invasion of Italy itself. The attempt was opposed by Marius who, in his fourth consulship (102 BC), engaged the great barbarian horde on the lower slopes of Mont St. Victoire, outside Aix-en-Provence. The resultant Roman victory is perhaps better described as a mass massacre, for over 100,000 of the enemy were killed and for decades afterwards local farmers attributed their abnormally rich harvests to the soil having been fertilised by the great quantities of blood spilled upon it.[27] For Massalia the most important – certainly the most profitable – result was a by-product of an enterprise of Marius during the campaign. Somewhere up the Rhône he established a base (Orosius[28] says at the confluence with the Isère, near Valence) which had to be supplied via the Rhône itself. The chief problem here was the difficulty of navigation around the mouth of the Rhône (p. 43 above), which Marius solved by having his men dig a ship canal, the Fossae Marianae, from the sea in the vicinity of Fos, to one of the nearest loops in the serpentine course then pursued by the river through the Camargue, so, he hoped, by-passing some of the worst bits and facilitating access from the Mediterranean to the Rhône. After the war was over this canal was gratefully presented to Rome's chief ally in the area, Massalia, which found the tolls levied on it a profitable source of income.[29] In the end it apparently silted up, sharing the fate of the rather better known canal from the Nile to the Red Sea.[30]

After that, little happened in our area that affected Massalia, or perhaps we should rephrase that as 'little that we know about', until the Roman Civil War. That 'little' includes, however, the governorship of M. Fonteius in Narbonese Gaul, now firmly and officially established as a province. It is significant because on his return to Rome in 73 BC he was put on trial for corruption and defended by Cicero whose speech on the occasion contains much material of value. Of course, Narbonese Gaul, the scene of Fonteius' alleged misdeeds, did not include Massalia within its jurisdiction, but there are many interesting and relevant sidelights. These are both historically factual and also illuminate Roman opinions of Massalia, though we must recognise that Cicero was himself a convinced Massaliophile and hence perhaps not entirely representative of Roman attitudes (to take an extreme example, one suspects that Cato would not readily subscribe to all his Massaliot eulogies); and in any case allowances must be made for the exigencies of forensic pleading. The speech remains a valuable work none the less.[31] Another minor event was Caesar's conquest of Gaul. Beginning in 58, and provoked by the Helvetii wishing to cross Narbonese Gaul (which at this time stretched as far north up the Rhône valley as Vienne and Geneva) en route from Switzerland to Aquitania, this mammoth series of campaigns added the whole of France to the Roman Empire. Massalia, however, was only marginally affected by these titanic events. Not being a military state, its contribution was apparently limited to moral support, goodwill, facilitating Roman communications up the Rhône, and generally shouting encouragement from the sidelines.

By this time the Massaliot *chora*, liberally interpreted, had greatly expanded. Sextius (the founder of Aquae Sextiae, Aix-en-Provence) had in 122, in crushing the attacks of a Ligurian confederacy, imposed upon the insurgents peace terms expelling them from the coastal regions (though they were moved back only to a distance of 8-12 stades (1-2 km) inland from the shore, which seems impossibly little) and turning over the confiscated lands to Massalia.[32] The details of this arrangement are too skimpy to give us a clear picture, but presumably what it came to in practice was that Massalia was recognised by Rome as controlling the entire littoral of Provence and the Côte d'Azur. As previously noted, a long series of ports, trading posts and full fledged cities lined the coast from Monaco to beyond the Spanish border. The individual political circumstances of each one varied, and are usually unknown, but the general pattern is clear. Along the coast was a belt of Hellenic foundations, of which Massalia was the undisputed spokesman and leader. They seemed to maintain a remarkable cohesion and uniformity. For one thing, we never hear of them fighting each other, a condition that in their home country was thoroughly endemic. All of this was Massalia's sphere of influence as recognised by Rome. The actual territory of Massalia itself was also recognised as being excluded from the Roman province, and many of the port cities may also have benefited from individual arrangements. There seems to be no way of telling, for example, whether at any given time somewhere like Agde was subject to the authority of the Roman governor at Narbo, or even that of Massalia.

Thus far, the history of Massalia has been one of success. Not herself militarily strong, her unwavering support of Rome had brought her rich economic, and even political, dividends. But what if Rome herself should become divided? This, of course, was what now happened. Effectively the outbreak of the Roman Civil War presented Massalia with two Romes, and she had to choose between them. The Massaliots, faced with this invidious choice, tried hard to avoid making it. Both Caesar and Pompey, they said, had been their benefactors, and it was not for them to decide between them. This attempt to stay neutral failed, as such attempts often do, and with Caesar on the spot in person (en route to Spain) and L. Domitius, the legally appointed governor of Gaul and a Pompeian, arriving in the middle of the negotiations, the Assembly of 600 was driven to declare openly which side it was on. Given the aristocratic (and hence legalistic) traditions of Massalia, it is not surprising that the choice fell on Pompey.[33]

Caesar himself did not remain long, just enough to put in hand the necessary preparations for the siege of Massalia that could no longer be avoided. Behind him he left D. Brutus in charge by sea, and C. Trebonius by land; in Massalia the defence was in the hands of L. Domitius, and the Massaliot Apollonides, who was President of the Assembly of 600. It is a striking example of how dependent we are on Roman sources for our history of Massalia that we know next to nothing about this man other than his name, and that comes to us only from the Scholiast to Lucan.[34] It was Apollonides who brilliantly led the Massaliots in the siege in which they withstood for a full six months the force of Caesar's army, and it is tempting to compare his obscurity with the fame of Vercingetorix, who at Alesia withstood Caesar for only six weeks.

The course of events is, to our eyes, astonishing. Massalia – not, as we have often noted, a city with a military tradition – conducted its defence on land with courageous and enterprising tenacity that cannot but stir our deepest admiration. By contrast, the war at sea was a complete fiasco, and the Massaliot navy came out of it little better than a laughing stock. However, it was at sea that the war began. Lacking a fleet, Caesar had a squadron of twelve ships hastily constructed up-river at Arles. It only took thirty days to build them, and the timber used was green and unseasoned – a rush job if ever there was one. Their crews were green too, so inexperienced that they did not even know the names of the various parts of the ships' tackle. Lucan, on the other hand, gives Caesar a fleet of triremes, quadriremes, quinqueremes and a sexareme as flagship, which cannot be reconciled with Caesar's own more modest description, just quoted.[35] On the other side, Massalia fielded a fleet of some seventeen warships, well equipped and competently handled, accompanied by a flotilla of whatever small boats they could hurriedly round up, in what seems to have been an early anticipation of the Dunkirk spirit.

There were two separate battles. In the first, the Massaliot navy sailed forth from the Lakydon to confront Brutus and his fleet just outside the harbour, off the Frioul Islands. Despite the superior manoeuvrability and speed of the Massaliot ships, it was the heavy, lumbering Roman craft that won the day, and Massalia lost no less than nine ships out of the seventeen, some sunk but some captured by the Romans and now added to their forces. In the second battle, this Massaliot loss should have been made up by reinforcements. Pompey, in Spain, did send reinforcements, a squadron of eighteen ships (which should have been enough to turn the scale) under a certain Nasidius. Nasidius evidently did not dare to come too close to Massalia, the city he was supposed to be aiding, and instead dropped anchor off Tauroentum (Le Brusc, near Toulon), sending word secretly to the Massaliots that he had arrived, and to come and join him. This they did, followed by the Roman fleet in hot pursuit. In the ensuing battle off Tauroentum the right wing was held by the Massaliots (their previous admiral, Parmenon, now being replaced by Hermon), who fought bravely and skilfully. On the left wing, Nasidius apparently found that the warlike enthusiasm of his crews stopped short of actual fighting, and the ships turned and ran. Caesar's account puts it simply – 'they were of no use at all'.[36] When it was all over, the Massaliot fleet had lost nine more ships, five sunk and four captured. The remainder returned to Massalia, one going ahead to bring the grim news, which was received with a wailing and lamentation that filled the whole city. For Massalia, the war at sea was now at a end.

The naval campaign is hard to evaluate, for it raises one enormous question. How does one explain the tiny forces involved on both sides? Size is a relative matter so let us put it into context. There were, in the first battle, seventeen ships against twelve. At this same time, Pompey was maintaining on the coasts of Spain a fleet of 500 vessels. The battle of Actium was fought by fleets of over 400 ships (mostly smallish Liburnians) on Octavian's side, and 200 on Antony's.[37] Two things are plain. This was no more than a minor scuffle that would hardly be worth mentioning in the history books did not Massalia's life depend on it. Moreover, this is so surprising that it would be incredible were it no so well attested. Massalia was a trading state and hence supposedly a sea power. The city was crammed with monuments to naval victories.[38] If Massalia's naval reputation was anything to go by, Caesar ought to have been afraid to send a fleet anywhere near it, let alone a clumsy, lumbering force of only twelve ships, hurriedly thrown together in a river (not deep-sea) shipyard, built of unseasoned timber and manned by seamen with no naval experience. Yet this handful of hulks, green timber manned by green crews, took on the whole might of the Queen of the Western Ocean – and won. While Massalia, at this crisis in her history, with her very life at stake, at a time when any serious fleet was to be measured in hundreds, could put in the water, as a maximum effort, a mere seventeen ships. If this was the best Massalia could do, it is plain that at this period a bystander on the waterfront could not even, on the evidence of a glance at the Lakydon, utter the traditional declaration, 'The fleet's in!' You'd have had to look for it with a microscope. How did this state of affairs come about? The normal explanation is that Massalia had neglected and run down the navy after the Punic Wars, so that when, in Caesar's siege, a desperate need for a fleet arose, it was too late. They hadn't got one.[39] This in turn raises two questions. The first is, why did the Massaliots let their fleet get into such a state? The orthodox answer is that once Roman power in Provence was securely anchored by the establishment of bases such as Aix, the Massaliots felt (rightly) that they could rely on the Roman legions to control the Ligurians, brigands, and the like, without having to get mixed up in it themselves. But why did this military neglect spread to the fleet? It is illogical, and Clerc can only suggest that, though it is 'surprising', maybe it was because they were so concentrating on commercial development (particularly, it may be, on the overland routes across Gaul) that they forgot about the need for a navy to support and protect the merchant marine. Such an attitude is not only stupid and short-sighted, but there is an even greater objection. Historically, it very seldom happens. States depending on sea trade nearly always have accompanied it by the maintenance of a powerful navy, from ancient Athens to the nineteenth-century British Empire. Why was Massalia an exception? One can of course speculate – improvidence, greed, even stupidity: hypotheses, unsupported by factual evidence. When Clerc calls the situation 'surprenante' it is a clear statement that this is a problem yet unresolved.

But the second question is worse. How do we know that there was ever a decline in the Massaliot navy at all? To decline, that navy must first have been large and efficient, but where is the evidence for that? Evidence of a sort there is. Massalia certainly enjoyed a good reputation at Rome for services rendered, particularly during the Punic Wars but the relevant literary references, vaguely, and sometimes even effusively laudatory, deal largely in generalities. Specifics are largely lacking, and it is very hard to point to anything important that the Massaliots actually did, particularly by sea. It is therefore reasonable to point out that their chief historian, Michel Clerc, delivers himself of a somewhat uncomfortable contradiction: he cannot understand why the Massaliots allowed their fleet to decline, finding it surprising, while at the same time he emphasises that there is no firm evidence that it ever achieved much to start with.[40] We therefore have to ask, since the only real evidence we have for the size and activities of Massalia's navy is the performance of those seventeen ships during Caesar's siege, why should we assume that it was ever anything different? To this question, seldom plainly asked, there can be only one reply: 'Well, it must have been.' What this comes down to is that the evidence for Massalia's naval excellence rests on its reputation, not the other way round; and the only time that reputation is put to the actual test, it is found to be empty and worthless. I am inclined therefore to feel that the role of Massalia's navy has been greatly exaggerated throughout ancient history. I must make clear two things. First, this does not apply to Massalia's merchant commerce, nor to explorers like Pytheas. Second, I am not attacking modern commentators. It seems to me that in this matter, the ancients too were taken in by Massalia's public image (though Caesar knew better). The example from naval affairs is striking, but as we consider other fields we shall find more evidence that in the ancient world Massalia, a past-mistress of public relations, was a city that not only rested on its laurels; on closer examination, the laurels are found to be artificial to begin with.[41]

After the miserable performance of Massalia by sea, it is nothing short of astonishing to turn to the siege by land. Massalia did not have a large army. Native Massaliots were liable to military service, something like the *ephebes* with which we are more familiar at Athens,[42] but could not fill out the ranks to anything like the numbers required. The bulk of Massalia's army accordingly seems to have been Ligurian mercenaries and auxiliaries, with a stiffening of Massaliot officers,[43] the Albici (a Ligurian tribe living around the modern Riez, in the hills overlooking the upper Durance valley near Manosque[44]) being particularly loyal and prominent: they evidently also served on board ship during the inglorious Massaliot campaign by sea. Yet in Massaliot eyes the army ranked as the Senior Service, its general being the Commander-in-Chief of the city and outranking the admiral of the fleet, who was subordinate to him. In case of need there was a *levée en masse* of the population, and the army was kept in a constant state of readiness by regular drill and exercise. It does not seem to have suffered the same neglect as the navy, and Strabo makes a comparison in point of general military efficiency with Rhodes and Cyzicus, cities he admired in this respect.[45] Logistics were looked after by a series of armouries, which again aroused the admiration of Strabo, in which were stored arms for issue to the citizen-soldiers when they were called up, war-engines (a branch of the service in which Massalia evidently excelled), and strategic supplies of grain.[46]

On the other side, the besieging Roman forces were at first personally directed and led by Caesar. For a month he remained at Massalia, then left for Spain, where he was urgently needed for the prosecution of the war against Pompey. C. Trebonius, one of his senior officers, remained in charge, to execute the plans outlined by Caesar. The Roman base camp was established on the Butte St. Charles, on the site now occupied by the SNCF railway station. Since the city was on a peninsula the assault was directed only against its third, landward side, no attempt being made to attack from the sea.[47] The attack was a two-pronged one, directed at La Joliette and at a point a little north of the modern excavations. It took the form, as did most Roman sieges, of the slow but inexorable construction of engineering works – ramps, terraces, siege towers, and the like – designed to undermine the city walls and to create a breach. The defenders countered with sallies in which the besiegers' equipment was repeatedly burned and destroyed. In particular, Caesar spends a lot of time describing an impressive siege engine on rollers (*musculus*), by which the Romans were enabled to undermine the foundations of the city's fortifications. At this point, a truce was declared – Caesar says the defenders asked for it – under cover of which the Massaliots sallied forth,[48] at a time when the Romans were evidently enjoying a siesta and a particularly violent Mistral was blowing, and set fire to everything they could get their hands on. Fanned by the wind, the flames devoured most of the Roman siege works (including the *musculus*), and when the infuriated Romans chased the marauders back inside their walls and set about rebuilding their burned-out siege works, it was only to find that they had no wood to do it with, since they had felled all the trees in the vicinity to provide the necessary lumber the first time round and there were none left. Nevertheless, by various shifts, such as using bricks and clay instead, the work went forward, while the besieged Massaliots, defeated by sea, with no hope of relief by land, their fortifications undermined, and now ravaged by disease through having been forced to eat grain that was unfit for consumption,[49] nerved themselves to face the inevitable surrender. Around the end of September, 49 BC, the capitulation was signed and with it, for all practical purposes, came the end of the Massalia we have been studying. Ahead lay Roman Massilia, which is something different. Apollonides, the Massaliot commander, had fought valiantly, whether one sees him as fighting for a free Massalia or for the doomed cause of Pompey. The end was the same.

The victory went to Brutus and Trebonius, Caesar's loyal lieutenants. And it is perhaps fitting to leave the last word with Michel Clerc, a great historian, but still a patriotic Marseillais: four and a half years later, on the Ides of March, these same two loyal lieutenants were to be found among the band of conspirators who knifed Julius Caesar when he was unarmed, and then later on themselves perished ingloriously in the ruin of the Roman republic that had vanquished Massalia.

Massilia after 49 BC

The above heading is accurate, for after 49 BC the city in effect fell under Roman control and the Latin spelling, Massilia, with an i, is the appropriate one to use. And yet Massaliot independence was not wiped out in 49; legally speaking, it was not affected at all. The terms imposed by the capitulation were perhaps humiliating for a proud city that not only had a long history but throughout it had been recognised as the undisputed leader and standard-bearer of Hellenic culture in the Western Mediterranean, but, as things go in civil wars, they were not brutal. The story of Massilia in the Roman Empire does not fall within the scope of this book, and the relationship of Rome and Massilia/Massalia will in any case be more fully dealt with in a later chapter (p. 135ff.), but we may fittingly close this one with a brief survey of what happened to the city at the end of the war.

Internally, Massilia retained full autonomy,[50] and there was no question, for example, of Rome sending there (as she often did) a praetor to act as judge (*ius dicere*). But though the Massaliots continued to appoint their own magistrates and to live by their own laws in what was, in effect, a small enclave outside the jurisdiction of the governor of Narbonese Gaul, even, for some time at least, striking their own coinage, to most of them their 'autonomy' (though perhaps comparable to that actually enjoyed by many Greek city-states) must have seemed but a sorry thing as compared with past glories. The city was disarmed, losing even the questionable naval might of the 17-trireme fleet that fought at the Friouls, and Caesar installed a Roman garrison of two legions to oversee future good behaviour. While he was at it, he also helped himself to the accumulated wealth of the city treasury. Politically, Massilia lost all control (and possible income) from her colonies except for Nice and the Lerin Islands, and nearly all her *chora*, at one fell swoop, became part of the Roman province. Indeed, in one of the Triumphs that Caesar celebrated in Rome for his accumulated martial successes, a float representing the conquest of Massalia featured in the procession – to the disgust of that greatest of all Massaliophiles, Cicero, who inveighed against the desecration in his Philippics.[51] Where Massalia really suffered, however, was economically. Narbo, the 'capital' of the Roman province, profited from the general increase and more formal organisation of the Roman presence in the region. Antibes too benefited from the eclipse of Massalia, but the chief beneficiary was undoubtedly Arles, which had always been a potential and sometimes an actual rival for the Rhône Valley trade, and now could expect increased Roman support and favour, for it had, of course, fought on the Caesarian side, and actually provided Caesar with the twelve ships that fought for him at the Friouls. The disbanding of the Massaliot navy may also have had an inhibiting effect on Massaliot merchant shipping.[52] Moreover, there was a wider issue. With the whole of Gaul now, in the post-Caesarian era, forming an integral part of the Roman Empire, we should probably see at work a 'Common Market' factor. Trade moved more freely, and Gallic imports, notably wine, could be brought in by any route found convenient. Geographically, of course, the most convenient route to the interior was still the Rhône; the difference was that Massalia had lost its privileged position as middleman or supplier, with the contacts both in Gaul and in Italy that had previously been necessary but now were less so. Nevertheless, this does not mean that Massaliot trade collapsed. The extensive nautical and commercial finds (amphorae, ships' equipment, harbour installations) of Roman date that have come to light, in the Bourse and Place Jules Verne excavations, and the Musée des Docks show that Massalia still counted as a trade centre. And as an academic and intellectual centre one might say that its greatest days were yet to come. But a patriotic Massaliot, looking a Caesar's 49 BC settlement, and thinking of the past, when his city, to borrow Wordsworth's famous description of Venice, 'held the gorgeous West in fee', surely must have felt that indeed his world had ended – and whether it was with a bang or a whimper really made very little difference.

7

Massalia – Politics and Economics

Political science was an invention of the ancient Greeks. It was thus not only familiar to them as a concept, but that concept was stamped with their own characteristic outlook and attitudes. That outlook liked neat, tidy schemes, and ones that were for preference also symmetrical in their elements. Thus in medicine we encounter the four humours of Hippocrates and in cosmology the four elements of the Presocratics, while in astronomy Plato and others speculated endlessly in their attempts to find a rational pattern in the heavenly movements that would impart an orderly sequence to the disorderly wanderings of the planets and so make these vagabonds respectable. In political theory it was much the same thing. There was a set list of ingredients that went into every constitution, and the constitutions varied chiefly in the proportions of each, the strength and extent of their powers. Unlike the planets, the constitutions were man-made, so, given this preconceived master-plan of what form they ought to take, they often in fact did conform to it so that the theory became self-perpetuating. Exceptions to the rule stood out, and the board of five Ephors at Sparta was accordingly celebrated as a particularly and peculiarly Spartan institution. Depending on the proportions in which these ingredients were mixed, there then existed a further set of categories by which the end result could be classified. Traditionally there were three of these categories, monarchy, aristocracy and democracy, each of which also had a bad or degenerate form – tyranny, oligarchy, and ochlocracy (mob rule). The terminology is not always constant or consistent, but it was generally recognised and accepted by political thinkers and theorists.[1] On this basis, Massalia is to be classed as an aristocracy and an extremely stable one. We never hear of any of those *coups d'état* that mark the history of so many Greek cities, nor yet of rumblings of popular discontent – though we must straight away qualify this by noting that on the internal history of Massalia for most of the time we never hear anything at all. A conservatively run state, then, with the government firmly and permanently in the saddle.[2] As such, it naturally commended itself to the philosophers and political theorists, whose tendencies were uniformly towards the right wing, and the Romans, for the same reason. In all of our ancient sources, accordingly, the reputation of Massalia stands very high, one might even say undeservedly high. We shall return to this later, but we may here note an important qualification.

7. Massalia – Politics and Economics

Massalia was a timocracy.[3] The term is ancient, and was a subdivision in the classification outlined above, being a state in which political rights and the degree of power attainable depended on individual wealth – in essence, an aristocracy with an economic rather than a hereditary basis. It would be tempting to see in it the supersession of the landed gentry by the *nouveaux riches* of commerce (and this undoubtedly did often occur) and hence view it as a natural development in a trading state like Massalia, but in fact its primary purpose usually seems to have been military. Soldiers in the citizen militias of Greek cities had to furnish their own equipment. Heavy-armed hoplite infantry had to buy their own armour, cavalrymen had to own a horse, and so on. The role in which they performed their national service was thus determined by their financial resources, and the citizenship rolls were divided up on this basis. By classical times the military connection was often no more than nominal, and the *Hippeis* in Athens and the *Equites* at Rome were not real serving cavalrymen, but rather citizens who formed a distinct class, based primarily on wealth, with distinct political privileges and responsibilities.

How far did the constitution of Massalia fit this profile? As usual, we cannot give a full answer, for our evidence is far too sketchy and fragmentary. Aristotle did actually publish a treatise on the *Constitution of Massalia*, but of it there survives only a tiny (and, for our purposes, worthless) fragment embedded in a series of love stories repeated by Athenians and recounting the affair of Protis and Gyptis. Our chief source is in fact Strabo.[4] His account is far from complete, but we can only be thankful that we have it. The following outline is based upon his description.

The chief governing body was a board of six hundred members, known as the *timouchoi*, drawn from among the nobles and holding office for life. Greek political theorists would find this a familiar ingredient, for the *boule* or council, approximately of this size (at Athens it was of 500 members, at Rome the equivalent was the Senate) was a standard element in ancient constitutions.[5] Of this six hundred, a rotating group of fifteen formed an executive committee to deal with general administration; of the fifteen, three were specifically responsible for the day-to-day running of the city, and the chairman of the three was therefore the closest thing existing to an actual head of state. The similarity to the better-known prytany system at Athens is striking. Moreover, mere wealth did not by itself automatically confer membership of the *timouchoi*. One also had to have produced children, and to have held Massaliot citizenship for the past three generations; and presumably one still had to wait for a vacancy opening up, created by the death of one of the six hundred members. The method of selection of the incoming *timouchos* – nomination, election, co-option, or whatever – is not known.[6] At some period unknown there seems to have been a modification of this constitution, but the details are scanty and, from our viewpoint, relatively unimportant. In all probability it was nothing more than an enlargement of eligibility for *timouchoi* to include

111

the *nouveaux riches* among the merchants, the second wave of wealthy traders (very likely owing their position to the introduction of coined money) whose families were not listed in the original rolls.[7]

The board of fifteen seem also to have doubled both as military leaders and as judges, (or, at least, chairmen of the courts, there being, as at Athens, no professional judges or separate judiciary, as we understand the terms), and we do not know how the juries, if any, were constituted. The laws they administered are described by Strabo as being Ionian in origin and inspiration, and publicly available for consultation – which he evidently thought uncommon enough to be worth mentioning.[8] Of the laws themselves, several are reported in the ancient sources, chosen, one suspects, chiefly for their sensational nature. I list some of these:

1. *No wine for women.* This was not a tradition unique to Massalia, for a similar prohibition evidently existed at Miletos, and also at early Rome. The Massaliot law presumably formed part of the city's Ionian inheritance.[9]

2. *Suicide legal, subject to official approval.* Valerius Maximus, whom we have to thank for a collection of some of the more colourful items of Massaliot legislation, assures us that anyone who felt that life was no longer worth living could make an application to the *timouchoi* arguing his case, and, if successful, would be provided with a dose of hemlock at public expense to facilitate the execution of his project – and, indeed, himself.[10]

3. *Execution of criminals by a sword kept rusty on purpose.* There is some doubt on this. Valerius does state that the sword was rusty, but it may be that this shows only how seldom it was used, so that it may be in fact evidence of moderation rather than severity.[11]

4. *No pornographic theatre.* There was of course an actual theatre building in Massalia, but productions were presumably restricted to more serious works. What was banned was mimes, a dramatic form that also had a very bad reputation at Rome, and which Valerius says was prohibited from the fear that the audience would consummate in reality the disgraceful acts they saw counterfeited on the stage.[12]

5. *No unauthorised cults.* The object of this prohibition was not so much religious as to get rid of beggars using it as an excuse to seek handouts, when instead they ought to be doing an honest day's work.[13]

6. *Foreigners to check their weapons with the police.* Apparently an officer was on duty at the gates to receive for safe-keeping all arms from visitors entering the city. They were handed back on departure. This may have been a security measure that originated after the failed attempt at a *coup d'état* by infiltrating armed Celtic natives (p. 94 above).[14] There were also a number of sumptuary laws, restricting expenses on conspicuous luxuries, as also a set limit for dowries and the cost of bridal dress.[15] Funerals likewise benefited from an enforced austerity. Two empty coffins (one for citizens, one for slaves) were kept on permanent stand-by at the city gates, and the deceased was conveyed to the cemetery on a farm cart.

Public demonstrations of mourning were forbidden, or rather limited to a small private wake for members of the family.[16] Rather more unusual was a provision that a freed slave could be re-enslaved, apparently on the grounds of having shown himself insufficiently grateful to his former master, and this could be done no less than three times over. There could be no fourth time, however. The argument apparently was that if the master had three times freed a slave and then on each occasion repented of it, by this time it was the judgement of the master that was called in question. After three false starts, he ought by then to have realised just what the slave was like, and not freed him yet again.

It will be seen that this farrago leaves us very far short of any comprehensive or even coherent account of the constitution of Massalia. Some of it we can perhaps fill in by guesswork based on the known practices of other Greek states, but there are many gaps, and in particular one crucial one. Where was the *demos*, the proletariat, in all of this? This was normally, even in antiquity, considered an essential ingredient in all constitutions. It usually formed an Assembly, or *ekklesia*, and though its power might vary from much to little, depending on the political emphasis in different cities, on really large issues, such as peace or war, it often had the last word. Not only is there no real trace of any such body at Massalia, but in what one hears of the *timouchoi* one gets the impression that they had both the first and the last word on everything, exercising the functions otherwise reserved for an Assembly. Given that the membership limit on the *timouchoi* was six hundred – this is one thing that does seem reliably established – this would mean that there would be many citizens, even well-to-do ones, permanently excluded from the conduct of affairs in their own city.

But our worries about the exclusion of the *demos*, the working class, must go further. Massalia was a trading state. We must be clear what that means. All the Greeks relied primarily upon agriculture. When we read of a city being commercially based, such as Athens vis-à-vis Thebes, what we mean is that it is more oriented towards trading than others that have no such orientation at all. But the peasants remain the mainspring of its economy and usually of its politics as well.[17] That said, we must yet recognise that in a trading state – and particularly, I feel, in Massalia – the commercial interests must have been important enough to win some sort of political recognition; and there is no sign of it here. Was it because, as at Athens, trade was in the hands of metics, resident aliens, who, prohibited from owning land, were completely shut out from the political process? There is no evidence for metics at Massalia, so we do not know. Was it that leading merchants became so wealthy that they combined in cabals, like the mediaeval trade guilds, and infiltrated the *timouchoi*? The argument has been put forward, but one remembers uneasily the objections that have been urged, maintaining that this reflects an anachronistic view of trade that was not shared by the ancient world.[18]

What does seem quite clear is that the class of the *timouchoi* seem to have considered Massalia as their own personal possession and this brings up again the role of the *demos*. The rare occurrence of the word in inscriptions is apparently no more than a technicality. In reality, the *demos* not only had no say whatever in the running of the city, but was apparently quite satisfied. There is no mention of Massalia ever having been struck by civil unrest, revolution, or even tyranny, that standard Greek safety-value for repressed proletariats. It is enough to make one almost doubt whether a *demos* ever existed at all. There are four arguments for its existence. First, a trading state, even if land-holding peasants are in a majority, must have at least a sizable minority of craftsmen who form a potential working class. The only valid argument against this would be if all crafts were in the hands of slaves owned by *timouchoi*. The second argument is the navy. Greek warships, being oared galleys, were labour-intensive. It was a Greek tradition that they never were manned by slaves, but by poor citizens, who, not being able to afford the armour required for service in the army, performed their national service at the oars of the triremes. The navy was thus a stronghold of the *demos* and democracy, while the nobles went into the army. This was especially true at Athens. A major seapower must therefore have had in its warships a very large number of poor citizens who – unlike the slaves and convicts who powered the galleys of later ages – where naturally minded to demand political rights, and in a position to make their demands stick. A major trading city like Massalia must accordingly have had a strong navy, and, at its oars, a strong *demos*. But we see no sign of it.[19] The third argument is the simple statistical one that from what we know all Greek cities did have a *demos* (and were expected to have one by the political theorists), and why should a state like Massalia, prominent in trading circles and a natural attraction to landless craftsmen, be an exception? Finally, we have one very firm and convincing piece of evidence, the testimony of Cicero. A stout friend of optimates everywhere and a devoted constitutional conservative, he yet, in a well-known passage, declares that 'If Massilia is governed with fairness and justice by a chosen group of its leading citizens, just the same the ordinary people are in a position that looks remarkably like slavery.'[20]

All of these arguments point to one seemingly irrefutable conclusion. At Massalia there really did exist a proletariat, a *demos*, it really was completely powerless, and over six centuries it never showed any signs of trying to change the situation. Such is the fact. Trying to explain why is a different matter altogether. One possible explanation in such circumstances is that, surrounded by constant pressure from the barbarian hordes (in much the same way that, later, Ovid felt himself surrounded at Tomi), the Massaliots avoided internal dissension in the face of the external threat. This seems to me unlikely. For one thing, it is a matter of history that, even faced with external threats, Greeks usually did find it very hard to stick together,[21] and it seems even more improbable that they could maintain this harmonious concord unbroken for six centuries. The other possible explanation lies in trade, and the profits to be made from it. By this argument, the trade with Gaul that passed through Massalia was so lucrative that, in effect, even the poor counted as rich, and were more than happy to perpetuate so profitable a status quo. It was, after all, a Conservative Prime Minister who called and fought a general election in Britain on the slogan 'You've Never Had It So Good!' – and won. The proletariat of Massalia, it may be suggested, felt the same way. On this however the evidence is contradictory. Commerce at Massalia certainly was booming, and in a normal Greek state that meant prosperity for the lower classes, even the metics. But Massalia does seem in many ways to be an exception to the ordinary Greek rules, and the trade it developed with the hinterland seems to have been largely aimed at and handled by the Celtic chieftains, so in Massalia it may also have had socio-political overtones and been more in the hands of the aristocrats than was customary. Failing a more profound analysis we should probably be wise not to build too much on assumptions that Massalia was different from other Greek cities when in fact we know so little about it. But it would seem reasonable at this point to leave the political picture and turn to the economics of this avowedly and admittedly trading state.

Economics

Its geographical position, as we have already seen (p. 57 above), marked Massalia out to be one of the great trading states of the ancient Greek world, if not even the greatest. It controlled the one sure route of access from the Mediterranean world to Gaul. The Greek Mediterranean was the chief workshop for the production of all the goods for sophisticated, civilised living. Gaul was one of the largest virgin markets that there was. No doubt the Greeks of Syracuse, for example, traded with the native Sicels, but a mere glance at the map, comparing the relative sizes of Gaul and Sicily, will put paid to any arguments on this basis. Gaul, on the other hand, was enormous in extent, well populated, easy of internal access (thanks to its rivers and lack of mountain ranges), and if the number of golden torques sported by its natives is anything to go by, rich. Once one got inside Gaul, inside the doorway represented by the Rhône valley, it was a trader's dream; and Massalia was the doorkeeper. There were, of course, other cities in the ancient world whose position on natural trade routes assured them commercial prosperity, such as Alexandria or Palmyra, but these were mostly located in the context of a developed local civilisation, so that there were other factors contributing to their preeminence as well as trade. But at Massalia, trade was the one thing that gave the city prominence. Some may see this as an overstatement, but I think it will stand. Trade with Gaul is something that we have already considered on a general level; we will now turn to look at the trading patterns of Massalia in particular, for the last century or so BC for which the evidence is most abundant. The essentials are easily stated. Wine and manufactured goods were imported from the Mediterranean, tin, grain, and slaves exported. Stripped to essentials even more basic, this probably came down to a simple exchange: wine for slaves.

Our evidence in turn comes from two main archaeological sources: coinage and amphorae. Coinage, and its spread, can tell us much about trade relations in general – in general, because, of course, when we find a coin there is no telling what particular commodity it had been used to buy. Wine was normally sealed in amphorae at the place of production – 'bottled', as we would put it – and not transported in bulk (i.e. any given ship might be carrying an enormous quantity of wine, but it would all be in individual amphorae). As practically every region made amphorae to its own local shapes and style, this enables us to look at the discarded amphorae, or the fragments thereof, at the place of consumption, and identify where it was getting its wine from. We must also note one major problem: slavery. Slaves were quite certainly a mainstay of the Celtic and Massaliot economies, but it is almost impossible to find out anything about them. Not only were slaves easily transported, walking along on their own two legs and leaving no archaeological trace behind them, but even literary or epigraphical references are very thin on the ground, as if this was a taboo subject that gentlemen did not like to talk about. Nevertheless, in considering the various forms of economic evidence, that is what we will start with.

Slaves

Throughout antiquity, the institution of slavery was never questioned by anyone, of any race, culture, colour, or religion.[22] Slaves therefore formed a normal and accepted commodity in the world of trade, and Gaul had the reputation of being a prolific source of them. What this presumably meant was that individual Celtic chieftains would barter prisoners taken from another tribe in border raids, or even members of their own tribe that they wanted rid of, for goods offered by travelling traders. The commonest, and certainly the most popular, such good was wine. We will postpone to a later page (see pp. 211ff. below) our discussion of wine and its impact on Celtic society, but here may note its close connection with the slave trade. Celts, it was believed, would do anything to get wine, and Diodorus, in a much-quoted passage, remarks how they would willingly exchange a young slave for a jar of wine. Diodorus perhaps exaggerates, but the main point is clear.[23] Slaves could also be acquired in two other ways. One was purchase, the slave being paid for either with coined money, or with gold or silver in bullion form. The other was by capture, either as a prisoner of war or as booty from a raid. In the Greek and Roman world there sometimes existed a further possibility, enslavement for debt, but this is not relevant to Massaliot-Celtic commerce.

What is the evidence, then, for an extensive Celtic slave trade? As noted, we have very little direct testimony, but we may yet come to some conclusions.[24] It will be most productive if we approach the problem not from the Gaulish but the Italian end, looking not for evidence of slaves leaving Gaul but at known figures for the Gaulish slaves who ended up in Italy. One of our best sources here is the revolt of Spartacus, for in his army he had a whole Celtic division, who refused repatriation to their native Gaul. We are here dealing with estimates, not known facts, but it is plain that, as a leading authority has put it, 'the Gauls accounted for a large proportion of Spartacus' band and, that being so, there must have been at least some hundred thousand Gallic slaves in Italy at the time.' To remain stable, such a figure would require annual replacements, bought, if there was no war and hence no prisoners. So, 'assuming there to have been 300,000 Gallic slaves in Italy – between 10 and 15 percent of the slave population – and allowing for a 7 percent rate of replacement, only one quarter of which could, in those times, have been assured by natural reproduction, a total of 15,000 slaves must have been brought from Gaul during each warless year'.[25] And this is for a period before Julius Caesar embarked on his Gallic wars, during which Gaul was generally free from Roman military incursions. The figures work out well enough. The Gallic population was big enough to stand this regular drain on it, and the cost would be more or less balanced by Gallic imports of Italic wine. True, this may be no more than what one of my students described in an essay as 'a sure guess', but we take it as a working hypothesis that, in the second and first centuries BC, at least, there was an Italic-Gallic trade axis, and that essentially it was an exchange of wine for slaves. This convenient system broke down when Caesar added Gaul to the Roman Empire, for, since the Romans could hardly enslave *en masse* the peaceable inhabitants of one of their own provinces, the slave supply from Gaul dried up. This in turn meant that the Gauls, deprived of their chief currency, could no longer pay for Italic wine, and had to start making it themselves, thus developing the domestic Gallic wine industry, which is still so prominently with us today. It should perhaps be added that though we are here dealing with a trade between Italy and the interior of Gaul, it would perforce be funnelled through Massalia, and thus, even if not carried on Massaliot ships nor in the hands of traders who were themselves Massaliot nationals, it was a mainstay of the Massaliot economy.

Wine

The other half of this equation was wine, which represented a vast commercial traffic until the final reduction of Gaul and its inclusion in the Roman Empire. When this happened, Rome no longer needed to pay for Gallic metals (such as tin), nor could they very well enslave the Gauls now living under their protection. The two trade equations on which Italian wine exports (through Massalia) to Gaul were based, wine for tin and wine for slaves, thus both collapsed, independently. The result was that, with-

67. Vines in Provence.

out wine from Campania, the Gauls, if they wanted to keep on drinking (and there was not doubt on that score), had to make their own, and this indeed proved the origin of the French wine industry. But in the earlier years, with which this book is concerned, Massalia had a ready market.

In antiquity the Celtic thirst was both gargantuan and notorious. For the traders it was a gold mine, for the Celts the wine represented, in Benoît's words, 'la monnaie d'échange la plus appréciée'.[26] The traffic in wine is best measured by finds both on land and in the cargoes of shipwrecks, where the original source of the wine is identifiable by the national type of the amphora in which it was carried. Wine was sometimes transported by sea in *dolia*, enormous jars for carriage in bulk, and for a long overland journey, such as that to Vix, it might be transferred at some point to wine-skins, less liable to breakage from the stressful jolting of cartage,[27] but usually wine was carried in sealed ceramic amphorae, filled at the vineyard of production and left in the amphora till it reached its destination. From the types of amphora found we may note that wine traffic at Massalia and its surrounding area falls into three separate periods chronologically (though the volume of wine handled in each is not necessarily the same). In archaic Massalia (600-500 BC) there were extensive imports from Etruria. These were soon replaced by a growing Massaliot industry, supplemented by imports from Greece, and this lasted till 175. Around 175 Italic imports, mostly from Campania and characteristically in the type of amphora known as Dressel 1, entered the market

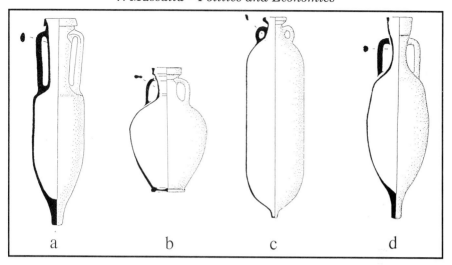

68. Wine amphorae were made in shapes characteristic of their place of origin. Four of the types most commonly found in the South of France are: (a) South Italy, Campania (Dressel I); (b) Massalia; (c) Carthage (probably for oil); (d) Spain.

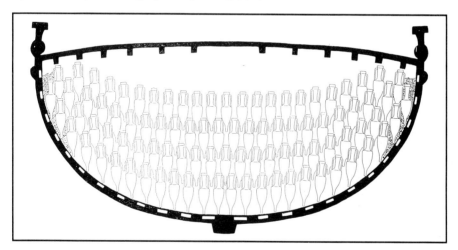

69. Cargo of (South Italian) wine amphorae, as stowed on board ship.

in a mighty flood that simply obliterated domestic production, and this lasted until the end of Massaliot independence and the subjection of Gaul by Caesar, a period of about a century and a half.[28] At Toulouse, not easily accessible by water from the Mediterranean, vast numbers of discarded Italic amphorae have been found, so a lot of wine got at least that far still in the original container.[29] Some statistics may help us to put this trade into context. A ship, excavated by underwater archaeology and known as the Petit Congloué wreck, was carrying as its principal cargo 15 *dolia* full

70. South Italian wine amphorae, showing stacking technique: in grounds of St. Raphael Museum.

71. Wine amphorae of various types: first century BC.

of wine. A *dolium* is a very large jar, much bigger than an amphora, with a capacity of 2,000 litres.[30] The wine being carried on this one ship thus came to a total of 30,000 litres, or the equivalent, in modern terms, of 40,000 bottles. This is not counting a supplementary cargo of wine carried in amphorae.[31] When one looks at these figures one is impressed by their size. We must not be, in view of what is to follow. Ships could carry up to ten thousand amphorae and the wreck of one such ship, dated to c. 80-60 BC, has actually been discovered off Albegna (in Liguria, between San Remo and Savona) in which the cargo consisted of five or more superimposed layers of amphorae, of capacity 26 litres each, to an estimated total of at least 10,000. This gives a total volume of 260,000 litres, or around 350,000 modern bottles.[32] On the basis of this and similar pieces of evidence, our leading authority on the topic has estimated that there was around 10,000,000 litres[33] of wine imported annually into Gaul from Italy, and mostly via Massalia. For those who, from a familiarity with the local wine store, still find it easier to envisage it in modern terms, that means 13 million bottles every year. At his rate it is reckoned that 'some forty million amphorae would have been unloaded in Gaul' during the century or so (basically the first century BC) for which evidence for this trade exists.[34] And each amphora contained 20-30 litres. Naturally the mind simply boggles at figures such as this. But it must be remembered that this figure is accumulated over a century and a half. At 10,000 amphorae per ship, a million amphorae comes to 100 shiploads, which, spread over two centuries, comes to only one boat every two years. Plainly, on a heavy trade such as this, traffic was much more frequent, and the figure of forty million begins to look less fantastic. Certainly a large part of France is littered with fragments of Italian wine amphorae, and at some sites the soil is literally stuffed with them. An eighteenth-century history of Toulouse tells us that 'the labourers there cart [the fragments] away to clear the earth but despite such labours, repeated over and over again since time immemorial, their ploughs continue to unearth them constantly and the plough-shares are continually blunted by the impact of this pottery'. At Châlon-sur-Saône 24,000 amphorae have been dredged up from the river bed, leaving an estimated 200-500,000 still lying there.[35] The actual route of importation of these overseas supplies cannot always be determined. Some may have come directly to local ports, such as Agde, or even up-river to Arles, while some may have come first to Massalia and there been trans-shipped, either to coasting vessels or forwarded by road. But they certainly formed a major factor in the economy of Massalia, or at least the territory, the *chora* of Massalia, if we apply to that its most elastic definition. And though, as the second century BC passed into the first, direct Roman competition through the new (and entirely Roman) port of Narbo and hence inland up the Aude-Garonne axis became more prominent, the Massaliot economy does not seem to have suffered greatly: the Celtic market, and the Celtic thirst, were apparently big enough to accommodate both Rome and Massalia at once.[36]

We will postpone to a later page (211ff.) a consideration of the wine trade as it manifested itself among the Celts, but may notice one possible political side-effect on Massalia. Despite its volume, the wine trade, was essentially a luxury trade, or more precisely, a chieftains' trade. The buyers of the wine were never ordinary Celtic tribesmen. Instead, wine was recognised as a prerogative of chieftains and princelings, a king's drink, and in Celtic society anyone with regal pretensions was expected to have a supply of it on hand to be served out to visitors, honoured guests, retinue, and fellow-tribesmen on appropriately festive occasions. It was a special drink, with a whole range of ceremonies and a cachet all its own that perhaps recall our own attitudes to champagne.[37] It may therefore be possible that since this was essentially a trade with aristocrats, those handling it at the Massalia end also came to enjoy a quasi-aristocratic status, or, alternatively, it was seen as an appropriate activity for existing aristocrats.[38] This could at least help to explain the paradox that has beset us – how did Massaliot society contrive to remain both rigidly oligarchic and comprehensively commercial, in the face of all normally accepted Greek historical theory? However, I am inclined to offer it only as a possibility, and one that I cannot myself see as more than an outside one.[39] It is quite common for the socially elevated to purchase luxury goods from sellers who yet retain the more lowly appellation of merchants, and for all their welcome on arriving at the hall of a Celtic chief, the Massaliot wine dealers might yet perhaps have found themselves directed to the tradesmen's entrance.

There remains the question of Massaliot wine, produced in Massalia or its territories, and either exported or consumed locally.[40] It also may be traced by the presence of its distinctive amphorae, their swelling bulbous bellies a striking contrast to the tall emaciated slimness of the Dressel I amphorae used by Campanian producers. Wine production around Massalia began when the colony was founded – it was always one of the first things Greek colonists set about doing, if their land could at all be induced to produce vines. This was supplemented by wine imports from Ionian cities such as Thasos, Cos, Cnidos, and, especially, Rhodes.[41]

Domestic Massaliot wine was first exported along the littoral and into the interior of Gaul as well as consumed in Massalia. This lasted through the Classical and Hellenistic periods, until this export trade was effectively swamped by the flood of incoming wine from Campania in the early second century BC. Massaliot wine, of course, continued in production for the internal Massaliot market and with the coming of the Empire – strictly speaking, outside our period, but worth noting – , when the Campanian imports declined, again enjoyed a more widespread market. In this period, it – apparently for the first time – penetrated to Rome, where it came to enjoy a somewhat ambiguous reputation. Pliny, listing and ranking in order the principal vintages of the whole Mediterranean area, says it is the best there is between the Alps and the Pyrenees, almost a classic example of damning with faint praise. He adds that it comes in two separate kinds, one of which is full-bodied (*sucosum*) and is used for blending with other wines. Athenaeus, in a much-quoted remark, says that it is 'rich and full-bodied', and that it is good, but not much of it is made. Martial, on the other hand, accuses it of having a too-smoky taste, and sees it as the kind of *vin ordinaire* you would pass off on some of your guests while keeping a better vintage for your own table.[42]

As well as conventional wine, the region also produced quite a lot of flavoured wine, the flavour coming from the addition of various herbs (the region, it will be remembered, was famous for its herbs). Lavender, coming especially from the Porquerolles (ancient Stoechades) was so used, as was thyme; thyme wine was evidently a local specialty, unknown in Greece. Silphium, for which Cyrene was famous (LSJ translate it 'saxifrage') may also have been used, to produce *vinum silatum*; so was myrrh.[43] It was apparently taken as an aperitif (*iantaculum*). Other flavouring agents included resin (the parallel with modern retsina requires no comment, though the ancient variety in this context, seems to have resembled pitch or turpentine more than pine resin), which was actually an item of trade; it was exported from Provence and has been found loaded as freight in the cargoes of shipwrecks at both Agde and Marseille.[44] Absinthe (translated – for the word is Greek – by LSJ as 'wormwood') was also well known, being described by both Pliny and Columella, though to those familiar with stories of its ferocious potency from the Paris of Degas and Toulouse Lautrec it comes as a distinct anticlimax to find it recommended as a cough mixture for the winter.[45] All of these herbal flavourings and many others were readily available at Massalia and seem to have been both popular and heavily used in making wine. The flavour was no doubt imparted by dipping or steeping the herbs in the wine, but we may note in passing that it is possible to save time and labour by simply planting aromatic herbs alongside the wine, which, as it grows, will pick up their flavour. This is done today, and may have been practised by the Massaliots.[46] The multiplicity of the flavours need not surprise us. Variety is a characteristic of the wine trade and, apart from these artificially flavoured wines, there would presumably be available, in Massalia as elsewhere, a range of imported vintages, both 'pure' wine and perhaps flavoured as well. Dion makes the point that people do have favourite brands and vintages, and hence the wine trade involves much more variety than a standardised staple such as grain, though no doubt choice was often limited by availability and a man had to drink not what he would like but what he could get.[47] To cloud the issue yet more, we must bear in mind that many of these herbs were held to have medicinal values, and hence wines flavoured with them may have been considered as essentially folk-remedies and tonics rather than drinks, the wine being a convenient, not to say pleasant, medium through which to administer the medicine, either by prescription of a physician or pressed upon the sufferer by well-meaning friends.[48] One probable offshoot of this would be the modern phenomenon of brand loyalty. In folk medicine of all things, people tend to have some particular remedy that they swear by, so this would be another factor – as indeed it is today in drug stores and chemist's shops – tending towards the multiplicity of brands handled by the Massaliot wine trade.

The extent of this trade, as judged by finds of Massaliot amphorae, was considerable, especially before the coming of Campanian imports at the end of the Hellenistic period, but it was more or less limited to Gaul. Along the Mediterranean coast, Benoit assures us, no Massaliot amphorae have been found beyond Genoa, to the east, and, to the west, beyond Ampurias and Majorca (though their sphere of export increased after the Roman conquest, including to Rome itself). Within the Midi finds are extensive, especially in Celtic oppida.[49] We may also note a further appendage to the wine trade. This was the trade in fine ceramics – in other words, the specialised vases and vessels that went with wine-drinking.[50] This includes jugs and goblets of various sorts, ladles, mixing bowls and so forth, and a lot of these were imported with the wine. Athenian black-and red-figure ware is found on quite a lot of Celtic sites, and this presumably made its way into Gaul via Massalia; for the fact that the Celts did not mix their wine but drank it straight, apparently did not stop them importing elaborate mixing bowls, as superbly represented by the great krater (mixing bowl) of Vix. One single shipwreck, dated to the late sixth/early fifth century, has yielded no less than almost 2,000 such pieces of fine ware (including 1,265 cups of one particular style of Ionian origin),[51] and Attic vases are to be seen in many provincial museums (including Vix, where they were found in the actual tomb itself).[52]

Coinage

When Massalia was founded in 600 BC, coinage was still something of an innovation, for it originated, in Lydia, only a hundred years earlier, perhaps less. Massalia began striking coins in the late sixth century and these played a vital part in the development of the Massaliot economy, though we must not thereby be led to underestimate the crucial role of barter. A great part, perhaps the majority, of the commercial transactions with the inland Celts were conducted without money changing hands at all, and this was common in the relations of Greek colonists.[53] The Celts, indeed, seem to have taken a long time in grasping the very concept of money. They were not short of gold, but seem not to have known what to do with it, wearing it as bracelets and collars, and storing it in temples. As for Massalia, the city struck coins in silver (which came partly from the district of the Aveyron, in southern Gaul, but mostly from the mines of Tartessos[54] (the Guadalquivir) in Spain), and in bronze; Massalia never, at any point in its history, struck in gold. The chief characteristic of its currency was its concentration on the production of large amounts of coins of small denominations. The drachma was the largest coin ever struck, while a glance into the coinage showcases of any Mediterranean museum will make it plain that the standard coin of most Greek cities was the tetradrachm, the four-drachma piece.[55]

The explanation is uncertain. One argument is that small change was much more useful in developing trade, and hence a lot of it was used. The contrary argument is that for any serious transaction, barter was still the rule, and many Celts may have for long hesitated to give away something of real practical value, such as a slave, in return for a few lumps of metal, however precious, in much the same way that many people today do not like to handle currency bills of very high denominations. The first Massaliot coins are, in fact, multiples or subdivisions of the obol, itself one-sixth of a drachma, and are struck in silver. They are well represented by a hoard of 2,130 coins inside a ceramic vase and unearthed at Auriol, near Marseille, in 1867, where they had been buried around 470 BC. A large number of these coins are imports from various issuing cities in Asia Minor (including some from Phocaea) but a good many seem to have been struck in Massalia; there are even some imitations apparently struck by Celtic neighbours, presumably those that had attained a certain level of sophistication. The coins themselves are mostly obols, and the selection gives a good idea of the types of currency circulating in the Massalia *chora* by the end of the Archaic Age.[56] The coins are anepigraphic, that is, they carry no inscription indicating the city of origin, and have a figured type only on the obverse, the reverse being incuse, imprinted only with the sunken stamp of a square punch. The metal is invariably silver, bronze coming into use only in the third century.

The next step was the striking of a coinage (still obols) with types on both faces. These coins, dated to the mid-fifth century, carrying on one face a profile head of some presumably divine personage, though the sex is not readily identifiable (which means, in effect, it is either Apollo or Artemis, both venerated at Massalia). The reverse commonly carries either a crab or a four-spoked wheel. This was a common way of publicly recognising close commercial or even political ties with another city: the crab was the recognised national emblem of Acragas, in Sicily, and the wheel, though hardly a national emblem, is the standard type on obols issued by Syracuse. These Massaliot obols also, for the first time, now often indicate their origin by carrying prominently displayed the letters MA, or (in Greek) MASS. A few, featuring the horned head of an aquatic divinity (a standard convention) even identified it by spelling out LAKYDON.[57]

The early years of the fourth century marked a further advance, with the issue of the first Massaliot drachmae. This coin, generally known as the heavy drachma, was struck to a weight of 3.70 g, the same standard as that used by Velia. The types now settled down to what was to become the standard types of Massaliot coinage, familiar through the Classical period. On the obverse appeared the profile head of Artemis, finely executed and surely modelled on the famous head of Arethusa that, from the skilled hands of the master-engraver Euainetos, was now appearing on the coins struck of Syracuse. On the reverse appeared in profile a lion, particularly distinctive by its very high-arching waist and hindquarters, and usually also the name MASSALIETON, 'of the Massaliots', often inscribed in the exergue (the bottom segment of the coin, under the lion's paws). This heavy drachma was only a very limited issue, and did not last long, but obols continued to appear in great abundance, struck to a (theoretical) weight of 0.61 g (= one-sixth of a 3.70 g drachma).

With the disappearance of the heavy drachma, the obol held the field unchallenged for a further 175 years. Then, between 241 and 218, the drachma reappeared, in great and lasting abundance but in a new guise. The types of Artemis and the lion were resurrected, but the weight of the coin much reduced, to between 2.75 and 2.50 g. These are generally known as the light drachmae, and the obol, remaining at 0.61, was now presumably exchanged at the rate of four obols to the drachma.[58] Finally, at the end of the third century, bronze coins appear, struck to a weight of 10/11 g (the value-ratio of silver:bronze at this period throughout the Mediterranean is around 1:120), the lion on the reverse being replaced by a charging bull. With minor changes, such as the introduction of bronze coins of smaller denominations, this system prevailed until Caesar brought to an end the independence of Massalia, and, with it, its coinage.[59]

What evidence does this Massaliot coinage have to offer for the patterns of trade? To start with, it has often been found along the coast of Provence and in the lower valley of the Rhône, where it comes as no surprise. Common also in the Celtic *oppida* of Languedoc and Roussillon, it has also come to light along the Loire and the Seine; in Spain it is found at Ampurias and elsewhere in Catalonia, and the most far-flung finds come from Switzerland, Jersey, and include three Massalia drachmae of late date found in Britain.[60] Given what we have previously said about the extent of Massalia's commerce, there is little in this that is surprising, but it does stand as a confirmation. Moreover, the large number of hoards of coins found at Celtic sites seems to indicate that the Celts sometimes simply amassed them as bullion, rather than as money for exchange and commercial use. Clavel-Leveque does not exaggerate in calling some of these accumulations 'des sommes extraordinaires'; the hoard discovered in 1336 at Tourves, between St. Maximien and Aix-en-Provence, numbered 4.2 million coins and weighed 2,400 kg, all in obols.[61] But this illustrates what is perhaps an even more significant factor in the financial policy of Massalia, the un-Greek insistence on coining only in small denominations. This coinage must have been oriented towards internal trade within Gaul, not international trade with Greece and Magna Graecia. And this trade seems to have been at a relatively unsophisticated, if voluminous level, as often happened in a colonial situation.[62]

There remains one problem that, though perhaps impossible to resolve satisfactorily, must yet, I feel, be faced. We have stressed the relative values of these various coins. But what were they actually worth? There are few things harder than trying to express ancient monetary values in terms of modern currency, yet the reader has surely some right to expect that the attempt will be made, for if it is not, then the whole issue is liable to become dangerously academic and abstract. Can we then hope even to indicate to what order of magnitude ancient coins correspond? Or, to use the American idiom, can we get even a ball-park figure?

Some points should be noted. First, in the ancient world there was no token money. Coins were always worth the weight of the precious metal contained in them and the state types stamped on their faces were quality-control marks certifying that the coin was of pure metal and of full weight. But the availability, and relative value of metals in the ancient and modern world are much too variable and far apart for this to be a basis of comparison. Second, any expression of value in modern terms begins to become inaccurate, under the influence of inflation, as soon as the book is printed; and when the reader comes across a statement, as he or she sometimes will, that some ancient coin is worth so many pounds or dollars, the very first step should be to look at the date of the publication of the book. Third – and in this I give only a personal belief of my own, but I think I am right – we tend to underestimate the value of ancient coins because we tend automatically to equate them with modern coins, and practically everywhere nowadays coins are of very low value, any larger amounts being covered by paper bills or notes. This mistaken equation is helped along by the small size of many ancient coins. In fact, the rule that is usually quoted is that one should equate the daily wages of an ancient and modern workman, but even this is far from precise, for not only did ancient economic conditions vary geographically and chronologically, but it takes no account of income tax, pension fund, week-ends off, or other realities of modern life. Still, in the Erechtheion building inscriptions from late fifth-century Athens, we do have a reliable figure that has the added benefit of simplicity. All workmen, such as carpenters and masons, were paid one drachma per day. Attempts to equate this to a modern figure reveal a further problem. Many scholars publishing such an equation seem to have no idea of what modern workmen actually earn, and, without finding out, e.g., what would be the current trade union rate for the job, produce a figure based on pure guesswork and rough impressions. Where they err, such guesses always err on the side of being too low, sometimes so ludicrously so that they would give any union organiser apoplexy.[63] The current rate for such workmen in Canada at the time of writing is somewhere around $120-150 daily, so a tetradrachm, so often quoted as the standard coin in ancient currencies, represents (in 1995 figures) something like $500, or £250. The obol, one-sixth of the drachma and the favourite denomination at Massalia, thus stands at something like $20 or £10. These figures are of course quite imprecise, but I think they do make a point when we speak of the Massaliot concentration on small denominations – even the obol was not the kind of coin you would offer to buy a cabbage in the market place. And for actual size, the smallest ones – smaller than the nail of your little finger – must have presented a problem for a people who not yet having invented pockets, often carried their small change tucked into their cheek.

8

Cultural Massalia

In antiquity, in all matters cultural and intellectual, Massalia had a very high reputation, one, indeed, that might, without exaggeration, be termed 'sky-high', at least until the fourth century AD, when its academic standing was replaced by the rising prestige of Bordeaux.[1] Indeed, this attitude has often carried over into modern scholarship as well. Two points should be clearly understood at the start. First, almost all of these plaudits are of Roman date, and usually of Roman origin. They do not refer directly to the Massalia of Hellenistic and earlier years that is the subject of this present study. And they are nearly all in the form of quotations from writers (notably Cicero) who had never themselves gone to Massalia, nor show any signs of ever having wanted to. Second, we are dependent almost entirely on secondary sources. Not only do ancient sources tell us that Athens was great, but we can see that greatness for ourselves by looking at the Acropolis and reading the works of the great Athenian authors. To a lesser extent we can apply the same reasoning to places like Miletos, Halicarnassos, and even Troy (for, Schliemann apart, surely Homer must count for something). But we cannot do this for Massalia. Essentially, the cultural pre-eminence of Massalia is something we are, perforce, asked to take on trust.

The view from Rome

Roman views on Massalia fall roughly into two categories. The first is political. The political stance of Massalia, at least in foreign affairs, won invariable praise in Rome, since it was invariably pro-Roman. Such comments, with equal invariability, date from the Roman Republic, for after the unfortunate misunderstanding whereby Massalia supported the wrong side, namely Pompey, in the Roman Civil War, the city, no longer independent, ceased to have any foreign policy at all. So all Roman views on the external politics (and there are very few on the internal) of Massalia antedate Caesar's siege and hence are relevant to our period. But views on Massaliot culture are different. Just as Athens retained its cultural supremacy in the Mediterranean long after it became politically negligible, so, on a lesser scale, did Massalia. The result is that much of our Roman evidence dates from the Imperial period. The danger here is that we may here be tempted into using it to illustrate the earlier, republican era, for

128

which it will only be reliable if we can show, or assume, that conditions were the same; and we have already noted how, at least in architecture, Augustus marked a new era in Massalia.

As to the picture in political history, Massalia was always a close ally of Rome, and the Romans appreciated it. In the Second Punic war we have already seen how Massalia did what it could to support Rome[2] and Cicero for one was always fulsome in his praise of it. Massalia was among our 'staunchest and most faithful allies', 'the people without whom we could never have reduced Transalpine Gaul', and 'to whom our generals owe their triumphs',[3] and the Romans backed up their praise with actions, going to the aid of Massalia when she was threatened by attacks from the Ligurians.

In the cultural field, Romans were attracted by Massalia on various levels. There was the idea of the far-flung outpost of classical civilisation, gamely fighting back the surrounding hordes of barbaric darkness.[4] More to the point, to Massalia were attributed all sorts of serious moral qualities, both in the abstract and as applied to the process of government, that were particularly admired, even if not always practised, by traditionally minded Romans. Honesty, fair dealing, self-control, responsibility – a Roman of the old school would smile at the suggestion that any of these virtues were to be found in a community of Greeks, famed rather for their feather-brained levity and unreliability – but he would make an exception for Massalia. It was, we hear, a favourite place of resort for educated Romans who wanted all the cultural cachet of a Hellenic ambiance joined to the political correctness of a conservative government firmly in the saddle and not a popularis in sight.[5]

We perhaps may look at the achievements of Massalia, military and cultural alike, with a more critical eye than did Cicero. Clerc, the great historian of Massalia, is less impressed with their military contribution. As he saw it, essentially what happened is that the Massaliots rested on the laurels of their aid to Rome in the Second Punic War. There was a kind of unwritten *entente*. The Massaliots assumed that the Romans would use their legions on land to deal with brigands, Ligurians and other enemies of the Massaliot *chora*, and in this they were more or less correct; generally speaking, the Romans did. But the Romans assumed that Massalia could be left to look after its own territory and the associated sea routes, notably that from Rome to Spain, and in fact the Massaliots, letting their armed forces, particularly the fleet, run down to a derisory level, proved incapable of it.[6] As for the Roman praise, often undiscriminating, of Massaliot culture and political ethos, Nenci not unreasonably postulates that a lot of this springs from history written by aristocratic, and hence Pompeian, senators, who tended to glorify Massalia for its opposition to Caesar.[7] In fact, the traditional Roman – one is tempted to say Puritan, or even Calvinist – virtues generally attributed to Massaliots must have awakened nostalgic reminiscence in right-wing Romans, particularly those of the first century of the imperial epoch. They probably felt that Cincinnatus could well have been a Massaliot, and how could they not admire such a city? That such a state of public affairs had not actually existed at Rome for a very long time was irrelevant, for that is the essence of nostalgia.

In matters cultural and intellectual, there is again a simple explanation for Roman praise of Massalia. All Romans were conditioned to believe in the superiority of the Greeks in matters of art, culture, or the intellect, the conditioning being done both by the Greeks (naturally) and by the Romans themselves. This of course did not mean that the Romans thereby set such skills on a pedestal, any more than a nineteenth-century colonial administrator in the British Empire, by acknowledging Italian supremacy in such things as opera and painting, would thereby scorn the skills of government or gentlemanly conduct.[8] What it did mean was that a Roman *expected* of Massalia, in W.S. Gilbert's words, 'intellectual eminence, or scholarship sublime'. And very often you see what you expect to see. The cynically inclined may also find some significance in the undoubted fact that almost all of this effusive praise of Massalia comes from Roman writers who themselves never went near the place. Certainly Cicero never did. He simply recommended it to everybody else. Still, it must be clearly stated that in this period not only the arts but what we may call the liberal professions, such things as architecture and medicine, were firmly in the hands of the Greeks, or at least men with Greek names. The qualification is important. That the Romans believed that all doctors were and should be Greeks – this is incontestable; Cato indeed complained of it, gloomily sneering (as was his wont) at the invasion of good Roman bodies by foreigners. But in individual cases the only evidence of Greek nationality is often the name, for that is all that we, or the Romans, know, and I cannot help wondering whether professional men would sometimes adopt a Greek-sounding name – 'Apollodorus', or the like – to facilitate their advancement in their chosen field. If so, then the Greek dominance of these professions becomes a self-fulfilling prophecy.[9] The issue is accordingly obscured, and with it the true cultural standing of Massalia. To this we now turn.

Geography

The sceptical reader must not be misled by the above into thinking that this is a mere hatchet job, an assertion that Massalia had no culture at all. Romans may have overestimated it, and I suspect that they, and their modern followers, did, but that real demonstrable manifestations of culture existed cannot be denied. We will begin with the first and most important of the Big Names. This is undoubtedly Pytheas, for there can be no overestimating him.

Pytheas of Massalia[10] certainly existed and certainly performed the feat attributed to him, a voyage of exploration to the northern seas. Of that there can be no doubt, nor of the magnitude of his achievement. He wrote two books on it, entitled 'about the Ocean' (*Peri tou Okeanou*) and 'Round

72. Statue of Pytheas on the façade of the Marseille Bourse.

the World' (*Periodos Ges*), and although the original text does not survive, large sections are quoted or referred to in other authors. Chief among these are the historian Polybius and, even more, the geographer Strabo, and it is ironic that most of these references from which spring our knowledge of Pytheas were written by their authors as violent attacks on his reliability. For Polybius, Pytheas was an unprincipled rogue and liar (Clerc appositely equates his reputation to that of Jules Verne or H.G. Wells), a condemnation then eagerly swallowed whole and repeated by Strabo.[11] His rehabilitation as a serious authority dates only from the work of Bougainville, a French mathematician of the eighteenth century.

The precise dates of Pytheas are unknown, but since he is evidently unknown to Aristotle, who died in 322, while known to Dicaearchos,[12] a disciple of Aristotle who wrote around 310, we may presumably date him to the late fourth century BC. We know nothing of his private life, nor even who he was, only that he was as much a scholar and mathematician as a mariner, for much of his work rested on his astronomical observations and computations of latitude, as calculated by the gnomon, an instrument like a sundial. His calculations were commendably accurate for he gave as the latitude of Marseille 43°3′ 38″ north of the Equator, while the true figure is 43°17′ 4″, an error of only about 50 km.[13] He was the first Greek to establish that ocean tides were caused by lunar attraction, though he may have been anticipated by local residents on the Atlantic coast, and accurately located the true North Pole in the heavens.[14] Moreover, not only were his writings in sufficiently wide circulation to be known to Polybius and to earn his denunciations, but they were specifically accepted by such outstanding figures in ancient mathematics and astronomy as Eratosthenes (third century BC) and Hipparchus (second century), who based some of their own work on that of Pytheas. Plainly his reputation stood very high among the great figures of ancient science, no matter what Polybius thought.[15]

On the status of his voyage there is some doubt. Did he sail as a private citizen, or was it an enterprise funded by the Massaliot government? Did he run the gauntlet of a Carthaginian blockade of the Straits, and twice at that – out and in – , or did he have Carthaginian authorisation and support? An even more original proposal comes from Roseman, that he travelled from port to port on the vessels of local fishermen and traders without a ship of his own at all, thereby profiting from their local knowledge and interpreting skills, perhaps taking three years or more on the trip. Leaving Massalia, then, some time in the late fourth century – Hawkes opts for 325 BC –, Pytheas passed Gibraltar and turned north.[16]

The route of his voyage is at first clear, though much debated on its northern extremities. What is clear is that he followed the coast north to Brittany and then, continuing north, circumnavigated Britain. Making landfall at Belerion (Land's End) he apparently proceeded up through the Irish Sea, possibly calling at the Isle of Man,[17] to the Hebrides, and thence (apparently avoiding Cape Wrath) directly across to the Orkneys. At this point comes a side trip to Thule (or, as it has become known since the reference in Seneca's *Medea*, 375-9, *ultima Thule*), at the ends of the earth. It is often spelled Thoule in Greek and Tyle in Latin, and is identified by Pliny, quoting Pytheas, as an island 'six days sailing north from Britain'. It is most commonly identified as Iceland, and sometimes Norway.[18] There seems to be no doubt whatever that, wherever it was, he did actually go there, for he recounts phenomena such as the 'congealed sea' (icebergs, pack ice) and the midnight sun which could only be encountered in far northern latitudes.[19] He then, in search of amber (a prized import), seems to have made for the Baltic. How far he got is again debatable: Heligoland and Bornholm are candidates for a Pythean visitation, and he may have got as far as Stettin (Szczecin), at the mouth of the Oder; on the other hand he may not have got very far beyond Jutland.[20] At some point he also visited Kantion, or Kent, though the actual sequence of these ports of call on his itinerary varies according to the reconstruction proposed.[21] From Britain back to Massalia presumably he followed the same route as outward, and when he arrived back he had completed a voyage longer than a return trip across the Atlantic. His achievement, both as a sailor and a scholar, was magnificent. He is perhaps the greatest single claim to intellectual supremacy that Massalia can boast, and he has well been called the Columbus of the North.

But his name does not stand alone. Indeed, on the Bourse building on the Canebière in modern Marseille there are displayed twin statues, one of Pytheas and the other of Euthymenes. Euthymenes has undoubtedly been eclipsed by his more famous contemporary (Pytheas and Euthymenes both lived around the middle of the fourth century BC), partly from the more sensational nature of Pytheas' voyage among the icebergs of the midnight sun, and partly because, unlike Pytheas, he did not leave any written account, or, at least, one that survived as well as that of Pytheas.[22] Euthymenes too was an explorer, and he too sailed out into the Atlantic (raising again the question of Carthaginian co-operation at Gibraltar), but, unlike Pytheas, then turned south, coasting along the African shore. This he followed for a very great distance, though how far is again, as with Pytheas, disputed. He certainly got as far as Dakar and Senegal; whether he got beyond, into the Gulf of Guinea towards Ghana, is much more problematic. One of the key points is that he says he saw a large river, which he thought was the Nile. This was not as unlikely as it sounds, for many of the ancient geographers were convinced that in the Sudan the course of the Nile took a right-angled bend towards the west, to a course somewhere in West Africa.[23] Moreover, asserted Euthymenes, in this river were to be found the same creatures that inhabited the Nile, namely hippopotami and crocodiles. Since Greeks believed that the Nile was the only place where you found crocodiles, the identification was reasonable. In fact, what Euthymenes saw, or heard of, was probably the River Niger, either at its mouth near Lagos, or near its source in Guinea, which is not far inland from the coast; and in between it does flow in an easterly direction, giving possible credence to the Nile identification, for that course, if persisted in, would indeed bring it eventually to the Sudan. But the really important point, of course, is that the observation of such a river would then be a valuable indication of how far down the African coast Euthymenes actually got. Unfortunately this still remains subject to question.

There remain three other names that should be mentioned before we conclude our survey of Massaliot exploration. One is Hanno, who, as we have noted,[24] was not a Massaliot but a Carthaginian, whose voyage down the west coast of Africa, and his published account of it, almost certainly served as a precedent and guidebook for Euthymenes a century later (Hanno living around the fifth century, and Euthymenes the fourth).[25] Our second name is Himilco, another Carthaginian (possibly the brother of Hanno – Clerc is tempted so to believe) who also explored the Atlantic, sailing northwards to Brittany, along the route later followed by Pytheas, since Hanno had taken the southern one, and the two explorers seem to have sailed around the same time, probably as a pair, dividing the northern and southern waters between them.[26] Their relevance to this book is that between them they must have furnished an invaluable corpus of information for the later Massaliot voyages. And we end with our third name, Midacritos – a shadowy figure if ever there was one. His very existence rests only on a single mention in Pliny, who says that he was the first trader to bring back tin from the Kassiterides (Scillies?).[27] He may have gone there overland rather than by sea, and even less is there any reason to associate him in any way with Massalia, though this is sometimes done.

Literature and other arts

When we turn to literature, and, to put it frankly, culture in general, the attested contribution of Greek Massalia is disappointing, even meagre. Its most important ingredient is undoubtedly the Massaliot edition of the works of Homer. The first recension of Homer was the Peisistratid (560-514 BC) one at Athens, but this was soon followed by a flurry of other editions, as other cities, apparently as a matter of national pride, wanted to have one of their own. Some of these are known by the name of the individual editor, but six are attributed simply to the issuing cities: Massalia, Chios, Argos, Sinope, Cyprus and Crete. Clerc has noted that, of the six, only half of Cyprus was hellenised, while Sinope and Massalia were at the (opposite) ends of the Hellenic earth. His explanation is convincing: it was exactly in these outposts of Hellenism that the settlers felt it most essential to inculcate in the education of the young the very core of their national identity – and for a Greek that was Homer: Clerc well compares the Koran, with all that it means and embodies for a Muslim (not that the two cases are identical, of course, but, given the quasi-religious authority attributed to Homer by the Greeks, they are close enough for the comparison to be relevant).[28]

In fact, that is almost the sum total of known Massaliot literary production, despite the reputation that the city acquired. It must be emphasised that after the taking of the city by Caesar things changed radically; possibly with the decline of an independent foreign policy and the inroads made into its commerce (especially that with Gaul) by Narbo, Massalia reacted by developing its intellectual resources. Certainly in the Roman Empire it rapidly acquired the undisputed prestige of a 'university city', a place of doctors, engineers, orators, philosophers, and mathematicians, though even this seems sometimes to have been exaggerated.[29] The truth of it is that though Massalia, as a Greek polis, doubtless appreciated and, within the limits of its resources, created Greek literature, put on the works of Sophocles and Euripides in its theatre, and so forth, its chief original contribution was probably more in the field of mathematical and geographical treatises, such as Pytheas' *Periodos*, reflecting the city's commercial orientation.

8. Cultural Massalia

Language

It is perhaps arguable whether the language of a country, as opposed to the content of what is said or written in it, is a basic element in the country's culture; certainly it is a matter on which little doubt would be entertained by a modern Frenchman. On the spread of the Greek language to the Gauls and its retention in Massalia long after the Roman conquest, we will speak later (p. 216 below). Hellenic Massalia probably spoke an Ionian dialect of Greek, as inherited from Phocaea, and in writing it used a Western Greek (i.e. early Ionian) alphabet.[30] There has been much controversy over whether or not traces of this or of the native Celtic survive in the vocabulary of modern Provençal and in place names in the region.[31] There is nothing in theory improbable about the idea, for ancient languages are notoriously tenacious in toponyms, as witness, for example, the large number of cities in North America still retaining their name in the language of their Spanish or French founders, or even the local native peoples (Los Angeles, Baton Rouge, Ottawa); in Australia the prevalence of aboriginal names is even more marked (Wooloomooloo (in Sydney)). In ordinary vocabulary, the derivatives would be found in technical terminology, especially as referring to seafaring and viticulture,[32] both activities alien to the ancient Celts and to which they were introduced by the Phocaean colonists, whose Greek terminology then became embedded in Celtic, so to survive into Provençal. But though the theory is reasonable it must be admitted that the consensus of modern opinion is against it having actually happened, explaining away Celtic/Greek resemblances as being either 'rhabillages' (p. 269 n. 4 below) or purely fortuitous.

Roman Massilia

Though the history of Roman Massilia, after Caesar's reduction of the city in 49 BC, does not really fall within the scope of this book, we may perhaps justify a brief survey, for this was after all Massilia's Golden Age. It sprang from two sources. One was a broad, general one. With the spread of the Roman Empire came a kind of stable universality that promoted provincial development. No longer did everything and everyone have to come from Rome, if they were to count. They might still come from old imperial families, but, like Victorian administrators of the British Empire, have been born in 'the colonies' without it diminishing their national status. The Emperor Claudius was never really considered a Frenchman though he was born at Lyon, nor Trajan (Italica, near Seville) a Spaniard. But as well as that, there was a new prominence, or at least acceptance, for men of genuinely provincial origin. Second, Massilia (for we are now justified in using the Latin spelling, with an i), as well as profiting by this general provincial upgrading, did also enjoy an individual renaissance of its own. It is at this period, if at all, that Massilia can claim the status of the 'University of Marseille'.

135

That the imperial Romans did in fact go to Massilia instead of Athens for liberal studies is undisputed. Strabo says they did, in so many words.[33] What they got there was largely a formal education in the pattern that had crystallised in the Hellenistic world – that is, rhetoric. Originally based on oratory, this had become an armchair study far divorced from the daily needs of trial lawyers and politicians on the hustings. Practising speakers such as Cicero scorned it for its artificiality, its stress on florid ornament and declamation on set topics far removed from real life and often drawn for mythology ('Should Helen be reproached for leaving Menelaos and running off with Paris, her paramour?'). This, they maintained, was no useful training for anyone, an eminently rational argument that I personally would find more convincing if it did not remind me of the firm conviction of the nineteenth-century British Foreign Office that a degree in Classics was the best preparation for colonial administration. Whatever the truth of that, it remains that when Romans went to Massilia for an education, rhetoric is what they got.[34]

Only one of these teachers of rhetoric is actually known to us by name, Volcatius Moschus. He was not himself a native of Massilia, coming instead from Pergamon, where he had studied rhetoric from Apollodoros, a celebrated rhetorician of the first century BC. Obliged to flee from Pergamon because he was accused of having poisoned somebody (and was not acquitted in spite of the best efforts for defence of Asinius Pollio, the associate of Caesar, Virgil, and Horace), he ended up at Massilia in 20 BC, where he rapidly carved out for himself an enviable niche in the academic world: when he died in 25 AD, in gratitude he left all his possessions to the City of Massilia.[35] Two other names are indeed known to us, Pacatus and Agroitas, since they are mentioned by Seneca, but next to nothing is known about them, including what was actually their connection with Massilia – Agroitas evidently left Massilia to establish himself at Rome, and Pacatus is mentioned only in an anecdote, as someone Agroitas once met walking down the street in Massilia.[36] This is thin evidence indeed! One of the few solid points that does come out of it is that, as Clerc makes clear, these professors evidently lectured and taught in Greek, but that need not surprise us. As Varro (d. 26 BC) assures us, in his day Massilia was a trilingual city, in Greek, Latin and Celtic.[37] Naturally this does not mean that all Massaliots spoke all three languages, just as in Canada, an officially bilingual country, there were (at least up till the 1980s) many highly educated English-speakers living in Montréal, a francophone city, who could not manage a word of French. All we can assume is that in Massilia all three languages were in regular use, and many Massaliots could speak at least more than one of them.

It does seem, however, as if Massaliot academe did develop its own specialisation. Concentrating perhaps less on literature than other cultural centres, it came to acquire a distinguished reputation in science (after the example of Pytheas) and, in particular, medicine. The fame of Massaliot doctors spread even as far as Rome, the best known being

Crinas (after whom the 'Wall of Crinas' in the Bourse excavations (p. 82 n. 46 above) was named). Crinas lived under the reign of Nero, and moving to Rome became successful, famous, and rich. In competition there with a certain Thessalus, who prided himself on being an innovator on the cutting edge of medical science, Crinas apparently favoured a more traditional approach, based on mathematics and astrology. He was at any rate successful enough to finance the construction of city walls at Massilia, and also to win a mention in Pliny.[38] His fame was, however, threatened by a further Massaliot doctor named Charmis, who also made a great impression at Rome with a new therapy – cold baths, which he prescribed even in the depths of January, and from which elderly ex-consuls emerged with their limbs frozen stiff.[39] There was also a certain Demosthenes Philalethes who was a well-known ophthalmologist, but any connection with Massilia would rest on a single mention in Galen of a doctor of that name having resided there, with no guarantee that it is the same person. Clerc,[40] however, wonders whether the very fact that Pliny, in mentioning these various names, often adds on 'of Massilia' may not of itself indicate that in medicine an origin, or at least training, at Massilia may not have carried a certain cachet, like 'So-and-so, of Oxford'. He may be right. There is also epigraphical evidence (in the form of tombstones of doctors, giving their profession) from other nearby cities, notably Nîmes and Narbonne.[41] It is quite probable that they got their medical training in Massilia, given its established reputation, but naturally there can be no proof of this.

In the field of Fine Arts, we search in vain at Massilia. No doubt there was a certain amount of monumental architecture, both such as testified to by the fragmentary Ionic capital already mentioned (p. 80 above) and by the many structures of Roman construction but Greek inspiration that dot Provence, such as the Maison Carrée at Nîmes or the Temple of Augustus and Livia at Vienne. If the architects of these had any kind of Greek training it is a reasonable guess that it may have been at the conveniently local bastion of Hellenism, Massilia. But, again, all we can rely on is supposition, and the only real conclusion we can draw has already been anticipated by the judgement of Clerc: 'The University of Marseille had something missing, a School of Fine Arts.'[42]

We may close with an aspect of culture that any Frenchman at least would not wish to see consigned to a neglectful silence, cuisine. Massaliot food and drink certainly conformed to the normal culinary profile of Greek colonies, with the emphasis on olives, wine, bread, and, as with most maritime cities, various forms of seafood (the most famous being Milo's mullets). These have all been discussed already when we were considering the resources of Languedoc and the Côte d'Azur. It remains only for us to add to the end of this menu, as a possibly incongruous dessert, ham and sausages.[43]

The Greeks in Provence and Languedoc

Massalia was the centre of Greek influence in the Western Mediterranean, the sun round which the other colonies and trading posts, great and small, willingly or unwillingly revolved. It is now time for us to leave Massalia and turn to some of these planets. Some general points should be made first. We speak of Greek influence, but we could equally well speak of Phocaean. Phocaea was the only Greek city active in the area, and, initially at least, the Western Mediterranean, non-Greeks apart, was a Phocaean lake. All Greek foundations directly or indirectly sprang from Phocaean origins, and it is understandable that sometimes our ancient sources use the terms interchangeably. The same thing seems to have happened with Massalia, the influence of which was so extensive, and so familiar that Roman writers would sometimes speak of sites as 'a Massaliot outpost', when all they really had in mind was that it was Greek. With small, minor sites, of which our knowledge is sometimes limited to one single passing reference in a late author, we should therefore be very careful about taking such a reference, unsupported, at face value. Because some location is referred to as, say, a Massaliot outpost, a *castellum Massiliensium*, this should not be accepted as conclusive evidence of its political status, that it was founded by Massalia nor that its inhabitants enjoyed Massaliot citizenship.[1]

It must also be accepted that while major sites such as Ampurias, Antibes, or Nice, have a known history and assured identity that can, so to speak, stand on its own feet, there are many minor ones known to us by name alone, with even the location a matter of conjecture. Sometimes we know of them because of an isolated reference in a historian, because something, say a battle, once happened there. More often our source is one of the geographers, who give lists of ports along the coastline, all – presumably – in proper sequence.[2] What then happens is that we have a name, otherwise unknown, to be located somewhere along a known stretch of coast between two securely identified sites. Usually there are only two possible ways of pinpointing the location, neither very reliable. One is to find a site that is topographically attractive to colonists – with, for example, a convenient acropolis and good harbour. If convincing archaeological remains, preferably architectural, are found, so much the better. The other

approach is by toponyms. Place-names are often embedded in the language of the local society, surviving countless invasions and new
settlements – in the USA, as we have noted, Baton Rouge survives as a
relic of the French settlement of Louisiana, Los Angeles and San Francisco
are both Spanish, and countless names are of Amerindian origin; 'London'
itself is a carryover from the 'Londinium' of the Romans, who may well
have based that on some native British name. So if we find, in more or less
the right area, a modern town bearing a name that looks a derivation of
the one in the ancient geographers, it is tempting to identify the two, even
with no further evidence. Thus when Stephanos of Byzantium mentions a
certain Pergantion, located somewhere along the coastline of the Maures,
it is natural to identify it as the modern Bregançon, particularly since this
location is highly defensible and has two sheltered bays.[3] And it is beyond
question that most ancient foundations actually do retain today a name
derived from that of the original city, as Antibes – Antipolis, Agde – Agathe
Tyche ('good luck'), Ampurias – Emporion, Arles – Arelate, or Avignon –
Avenio. This approach is not always foolproof, but neither can it be
neglected, particularly if, on tracing the name back to the original language, we can see that in that language it actually means something that
makes sense.[4]

Sometimes we also encounter the opposite problem, where we have an
undoubtedly classical site, well marked by archaeological findings on the
ground, but cannot for certain assign to it an ancient name even though
there are various possible candidates in the field. The best example of this
is Saint Blaise, a very extensive site between Martigues and Istres on the
west side of the Étang de Berre. It is known from Pliny that there was a
settlement named Mastromela in the region, and Saint Blaise is most
probably it (though the claims of both Martigues and Istres have been
urged), but there is no sure identification and the site continues to be
known by its modern name. We must also note that this site is almost
unique in that it was never built over in modern times and hence offers an
open, extensive vista of classical antiquities that will be familiar to the
traveller in Greece, Ionia, or Italy, but which he will rarely find in
searching for Greek antiquities in Provence. Pretty well all the other major
sites have remained in continuous urban occupation (the chief exception
is Ampurias), which usually means that identification, with a given name,
is certain, but the remains are very difficult to trace and excavate, being
all built over. Greek archaeology in Provence is thus often a matter of
hurried rescue excavations, spurred by the installations of drains or the
building of underground car parks, and enlivened by occasional test
trenches in somebody's cellar. With difficulties like these, all credit must
be given to those carrying out the work.[5] And finally, before leaving this
topic, we may note that there are also some known ancient names that
have so far successfully resisted any effort to pinpoint them in any
location. Rhodanousia, mentioned by Ps. Skymnos (208) and Stephanos of
Byzantium, has been very hesitantly located at Trinquetaille, the suburb

of Arles on the other side of the River Rhône, but all this conjecture really has to support it is that the name of the colony seems to link it somehow to the Rhône (Rhodanos), and Trinquetaille is, one supposes, as good a possibility as any (the best site on the Rhône being occupied by Arelate, Arles, itself). To the east, Tauroentum has also been the subject of peripatetic identification that has ranged all the way from La Ciotat through Les Lecques to Le Brusc, a distance of 27 km.[6]

We may now proceed to a consideration of the various sites. They will be taken individually, in geographic order. Beginning with Aleria we will work our way west along the coast from Marseille, then east to the Italian border, and finally inland. In all of this we will be dealing only with classical, i.e. Greco-Roman, sites. Celtic *oppida* will follow in Chapter 11 below.

Aleria (Corsica)

Aleria (ancient Alalia)[7] presents an organisational problem. Though a Phocaean colony and closely connected with our story, it was not on the mainland and hence cannot be logically included in either here or in Chapter 10. But though geographically it belongs to neither, it must be included somewhere, and since its foundation was very ancient (though not quite as ancient as Massalia), we may as well consider it here.

Aleria is half-way down the east coast of Corsica, or, to give it its ancient name, Cyrnos.[8] Less rocky and indented than the west coast, it offers much more in the way of arable plains and much less in the way of good harbours. Indeed, there is really no obvious harbour between Bastia in the north and the excellent roadstead of Porto Vecchio in the south,[9] and, in strictly nautical terms, the settlers seem to have picked just about the worst part of the whole of Corsica. However, as previously noted (p. 49), unless we are speaking of a small anchorage where ships put in for purely marine technical reasons (shelter, topping up drinking water), for a port to flourish there also has to be some commercial reason for going there, and this often boils down to what is in the hinterland. Aleria had behind it the best arable plain in Corsica, and behind that in turn there seems also to have been copper ore in the mountains. The island was also famous throughout antiquity for an export that seldom figures in modern economic analyses – honey. Without sugar, the ancients had no other sweetening agent, hence the importance of beekeeping; beeswax was an important byproduct, being employed in metal-casting (*cire perdu*), ceramics, and shipbuilding.[10]

The harbour – obviously there must have been one – was presumably on the river Tavignano (ancient Rottanos), and the adjoining Étang de Diane was supposedly, in Roman days at least, a naval base. This does not sound promising. One can never be too sure of the topography in an alluvial region, for it may have changed substantially since antiquity, but here, *faute de mieux*, we have to base ourselves on the situation as it is today. And a river port some 3 km or so inland can never have offered the same convenience to sailors as something like the Peiraeus or the Lakydon. Moreover, the river itself is little more than a glorified stream, with a depth of just over two metres – hardly enough for any deep-sea vessel.[11]

The site of the city is on a low plateau, oblong or oval in shape ('la butte d'Aléria'), not high enough to be spectacular but enough to be defensible.[12] It forms an escarpment, with the steep slopes, on the north and east sides, and overlooking the Tavignano and the inland plain. There are next to no architectural remains from the Greek (i.e. Phocaean) period, though excavation has turned up sherds of Phocaean grey pottery, vases of Ionian and Rhodian origin, and Attic black-figure; the extent of commercial relations is also attested by finds of ivory and Egyptian glass.

The departure of the Phocaean settlers after the Battle of Alalia (535), recorded by Herodotus, does not seem to have left the city deserted, as he implies. Chamber tombs are now constructed, often containing fine Attic pottery, and the town seems to have enjoyed a period of commercial prosperity while now inhabited by a cosmopolitan mélange of Etruscans, Phoenicians, native Corsicans, and left-over Greeks.[13] This 'communauté de civilisation' lasted till the start of the third century when Carthage profited from Rome's preoccupation with the war with Pyrrhus to take complete control of Aleria. This phase did not last long, and in 259 the city was finally taken by L. Cornelius Scipio and remained thenceforth part of the Roman Empire, with varying fortune depending on the vicissitudes of the civil wars marking the end of the Roman Republic: Aleria supported both Marius against Sulla and Pompey against Caesar. Caesar, passing

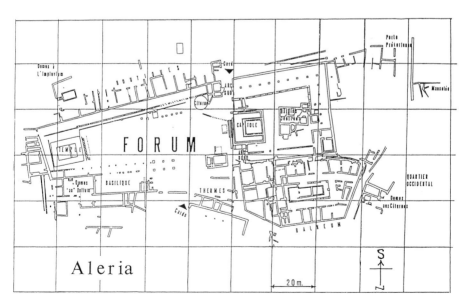

73. Aleria, Corsica: general site plan.

74. Aleria: general view of site.

75. Aleria: Forum.

through Corsica after his victory at Thapsus in 46 BC, evidently reduced the city without any of the difficulties he experienced in similar circumstances at Massalia. In the civil war following his death Aleria found itself on the wrong side, as usual, this time supporting Sextus Pompey. After sundry volte-faces it was surrendered to Octavian in 38 and, turning over a new leaf, recommenced life as the Colonia Veneria Iulia Pacensis Restituta Tertianorum Aleria.[14]

The site is at present covered with extensive architectural remains, but these are all of Roman date (Figs. 73-5). They are centred on a Forum, 92 m long and of roughly oblong (more precisely, trapezoidal) shape, dating from the Sullan settlement. The two long sides are occupied by stoas; at the east end there is surviving the podium of a temple, probably dedicated to Augustus and Rome, and at the west end stands the Capitol, or praetorium. Immediately to the north of it, as an attached dependency, is a bathing establishment, with cisterns and the usual hypocaust: it was apparently not a public bath in the usual sense, and may have been part of the governor's private apartments.[15] There is also a large public bath of traditional design, albeit here in somewhat elongated form, at Santa Laurina, outside the city centre and alongside the river, at the bottom of the acropolis hill. Much of the site remains still to be excavated, though enough has been uncovered to show that the street plan, at least to judge by the forum, was irregular, with no sign of grid-planning.

Diodorus also records the existence of another early Greek city called Nikaia (i.e. the same name as Nice) but nothing is known of it.[16]

Saint Blaise

Saint Blaise is the name of a small chapel located in the commune of Saint-Mitre-les-Remparts, 12 km north of Martigues, and has given its name to the adjoining Greek site. In late antiquity the site was known as Ugium. During our period we often come across the name Mastromela or Mastrabala, appearing in our sources and associated with this area. The Limne or Stagnum (= marsh) of Mastrabala seems to be established as the ancient name for the Étang de Berre[17] and it seems that a settlement name Mastromela also existed somewhere in the area. This may well have been the site that we call Saint Blaise, though we must also record the existence locally of a town named Maritima Avaticorum (Martigues?), and in any case the most recent excavator of Saint Blaise has opted for the ancient name of Heraclea.[18]

Located on a plateau between the Étang de Clitis and the Étang de Lavalduc, Saint Blaise seems to have had no direct waterborne communication with the sea, though access, by a paved road, cannot have been lengthy or difficult.[19] The city, or settlement as it then was, seems to have been founded very early, perhaps slightly before Massalia itself; and it certainly saw native Celtic inhabitation even before that. With the arrival of the Greeks Saint Blaise became a kind of joint Etruscan-Greek-Ligurian trading centre, and until about 520 it apparently co-existed in parallel, if not in actual competition, with Massalia. From 520 on, it fell under the influence of its stronger neighbour.[20] Indeed, in view of its position, it is hard to see how Massalia could have carried on a successful trade up the Rhône valley if Saint Blaise had been powerful or hostile, for it lay directly between the two. There was a further problem as well. Saint Blaise seems not to have had any merchant shipping of its own[21] and the South Italian wines that formed a staple of its import trade (as they did of Massalia's) were brought there in Etruscan ships. This trade suffered from the general decline of Etruria in the fifth century, particularly after its defeat at the battle of Cumae (474 BC). Massalia was not affected as it had its own ships and was in general more closely connected with the whole milieu of Greek long-distance commerce. Saint Blaise thus in effect entered into the Massaliot zone of influence and control, probably representing about the furthest extent of the Massaliot *chora* (depending on how one defines that nebulous entity). As an outpost of whatever sort of Massaliot power it still knew a high level of prosperity in the Hellenistic era, declining only in the first century. At this point, for whatever reason, the site was abandoned; whether as a result of military assault or voluntary migration is not clear, but the opening of the Fossae Marianae gave Massalia a direct waterborne route to the Rhône, obviating the need for any trans-shipment by land that may have been the basis of much of Saint Blaise's importance. The site then lay abandoned until the mediaeval era, when the collapse of the pax Romana and the anarchy of barbarian incursions turned the eyes of the peasants in the plains once again up to the defensible heights of Saint Blaise. The rebuilt settlement became the mediaeval Ugium. Though its name is evidently preserved in the name of the nearby Étang de Lavalduc (*La Vallée d'Ugium*), the site was never subject to continuous urban occupation, and today remains as one of the few Greek mainland sites in South France open to general excavation: the others are Glanum and Olbia, and, in Spain, Ampurias.

The site itself is roughly triangular, the chief entrance being at the north-east corner on the low saddle joining the site to the chapel of Saint Blaise, though a gate and two minor posterns are to be found along the preserved ramparts of the eastern side. The walls, preserved along this stretch to a length of about 400 m, are of Hellenistic date and impressive appearance. Their ashlar blocks carry on their outer face a roughly tooled herringbone pattern (Fig. 80), a technique that we also encounter in mainland Greece: an analogous treatment is to be observed at Glanum, Olbia, and on the blocks of the Wall of Crinas at Marseille. The blocks also carry engraved mason's marks, in the form of letters, often archaic and occasionally even retrograde, from the Greek alphabet.[22] The excavators see in all this signs of probably Sicilian workmanship. More striking is the fact that the walls were crowned with a series of crenellations ('*merlons*') (Fig. 79) with rounded tops, a feature rare if not unparalleled in Greek military architecture and apparently derived from Phoenician work;[23] in

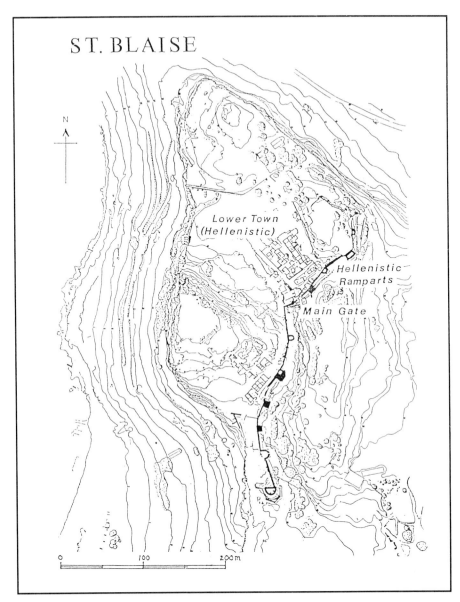

ST. BLAISE

N

Lower Town
(Hellenistic)

Hellenistic
Ramparts

Main Gate

0   100   200 m

76. St. Blaise: site plan.

the eventual destruction they were hurled down from the walls, and lie in a row on the ground outside. The wall was also strengthened with square towers, and though its height can only be guessed at, the best guess would appear to be around 6 m, with 9 m for the height of the towers. Thickness was 2-3 m, and, as so often, an ashlar facing contained a rubble core.

Inside the circuit of the walls as yet only a small section of the settlement has been excavated. No public or monumental architecture has been

77. St. Blaise: general view of site.

78. St. Blaise: Main Gate, from outside.

79. St. Blaise: crenellations (*merlons*) from the battlements of the ramparts.

80. St. Blaise: 'herringbone' pattern on masonry of ramparts.

found, though the general feeling of Hellenistic sophistication (such as in the fine finish of the ramparts' masonry) would surely imply such standard ingredients as an agora, and several cornice blocks, stylistically datable to the second century BC and evidently coming from a large building, have been found built into the wall.[24] A number of houses have been uncovered. The streets formed a rough grid-plan, and were of beaten earth, unpaved.

Fos

Very little can be said about Fos. In all probability it was a place of some consequence in antiquity, both as the port serving Saint Blaise and as the terminal of the Rhône Ship Canal, the Fossae Marianae, which gave it its name, but all has now been wiped out by the development of the modern port for supertankers. In all honesty it must be admitted that, from what one can tell from skimming through old records and archives, there does not seem to have been much there for the modern developers to obliterate, even allowing for a local tendency to ascribe anything looking even remotely old to the golden days of classical antiquity. Offshore explorations by underwater archaeology have been rather more fruitful, discovering not only a cemetery and 'des structures bâties qui appartiennent certainement au port romain de Fossae Marianae', but also some shipwrecks, one of which is well enough preserved to offer valuable evidence of shipbuilding.[25]

Fossae Marianae

For this we are almost entirely dependent on ancient sources, though at the height of Massalia's power, the canal must have had considerable economic importance. The digging of the canal is firmly dated, for the work was done by Marius' soldiers in 105-102 BC.[26] Its course is largely conjectural and conjectures have not been lacking, even including suggestions that it went all the way to Arles. This is not quite as crazy as it might seem, for it was thought worthwhile in modern days to build just such a canal (now disused) from Fos to Arles, running for some distance right alongside the river Rhône that it was intended to replace.[27] Almost certainly, however, the Roman canal was something shorter and less ambitious. Its outer terminal seems to be reliably located at Fos, but where did it go from there? We may surely postulate that it cut straight across the Rhône delta to pick up the Rhône wherever it was nearest – the navigational difficulties on that river were evidently concentrated on its actual mouth (sandbars, difficulty of finding the channel, and so on), so once you had successfully by-passed the mouth you would bring the canal into the Rhône as soon as possible. Matters are complicated by the fact that the Rhône has changed its course since antiquity, but the old river-bed can be traced (Fig. 27). It was much more sinuous than today, entering the sea about 10 km west of its present mouth and then crossing the present river in a wide, S-shaped loop, the Boucle de l'Escale, before rejoining the present course somewhere near Le Sambuc. What the canal had to do, therefore, was cut straight across to join the Rhône at its nearest point, and that was the Boucle de l'Escale. This would give a canal 7 km long, and we may accept it as the reality.[28] Strabo evidently thought that the canal discharged into the sea, like a river, which implies that it was thought that some of the current of the Rhône either could or should find its way down it. If this was intentionally thought out, it may have been hoped that the flow would keep the canal scoured out and free from silting. If so, it didn't work, and by the time of Augustus it seems to have silted up enough to frustrate its intended purpose. Massalia was no longer the commercial power that it had been, and probably lacked both the resources and the motivation to maintain the canal; and in any case, dredging in the ancient world is an operation of which we know nothing, but which cannot have been easy – originally digging the canal, in the dry, before the water was admitted from either end, must have been a much simpler task.[29]

Ostium Massiliense

The very name Ostium Massiliense is enough to make one pause. 'Port Massalia' – was Massalia not itself a port? Was the Lakydon not a harbour? Such a place apparently existed, however, and under that name. No archaeological remains of any kind have been found, but it was certainly a river port, on the main stream of the Rhône, and has most probably been located at St. Bertrand, on the route of the present Canal du Japon.[30] The evidence for its existence is twofold. First, it appears marked in on the Peutinger Table, a preserved map, in very stylised form, of the roads of the Roman Empire. Second, in the form Gradus Massilitanorum, it is mentioned in the Antonine Itinerary (507), as lying between Fos and Arles, 16 miles from the first and 30 from the second.[31]

Normally one would assume that such a port would be located where the Fossae Marianae joined the Rhône, so that the canal would have Fos at one end and the Ostium at the other, at the junction with the main river. The recorded mileage, however, will not match, and dictates that the Ostium be placed downstream a considerable distance, between this junction and the sea. This in turn means that it would be just about useless for traffic arriving by the canal and proceeding on up the Rhône. If it were upstream things would be different, but as it is (Fig. 27) ships would have to make a pointless diversion down the river and then back again, just to pass by the Ostium. The lesson to be drawn from this is surely that its *raison d'être* was quite independent of the canal, and that it may even have been built after the canal had itself silted up and become disused. Why it should have been thought advisable to establish a river port here is open to question. Perhaps it was for the trans-shipment of goods between river boats and deep-water vessels, but that need was already catered for by Arles (and, after the subordinate status accorded Massalia following

Caesar's settlement, why the insistence on the Massaliot connection?). A further problem is that the Peutinger cartographer evidently thought it a place of prime importance, for he graphically represents it by a stylised semicircular harbour, a convention he otherwise reserves only for Ostia, the Port of Rome. Indeed, on the Peutinger Table, the Ostium looks like the most important place on the whole seaboard, and much bigger than Massalia itself. Of course, it may well be no more than one of these ambitious schemes in which subsequent reality somehow fails to live up to the grandeur of its authors' concept. And in any case all the evidence is late, so the Ostium, whatever it was, may fall outside our period.

Lattes

Lattes, the ancient Lattara, is a minor site as yet little known, located on the River Lez some 6 km or so to the South of Montpellier. In antiquity the river was navigable, at least for *utri* and small craft, and possibly Lattes served as a port of arrival or trans-shipment for deep-sea traffic. There are no references in literary sources, so we do not know who founded it (if it did not indeed grow up spontaneously) or when, but archaeological evidence suggests an extensive trade with the Etruscans beginning around 550 BC, before which the site has no discernible history (other than some Stone Age finds), and lasting till around 500, when Lattes fell under the economic, if not political, influence of Massalia. From then on, wine amphorae indicate an extensive trade in this staple commodity both from

81. Lattes: general view of site, from the museum.

Massalia itself and, no doubt through Massalia, from the prolific vineyards of South Italy. Excavation has so far, at time of writing, revealed the main street and a number of houses arranged in a grid orientation around and along it. The docks were wooden wharves along the west bank of the river, and no monumental buildings have yet been found. It is 'included in this book because the site is not encumbered by modern building and so it does seem possible that future excavations will entitle it to a greater and more prominent role in our story than it enjoys at present.[32]

Glanum

It is customary to call this city by the Roman form of its name, Glanum, and I shall do so in this book. In Greek form, Glanon also existed, and coins have been found, though rarely, bearing the inscription in Greek, '*Glanikon*', 'Of the Glanikans'. Pliny lists it as a city enjoying Latin rights in the Roman province of Narbonne, and the geographer Ptolemy mentions it as one of the settlements of the Salyii (i.e. Celts/Ligurians). A funerary *cippus* identifying a certain Aebutius Agathon as Treasurer of the Glanikans confirms the identification, and Glanon is marked as a way station on one of the roads on the Peutinger Table.[33] We may note that while neuter place-names, ending in -um, are the standard rule in Latin, the Greek equivalent, in -on, is very rare, though it does occur (e.g. Thermon, in Aetolia). Thus while Glanum will raise no eyebrows as a Latin version of an already-existing Glanon, Glanon itself is much more unusual, and I am inclined to see in it a possible Hellenisation of an earlier aboriginal name.

The site itself is at the entrance to a gorge giving easy passage across the ridge of the Alpilles. It is about 30 km east of Arles, and 1 km south of the modern town of St. Remy de Provence, the actual site itself being locally known as 'Les Antiques'. This raises a problem. In a case like this, historical studies generally stress how the location of the city was determined by communications, the convergence and divergence of natural routes. This has been done for Glanum, and in a recent publication F. Salviat ascribes to it a 'position priviligiée', at 'le point de jonction de deux voies importantes'.[34] One is the Roman road via the Montgénèvre col and the Durance valley, which crosses the Rhône at Tarascon and so on to Spain. The other is the much later Via Julia via Ventimiglia, Fréjus, and Aix, which seems to have crossed La Crau to Arles, and thence by pontoon bridge across the Rhône to join the older route at Nîmes. I am reluctant to query the authorities on this, who are literally on their own ground, but feel I must share with the reader my own personal sense of disquiet. It seems to me that Glanum is not on a natural route to or from anywhere. It did of course command the gorge through the Alpilles, but this would seem a natural route only for local traffic, from one side of the Alpilles to the other. For long distance travel, the trouble is that the Alpilles form a long, straight isolated ridge running east-west. The main routes run east-west too, passing along either side of the ridge, and converging on Arles or Tarascon after it is passed (Fig. 19). If the ridge ran north-south, at right angles across the natural trade routes, then a pass through the middle of it would be a great convenience, and the tolls and trade enriching those who controlled it would doubtless make the site, in Gaisford's memorable and oft-quoted phrase, 'a position of considerable emolument'.[35] The same argument would hold good for the ridge in its present orientation if there was no way round it. But in fact it is not all that long and north-south long-distance traffic would simply by-pass it by going round either end without looking for a gorge through the middle – particularly so since the way from Avignon to Aix (the route of the present R.N.7) is flat, straight, easy, and shorter; and the natural north-south route round the other end is, of all things, the Rhône valley, the main highway of the whole of Gaul. Thus from practically anywhere passing through Glanum necessitates a diversion – not a long one, for it is not a nowhere-place at the back of beyond, but a diversion none the less. Indeed, this is still true today. If you are at Glanum it's because that's where you wanted to go. You do not pass through it on the way to somewhere else. Naturally, this does not apply to local residents living in the foothills of the Alpilles, who might welcome a nearby short cut to the other side of the mountain, and of course it is true that from Glanum there *was* convenient access to Massalia, Arles, Apt, and other centres, if you happened to be at Glanum to start with. For others, one cannot but recall the old joke about the directions given by the rustic: 'If you wants to get to there, sir, I wouldn't start from here.' And even local traffic must have been inhibited by the fact that the south end of the gorge debouched on to La Crau, in antiquity a desert area where nobody much lived or would want to go to. All of this, of course, is not to deny the existence of trade routes in the region. St. Remy, a mere kilometre away, is on the natural route for travellers heading for the Rhône crossing at Tarascon. But Glanum, by that very small margin, is not. One possible solution to the problem would be that there has been an inaccurate identification, and that the real town of Glanum is buried somewhere underneath St. Remy (where it would be a minor but natural way station on the road to Tarascon, as shown on the Peutinger Table), the 'Les Antiques' site being an outlying suburb owing its importance and development not so much to commercial traffic through the gorge as to a local religious sanctuary, of 'Les Mères Glaniques'.[36] So radical a solution, however, will be attractive mainly to the adventurous of spirit.

The site itself is also highly unusual, though only if one considers it as an orthodox city or Celtic *oppidum*; as a religious sanctuary it makes much more sense. Located at the bottom of a gorge, it has the distinction of being, in military terms, probably the most indefensible site in the whole Roman Empire. The heights commanding it on each side are so close that pretty well the whole settlement would be open to bowshot from above, or even to boulders rolled down the slope, and particularly so since the layout of the town forms a strip development along the bottom of the valley and no part of it is out of range from the hills. The fortification is bizarre, being limited to a crosswall (with fortified gateway) blocking the narrow entry to the gorge proper (plan, Fig. 82). The wall is only some 25 m long, and apparently was never any longer, that being all that was needed to block the thoroughfare. But there is no sign of any second wall at the other end of the gorge, or indeed anywhere else at all, so this could not have offered a serious obstacle to any determined assault. Moreover, the wall protects only the religious sanctuary, leaving the residential part of the town quite outside its somewhat questionable protection. This is not how towns are fortified.[37] Moreover, the location of the site must perforce go back to its earliest inhabitants, and one thing we do know about the Celts and Ligurians is that they built their *oppida* on defensible high ground, not in the bottoms of deep valleys. Indeed, one of the phenomena we regularly encounter in Roman Gaul is that the Gauls originally lived in hill villages, then moved down into the plains to enjoy the benefits of the Pax Romana, and finally, when the Empire collapsed and the Pax with it, back up into the hills again. One need only compare Glanum with Entremont, Ambrussum, or Ensérune[38] to realise that, as an ordinary city founded, whether by Greeks or Ligurians, for the ordinary purposes of commerce and agriculture, Glanum is open to very serious question. If, however, we see it as an important religious sanctuary, a dependency of a real town located elsewhere but nearby, and not yet uncovered – that is a different matter. This, of course, is pure hypothesis, but I find it sufficiently interesting at least to set it before the reader.

Glanum is often described as a Celtic/Hellenistic/Roman site.[39] There is no real problem with this. All three peoples certainly did contribute to it, and in that order. Where the questions arise is in deciding how much each contributed, within what dates, and whether they overlapped. There is no difficulty with the Romans. From 49 BC (the fall of Massalia) onwards, Glanum was a fully Romanised city within the province of Narbonese Gaul. The trouble comes in the period before that. Was Glanum (or Glanon, as we should perhaps now call it) primarily a Massaliot colony of the Hellenistic period, perhaps even under Massaliot political control, but with Ligurian elements inherited from an earlier native occupation that continued on, co-existing in a junior role after the arrival of the Greeks; or is it the other way round – a Ligurian (i.e. Salyan) settlement that from the second century on so immersed itself in Hellenistic influences (especially architectural) that it came to look like a Greek city even though it was still Ligurians who were doing it all? The first interpretation was that of the excavator, Henri Rolland, who proposed a three-phase chronology: Glanum I, the Ligurian-Hellenistic period, from the second century and earlier, ended with the brutal destruction of the city around 100 BC. Glanum II was a short, transitional period of fifty years of Romanisation, largely by the legions of Marius; and Glanum III, 49 BC to the final destruction of the city by invading Germans around 270 AD, represents the fully-fledged Roman Glanum of the Empire. The counter-view, that the

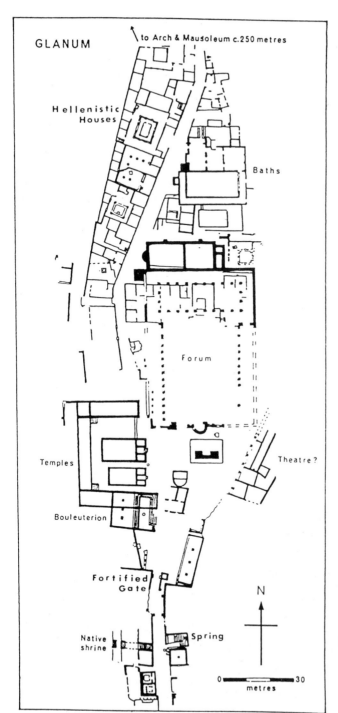

GLANUM

to Arch & Mausoleum c.250 metres

Hellenistic
Houses

Baths

Forum

Temples

Theatre?

Bouleuterion

Fortified
Gate

Native
shrine

Spring

N

0   30
metres

82. Glanum: site plan.

site of Glanum I was not only a highly developed Ligurian city, but one that became the focus and centre of Ligurian resistance to Rome after the fall of Entremont, is championed by Anne Roth Congès. In this version, the Greek presence at Glanum is very much downplayed, being limited to the Greeks providing the architectural inspiration for the town's various monuments in that the Glanic Ligurians built copies of Greek originals existing elsewhere, and, perhaps a few Greeks actually living on the site.[40]

The site itself is V-shaped, like a funnel, as development sprang up around and spread back from the narrow entrance into the gorge. Through the gorge ran a roadway which, continuing north, formed the main street of the town. Given the long and narrow site, hemmed in on both sides by high ground, there are no cross-streets, and no question of grid-plan. On the right-hand (i.e. west) side entering the gorge, a stairway gives access to what was evidently the sanctuary of the goddesses known as the 'Glanic Mothers' (Les Mères Glaniques). There is no shrine, but inscriptions confirm the identification, including a dedication of Roman date from a certain Marcus Licinius Verecundus, a retired legionary, to the deity Glan (Glanis?), which presumably accounts for the origin of the name Glanum.[41] This primitive, rocky sanctuary seems to have been the real *raison d'être* of Glanum, and the nearby fortified gateway (see Fig. 82), useless for protecting the town, was at least facing the right way to protect the sanctuary, i.e. against anyone coming from the north.[42] The gateway is a source of doubt, for it carried curved crenellations (*merlons*) of the type we previously encountered at Saint Blaise, raising the possibility of Greek

83. Glanum: the site, looking south.

155

84. Glanum: the south end of the site, looking north. The standing columns of the temple are reconstructed.

85. Glanum: peristyle, Hellenistic house.

influence or even presence at Glanum, a possibility reinforced by the presence at Glanum of wall blocks with their surface worked in alternate bands of roughly tooled chevrons, also a technique familiar at Saint Blaise (see Fig. 80) and Marseille itself (Wall of Crinas).[43]

Proceeding further north (i.e. falling back from the gorge and towards St. Remy), we come to 'Le Centre Monumental Gallo-Grec'. Glanum may have been a sanctuary rather than an orthodox city, thus explaining some of the problems of siting and location, but there is no denying that around the second century BC it acquired many of the standard ingredients of Greek urban development. A *bouleuterion*, more or less square in shape and recalling that of Priene but, unlike Priene, not roofed, fronted on to a smallish agora.[44] Continuing to the north along the main street, now largely paved with flat stone slabs which double as the cover slabs of a monumental drain running under it, we come to a striking residential quarter. Its chief feature, on a wedge-shaped plot of land bordering the west edge of the street, is a series of luxurious houses ('Maison des Antes, Maison de Cybèle et d'Atys'). Of the peristyle type (and incorporating what may be a small, colonnaded shopping centre), they are of a plan made familiar by the houses of Hellenistic Greece, particularly on the island of Delos,[45] and repeated at Ampurias. Their Corinthian pilasters, mosaic floors and colonnaded peristyles testify not only to the wealth of their proprietors, and hence of the community as a whole, but to the strength of the Hellenic influence. Even allowing that the local Celts may have been more sophisticated and receptive to innovation than we normally give them credit for, I at least find it very difficult to look at these dwellings so characteristically Greek and then believe that Glanum was a completely Celtic town with no Greek element in its population.[46]

At the same time, there can be no denying a Celtic presence. Quite a number of inscriptions, dating from as late as the first century BC, are in the Celtic language, written in Greek script. They are mostly funerary stelai, giving little more than the names of the deceased (but making it very clear that these were Celts (or Gauls)), though there are also dedications, in Celtic, to the 'Mères Glaniques'. There are also sculptures of male figures (presumably chieftains) sitting cross-legged, a characteristic Celtic pose.[47] More striking was a lintel or architrave block, carefully carved with decorative mouldings and carrying hollowed-out oval recesses evidently designed to accommodate human skulls, fixed to the stone by iron spikes, the points of which still survive, embedded in the masonry. This exhibition of the skulls of slain enemy warriors ('les têtes coupées') was a well-known Gallic practice and provides irrefutable evidence of a native presence in Glanum. Actual skulls, perforated where the spike affixing them had passed through the cranium, were found on the floor of building LVII, the 'Prytaneion' (?).[48] From the same location came a series of figured capitals bearing, between Corinthian-type volutes at each corner, portrait heads representing Pan, Apollo, Hermes, Dionysos, an allegorical Africa, a monocular Cyclops, various Celtic heroes, and a number of unidentified

157

women. The style has been identified as 'Salyan art at its peak'; though the presence of 'Africa' may also hint at Carthaginian influence, a conjecture supported by the curved crenellations (*merlons*) on the fortified gateway.[49] What all this confirms beyond any question is that in Glanum there was a strong Celtic element in the population, no matter how close the control exercised by the (Massaliot?) Greeks, just as the houses seem to substantiate an equally strong Greek element. None of this should come as a surprise.

The visitor to the site may well find a further factor somewhat confusing. As we see it today, the site is largely a Roman one, with forum, basilica,[50] temples to Roman objects of veneration (notably the imperial family), baths, and, most of all, the prominent triumphal arch and funerary monument that gave the site its local name, Les Antiques. None of these concern us within the compass of events covered by this book, but they must be mentally thought away – not an easy feat – before one can get down to the relevant Greco-Celtic Glanum.

Agde

Adge is a river port, on the River Hérault, near Béziers. Skymnos lists it as a Phocaean foundation, but, as we have noted, this should perhaps be taken not too literally and may mean no more than that it was Greek. Also mentioned by Mela and Ptolemy,[51] its Greek name was Agathe Tyche ('Good Luck'), and modern Agdiens are daily reminded of it by an imposing statue of this influential patroness set up facing the ancient ramparts, with her name inscribed in Greek on the base.[52] Although I have described

86. Agde: air view. The ancient city lay along the bank of the river; its extent inland is marked by the tree-lined, sickle-shaped boulevard, in centre-left of the picture.

87. Agde: the River Hérault; the Cathedral of St. Etienne (square tower, centre) approximately marks the centre of the Greek colony.

Agde as a river port – which it was, because it was on a river – it was not a river port in the sense that, say, Arles was. It was not inland but only 4 km from the open sea, and in fact might almost be said to have been on an estuary – something scarcely existing in the tideless Mediterranean. It thus had a much closer contact with deep-sea traffic than many river ports, and, indeed had an exceptionally favourable site in terms of communications. It was a natural port of call for coastwise shipping, running along from Massalia to Spain, and also on the overland coastal route, the 'Voie Héracléenne', which paralleled the shore. A route heading straight inland took one up the Hérault valley to the heart of the Cevennes while another forked off to the west (in the direction of Toulouse) to Aquitania and, eventually, the Atlantic coast on the Bay of Biscay. There was also a hinterland (around Lodève) and a rich coastal plain that were themselves fertile generators of trade. One of its chief exports was basalt millstones, and it imported wine from Massalia.

The ancient site was on the river bank, in the centre of the modern town, and was a relatively small one – at least as compared with something like Massalia. Although there have been excavations within the ancient city, these have perforce been small and localised, it being a modern built-up area, and the most outwardly obvious archaeological testimony to Agde's past is its ramparts. The most prominent ancient stratum of these dates to the second century BC, but is built on fourth/third century foundations.

159

The city apparently fell under Massaliot control and/or occupation towards the end of the fifth century BC.[53] Moreover, the surrounding land is centuriated, i.e. the divisions between landholdings are mapped out and surveyed on a regular geometric plan, with the division lives following the same orientation as the Agde street plan and hence linked to it. Centuriation is a Roman rather than a Greek practice, but this at least suggests the extent of the territory assigned to the city, in Greek as in Roman days. The centuriation extends as far inland as the Via Domitia, which ran through Béziers.[54]

Arles

The ancient name of the city was Arelate, but this does not occur in surviving literature any earlier than Caesar, who refers to it in connection with the siege of Massalia. Avienus tells us the old name of the place was Theline, while Ps. Skymnos mentions a Greek city on the Rhône called Rhodanousia. Theline is a possibility as the original name of Arles, but nothing more is known about Rhodanousia: it sounds like a name artificially coined by someone from the Rhodanos river ('Rhôneville') and if it has to refer to anywhere in particular Arles is the most prominent candidate, but that is as far as it goes and we must question whether such a place ever existed at all. In any case, it is not to be taken seriously.[55] Most of the antiquities of Arles are of Roman date (theatre, amphitheatre, cryptoportico, baths) but excavations at the Winter Garden site, beside the Boulevard des Lices, has revealed architectural remains dating back to the sixth century. This confirmed the hypothesis, previously based on extensive pottery finds, that there was a strong Greek presence in Arles going back almost as far as the foundation of Massalia.[56] Presumably Massalia was the source of this Greek presence, though, as so often, it is impossible to be specific on the political situation, and the best we can do for Arles is to declare it, like Glanum, a mixed Greco-Celtic settlement.[57] The one thing that remained unchanged in both its Greco-Celtic and Roman periods was its position, as the lowest feasible crossing of the Rhône (Fig. 20). During the earlier years this was presumably achieved by ferry. In Roman days there was a pontoon bridge, serving the Via Julia, from Ventimiglia (once that was opened) and the older route via Apt from the Col Montgénèvre and, across the Rhône, the Via Domitia on to Spain.[58] Arles was also prominent as a port, and as such was in competition with Massalia. Massalia may have controlled sea traffic, particularly at the period when the Fossae Marianae were in operation, but Arles likewise controlled the River Rhône and access to it from the sea. Docks and harbour installations have been found in the west bank suburb of Trinquetaille, and, as we have previously noted, its shipyards, though doubtless more experienced in the construction of river boats, yet were capable of turning out in 49 BC for Julius Caesar a fleet of 12 ships which defeated the entire Massaliot navy.[59]

160

Avignon

The Greek name of Avignon was Aouenion, Latin Avennio. Like practically all such settlements, pottery and other finds show continuous indigenous occupation going back to the Bronze Age and even the Neolithic. Pliny and Pomponius Mela both mention it, but as an *oppidum* of the Cavares, a local Celtic confederacy. Stephanus of Byzantium calls it a Massaliot city, but that may mean no more than that a lot of Greeks lived there, and should not be taken as evidence of political control by Massalia.[60] One should not be misled by its strikingly strategic position at the confluence of the Rhône and the Durance, for in antiquity the Durance followed a more southerly course, entering the mainstream near Tarascon. There was certainly a crossing of the Rhône at Avignon, presumably by ferry, though a pontoon bridge like that of Arles has also been suggested.[61] A further indication of Greek influence is the local minting of coins carrying the city name in Greek, and the finding of a major hoard of Massaliot obols. Perhaps, as a very minor point, we may also note that Avignon represents the northern limit of olive cultivation (Fig. 35). All in all, Greek Avignon is indeed a very shadowy place. No doubt it did indeed carry a certain volume of trade from Massalia, either overland direct or via Arles and the Rhône valley but its great days, as a Roman city with Latin rights (Pomponius Mela, *loc. cit.*, lists it as the third richest city in Gaul) were yet to come.

Cavaillon

Cavaillon (Latin Cabellio) had a history very like that of Avignon. Originally a Celtic *oppidum* of the Cavares that had a subsequent history of prosperity under the Romans, it is included here solely because, once more, Stephanus of Byzantium identifies it as a Massaliot city.[62] Like Avignon, it was on a river crossing, where the Via Domitia from Montgénèvre (and presumably whatever rough track was its Celtic predecessor) crossed the Durance; like Avignon it minted coins with Greek inscriptions, and also produced grave stelai with Gallic names in Greek script. There is not much more to be said about it. We may reasonably infer that it saw a good deal of Greek cultural and commercial influence, but that is about as far as we can go.[63]

Port-Vendres

The Latin name for Port-Vendres was Portus Veneris ('Port Venus'). Because of the name it has also been identified with Aphrodision, a nearby sanctuary mentioned by Strabo. Portus Veneris is mentioned by Pliny and Ptolemy, and marks the boundary, now and then, between Gaul and Spain. Avienus apparently refers to it under the name Pyrene.[64] Although it was regularly frequented by Massaliot traders from the sixth century

88. Port Vendres: waterfront. No classical antiquities are preserved in the town, its chief interest being topographical – the very well-sheltered harbour.

on, little is known of it historically, and there are no local remains of classical date. The chief evidence is again as so often, topographical. Port-Vendres was certainly a Greek outpost, and was a natural calling point for seafarers before rounding the headland and Port-Bou (which followed the projecting end of the Pyrenees ridge) on their way to Ampurias and so, eventually Tartessos. This was an important sea route for Massaliot and Phocaean traders and must have carried a reasonable volume of traffic. Equally striking is the fact that Port-Vendres is an outstanding natural harbour, something rarely found on the Languedoc coast. Indeed, as one looks today at the land-locked port, sheltered by its surrounding hills, it is hard not to see a parallel to the Lakydon at Marseille. Given the presence of so superb a refuge from bad weather on a heavily travelled route at a point where it rounds a projecting and exposed promontory, it is surely inevitable that Massaliot sailors often called there and that it formed an important link in their commercial network.[65] (See Fig. 88.)

Rhode

Rhode (or Rhodanos) is the modern Rosas, just south of the Spanish border, a kind of Hispanic counterpart to Port-Vendres. There is next to no archaeological evidence; what we do know comes from literary sources and may not be entirely reiable. On two counts Rhode stands out of from all the other Greek foundations we have been considering. One is chronological. Strabo says the settlement was founded before the First Olympiad

(776 BC), and an ancient tradition puts the foundation back to the late ninth or early eighth century. The first Greek colony in the west has always been said to be Cumae, near Naples, but though the ancients themselves usually ascribed to it a foundation date of around 1000 BC, the real date was around 750. Rhode, on this basis, came first, and so becomes the earliest Greek foundation in the west. The second count is that, alone among all the Greek colonies and outposts in the Western Mediterranean, Rhode had nothing at all to do with Phocaea. It was founded by Rhodes, and, we are told, 'always maintained its Rhodian character'.[66] It was not entirely as isolated as it sounds, the one non-Phocaean foundation in the region. First, there was an early-established Rhodian trade route to South Gaul and thence up the Rhône valley (for tin and amber) which operated via the Balearics; Rhode was a natural way-station on this route. Second, once the Phocaeans arrived and opened up the area, Rhode seems to have thrived by the association with them – in short, blood proved thicker than water, and in these remote recesses of the Hellenic world being Greek proved more important than not being Phocaean. In fact, Rhode was the first Western Greek city to coin in silver and its coins, and local imitations of them, have been found widely spread through Gaul, and it ended up being more closely involved in the Phocaean trade sphere of Massalia-Ampurias, particularly Ampurias, which was closer. All this seems to have come about amicably.[67]

Ampurias

Ampurias (ancient Emporion) was founded by the Phocaeans; whether directly from Phocaea or as a sub-colony founded by Massalia is uncertain. Chronologically, there seems to be no doubt that Massalia came first. Ampurias and Aleria (in Corsica) seem to have been founded around the same time, and there is really no telling in what order.[68] Nor is it very important. A third link in this chain was the colony of Mainake, near Malaga in South East Spain, and the last Greek port of call on the route to Tartessos. Both Skymnos and Ps. Scylax mention Ampurias, giving a sailing time of two days and one night from Massalia.[69]

The first Greek foundation (585-75 BC?) was on a small island just off the coast (see p. 38 above); today it forms part of the mainland, and carries the village of Saint Marti d'Empúries. In antiquity its original name may have been Cypsela, but this soon became Palaiopolis, 'The Old City', as population pressures led the colonists to move, around 550 BC, to a mainland site some 500 m to the south, at the mouth of the small River Fluvià; logically, this second location is often spoken of as Neapolis, 'The New City',[70] but this title seems to have been bestowed by modern archaeologists and there is no ancient authority for it. Both sites were quite close to Rhode, which they, 12 km away, visibly faced across the bay.

Ampurias probably saw its population grow from the arrival of refugees from Phocaea after the Persian destruction of that city in 540, more

89. Ampurias: air view; Neapolis, the site of the Greek colony, is in the lower centre; the building at its further side is the Museum.

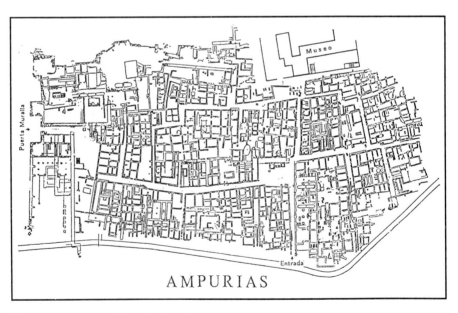

90. Ampurias: plan of Neapolis, the Greek site.

91. Ampurias: general view of excavations (Neapolis).

refugees from Aleria after its abandonment following the Battle of Alalia in 536-5, and yet more again from Mainake, destroyed around the end of the century by the Carthaginians. The removal of these trade rivals and the temporary commercial recession from which Massalia suffered in the fifth century combined to bring to Ampurias a trade boom that made the fifth-third centuries BC the brightest in the city's history. Especially interesting was the relationship between the Ampurias Greeks and the local indigenous, i.e., Iberian, population. The natives occupied a compound named Indika (from the name of the local Iberian tribe, the Indikétes). Interpretations vary. The two separate foundations, we are told, show that 'no love was lost between them'. Alternatively 'Patriotic modern Spaniards infer from the evidence that the Greeks were a mere outnumbered enclave, and that the Iberians preserved their independence'. Thirdly, we may see in it evidence of peaceful cohabitation in a spirit of amity that forms a striking contrast with Greek-Ligurian relations at Massalia. Whatever the relationship, one thing seems clear. The two sides were in close commercial contact, and Ampurias was the chief gateway through which passed Massaliot trade with the interior of Spain. The city was noted for its manufacture of linen, and produced large quantities of rushes, probably used in making ropes and basketry.[71] Eventually the two settlements merged, which is why in Latin the Greek Emporion (= 'Trading Post') is referred to in the plural, Emporiae. In the meantime, a wall divided them, with a single gateway through which

165

92. Ampurias: atrium and impluvium of Roman house (Villanueva).

93. Ampurias: Hellenistic house-floor with mosaic inscription in Greek ('Sweet Dreams').

permanently stationed sentries peered suspiciously at whatever they could see on the other side. After the Second Punic War, in 195, the surrounding countryside became a Roman province (its first governor was Cato), warmly cherished for its production of gold and silver in large quantities. In the Civil War it opted for Pompey, and so to the victorious Caesar Ampurias seemed a good place to settle his veterans, whence they could keep an eye on disaffected locals. This colony was attached to the Greek Neapolis as a separate and very large addition, outside the Greek walls.

Today, the site is a large one. The Greek city is surrounded by a Cyclopean wall and contains remains of temples of Ascelpios and Zeus Serapis, an agora, stoa, and a large number of private houses. Outside it the later Roman city, ten times as big, features a forum, an amphitheatre (outside the walls) and several luxurious houses of Hellenistic type. Some of their floor mosaics carry Greek inscriptions (my own favourite is the bedroom marked *hedu koitos*, 'sweet dreams'), showing that even in Roman imperial days a pervasive Greek influence survived.

Hemeroskopeion, Mainake

These two sites may conveniently be considered together.[72] They were Greek trading posts on the Iberian coast, somewhere between Ampurias and Gibraltar, and, beyond literary references, little is known about them. The very name is an evocation of frontier life on the outer marches of civilisation – Hemeroskopeion may be roughly translated as 'Fort Look-out'. They must have been very minor places indeed, except that, being on the coasting route to Tartessos, a famed source of commercial wealth, they doubtless offered a welcome port of call to ships looking for a safe overnight anchorage where they could refill their water jars.

Hemeroskopeion is mentioned in Strabo and Avienus, and may have been on or near the site of the modern seaside resort of Denia. It was known for its iron mines. Mainake occurs in Avienus and Ps. Skymnos and was somewhere down near Malaga. Like so many other cities, it was confidently described as having been founded by Massalia; it is likewise, but more reliably described as the most remote Greek settlement in the Western Mediterranean. Mainake was destroyed by Carthage sometime around 500 BC.[73] Strabo also mentions that Hemeroskopeion was one of a group of three small Massaliot foundations, but without saying what the other two were. They were named by Artemidoros, Poseidonios' source, and evidently were Akra Leuke (Alicante) and Alonis (Benidorm).[74]

Tartessos

Tartessos was not a Greek settlement. But it was a vital factor, perhaps more so than any other, in the trade patterns of the whole Western Mediterranean, and without some consideration of Tartessos it is impos-

167

sible to understand fully the pattern of development of the Western Greek colonies, including Massalia itself. Tartessos was on the Atlantic coast of South West Spain, beyond the Straits of Gibraltar and in the general neighbourhood of Cadiz. There are no archaeolgical remains, since there is no site clearly identifiable with the name, and we must rely solely on literary evidence. This is not clear-cut either, for by 'Tartessos' some authors evidently refer to a city while others use the name for the whole surrounding region. Some, notably the lyric poet Stesichoros, even identified Tartessos with a river, the modern Guadalquivir (ancient Baetis). Those who saw it as a city usually identified it with Cadiz (the Roman Gades), convincingly located near the mouth of the Guadalquivir, though some thought it was on an offshore island.[75]

Tartessos was important for its mineral wealth. To the Greek traders of the Archaic Age it represented a distant and shadowy Eldorado, the crock of gold at the rainbow's end. In later times they would undoubtedly have told how in Tartessos the streets were paved with gold: as it was, they contented themselves with tales of how their ships' anchors were made of silver. In fact, there was some basis for this. The area was productive in copper, notably from the Rio Tinto mines later worked by the Romans, silver, and sometimes tin, possibly re-exported after importation from Cornwall and Brittany (p. 143 above). Although the site of Tartessos City has yet to be identified (and it has been energetically and doggedly sought), a considerable amount of gold jewellery and other treasure has been found in the region and is now in local museums.[76]

The striking thing about Tartessos is how early in Greek history it came to be exploited. One looks at the map and instinctively feels that, situated at the ends of the Mediterranean earth (if one may so put it), it must have been one of the last places the Greeks got to, and settlements like Massalia must have antedated any contact with it, because they were closer to home. This is not so. Colaios of Samos got to Tartessos around 660 BC, long before Massalia, or any other Greek colony in the area, was founded, and trade with it was already established in that century. Plainly, we should see Massalia, Ampurias, Mainake, and the like – at least partly – as stepping stones set in place to guard and reinforce a trade route already in operation, rather than as independent foundations from which Tartessos was then subsequently discovered. And in any case, it was not only the Greeks who were interested in this area. The Phoenicians too were aggressively prominent in pressing their claims, and indeed ended by winning – around 500 Mainake was destroyed by them, Tartessos became essentially part of the Carthaginian empire, and, at least if we are to follow orthodox doctrine, the Straits of Gibraltar were closed to all non-Phoenician traffic.[77] The Phoenicians one always hears of in this connection are, of course, from Carthage, but their activities were evidently shared by their kin from the Levant. Tartessos may be the Biblical Tarshish,[78] which was the destination of the ship that Jonah caught from Jopa, before his adventure with the 'great fish'. This eastern connection came to an end in 573 with the destruction of Tyre (which had founded Cadiz) by Nebuchadnezzar.

Tartessos, during the seventh and sixth centuries, was ruled as a kingdom by a local dynasty, and, surprisingly, we know rather more of its history than we do at, say, Ampurias. This is largely because it enjoyed close and friendly relations with the Greeks (not just the Hellenic colonies of the west, but their mother cities also; the long distance does not seem to have been a serious impediment in dealings with the Tartessians), and so appears in literary sources. Its best known monarch was Arganthonios, who out of friendship with the Phoceans gave them the money to fortify their city against the Persians, thereby rating a complimentary reference in Herodotus, who modestly thinks that he passed away in an untimely death at the early age of only 120 (670-550 BC) – the lyric poet Anacreon more generously allows him to have lived to be 150. There was also a King Theron, and a Habis, 'who taught agriculture, promulgated laws, and finally converted himself into a god'.[79] The general area also appears frequently in Greek mythology, notably in the adventures of that most peripatetic of Greek demigods, Heracles. 'Tartessos' is not actually mentioned by name in any of the Heraclean myths, but the Garden of the Hesperides and the Cattle of Geryon, two of his celebrated Labours, are set in the region.[80] Tartessos also had epic poems and a law code written in verse, and adopted a form of Greek alphabet (though the language they spoke is as yet unknown). The inhabitants claimed that the content of these documents dated back some 6,000 years. They seem to merit the summing up of MacKendrick, 'an old and cultured people, a prosperous empire of hospitable men of peace'.[81]

10

The Greeks on the Côte d'Azur

The study of Greek foundations east of Marseille faces a problem we encountered only rarely towards the west. We are often dependent on itineraries (notably the Antonine itinerary of 150 AD) which list the various ports of call along the coast. This gives us the names of quite a few small ports, but without any detailed clue to their location other than their sequence in the list. Many of these settlements are of Roman date, but prosperity under the Romans of course does not rule out previous existence, or even an origin, under the Greeks, particularly if the place-name itself sounds Greek. The problem is matching the recorded name with an actual geographical location, and often this is perforce reduced to pure guesswork. Usually we know nothing of the history of the place, other than perhaps a brief note 'founded by the Massaliots', nor is archaeology all that great a help. All of the coast of Provence and the Côte d'Azur was settled, after a fashion, by the Ligurians, and once the Phocaeans came on the scene there can scarcely be anywhere with a convenient anchorage that did not see the occasional Greek trader, or even Greek settler. Thus there is practically nowhere along the coast innocent of minor finds of Greek coins and amphora sherds. This problem scarcely exists west of Marseille, where we have instead a succession of clearly identified sites marked by major architectural remains, such as Saint Blaise, Glanum, or Ampurias. Not until we get to Hemeroskopeion and Mainake in Spain do we encounter the problems of matching a whole string of bare names in an itinerary to actual sites on the ground, guided by nothing more than topographical probability occasionally eked out with tantalising references in Victorian antiquarians to fragmentary ruins supposedly visible in their day and long since gone.

This, however, is precisely what now confronts us. On the entire coastline from Marseille to Antibes (180 km or so) there is only one site, Olbia, near Hyères, where there are actual remains of buildings and a city of Greek date and known Greek identity (Fréjus, despite its extensive antiquities, being exclusively Roman). Nevertheless we have some eight or nine names that have somehow to be fitted into this virgin framework, sometimes on the basis of evidence as flimsy as a *prima facie* resemblance between a modern name and a recorded Greek one, which itself may have been a *rhabillage* of some Ligurian original. This is insubstantial stuff indeed, but in the absence of any other indications it is better than nothing, though not much.[1] As one leaves Marseille, then, and moves eastward along the coast, one finds oneself in a dead end. The narrow coastal plain, hemmed in by the mountains, comes to an end at Cap Croisette, and further progress along the coast, at least by land, is limited to footpaths and rough tracks. The first inhabited locality, with access only from inland, is Cassis.

Cassis

Cassis was the ancient Charsis, so mentioned in the Itinerary of Antoninus (150 AD). The port was probably on the site of the beach, just east of the modern harbour, but no remains have been found apart from an altar dedicated to a local protective deity, Tutela Charistana, though the antiquarian C. Lenthéric noted that 'at some distance from the port one still finds in the cellars fragments of the walls of the old quay, which serve as supports for the modern vaulting'. The long, narrow and spectacular calanque of Port Miou, so close as to be almost a part of Cassis, has sometimes, but improbably, been identified as the Portus Aemines, a seaport mentioned in the Antonine Itinerary, which is more plausibly to be sought further east, around Le Brusc. Cassis was in antiquity chiefly famous for its coral, which was held to be superior in quality to that produced by the Balearics, Sardinia, and North Africa. There were also extensive limestone quarries, and inscriptions cut on Cassis stone have been found as far away as North Africa. All of this evidence pertains to Roman occupation, but it would seem unlikely that there was not also some sort of Greek presence during our period.[2]

La Ciotat / Citharista

The Antonine Itinerary mentions as its next stop east of Cassis a harbour named the Portus Citharista. This seems to be the modern port and shipbuilding centre of La Ciotat. There is also the small mountain village of Ceyreste some 3 km inland. Evidence is very slim, but it would seem likely that Ceyreste was the city of Citharista (a Greek foundation, if the name is to be trusted), and the present La Ciotat its harbour, on the analogy of Athens and the Peiraeus. La Ciotat is probably a derivative of some Latin title that the place acquired as a *civitas*. Lenthéric assures us that, in his day, 'there are still some ruins to be seen at Ceyreste', but even then they were very fragmentary and seem to have been mainly ancient blocks found lying around the fields and built into stone walls. At La Ciotat the site of the ancient harbour may have been preserved in the Provençal toponymn, 'La Cioutad, bort (= 'port') de nostre cioutad', but Lenthéric wisely reminds us that 'it is, undoubtedly, somewhat imprudent to venture too far afield with the etymologists', and perhaps we would more judiciously limit ourselves to echoing his categorical verdict on the place: 'There is nothing to attract the artist, the archaeologist, or the scholar.'[3]

94. La Ciotat (ancient Citharista): now largely occupied by a shipyard building supertankers, the site is surrounded by mountains and cliffs that give the Greeks a sheltered harbour.

Tauroentum

The location of Tauroentum has been disputed more than that of any other ancient site in Provence. Mentioned by Strabo and Ptolemy in its Greek form, Tauroention, it is identified by the first as a city belonging to the Massaliots (along with Olbia, Antipolis and Nice). Scymnos, Stephanos of Byzantium, and Mela list it as Tauroeis, and Caesar calls it Tauroenta, a 'castellum Massiliensium'.[4] Its position, not otherwise defined, has been keenly sought and identified on the twin basis of topographical probability and enthusiastic local patriotism. The site was once identified as La Ciotat, but the two chief claimants are Les Lecques (near St. Cyr, on the Bay of La Madrague, a short distance east of La Ciotat) and Le Brusc, south of Sanary and on the western side of the promontory of Cap Scié. Les Lecques can boast a museum extensively signposted in the area as the 'Musée de Tauroentum' and built amid an impressive set of architectural remains, but they are those of a Roman villa, and the Le Brusc site seems to be now generally accepted as the true one, though that does not stop the Princeton Encyclopedia listing it in the inverted commas of scepticism as 'LE BRUSC ("Tauroention")'.[5] Tauroentum seems to have been more than a mere trading post. Stephanus of Byzantium calls it a Massaliot colony (*apoikia*), Caesar a *castellum*. Clerc considers the possibility that it may have been founded directly by the Phocaeans, on the authority of Apollo-

172

dorus, Stephanus' source, and it certainly appears on the Antonine Itinerary as an official port of call for the Roman navy between La Ciotat and Toulon. The name also has been much discussed, since it exists in several different forms – Tauroeis, Tauroention, Tauroentum, to say nothing from analogies drawn from Tarentum (Taranto) and Tauromenion (Taormina, in Sicily) – and it has even been derived from a bull's head blazon on the mainsail of the ship carrying the founding settlers. In fact, it most probably is a *rhabillage* of some native Ligurian name. Some not very spectacular remains, of varying dates, are preserved at the Le Brusc site – a masonry rampart, an aqueduct, floors of houses and 'crude mosaics of Hellenistic date'.[6]

Nothing is recorded of the history of Tauroentum, and its one appearance on the world stage remains as the battlefield chosen by the Roman and Massaliot fleets for their first engagement in Caesar's siege of Massalia (p. 104 above).

Portus Aemines

Like so many of these small settlements along the Provence coast, this is known to us only from literary sources, usually itineraries, and all we can do is make a hopeful guess on the basis of topography and pass on. Even archaeology is no great help, for there was enough trade passing along this coast for just about any minor hill or bay to produce at least a few coins and amphora fragments. Portus Aemines is listed on the Antonine Itinerary. Benoit identifies it as possibly Bandol. That is about as far as we can usefully go.[7]

Alonis

Alonis is listed by Stephanus of Byzantium as 'an island, and city belonging to Massalia'. This tells us little, and it has been suggested that there may be some confusion here with the Alonis in Spain mentioned by Mela. Benoit suggests as a location Saint-Mandrier, which was at one time an island though now a peninsula; it is at the mouth of Toulon harbour.[8]

Toulon

Toulon is a surprise. It is one of the only two large modern cities in the area that cannot boast a Greek past (the other being Cannes). In Roman times it was known as Telonium, or Telo Martius, and is referred to both in the Antonine Itinerary and in Silius Italicus, so there must have been something there, but that is as far as our knowledge goes. When one looks at the great natural harbour of Toulon, surely one of the finest in the whole Mediterranean and not for nothing long established as the principal base for the Mediterranean fleet of the French Navy, it is hard to imagine that the Greeks, or Phocaeans, looked upon such a superb roadstead and were

95. Toulon (ancient Telo?): no ancient remains have been found, possibly because they lie under the modern city or the French naval base.

not interested. It may be, however, that this great land-locked bay was simply too big. It is a question of shelter. The seaward side of the bay is so far from the protecting mountains of the landward side that it is exposed to northerly winds (which include, of course, the Mistral), which have time and space to swoop down to sea level after crossing the shoreline at the modern city of Toulon. For the needs of the ancient sailor, a much smaller and more closely sheltered anchorage, like the Lakydon, would answer better.[9] There is also a further possibility: that, in the absence of any extensive or organised excavation, whatever antiquities do exist may still be hidden under the modern city.

Olbia (Pomponiana?)

After some of the entries listed above it is a relief to find an actual archaeological site firmly linked to a firm identification. Olbia (= 'Fortunate') was not too uncommon a name among Greek colonies, the two other most famous ones being Olbia in the Ukraine and Olbia in Sardina (which, as the ferry terminal for mainland services from Civitavecchia, still retains its ancient name).[10] No less than nine other cities of the same name are listed by Stephanus of Byzantium, and the present Olbia is mentioned by several of our ancient sources; Strabo specifies that it was a Massaliot

city. The site was firmly located and excavated only in 1947-50 and
1956-73, by J. Coupry, at L'Almanarre, near the Giens peninsula between
Toulon and Hyères.[11] From the absence of any earlier pottery sherds, we
may deduce that Olbia was founded around 350 BC, probably to reinforce
the security of Massaliot coasting traffic and land control of the littoral
against Ligurian expansion. In spite of Strabo, it was probably not a 'city'
in the political sense, a developed and independent *polis*, but rather a cross
between a trading post and a fort; politically, it was probably a dependency
of Massalia, with a population of around 1,000 (or 200-300 able-bodied
male adult citizens).[12]

The site is square, each side being 160 m long, surrounded by a circuit
wall of which considerable stretches survive on the east, north, and west

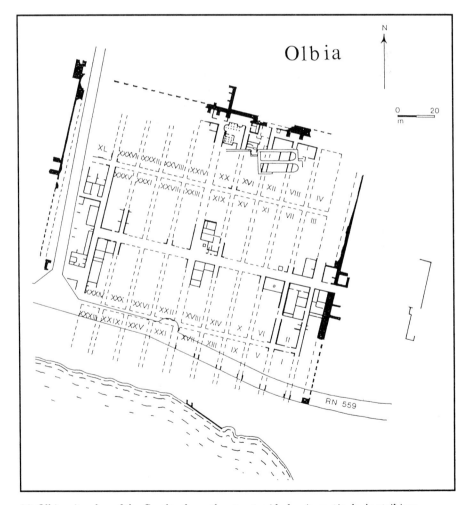

96. Olbia: site plan of the Greek colony; the street grid plan is particularly striking.

97. Olbia: excavated street (between blocks XL and XXV on the plan, Fig. 96), looking south.

sides. The south side has been eroded by the sea, also destroying most of the harbour works. Inside the walls, the city is laid out on a rigorously observed grid-iron plan of the best Hippodamian pattern that divides it up into 36 blocks of traditional Greek oblong format. The two main streets (4 m and 5 m wide) intersect at a central crossroads, as in a Roman camp, and at this key location is sited a large public well in ashlar masonry. A monument abutting on the north circuit wall carries a block with the inscription, in Greek, 'Of Aphrodite', giving some insight into the religious beliefs of the inhabitants.[13] The walls of the numerous houses and shops in the excavated section are preserved to a height of 70 cms or so, and, after a destruction layer of the mid first century BC (perhaps associated with the Roman siege of its mother city, Massalia, in 49 BC), there is superimposed a stratum of Roman occupation including a Roman bath complete with hypocaust. The east gate (there is a gate in the middle of each side of the city) is heavily fortified, and apparently led to the harbour. Of the harbour itself some vestiges remain, now isolated from the city by erosion and the building of the coastal road.

The most striking thing about Olbia is its rigorously regular layout. Other Greek cities have the Hippodamian street plan, but the geometrically square city plan is rare if not unparalleled among Greek foundations. True, the land is more or less flat so that there is no need for the walls to follow an irregular course dictated by the needs of military defensibility, but the terrain was just as flat at, say, Mantinea or Poseidonia (Paestum) and the resultant city outline is oval or polygonal. At Olbia the feeling is one of emphatic artificiality, a town-planner's version of modular construction. Even the width of the blocks of houses, 11 m, was exactly five times the width of the streets separating them (2.20 m). Plainly the settlement was conceived from the start as a complete unit, rather than gradually built up, and conceived in military terms: as its excavator well describes it, it is a 'forteresse carrée, à rues orthogonales, et de plan apparement exemplaire'.[14] The resemblance to Roman camp-planning, which itself carried over into town-planning, is striking, and, given the relatively late date of the foundation of Olbia and the contact that Massalia must by then have been beginning to establish with Rome, one wonders whether one should see here some sign, however tenuous, of Roman influence.[15]

We close with a note on the territory of Olbia. Most colonies, even military ones, have been sited with some sort of arable land available so that the settlers can support themselves. Normally this would not have been a problem, for the terrain around Olbia is not particularly unsuitable nor, apparently, the settlers particularly numerous. But, by all accounts, Olbia was founded largely to contain the warlike impulses of the Ligurians, and they had built a fortified *oppidum* at Costebelle, only 2 km north of the city. With hostile forces so close, the Olbians could not have relied too much on the agricultural resources of the mainland. Coupry suggests that this vacuum was filled by the Stoechades, the modern Iles d'Hyères (notably Porquerolles), which Strabo specifically says were farmed by the Massaliots (by which perhaps we may understand 'Olbians'?),[16] but they are not all that close or convenient of access: what colony would rely on its food supplies having to come across the sea for however short a trip, with sailing suspended or at least restricted during the winter months, and on a course in the teeth of the prevailing Mistral? Naturally, this argument may reinforce the military purpose of the foundation – farming or no farming, Olbia was there because that's where the Ligurians had to be stopped, hence also the military format of the town plan.

There is also the possibility that there was some farming on the Giens peninsula, though it was probably more important for its salt-pans, and in any case Giens was probably at that time an island, leaving it problematic how much of the peninsula than existed. Some certainly did, for on it at the location known as Acapte there was a sanctuary of the deity Aristaios, at which have been found a large number of votive offerings, including vases of Hellenistic date and carrying inscriptions in Greek. Sometimes these give simply a name, but occasionally will run to a line or two of verse. One such records its donor as Aristodemos, son of Dionnis, of Massalia (Massaleus).[17]

Pergantion, Heraclea Caccabaria

On leaving Olbia we plunge once more into the listings of the geographers and the itineraries, pretty well unsupported by any archaeological evidence.

177

98. Brégançon (ancient Pergantion): fortifications by Vauban. On-site investigation is complicated by this being the official summer residence of the President of France, and evidence for an ancient settlement is largely topographical rather than archaeological. The paved circle is a helicopter pad.

Pergantion is listed (*s.v.*) by Stephanos of Byzantinum, but he tells us nothing about it. Its site, largely because of the name, is identified with the modern Brégançon, the cape separating the Bay of Hyères from the Bay of Bormes. The site is a small rocky islet, today connected to the mainland by a causeway, occupied by a sixteenth-century fort. Casual access is inhibited by the fact that it is now an official residence of the President of France (with a helicopter pad built alongside the causeway), but on topographical grounds alone we may surmise that it may have been appealing to ancient mariners. Even if the causeway was not there in antiquity, presumably the reef on which it is built was, providing in effect two harbours, one facing each direction. This configuration, providing a sheltered roadstead no matter which side the wind was blowing from, thus had obvious attractions. There seems to be no reason, however, to believe that the place was ever very large or important.[18]

Heraclea Caccabaria is mentioned in the Antonine itinerary; today it is identified, with reasonable probability, with the small seaside resort of Cavalaire. Its name ties it in with the widespread cult of Heracles in the region (p. 190 below), while the 'Caccabaria' half, being entirely non-Greek, is apparently of Ligurian origin.[19] It probably handled a good deal of export trade from the iron mines in the Maures. Little has been uncovered archaeologically but on what evidence there is the ancient site had been located at Pardigon, 2 km north-east of Cavalaire.[20]

Athenopolis (Saint-Tropez)

Proceeding eastward along the Corniche des Maures, our next stop is at Athenopolis. For this again we depend on literary sources, though not itineraries: this time our evidence comes from Pliny, Mela, and Varro,[21] under the title Athenopolis Massiliensium. Its most likely identification is Saint-Tropez, though other locations have been suggested.[22] The actual settlement was most probably on the site of today's Old City around the Hotel de Ville, or possibly on the Citadelle hill; there is a small but sheltered beach, 'La Puncho', that would serve as a harbour. Like Citharista, Athenopolis is referred to by our ancient sources as a city, which ought to put it on a higher level than a mere trading post or fort. If it is in fact a Massaliot foundation, this would be consistent with its name, there being at Massalia a well-established cult of Athena, with a temple (p. 79 above). The modern name, Saint-Tropez, also demonstrates a classical connection of sorts: it is traditionally derived from the Christian martyr Torpes, an officer of Nero's court beheaded in 68 AD for his Christian convictions, whose body, cast adrift in a boat, eventually came ashore at Saint-Tropez and was there sumptuously interred by a rich Christian widow.[23]

99. St. Tropez (ancient Athenopolis): the modern yacht harbour.

100. St. Tropez: air view. The ancient settlement was most probably centred on the two small curving beaches, left centre. The preceding Fig. 99 was taken looking across the large pleasure harbour to the right.

Agay

There probably were one or two small ports along the rocky coast of the Esterel between Saint Tropez and Antibes, but evidence for them is minimal. Fréjus (ancient Forum Julii) seems to be ruled out despite its plethora of Roman remains: its harbour was one of those artificially excavated ones (such as Ostia) that were favoured by the Romans but not the Greeks (p. 238 n. 17 below), and no archaeological remains of Greek date have apparently been found. Greek shipping certainly did ply along this coast, as is testified by the finds of underwater wrecks, quite apart from any other consideration. As for ports, a certain 'Agathonis Portus' is mentioned in the Antonine Itinerary, and in the eighth-century AD Chronicles of the Lérins. Its chief claim to our notice in this book is that name looks Greek, and is mostly probably to be linked to the modern port of Agay (on the analogy of *Agathe Tyche* = Agde). Agay at least does have a very sheltered harbour on a rocky and wild stretch of coast where the prudent sailor feels sorely in need of one, and so might be expected to have been used by Greek mariners.[24]

Aigitna

Aigitna was somewhere in this region, for Polybius mentions it in his account of Q. Opimius' campaign against the Oxybii in 154 BC. Where it was is a different matter. As Rivet points out, it has been located at Cagnes, Villeneuve-Loubet, Biot, Golfe-Luan, Cannes, La Napoule Théoule, Agay, and Fréjus. Rivet himself thinks either Cannes or Théoule most likely, basing his arguments chiefly on the presumed position of the Ligurian tribes Opimius came to fight, but one cannot improve on his realistic invocation of Walbank: 'The information available does not, however, seem adequate to give certainty to any proposed identification of the places mentioned.'

Strabo also records the existence somewhere along this coast of a 'Harbour of the Oxybii'. It cannot be identified either, though a number of scholars have naturally been tempted into trying.[25]

Cannes

Cannes shares with Toulon the questionable distinction of being one of the only two major modern cities in the area completely devoid of any discernible evidence whatever for an ancient past. A few Massaliot coins found on the beach prove nothing except the vaguest of trading connections. Quite

101. Cannes: the Greek city, if any, was probably to be found here in the Old Town, on top of the hill named Suquet.

181

probably there existed on the site during the Greek era some minor fishing port, and if there was any real settlement it was probably to be found on the heights of Le Suquet, overlooking the bay, and today occupied by what in Cannes passes for the Old City, crowned by an eleventh-century tower. Attempts, of questionable reliability, have been made to identify Cannes with the ancient Aigitna, and in Roman days it was apparently known as 'The Massaliot Fort' (*castrum Marselinum*).[26] The fact is that there is little natural reason for a settlement to be founded on this precise location – in Roman days the main road passed it by some distance inland and the chief stopover on it was at a place called *Ad Horrea* (Mougins?), and in antiquity as today it was rather a resort area favoured by the villas of the rich, attracted by the pleasant climate and scenery, rather than an orthodox commercial town. In this it has been well compared to the Bay of Naples as a centre of luxurious ease, and Lenthéric's concise evaluation was probably as true of Roman days as of his own: 'Cannes is a place where the necessity of hard work is unknown.'[27]

The Lérins

The Lérins are two small islands off the coast of Cannes. Unlike Cannes itself they do have an ancient pedigree, being mentioned in Strabo, Pliny, and Ptolemy,[28] and were supposedly named after a mythical hero Lero. We encounter the same name in the Dodecanese, between Patmos and Cos, so this may perhaps be further evidence of early Ionian influence in this region.[29] Strabo specifies that they were inhabited, and the Antonine Itinerary mentions them as a natural port of call between Antibes and Fréjus. On the larger of the two islands, Sainte Marguerite, a bilingual Greek and Latin inscription in honour of Pan testified (it is now lost) to a classical presence, and it seems a reasonable inference that the Lérins were a more important place than Cannes itself. The port was apparently located at the western extremity of the island, where traces of a break-water have been found, and in the Fort Royal excavation has uncovered 'an impressive series of structures, including not only buildings with mosaics and wall paintings, baths, cisterns, and a series of cryptoporticoes, but also some fortifications, apparently of the first century BC, with internal bastions'.[30]

Antibes

With Antibes, the ancient Antipolis (and, in Provençal, Antiboul), we leave behind us the long string of small, scantily-documented fishing ports – often no more than a convenient beach – and come to a well-authenticated major city.[31] Strabo mentions only four 'Massaliot cities' as existing along this coast, and Antibes is one of them. He does not give a date for its foundation, but pottery finds support an early date, around the sixth century; there is no way of telling whether it was founded by Massalia or

102. Antibes: distant view; the ancient city was on the projecting peninsula, and its harbour (the Anse St. Roch) on the far side of it.

directly from Phocaea. It is also listed by Mela, and by Ps. Skymnos as the most easterly (*eschate*) possession of Massalia, and events in its later history brought it to the attention of Livy and Polybius,[32] with the expedition of Q. Flaminius in 154. In that year increasing friction between the Massaliot-led Greek settlements and the native Ligurians (who were much given to piracy) led to a Roman attack on the Oxybii and the Deciates, the two chief Ligurian tribes in the area. Antipolis, in the territory of the Deciates, found itself in the theatre of operations, and probably took an active part in them. Massalia profited by the resultant carve-up of the Ligurians' land, and Antipolis fell under the influence and control of Rome, in due course becoming part of the province of Gallia Narbonensis, and within it achieving the status of a municipality[33] with Latin rights.

The name Antipolis has itself generated abundant speculation. It is good, grammatical Greek and means 'The City Facing'. The question is, facing what? The usual answer is, Nice. I do not myself find this convincing. Nice and Antibes are on the same stretch of coastline, and while you certainly can see Nice from Antibes, one would not naturally describe it as 'facing'. What is facing Antibes is the open sea, with nothing visible right to the horizon. True, two sites might perhaps be described as facing each other across a bay in the same coastline, but only if it was a really deeply curved one. One could, for example, imagine the term being applied to Naples and Sorrento – not that it apparently ever was – but the coastal

183

indentation between Antibes and Nice is nothing like the Bay of Naples. Nor, though Antibes is thought to have acquired its name from its facing Nice, does this work the other way round: nobody has ever described Nice (which does not have a name to explain away) as being opposite to Antibes. 'Anti', in fact, is a common prefix in Greek toponymns, but a brief consideration of them does not support the Antipolis explanation. The best known is the Rhion/Antirhion pair, that really are facing each other, on opposite sides of the Gulf of Corinth, and one also finds it in pairs of islands, such as Kythera/Antikythera, or Paxos/Antipaxos. All of these are separated by an actual strait and do not in the least resemble the Antibes/Nice situation. The chief importance of the 'City Facing' hypothesis is it imposes a relative dating on both Nice and Antibes, for plainly the latter could not have been called 'The City Facing Nice' if Nice was not already there for it to face; this would therefore mean that Nice must have been founded first, but if we reject the 'City Facing' interpretation – and I do – then this argument also collapses

A variant of this explanation is that what the City was Facing was not Nice but Corsica. This also seems improbable, though not impossible. The normal shipping route from Velia and, beyond that, Greece (or even Phocaea) ran up the coast of Italy as far as Elba, then across to Cap Corse, the northern extremity of Corsica, and thence across to pick up the mainland again at Nice or Antibes.[34] This is a reasonable explanation, in so far as Greek mariners would normally touch at Corsica first and to them the point of their mainland landfall could naturally present itself as the City Facing because it was the next point on their voyage, while most modern travellers come the other way, from the mainland to Corsica, and to them it is Corsica that they would naturally think of as the Opposite Shore, rather than the mainland from which they started. But militating against this explanation is the long distance from Corsica to the French coast. From Cap Corse to Nice is 175 km (indeed, it is much closer to mainland Italy, only 90 km), and modern steamers take 6-7 hours on the run. This is surely too far apart for the two ports to be considered as natural twins, with one named after the other on the Rhion/Antirhion principle. They are not even in sight of each other, let alone 'just facing'.

This leaves us with a simple explanation. 'Antipolis', in spite of being a good Greek name, in its own right, is most probably a *rhabillage*, an adaptation into a recognisable Greek form of some original name in Celtic, which cannot now be recovered. The same thing may well also be true of 'Nikaia', Nice.[35]

The ancient Greek city was built on the narrow strip of high ground between the present-day Cours Massena, with its covered market, and the sea, thus including both the Cathedral and the Chateau Grimaldi. The face of the sea-front along this stretch is rather abrupt, and the port was doubtless to be found at the Anse St. Roch immediately to the north, which offered a shelving shore on which ships could be beached. The Roman city was rather larger, and included a theatre (now underneath the bus

103. Antibes (ancient Antipolis): the ancient city formed an elongated rectangle along the sea wall, centred on the Chateau Grimaldi and the Cathedral, the two towers rising beside the sea. The ancient harbour lies beyond top left.

104. Antibes: the sea wall; masonry blocks from the Greek city walls have sometimes been identified low down, at the break of the waves.

station), an amphitheatre, baths, and two fairly short aqueducts. Greek remains are almost limited to a few courses of large ashlars at the base of the sea-wall near the Cathedral (and their dating though probable is not wholly certain), and several similar 'blocs à bossage' in the foundations of the Cathedral itself.[36] Unfortunately, the ancient city has been entirely built over, so archaeological excavation has always been very difficult, largely a matter of uncovering fragments of walling and foundations under the floor of the cellars of existing buildings and then, if possible, mentally joining them all up. Thus most of the archaeological reports are not readily comprehensible by the amateur (and, I suspect, sometimes give pause even to the professional).

Small finds, on the other hand, are relatively abundant, particularly pottery sherds and inscriptions. The most celebrated of the latter is the 'Antibes stone', 'le galet d'Antibes', a natural flint worn by erosion into the shape of a roller, 64 cm long and carrying a four-line inscription in archaic Greek script in which a certain Terpnon, a 'servant of holy Aphrodite', calls down blessings on those who set up the stone.[37] From this it may be inferred that at Antipolis there was a temple, or at least a cult, of Aphrodite; confirmation of a sort is offered by the discovery at Oblia of an altar inscribed with Aphrodite's name, in Greek.[38] Antipolis also struck its own coinage, with a head of Aphrodite and, on the reverse, Victory crowning a trophy; the inscriptions carried were ANTIP[OLITON] and LEPI[DOS]. Plainly relating to some period when Antipolis was free of Massaliot suzerainty, these coins are extremely rare, in contrast to the large number of Massaliot ones found locally. The reference to Lepidus presumably dates them to the Roman period, though the script is still Greek.[39]

In trade, Antipolis must have been a key point on both the coasting route between Massalia and Etruria and the long-distance route from Greece via Corsica, and one may postulate for it a healthy local commerce on the basis of its position alone, devoid of any other evidence. Its fish-sauce, a product of the tunny fisheries, earned it an honourable mention from Martial, and a number of viviers, artificial fish-ponds, have been found and published. Further evidence of its maritime commerce is to be seen in the anchors, amphorae and other material from shipwrecks excavated by underwater archaeology and now exhibited in the museum housed in the Bastion St. Andrée.[40]

Nice

The location of ancient Nice makes it plain that trade was the primary motive for its foundation. Like Antibes it offered a natural landfall for ships coming from Corsica and beyond, and coastwise communications would normally be sea-borne. Inland, it is doubtful if there was enough arable land to support a colony – Mela (2, 77) stresses that the mountains come right down to the coast: 'Nikaia tangit Alpes' – and so it does; and

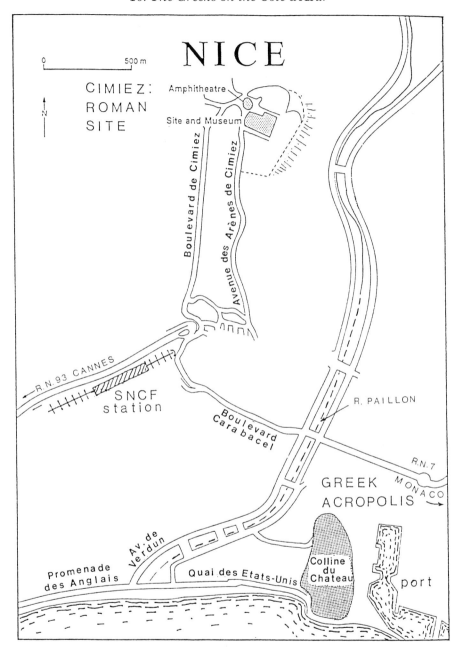

105. Nice (ancient Nikaia): sketch map showing the location of the Greek city and, top, of the Roman Cemenelum (modern Cimiez).

what there was of it was probably under control of the Ligurians, who, as noted below, were only 2 km away. The valley of the Paillon, however, opened a long-distance inland route that could eventually bring the traveller over the Alps by the upper valley of the Roya and Col de Tende, and hence down to Turin and the valley of the Po.[41] Nice also presents us with the same problem as Antibes, the origin of the name. Once more, Nikaia, its ancient name, is perfectly good Greek, being the feminine singular of the adjective formed from Nike, Victory (the feminine noun understood with it being polis, 'city'). A rough translation is thus Victory City, 'La Victorieuse'. Once more, attempts have been made to link it to some particular historical victory, as attempts were made to make sense of Antipolis.[42] This, however, now seems improbable, and it would appear rather that we are once more dealing with a *rhabillage*. That means that, there being no link with historical events, we should neither be driven to find one nor seduced into using it as historical evidence for, say, the date of foundation. There is just no connection with anything recognisable, and the original name cannot be recovered.[43]

As with Antipolis, ancient evidence is copious, if not detailed. Pliny lists it as a Massaliot foundation, and Strabo adds that they founded it to secure the sea routes from depredations by the inland 'barbarians' (i.e. Ligurians). Certainly Nikaia seems to have been firmly under Massaliot control, remaining so even when Antipolis broke free of it in 154, during Opimius' campaign.[44]

106. Nice: the view familiar to most visitors, the Promenade des Anglais, with its luxury hotels.

107. Nice: the harbour, used by the Greeks in antiquity and still in service for steamers to Corsica. The Greek site was on the Colline du Chateau, the wooded hill immediately beyond the harbour (centre left). Beyond that, the Promenade des Anglais (Fig. 106) runs on into the distance.

108. Nice, Cimiez: the Northern Baths (Roman, third century AD).

It is generally presumed that the ancient Greek site was on the raised plateau known as the Chateau, after a castle on it that was destroyed in 1706; offering to the west a fine view along the Promenade des Anglais, on the other side it overlooks the port. On three sides the approach is precipitous, making it a good natural acropolis, with a sheltered harbour alongside it. Strabo says it was a fortified strong-point, and excavation has produced pottery ranging in date from the second century BC to the fourth century AD.[45]

Some 2 km north of this lies the modern Cimiez, the ancient Cemelenum. Originally this was a Celtic (i.e. Ligurian) *oppidum*, occupied by the Vediantii. No doubt its proximity kept the Greeks at Nikaia constantly looking over their shoulders at their 'barbarian' neighbours – 2 km is not very far, and relations with the Ligurians were, as a rule, anything but cordial. Eventually it became the site of the later Roman city, and today preserves the remains of an aqueduct, two sets of baths, a small amphitheatre, and a stretch of the *decumanus*. Originally an army base, it became the capital of the surrounding region (Alpes Maritimae), and ended up by achieving the status of a municipality with Latin rights under Nero. There is now an attractive museum on the site.[46]

Monaco

It comes as a surprise to find that Monaco, today perhaps the most sensationally glamorous spot on the whole coast, has a history as long as it is undistinguished. It is first mentioned by Hecataios, as quoted in Stephanus of Byzantium, which puts it right back to the sixth century BC, and later references are to be found in Strabo and even Virgil.[47] The connection is to be found in the ever-present Heracles, who was apparently worshipped locally in the guise of Heracles Monoïkos, whence 'Monaco'. That the city was named after Heracles need not surprise us. Indeed, what is surprising is rather the number of places that were so named, for even those fully acquainted with the popularity of this hero seldom realise just how popular he was. The number of places named after Heracles in the ancient world has actually been counted, and the total comes to sixty-four. 'Monoïkos' is a different matter. The word has nothing to do with the Greek word *oikos*, a house, for the oï is not a diphthong, and is apparently a strengthened form of *monos*, 'Heracles, the one and only'.[48] It was evidently a Greek foundation if the name is to be trusted, and Strabo says it is the furthest and last port reached by Massaliot coastwise navigation. It was a wretched and poverty-stricken place (though Hecataios does call it a city, *polis*, not a trading post), a small, rocky harbour overshadowed by high and bleak mountains. To modern ears there is something bizarre about Monte Carlo pleading poverty, but such indeed is its history, and not only in antiquity; unlike places like Cannes which even in Roman days were centres of luxurious resort for the wealthy, Monaco did not become rich, or even accessible, until the building of the coastal railway. Before

10. The Greeks on the Côte d'Azur

109. Monaco: the form, a rocky promontory with a harbour on each side so that one was always sheltered, seems to have been favoured by the Greeks, and is here very evident. The tall, long building overlooking the sea is the Museum of Oceanography, and the hollow, rectangular one on the neck of the peninsula is the Royal Palace.

110. La Turbie: the 'Trophy of the Alps' (i.e. the Monument of Augustus) dwarfs the buildings of the surrounding village.

that the natural route of coastwise communications was that followed by the Via Julia, some 3 km or so inland and up in the mountains, conspicuously marked by the truly enormous monument set up by Augustus at La Turbie to mark for travellers the point at which they crossed from Italy to Gaul.[49]

The history of Monaco is almost a complete blank. A few Carthaginian coins have been found, showing that from the early fifth century onwards Carthaginian traders passed by from time to time; but they did that almost everywhere, and their coins have been found in Switzerland and even at Creil, just north of Paris, so not too much should be read into it.[50] Nevertheless, for some time scholars were eager to emphasise the Carthaginian connection, often concentrating on the ubiquitous Heracles and seeking to link him to the Punic divinity Melkarth.[51] On Roman history, or even Gallo-Greek, Monaco scarcely impinges. Not only the Via Julia, when it was built, but also the traditional mountain tracks of the native Ligurians, by-passed Monaco, following the easier route along the crests of the Alpine foothills – i.e. through La Turbie – leaving Monaco not only a dead-end but one that you could hardly even get into. Indeed, we would normally pass it over without even a second thought were it not for its modern celebrity.[52] This, of course, does not mean that it had no history, only that one may presume it was involved in and affected by historical events known to have occurred in that area, such as Opimius' expedition

111. La Turbie: the 'Trophy of the Alps', marking the highest point of the Via Julia, and the border between Italy and Gaul.

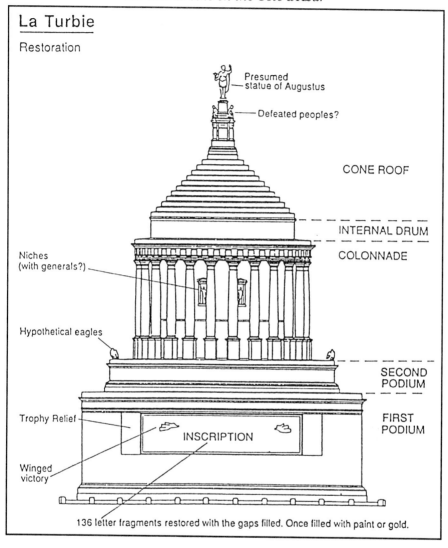

La Turbie

Restoration

Presumed statue of Augustus

Defeated peoples?

CONE ROOF

INTERNAL DRUM

COLONNADE

Niches (with generals?)

Hypothetical eagles

SECOND PODIUM

FIRST PODIUM

Trophy Relief

INSCRIPTION

Winged victory

136 letter fragments restored with the gaps filled. Once filled with paint or gold.

112. La Turbie: reconstruction of the monument; the inscription listed all the Gallic tribes now pacified by Augustus.

in 154, but there survives no mention of the name Monaco in any account of them. The other source of written evidence is epigraphical. As one would expect, quite a few inscriptions have come to light, but they all are of Roman date and throw light on a later period of history than that encompassed by this book.[53]

193

11

The Celtic Neighbours

Any account of the native peoples with whom the Greeks, and later Caesar, dealt is liable to be clouded by terminology. It will be best therefore to begin with a short summary of the situation.

The Celts were a people originating in Central Europe who, for our purposes, enter on the stage around 750 BC. Their culture is divided into two periods, the first being the Hallstatt culture, drawing its name from a site near Salzburg, in Austria; this lasted approximately from 750 BC till 500. Around 750 these Hallstatt-Celts arrived in what is now France, and were soon well established in Provence.[1] We are now in the Iron Age, which in Provence began around 900 BC. The Celts entered on their second phrase, the La Tène culture (named from a site near Lake Neuchâtel, in Switzerland), which ran from 500 till the beginning of the Christian era, when submersion in the Roman Empire rendered all such distinctions academic.

We turn to the Ligurians. This was the general name given by the Greeks in the sixth century and later to the native inhabitants of the Côte d'Azur and Provence (the local tribe settled around Massalia being known as the Salyii). As such, it is often the term used by ancient sources when speaking of peoples whom we would instinctively refer to as Celts or Gauls. They do not give them a good press. Described even by Benoit as 'la "Barbarie" Ligure', its inhabitants are represented as wild hill-billies who spent most of their lives scratching out a precarious existence from a harsh and stony land, and from time to time relaxing only in the most soul-revolting social customs, to be recorded by the civilised in tones of incredulous stupefaction.[2]

This leaves us with the Gauls. The name seems to come into use around the third century, and is applied in general to the inhabitants of modern France. Indeed, in many books it is employed more or less interchangeably with 'the Celts', referring – where there is any difference at all, which often there is not – to the same people, in one of their later periods. In this book I have generally referred to Celts rather than Gauls, for though I am not sure I can always achieve accuracy I can at least aim at consistency. Roman sources, or sources of Roman date, naturally always speak of the Gauls, and that is the name that subsequently stuck and so became familiar to us. The Gauls who in 390 invaded Rome and in 279 took Delphi were, strictly speaking by our rules, La Tène Celts, but that is not what the Romans called them. Indeed, the Gauls at one time or another went on the rampage through a good deal of Europe, getting even as far as Asia Minor, where some of them settled permanently. The Greek for Gauls being 'Galatai', they became locally known as Galatians, under which title St. Paul addressed to them his celebrated epistle.[3]

To the reader all this may well sound somewhat confusing, but it need not be so. The distinctions are real, but not relevant to our purpose. This book is about the Greeks, not the Gauls, and to the Greeks the Gauls were all more or less the same: they were the natives they had to deal and trade with, starting not very far from the comforting presence of Massalia's walls. And when Rome was invaded in 390 the Romans did not take time to determine whether their unwelcome visitors were of the Hallstatt or the La Tène variety. Gauls were Gauls, and that was that. And though in other works on the subject the reader may come across different names for even the same Celtic or Gallic peoples, this should not be too great a source of worry or confusion. I have, in this book, normally used the term 'Celts', save in special cases where I felt it inappropriate. Let us now turn to this Celtic – Gallic – Ligurian – indigenous[4] population that surrounded the Greek colonists.

The civilisation of the oppida

In our period, the Celts, or at least those of them with whom the Greek colonists were in contact, mostly lived in *oppida*. *Oppidum* is a recognised archaeological term for a type of Celtic settlement of this period,[5] and usually took the form of a fortified encampment on a defensible hilltop. Later on, with the coming of the Pax Romana and its tranquil prosperity, these hilltop *oppida* were generally abandoned and their inhabitants descended to found in the plains below a new settlement less defensible but more accessible; with the fall of the Roman Empire the position was then reversed and they went back up into the hills again. On the *oppida* one can no more generalise than one can on towns and cities, but some remarks may be relevant. Some of them we should perhaps call villages rather than towns. Some were sanctuaries and towns combined. And some were fortified strong points, chosen because they controlled the routes through some valley or pass. In this regard, a particularly common plan was a rocky projecting spur, protected on three sides by cliffs, and on the fourth, the normal approach, by fortification and circuit walls, forming a veritable acropolis. These *oppida* are extremely numerous, often no more than 10 km or so apart, and given the probable density of the population, some of them must have ranked as what we would call villages rather than towns proper. There is much that we do not know about the Celts, for they left no written records, and it may well be that even in Celtic the *oppida* had no recognised names, though of course the various tribes did, and their habitations may have been known locally as 'the Segobriges' village', or something of the sort. Be that as it may, we do not know the native name

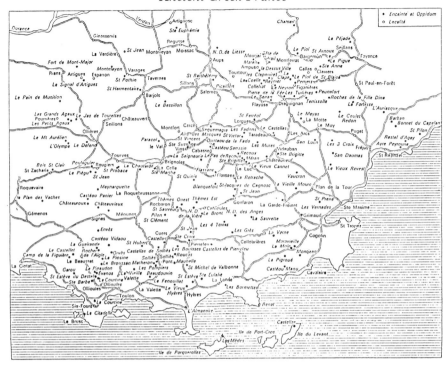

113. Celtic *oppida* in the Var, from La Ciotat to St. Raphael.

for any of these *oppida* (whereas we can often at least guess at what the Greeks or Romans called their foundations), and they are always referred to nowadays by the name of some modern local feature: thus in the scholarly publications the Celtic *oppida* always have modern French names, while classical sites may be mentioned by their Latin or Greek name.[6]

There can be no general description of the *oppida*, universally applicable, for, as one would expect, they are far from uniform. Yet a few comments may be helpful. That they were numerous has just been mentioned, but not quite how numerous. In fact, over 750 of them have been identified in the regions of the Var, Alpes-Maritimes, and Gard alone, though some of these enjoyed only a short existence and few have been actually excavated (probably the commonest means of identification being air photography). In size, they cover from 3 to 20 acres (1-8 hectares) and date from the sixth century BC (and even earlier) down to the Roman era. Some, including Ambrussum, Nages, and Entremont, three of the most important, were founded only in the fourth-third centuries, and quite a few new ones were still being built even in the first century BC. The most striking feature that the *oppida* exhibit is their fortification walls. Not only were these often stone-built, instead of the rough wooden stockades one might expect, but they often demonstrate a high level of sophisticated military architecture, with the curtain walls reinforced at frequent intervals (7-15 m) by projecting towers, their plan usually being not square but rounded, as in the best Hellenistic models. The ramparts were stone-faced, with a core of earth or gravel, though Caesar describes a type (the *murus gallicus*) strengthened by an internal framework of roughly cut beams creating a half-timbered effect. The best known examples are at Entremont, Constantine, Ambrussum, and Nages, but doubtless there were many others. The masonry differs from Greek practice in that it is built up of roughly trimmed and coursed small stones rather than large cut ashlar blocks (though some fine Greek-style ashlar work is to be found in the towers of the *oppidum* Mauressip (Gard, near Nîmes)). The defences also feature such tactical refinements as posterns, sallyports and ditches.

Inside, the houses run the gamut from single-room shacks to more highly evolved plans with an interior partitioned into several rooms, reflecting the traditions of Mediterranean societies. Walls were of stone or mud brick, and a quadrangular ground plan came to prevail over the earlier curvilinear format, doubtless caused by the increasing use of stone. Posts sometimes were installed to support the roof, thatch or tiles. Economic specialisation is indicated by the occasional presence of oil presses or blacksmith's tools, permitting the identification of shops and forges. Streets, usually of beaten earth, were sometimes (as at Ambrussum) paved, and, in the more developed *oppida*, might be laid out on a grid plan (as at Entremont). They do not seem to have had any monumental centre or public buildings, and the greatest expression of communal pride and identity is to be found in the city walls and ramparts themselves, which of course were to be seen as a public exaltation of the warlike valour that, hopefully, was the chief virtue and characteristic of the inhabitants. That they also had a practical value is attested by the large numbers of ballista-balls and sling-stones often found alongside them, relics of various assaults and sieges.[7]

Principal *oppidum* sites

Entremont

It seems reasonable at this point to comment individually on some of the leading *oppida*, not perhaps those most prominent in Celtic civilisation as a whole but those with which the Massaliots came into closest contact. First must come Entremont, the Salyii's capital. This is a large site, a veritable city, and it is to be found in the northern suburbs of Aix-en-Provence, just off the highway RN7.[8] In shape it is a triangular plateau, protected by cliffs on the south-west and south-east sides, while the long and more vulnerable north side is heavily fortified. The defences take the form of a stone-faced rampart 3 m thick, with rubble core, preserved to a height of 4.5 m. At 20 m intervals are a series of projecting towers, roughly

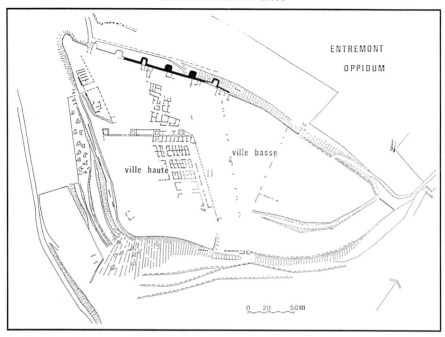

114. Entremont: site plan. The city of Aix-en-Provence lies 1 km to the south.

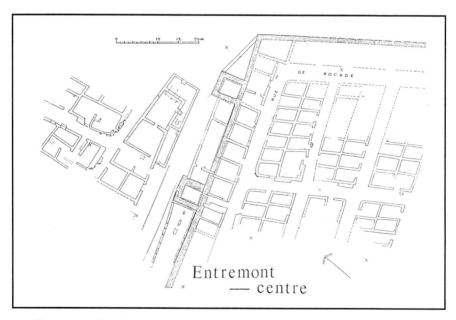

115. Entremont: plan of centre (upper town).

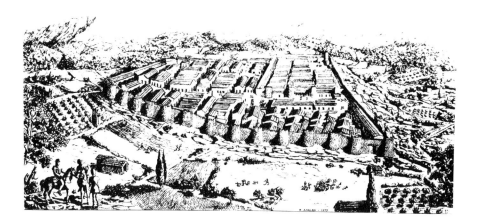

116. Entremont: reconstruction of the Celtic settlement.

117. Entremont: curtain wall and rounded towers.

rectangular but with curved corners giving them a rounded appearance. They are to be compared with the rounded towers of Nages, Constantine, and Ambrussum, and probably reflect Greek influence.

The city inside the walls is divided into two sections: the Upper Town and the Lower Town,[9] alternatively designated Habitat 1 and Habitat 2. The Upper Town was originally interpreted by Benoit, the excavator, as a kind of sacred/aristocratic compound, reserved for a priestly élite of warriors, while the Lower Town was occupied by the less prestigious commercial and agricultural classes, but this no longer seems to have been the case. It now seems that the Upper Town was the original foundation, dated to around 180-170 BC, and the Lower Town was a subsequent expansion, around 150-140. The expansion left a section of the Upper Town's original walls now enclosed within the expanded city and no longer fulfilling any useful military function; instead, the space between two of its projecting towers (four are identifiable) was now adapted to serve as a portico or stoa.

The most striking feature of the city, however, is the organised regularity of its street and house planning. One must completely set aside any preconceptions based on random agglomerations of primitive huts. This is a city laid out on a grid plan, with uniform blocks and cross-streets, closely resembling the Greek Hippodamian system, but with the orientation slightly skewed, resulting in blocks that are parallelograms rather than rectangles: this slanted plan is designed to accommodate the exigencies of the site, and its rationalised standardisation is particularly noticeable within the confines of the (earlier) Upper Town, or Habitat 1. The streets are paved with cobblestones, and ruts attest to their use by carts. By ancient standards, they are broad, and at the intersections the corners of

118. Entremont: houses of upper town.

119. Entremont: houses of upper town.

the buildings are curved, possibly to facilitate the passage of wheeled vehicles making the turn. All this, of course, implies a high degree of sophisticated planning. The houses, though not completely uniform, are not far off it, each block being divided up into two rows, back to back, each of six or seven narrow compartments. Most of them are single-room dwellings, for sophistication has not in general got as far as partitioning and internal subdivision. The Lower Town is later in date, and there one sees a good deal more flexibility in the use of space. The blocks are about twice as large, as are also the individual houses, now subdivided into two or three connecting rooms. There was probably also an upper storey, the ground floor being used as a workshop or storeroom for cattle and farm produce, a practice common in primitive building and still far from unknown today. The small finds also show evidence of commercial and industrial activity, such as weaving, metallurgy, olive presses, glassworking, milling, and baking. Extensive finds of Massaliot coins, amphorae, and imported fine pottery indicate a extensive trade with Massalia.

The obvious question is, whence did the Salyii derive this rational and organised town-planning, and the obvious answer is that it is a demonstration of Greek influence. Of the Greek colonies, Massalia was the closest, but little is known of its archaic street plan. Olbia, with its rigid grid-pattern, offers a much more plausible model, but this is far from certain, and Entremont may well reflect rather an independent native development, little influenced by outside sources.[10]

201

Celtic religion seems in general to have been celebrated in the open air, and usually in the woods, under the auspices of druids and the like, so we must not be surprised at the absence from Entremont of temples or other ecclesiastical monuments. However, a portico in the middle of the town does seem to have been set up as a kind of war memorial or sanctuary dedicated to dead local heroes, their prowess proudly commemorated by representations of those whom they had slain, in the form of decapitated heads adorning the monument. This was a traditional practice, fondly loved by the Celts, to which we shall return in a more general account of their society (p. 210 below).

Ensérune

Ensérune is 14 km south-west of Béziers, and about 40 km inland from the port of Agde, which in antiquity must have been its main supply route though it also commands the main east-west overland route, later developed by the Romans as the Via Domitia to Spain. The site is an unusual one, occupying the crest of a long ridge overlooking, somewhat precipitously, the plain on either side. The town thus becomes an elongated, narrow strip, an example almost of ribbon development rather than the more usual globular layout. Occupation began around the sixth century, but it was not until Ensérune II (c. 425-220 BC) that we see evidence of organised urbanism, with stone-built houses laid out on a grid-plan. On destruction of this city (by Hannibal as he passed through *en route* to Italy?), the site was immediately rebuilt and reoccupied as Ensérune III, which lasted until it too was destroyed, around 100 BC.

Given the exigencies of the terrain, the houses were arranged in *insulae*, blocks of unusual form, long strips of row or terrace housing, each containing up to a dozen or so houses, served by a road running along one side. Though architecturally unimpressive, by the standards of, say, Glanum, they adopted such sophistications as tiled roofs, stucco, and waterproof cement, and there are several examples of interior stone columns, complete with a rudimentary capital (possibly inspired by Ionic?).[11] Another noteworthy characteristic is the frequent use of silos and

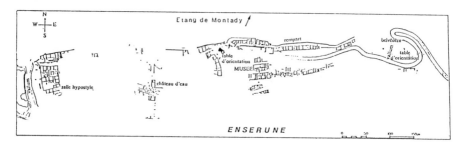

120. Ensérune: plan of site.

121. Ensérune: Hellenistic-type house and, beyond, the dartboard-shaped marsh of Montady.

122. Ensérune: houses.

203

cisterns, for the storage respectively of grain and rainwater – often, not knowing what any particular one contained, we cannot tell which we are dealing with. In shape they are often tall and narrow, and sunk into the floor or ground ('bottle cisterns'), but we also find two, lined with ashlar masonry, that are oblong with rounded ends and two square internal piers to support the covering. This type of cistern has many parallels at Ampurias, though probably of Roman date.[12] In some of the houses the subterranean cisterns and silos are replaced by *dolia*, large storage jars. There was also on the site of a fresh-water spring, today called the 'Agoutis', and still flowing, but it is questionable if this was adequate for the needs of Ensérune III, necessitating the construction of a terrace near the centre of the town a network of some forty-five interconnecting cisterns with a total capacity of around a million litres.

Inscriptions, in the form of graffiti,[13] show that the language spoken at Ensérune was Iberian, a tongue commonly found in Catalonia and Roussillon, and apparently persisting at Ensérune even after the eventual Roman conquest. Commercial relations with Greece and Campania, either direct or via Massalia, were evidently close and extensive, judging by pottery finds, and the city formed a natural centre for trade exchanges between the Mediterranean, and the Cevennes and the interior of Gaul, a Celtic version of the similar but Hellenic role played by Agde.[14]

Before leaving Ensérune we may also note the most spectacular feature of the whole locality, even though it is of mediaeval, not classical, date. This is the large circular marsh of Montady, of which Ensérune offers a superb panoramic view on the north side. The marsh (or étang) was drained in 1248 by the archbishop of Narbonne and the reclaimed land divided up into numerous segments like slices of a pie, giving the whole a very eye-catching resemblance (which it still retains) to an enormous dart-board. This forms a very prominent backdrop to many views of the site, and once seen is entirely unmistakable.

Nages

Nages is a site explored fairly recently, first published in 1962 and located 16 km west of Nîmes.[15] The site is a large one, measuring around 400 x 200 m, and is in the form of a barred spur, i.e. a projecting height protected on three sides by precipitous slopes and with the fourth one, the normal direction of access, heavily fortified. This was an arrangement often favoured by the Celts, and the reader will note the parallels with Entremont. After a first and very primitive settlement, Nages II was founded around 230 BC; it in turn was partly destroyed around 120-100 BC, and replaced by Nages III, which lasted until it was abandoned in the Augustan era, around 10 AD. Perhaps the most noteworthy feature of Nages II is its massive ramparts, preserved in places to a height of over 4 m, and in places up to an incredible 7 m thick, stone faced with an earth and rubble core. At intervals along the walls is a series of equally massive towers, of the rounded configuration that we meet also at Entremont, Ambrussum, and Constantine: an especially impressive pair flank the main gateway.

Inside, the city is laid out on a grid plan, the houses being of dry stone construction. The roadways were of generous width, some 5 m, but when under Nages III, the size and number of the houses was greatly increased (and, presumably, the total population), part of the extra space needed for the expansion was found by cutting the width of the streets in half, to 2.5 m. A temple, presumably under Roman influence, was constructed around 70 BC, but, as the excavator has put it, 'the actual civilisation of the third city was Gallo-Greek'.[16]

Ambrussum

Ambrussum is a way station on the Via Domitia, and is mentioned in the Peutinger Table.[17] It is between Nîmes and Montpellier, near the small town of Lunel and located on a minor road from the village of Villetelle. For the Roman road, it was a crossing point on the River Vidourle, spanned by a bridge of impressive dimensions, of which one massive arch and several piers survive. On the banks of the river is the Lower Town, a complex of Roman date, and overlooking it a raised triangular plateau carrying the Celtic *oppidum*, which has been only partly excavated and cleared. Its main features are the ramparts, which are very much on the Entremont/Nages model, with rounded towers every 10 m or so. A rather more striking feature is the excellence of the paved streets through the

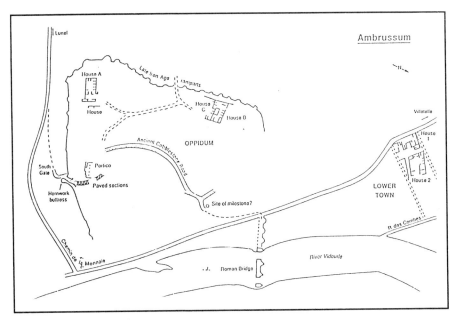

123. Ambrussum: site plan.

124. Ambrussum: paved roadway.

125. Ambrussum: paved roadway, showing Y-junction and grooves for wheels of carts.

126. Ambrussum: curtain wall and rounded towers (compare Fig. 117).

town, which are up to Roman-road standard, though paved with small, closely-packed elongated stones rather than the polygonal basalt blocks traditional in Roman road construction. Continuous grooves or ruts have been carved in the surface to accommodate the wheels of vehicles and keep them on course; alternatively, they may have been worn there by simple wear and tear of frequent passage, but they seem to me to be much too regular not to be artificial and deliberate. In the orientation of the streets there seems to be no attempt at a grid plan.

Other sites

There are far too many Celtic *oppida* in the region, running into the hundreds, to be individually mentioned, but we may perhaps briefly note some the more prominent ones in the immediate vicinity of Massalia, with which the Greeks might be expected to be in close contact. *Constantine* overlooks the north shore of the Étang de Berre, 1 km north-west of the Chateau Calissanne on the D10 road, and is noteworthy principally for its ramparts, a 300 m stretch of which survives, with rounded towers of the same type we have met at Entremont, Nages, and Ambrussum. It derives its name from the homonymous Roman emperor, a golden statue of whom is reputedly buried somewhere around. *Roquepertuse*, on the D20 near Velaux, between Aix-en-Provence and Rognac, has no remains still visible on the site, and is known chiefly for various Celtic sculptures, notably the 'têtes coupées' portico, to be discussed below (p. 212). We may also mention in passing *Les Pennes-La Cloche* (with foundations of a number of houses, this time not on a grid-plan), and *Le Baou-Roux* (at Bouc-Bell-Air); both are in the outer suburbs of modern Marseille, along the main road to Aix,[18] while at Martigues (at the sea entrance of the Étang de Berre), evidence of habitation from the eighth century on is found on the island that forms the centre of the modern town. The site carries some primitive Celtic huts, preserved and restored as a museum behind glass.

Celtic society

The standard view in antiquity was that the Gauls (i.e. Celts) were barbarians, and the worst of them were the Ligurians, who were so repulsive as to make the rest look civilised by comparison. No horror was too dreadful to be attributed to them and Liguria as a region was so ghastly, and its inhabitants so frightful, that even armies avoided going there; the French historian Papon, writing, be it noted in 1777, thought them on the same level of culture as the Americans.[19] We need not emphasise the obvious, that this picture, even if it preserves a substratum of fact that acquits it of total falsity, is wildly exaggerated. It comes about partly from the superior civilisation of the Greek colonists, at least as viewed through their own eyes, though modern anthropologists might not support the moral judgement implied. And the Romans, in matters of culture, were happy to take the Greeks at their own evaluation of themselves, so that Roman sources also re-echo admiringly the tenacious gallantry of the civilised Massaliots holding at bay on their frontiers the brutalised hordes of darkness.[20] Moreover, the Ligurians had a long history of brigandage and piracy,[21] which naturally got them a bad press from a trading state like Massalia.

Still, there is no denying that the Ligurians lived a rough and hard life in a harsh environment. Diodorus sees them as troglodytes, living in caves rather than huts or cabins, and Strabo retails from Poseidonios a story of a pregnant Ligurian woman, working on a farm for a Massaliot employer, who took a short break in a corner of the field to deliver her baby and immediately returned to work so as not to lose her day's pay.[22] Against this depressing picture, however, we must remember to set the developed urbanism already noted at Entremont and similar sites.

Politically, Celtic society was tribal, under the rule of local chieftains, and though relatively large groups may share a common name or identity, such as the Salyii or the Arverni, one cannot assume that they always acted with a coherent and cohesive unity, just as it is equally plain, as in the migration of the Helvetii, that sometimes they really did. But essentially it was a civilisation of tribal chieftains, such as Caesar found when he invaded Gaul. Economically, Gaul was rich, or at least potentially so. Most of it was open rolling country, fertile and readily arable, with no equivalent to the Alps, or even the Italian Apennines, nor yet to the dank Teutonic depths of the Black Forest in which Varus lost his legions. Socially, the Celts impressed the Greeks and Romans with their unstable exuberance, dancing and singing one minute and slaughtering each other the next.[23] Indeed, the national recreation seems to have been drinking, and the national sport, fighting. Religion was largely in the hands of the Druids, though at the principal ceremonies Bards, singing sacred hymns, and Soothsayers (*vates*) were also in honoured presence.[24] The Druids also acted as judges, and were believed to be learned in moral philosophy, maintaining that the soul was indestructible and returned to earth in another body (i.e. metempsychosis). Worship was particularly directed to two main targets. One was nature, itself subdivided into two principal manifestations. The first was water, and cults of aquatic divinities were firmly established at various springs. The best known is perhaps that at Nemausus (Nîmes), celebrated for its fountains long before the arrival of the colonising Romans, and even drawing its name from the eponymous local deity of the spring, but one finds a similar situation at Glanum, Uzès (source of the water supply for Nîmes), and many other locations. The second was mountains, the cult usually bring established on the very peak. The most celebrated example was the summit of the great massif of Mont Ventoux, near Carpentras, where dedications have been found to the divinity Vintur, a name also known from other sites in the Luberon area. As with the springs, many of these cults were perpetuated into the Roman era, sometimes under the same name. Another common Celtic cult was that of 'The Mothers', sometimes linked to the classical worship of the Dioscouroi,[25] but in general the religious practices of the Greeks seem to have had very little influence on the Celts.[26]

The other object of ritual devotions was death. Human sacrifice was part of their religion, sometimes allied to divination – a favourite method was to stab the designated victim in the back and then to draw auguries from the writhings of the dying body.[27] Cremation was at this time the rule in Celtic Provence, and vases and other artefacts were often interred with the ashes of the deceased as grave offerings in the tomb. The form of the grave itself varied from place to place, often taking the form of a small chamber or cist with a stele or headstone, though the superb burial chamber of the Celtic princess at Mont Lassois, near Chatillon-sur-Seine, containing the enormous Vix krater, should remind us that more ambitiously splendid arrangements are not to be ruled out. But there was one aspect of this cult that made an enormous impression on the Greco-Roman settlers, and deserves special attention. This was the 'têtes coupées', the decapitated heads.

The ritual probably originated in the Celtic practice of decapitating enemies slain on the field of battle, much as American Indians reputedly did with scalps, and carrying the severed head, or heads, around with them, partly as a public celebration of their martial prowess, and partly,

127. Entremont: Celtic sculpture of 'têtes coupées' (decapitated heads), re-used as threshold block.

210

as Voltaire would doubtless have put it, 'pour décourager les autres'. When they went home, the heads were nailed up around the doorway, there to stay indefinitely as a sort of private war memorial. The custom was deeply ingrained in the Celts, who would not only take pride in showing to visitors their collection of heads, but so prized them that they would not sell them even for their weight in gold.[28] There is also archaeological evidence for this practice. Skulls have been found with holes pierced to receive the nails; sometimes they were held in place by an iron ring around them. Nor were these ornaments to be found only on private houses. Excavation has showed that a display of skulls decorated the main gate of the Celtic oppidum of La Cloche, at Pennes-Mirabeau, only a few kilometres out of Massalia. The Greek settlers, particularly traders, must have been quite used to seeing them, almost as it were, on their doorstep, and one might wonder what was their reaction to it – except that we do not have to wonder, for we have been clearly told: Poseidonios, who lived there, says at first he loathed it, but afterwards he got quite used to it and it no longer worried him.[29] From the Celtic site of Roquepertuse (p. 208 above) comes a stone portico of two pillars and a lintel with a number or niches carved in it. The niches were mostly occupied by skulls, though a few were left vacant, presumably in a macabre anticipation of the modern advertising gimmick, 'Watch this space'.[30] The love of 'têtes coupées' was also reflected in sculpture. Celtic sites often feature sculptured effigies of the local dead, presumably as memorials to deceased heroes and warriors, though a well-known statue from Entremont (Fig. 129) shows a chieftain apparently still alive but exhibiting, with calm pride, a heap of no less than six severed heads piled up in his lap. Individual bas reliefs also show arrays of heads and faces; the dead, which are numerous, can be distinguished from the living by the Celtic sculptural convention which represents the faces of the dead with the eyes closed.[31]

Other features of Celtic society need not detain us, for they are outside the scope of this book. There is one exception, however, for it closely affected the relations of the Greek colonists and their native neighbours in a way that we do not find in other lands settled by the Greeks. This is the wine trade. We have already emphasised its importance in the Greek context (p. 117 above). We must now consider how it operated among the Celts.

The Celts (or Gauls) were famous in antiquity for their drinking.[32] By tradition their national beverage was beer,[33] but once the Greeks arrived, bringing with them their own national beverage, wine, the Celts were not slow to take advantage of it. Unlike the Greeks and Romans, they drank the wine straight, unmixed with water. One is tempted to say that they knew a good thing when they saw it, but the practice aroused the condescending scorn of the Greeks and Romans, who considered such unbridled self-indulgence fit only for barbarians.[34] The picture of Celtic alcoholic excesses, as painted by our ancient sources, notably Diodorus Siculus, is an intriguing one. The Celts regularly drank themselves under the table,

128. Celtic portico from Roquepertuse (near Aix), featuring niches to accommodate skulls.

and ended up either fighting or flat out. They would do anything to get drink, and one can hardly avoid the speculation that some of them, at least, were, in a proper clinical and medical sense, alcoholics. Certainly Diodorus thought that, in the absence of wine, they would hurl themselves upon any liquid with remotely alcoholic connections, however fanciful, even to the water used to wash out honeycombs. And the Nervii, who lived in the Pas de Calais, in a remarkable anticipation of American prohibition,

212

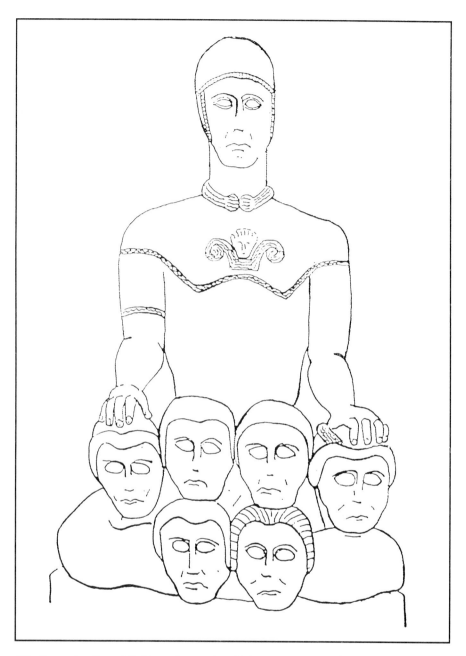

129. Reconstruction of Celtic sculpture, in which a warrior proudly exhibits the severed heads of six of his adversaries; the reconstruction seems quite certainly accurate.

actually banned all alcohol from their territory, and that explicitly on moral grounds, because of its bad effects on society.[35]

We have already noted that wine soon because well established among the Celts as a chieftain's drink, while the ordinary clansmen contented themselves with beer and herbal infusions. This seems only to have given it an added cachet or prestige. True, wine was expensive, but Gaul was not, by Greco-Roman standards, a poor country, nor was it short of a multitude of chieftains who would feel they had to buy it. Any self-respecting princeling would have to keep a supply on hand to serve to his guests, for if he did not it would be seen as a reflection not just on himself, but on his tribe and his people, which would be much worse. Because of this, wine was always surrounded by an aura of glamour, and, as Dion well put it, you 'honoured it with a splendid presentation'.[36] This meant not only wine of high quality (though at least some of the Gauls may not have been able to tell the difference, particularly as the evening advanced), but it was served with the finest imported vases and all associated paraphernalia. This has never been so well illustrated as by the magnificence of the famous Vix burial.[37] The enormous Vix krater has been much discussed as an item of trade and a work of art, but little consideration has been paid to what it was to be used for.

The first thing to note is that the Vix krater was unnecessary and grossly impractical. It was unnecessary because, since the Celts did not mix their wine (and probably looked down on anyone who did as unmanly), no krater was needed at all; and anyway it is the wrong shape to be a mixing bowl. It was impractical because of its enormous size. With a weight of 208 kg empty and requiring very careful handling because of its fragility – the sidewalls are eggshell-thin, only 1 mm thick – it would take several men to move it. Its capacity is 1,100 litres,[38] and since a litre of wine weighs, very approximately, 1 kg, the krater, when full, would be entirely immovable, with a weight of 1,300 kg. If you did try to move it, very probably the handles would tear off.

The second objection arises when we consider the Vix krater, as it were, in action. It was presumably intended for use at feasts, where the entire contents would be consumed at one sitting – it is hardly a suitable vessel for keeping leftovers standing around for several days, getting lower down and harder to reach every day, with no tap at the bottom. And even a single grand feast presents logistical problems. Reckoning consumption at one litre per man (probably reasonable for men who, whatever their appetite, did not drink wine regularly), that means a guest list of up to 1,000. The reader is now invited to envisage one thousand thirsty and drunken Celts around the Vix krater, all trying to get at it at once. This, of course, is precisely why today at large receptions there are usually a number of bars or punch bowls, to facilitate service and avoid bottlenecks, and one is tempted to wonder whether the Vix krater became a burial offering exactly because it offered a heaven-sent opportunity to get rid of a magnificent but useless white elephant.

But all this is no more than a half-truth. The reality is that the krater had an honoured place in the regalia of the ruling house of Vix and was in itself a splendid celebration of the god Dionysos in his liquid incarnation, to say nothing of a visible expression of some of the things its owners thought made life most worth living. Impractical or not, it stands as a proud acknowledgement of the honoured place held by wine in their scale of values and priorities, and hence of the wine trade with Massalia. Wine was, indeed, as Benoit says, 'la monnaie d'échange la plus appréciée'.[39]

From the combination of the Vix krater and Diodorus' comments on Celtic drunkenness we may make various observations. First, the volume of wine imported into Celtic Gaul must indeed have been enormous, fully supporting the archaeological evidence of the multiplicity of amphorae found at places like Toulouse (p. 119 above). Imports into Vix alone must have been substantial if the krater was to be used anything like regularly. It contained 1,100 litres and an amphora 20-30, so it would take 40 or so amphorae to fill it once; and they all probably had to come from distant Campania, and via Massalia. And how many more Vixes were there in the country, that we do not know about? Second, there was (p. 117 above) a close relationship with the slave trade. It was the slaves that paid for the wine. Third, wine, unlike tin or salt, was a luxury product and after so long a journey from it source was doubtless very expensive, yet the Celts, it seems, simply had to have it: it was an assured market. Fourth, a trader selling his wine would presumably lavish upon his customers copious samples of his merchandise ('what you taste is what you get'), and it would be a poor businessman indeed who could not get a good price selling alcohol to an alcoholic whom he had actually got drunk at the time of sale. This puts wine sales on to a completely different footing from any other commercial exchanges, and if they were even half-way competent at their craft the Massaliot and other Greek salesmen should have soon realised that they were on to a gold mine. Presumably this is one of the things the Nervii were objecting to when they introduced prohibition.[40]

Hellenisation of the Celts

The extent to which the Celts were 'civilised' by the influence of Massalia has been much discussed. The distinguished historian of Provence, Fernand Benoit, devoted an entire book to it, appropriately entitled *Recherches sur l'hellénsation du Midi de la Gaule*, and there have been other studies. More recently a volume of studies on the subject 'Marseille et la Gaule' has concluded with the observation that the term 'Hellenisation' is out of favour, and even 'acculturation' is avoided. Presumably it is even more politically unacceptable to speak of 'civilising' the native Celts, on the grounds that that would be disrespectful to their indigenous culture, so it is not easy to find a word to describe what the Massaliots did to them.[41]

Archaeological work on the question has chiefly taken the form of studies, often very long and detailed, of ceramic fragments, reflecting trade patterns. Though a valuable approach and often, in the absence of written records, the only one possible, such studies are to the non-specialist rarely attractive or even comprehensible. An alternative approach is philological: does Provençal retain linguistic elements taken over from the Greek of the settlers, thereby demonstrating a hellenising penetration? This controversy, once waged with zeal and dedication, seems to be no longer a serious issue. The arguments were that many words in Provençal resembled something in Greek meaning the same thing. The basis was one of vocabulary, not grammar, and concentrated on place-names; also on technical terms in fishing, seafaring, and viticulture, arts presumed to be unknown to the native Celts and passed on to them by the Greek colonists. The counter-argument is that such resemblances are fortuitous, and are to be seen merely as 'faux Grec', from which no historical inferences can be drawn.[42] What is absolutely clear, on the other hand, is the spread of the Greek alphabet. Apart from Greek colonies on the coast, full-scale inscriptions in Greek language are rare, but the use of the Greek alphabet by the Celts for writing things in Celtic rapidly became very common.[43] Often it was no more than grave stelai, on which the names of recognisably Celtic personages were inscribed, so that they may reasonably be called Gallo-Greek inscriptions. Strabo, indeed, specifically says that the Gauls (i.e., Celts) wrote their contracts *hellenisti*, which most commentators have taken to mean that they wrote them 'in Greek', though it has been objected that this might mean 'in Greek letters' though not necessarily in the Greek tongue, or even 'after the Greek fashion'.[44]

Moreover, when Caesar, campaigning among the Nervii, wanted to send a letter to his lieutenant Q. Cicero, he wrote it in 'Greek script', 'litteris Graecis', as a security measure to stop the Gauls reading it. On the other hand, Caesar also tells us that when in 58 BC the Roman army invaded the land of the Helvetii they found tablets written in Greek script that evidently formed a kind of census roll for purposes of military service, and that the Druids of Gaul used Greek script for their public and private accounts, even if one in particular, the Druid Diviciacus, evidently knew no spoken Greek since he had to use an interpreter for his interview with Caesar.[45] It will thus be seen that the evidence for Greek linguistic penetration of Gaul is not entirely clear, nor presumably, was it uniform: one would expect a great deal more Greek towards the south of Gaul than in the lands of the Nervii, alongside the English Channel. Nor does official use of Greek by the Druids presuppose a colloquial fluency in it – there must be many modern Catholic priests who, while celebrating the Tridentine Mass every Sunday, would not feel comfortable sustaining a conversation in Latin. And there may have been many people, Celts and Romans alike, who knew a phrase or two of Greek for conventional salutations, but nothing more, just as we should not assume that an Englishman is fluent in French because he says 'Au revoir!' We must also remember that the Massaliots did reciprocate. Our evidence comes from a much later period, the Late Roman Empire, but at that date, we are assured, Massalia was a tri-lingual community, with Greek, Latin, and Celtic all in regular use.[46]

A further potent element in the influence exerted over the Celts by the Massaliots was coinage. The Massaliots, and other Greek colonies, did, of course, strike coins themselves, but quite apart from that there were other coins that, from around the late fourth century BC on, came into wide circulation in Celtic Gaul. The model was the Philippeios, the standard coin issued by Philip of Macedon, carrying as types the head of Apollo and, on the reverse, a two-horse chariot, with Philip's name in the exergue beneath it. The number of these coins produced was colossal, and their area of circulation vast – hoards have been found in Greece, Russia, near Constantinople, Turkey, Cyprus, Syria, Egypt, South Italy, Sicily, and Gaul. Not only did the Celts seize eagerly upon them when, presumably through the agency of Massalia, they became available, but they set about minting their own imitations of them, going even so far as imitating the imitations, resulting in a whole series of coins in which the progressive deterioration of the artwork culminates in a representation of the Apollo and the chariot of the original types that cannot really be called anything but an abstract, so unrecognisable is it.[47]

The normal metal of this coinage was gold, rather than the silver and bronze of Greek cities, and this fitted well with Celtic familiarity with that metal. Naturally, such coins were only used for major transactions, or as hoarded capital. A further remarkable example of Greek influence is to be found much later, in the Roman period, in some of the low-value bronze coins issued by Celtic peoples along the coast of Languedoc which not only imitated established Greek types, with legends in Greek script, but sometimes carried the Greek title *basileus*, 'king', applied to the local Celtic chieftain.[48]

We thus see that the Hellenising influence on the Celts was largely commercial, as one would expect. It seems to have brought no political change, for those who profited from it were mainly the chieftains. For them, Massaliot commerce and the good things that it brought were in general welcome and, with one or two exceptions that we have noted, there seem to have been few Greek-Celtic conflicts. The Greek contacts did not lead to any democratisation of the Celtic tribes, for, after all, the demos seems to have been something of a dead letter even at Massalia itself. There was plain influence in architecture, both in the ramparts and the domestic insulae of places like Entremont, to say nothing of the reproduced classical capitals of Ensérune and the Delos-style villas of Glanum, though we must remember that this went hand in hand with such typically Celtic celebrations as the severed heads decorating the main gate of La Cloche (p. 211 above). In religion, Heracles was always popular, and Aphrodite, apart from her imported cult as maintained by the Greeks, evidently blossomed forth as 'Aphrodite of the Pyrenees', in a sanctuary, marking the frontier between Gaul and Spain; otherwise the Celts seem to have escaped Greek religious influence.[49] In writing, they adopted the

Greek script, *faute de mieux*, for though an Iberian script (half-way between a syllabary and an alphabet proper) did exist, it never caught on much beyond south-west Languedoc, so that for most Celts the Greek script was the only form of writing they knew. It appears first on objects, inscribed with a proper name, often that of the owner, and later graduates to use in lists and official documents. One presumes that there existed some form of Celtic literature, but it would be purely oral and presumably thus went uninfluenced by Greek literacy. One thinks of the use of Linear B in the Minoan and Mycenaean civilisations and its total lack of impact on, e.g., the Homeric sagas. Finally, we must be careful in accepting various statements in ancient sources emphasising how Massalia civilised Gaul. Many of these date from the Roman period, when Celts and Massaliots alike lived in the same political country, and some, originating in Massalia, were, one suspects, simply exaggerated.[50]

12

Conclusion

We conclude by trying to come to some evaluation of Massalia and the Greek cities of southern France. How important were they? What reputation did they have? What contribution did they make? We have already spelled out in the Introduction (pp. 1-6 above) some of the problems encountered in this search, just as our answers will involve repetition in summary form of some of the points already made, so it will not be too easy; but we must do our best.

In foreign affairs, Massalia was Rome's stout and unswerving ally. In particular, her navy won Roman plaudits as the strong maritime shield guarding Rome's land-bound legions. This may have been overstated and overestimated. It was always useful to a land-based power to have at its disposal a friendly navy, if only to hold in check any enemy navy, but it was not essential. In the last analysis, an army could always beat a navy, in the long run at least, because ancient war galleys were so full of rowers to provide oar-power that they had no storage or living space for their crews. This effectively limited the vessel's range and endurance in a way to which later fleets, such as those of Nelson's day, were not subject. The fleet was thus regularly and frequently dependent on access to its base, so that an army could always control or defeat a fleet simply by capturing all its bases. This was exactly what Alexander the Great did, when, without a single warship of his own, he nevertheless managed to subjugate the entire eastern Mediterranean, easily reducing such sea-powers as the Phoenicians. And, in her imperial days, Rome herself maintained her Empire with a navy that was little more than a glorified coastguard service (for the same reason – she occupied all the land bases); but she never tried to do without an army. So we may guess that while, in her efforts to control the western Mediterranean, Rome certainly had her task much facilitated by the support of the Massaliot fleet, she would, if deprived of it, probably have managed it anyway. And in any case we have reason to doubt whether Massaliot naval prowess was all that it was cracked up to be. Certainly at the end of her independent existence, Massalia's fleet proved a broken reed, raising the twin possibilities that all those war memorials that filled the streets in commemoration of great naval victories reflected nothing more than undignified minor scuffles with pirates, or that a once-great fleet had been run down after the Second Punic War to a very low level in the absence of any outside threat.[1]

219

By land, one again gets the impression that Massalia must have been a priceless ally, planted firmly astride communications with Spain. Here again we may be misled, by modern routes and a glance at the map. In the Roman Republic, routes did not run along the shores of the Côte d'Azur, where the terrain was far too difficult, but inland from Turin over the Montgénèvre pass and thence down the valley of the Durance. The real key point was Arles (Arelate), or perhaps Tarascon, at the crossing of the Rhône, whether by bridge or ferry, whence the route ran on to Nîmes (Nemausus) and Narbonne (Narbo). Massalia was a dead-end in the Roman road system, served by a short spur branching down from Aix-en-Provence, and this remained true even after the opening of the Via Julia along the coast from Genoa and Monaco. East-west communications by road bypassed Massalia, and did not even go through her territory.[2]

On the other hand, Massalia was ideally located as a seaport, and this worked two ways. One was for coasting east-west traffic, which did follow the shoreline, and found Massalia a useful anchorage for a stopover. The other was for seaborne traffic arriving from Greece or Italy and there trans-shipping to riverboat or road to continue up the Rhône Valley to Gaul and northern Europe. Since heavy freight was never carried by road if a waterway was at all possible, this meant that to Rome Massalia was important in economics (in so far as Rome ever took formal official interest in such things) and for individual personal travel, but not militarily, for armies normally marched by road: that's what the Roman roads were built for.[3]

There was also the vital and pervasive role played by Massalia in the dissemination of classical culture throughout the world of the Celts, who, if not assimilated, at least became aware of its existence, thus softening them up for subsequent Romanisation, or, as it has been (perhaps dubiously) phrased, 'civilising the impressionable barbarians'.[4] Apart from general cultural influences, this 'civilising' was conveyed by three main media. One was wine, which, for good or ill, indisputably lent a new dimension to the Celtic way of life (p. 211 above). The second was coinage, a Greek (or perhaps Lydian) invention that must have gone far to revolutionise Celtic trading and the Celtic economy; in Greece itself, given the large-denomination currency in wide circulation,[5] much of it must have been used for savings and major payments, while the small-denomination coins that formed the bulk of Massalia's issue would plainly facilitate local trade with Celtic tribes. The third was the use of the Greek language, and even more, the Greek script which in effect made the Gauls literate. Strabo notes that they wrote contracts and such formal documents in Greek, while Caesar notes that not only did the Helvetii keep their census lists in Greek script, but that Greek was used in accounts, private and public, by the Druids.[6] Of course, they would have found it hard to write in anything else, given that the Celts had no effective script of their own, and Latin had not yet arrived with Romans. But we must not be sarcastic. Roman writers, especially of the later period, do insist on the pervasive and tenacious impregnation of southern Gaul by Greek civilisation and the Greek spirit. Massilia is 'a school for the barbarians', we are told, in words echoing Thucydides' proud boast that Athens was an education to all Greece. The Celts were so transfigured by it that 'it looked as if it were not the Greeks who had emigrated to Gaul, but Gaul that had been transferred and set down in the middle of Greece'. The Gauls were philhellenes, and lived by the Greek way of life, indeed to such an extent that the cartographer who drew up the map of the Roman Empire known as the Peutinger Table, in the age of Theodosius (fourth century AD), marked the region between the Rhône and the Durance with the name 'Gretia', Greece.

To evaluate Massalia from a modern viewpoint is a lot more difficult. How important was Massalia, according to current scholarship? French scholars have done a lot of work on this, but almost entirely centred on one particular aspect of it, the influence of Massalia upon the native Celts of the interior. Since Benoit and earlier, the 'Hellenisation of the south of Gaul' has been the subject of much study, and, at the time of writing, still is. The question is not easily resolved, particularly in view of the shifting data: not only did Massalia develop, socially, economically and otherwise, but so did the Gauls. The picture of inter-relation that obtained in the sixth century was not the same as that in the fourth, nor yet again in the second.[7] But what did the Greeks themselves think, especially during the years of Massalia's greatness? The evidence is minimal, despite Goudineau's favourable verdict,[8] but there is one factor that surely a Greek at least could not have considered very creditable: apparently, according to the list of victors in the Olympic Games compiled by Sextus Julius Africanus, nobody from Massalia ever won anything at Olympia during the entire millennium of the games' existence, 776 BC – 385 AD.[9] Africanus does not list every Olympic victor, in all events. Usually he contents himself with noting the winner of the stadion race, the 200 m sprint, which was the most prestigious event, occasionally adding details of other events when, in that particular year, there was something unusual or memorable about them. So we cannot say that 'nobody from Massalia ever won anything at Olympia', only that nothing of the sort appears in the results listed by Africanus. But this is as good a sample as any, and if Massalia really was a great Greek city one would expect its name to turn up somewhere in the list, alongside entries such as Athens, Sparta, Syracuse and Miletos, to say nothing of relatively minor states such as Croton, Thurii, and Himera that seem to have managed to turn Olympic victories into a kind of recognised and successful domestic industry. Surely Massalia ought to be mentioned in there somewhere. So far as I can see it isn't, and I cannot think that an ancient Greek would be favourably impressed by that absence.

But, apart from its relations with the Celts, what was the reputation, the status of the independent Hellenic Massalia in the ancient world, before the Roman conquest? The chief problem is undoubtedly the absence of any firm primary sources, so that we have to fall back on secondary

221

material. We do not have a single paragraph, let along a complete book, actually written by a Massaliot (unless we count those five Massaliot grave monuments in Athens (p. 3 above)), and, apart from pottery, original material in any form is spread far and wide, and unquestionably thin. Of what there is, I have tried, up to this point, to give a comprehensive survey. But there is really no existing volume of material to put forward bearing on the question that begins this paragraph, no accepted version. But then again, that is not really a reason for trying to avoid answering it, so we will have to do our best. There are two possible approaches. One is to invite the reader, now that he has been given what I hope is a balanced and yet comprehensive, if abridged, overview of the relevant evidence, to form his own judgement, and I would most earnestly encourage the reader to do so. The second is for me to set out what I myself think, and this I will now do.

We must therefore begin with a clear warning. Up to now this book has been based on factual evidence and accepted, or at least published, inter-pretation. This will no longer be true. What follows are my own personal opinions, often guesswork, often perhaps unreliable, and the reader is cordially invited to disbelieve them if he sees fit. But it is better than leaving these pages blank.

Working backwards, I begin with Roman Massilia, for this is the clearest case to answer. There can be no doubt of Massilia's intellectual and cultural supremacy, for far too many educated Romans testify to it, and many of them practised what they preached by either going there or at least sending their children there to be educated. A similar if less emphatic judgement must be passed on the independent Massalia of the closing years of the Republic – less emphatic because some of the leading Roman expatriates there were, like Milo, exiles, whose choice in the matter was somewhat limited, while the extravagant praise of someone like Cicero would carry more weight if he had ever shown signs of wanting to go there, even for a short visit; though, in his defence, it must be admitted that, Pausanias notwithstanding, Romans did not often share our taste for vacations abroad (Greece and perhaps Alexandria excepted) and usually travelled in foreign parts only when so required by some military or administrative responsibility.

We turn to some of the weaknesses of Massalia. We have already noted that while the city was crammed with war memorials, the effectiveness of its navy, on which so much of the city's reputation rested, had by the first century BC declined to a level nothing short of the ludicrous (p. 105 above). Architecturally it was undistinguished. Augustus proverbially found Rome build in brick and rebuilt it in marble, but Massalia plainly had a long way to go before it reached the brick level. Greek domestic architec-ture was admittedly of great simplicity (when the Greeks burned Sardis during the Ionian revolt, it was apparently a place of mud brick and thatched roofs, though a Persian provincial capital), but it does look as if architecture had improved by the end of the Hellenistic period. One looks at the uniformly fine, even luxurious, houses of Delos, and wonders why, in an equally great commercial centre such as Massalia, their counter-parts could be, and regularly were, blown down by a strong wind (p. 238 n. 14). True, there was the Massaliot treasury at Delphi, but treasuries at a Greek national site were not always an index to a city's true importance. Olympia, for example, had treasuries of Sicyon, Gela, and Metaponto, but none of Athens. And one cannot easily dismiss the modern parallel of many poor and underdeveloped countries which seek to acquire prestige by building a luxuriously gleaming international air terminal amid sur-roundings of abject poverty and squalor. A single building is not a reliable index to a country's overall standing.

There is also the question of location. Massalia was at the very ends of the Greek earth. Only Ampurias and those shadowy outposts, Hemero-skopeion and Mainake, were further, and none of them ever were in the same league as Massalia, or ever claimed to be. Given the short sailing season of the Mediterranean summer and the uncertainty of ancient shipping, it is likely that a ship, or traveller, could not rely on fitting in more than one round trip per year between Massalia and Greece, or Phocaea.[10] Not only would the Massaliots be very conscious of the remote-ness of their city, but so presumably would be the rest of the Greeks. From the history of later empires we know what often happens in such circum-stances. The colonists go to great lengths to behave in accordance with the traditional forms of their motherland's culture – hence all the jokes about Englishmen dressing for dinner in the midst of the African jungle, after-noon tea on the polar icecap, and so on.

The object of such behaviour is partly to assure outsiders and visitors that despite the difficulties imposed by their isolated location they have not gone native and are still civilised, just like 'the people back at home', and partly – perhaps even more important – to reassure themselves of the same thing. Appearances must be kept up. Thus in the USA, during the great nineteenth-century migration westward along the Oregon trail, the thousands of covered wagons were often laden down with antique furni-ture, dinner sets of fine china, and other appurtenances of civilised living, which the settlers planned to install in their new homes (and which always had to be abandoned at some point as they faced the great hardships of the journey). Likewise in the Klondike, as far as one could get from sophisti-cated living and still be in North America, Dawson City regularly staked its claim to civilisation by putting on performances of grand opera, while carefully dressed and coiffed ladies operated a strict rota of 'at homes', taking turns, week by week, to pour the tea from cherished silver teapots.[11] I have a suspicion that, in the sixth-third centuries, much of Massalia's much-praised Greek civilisation may have operated on the same level.

The next point to consider is the attitude of those 'at home', in mainland Greece or Phocaea. Again, following our modern analogy, a common reaction to colonists in, or from, these far-flung outposts of empire, is admiration, sometimes tempered with secret and patronising amusement. What one finds much more rarely is acceptance. One is therefore liable to be faced with the colonials insisting on their local manifestations of culture, publicly received with expressions of admiration, but, once they have left, brushed aside and forgotten, possibly even with an occasional smile half-hidden behind the hand. I have elsewhere (p. 3 above) suggested that modern scholars often pay only lip service to the eminence of Massalia, readily brushing it aside as they pass on to the next chapter. I now suggest that perhaps the ancient Greeks did the same thing. This would certainly account for both the frequent paeans in praise of Massalia and the absence of anything solid to base them on. We have already noted that, as a frontier city, Massalia has been, unconvincingly, compared with Winnipeg. If we are to look for a Canadian parallel, Dawson City, in the Klondike, still seems to me more appropriate.

From this arises a by-product. Granted that Massalia enjoys this high reputation, and, in the Roman period, fully deserved it, I wonder whether this may not retroactively affect our assessment of the Greek Massalia – we assert that it *must* have been great, because, on the basis of later evidence, that is what we expect. Thus, as noted by Clerc (p. 267 n. 29 below) quite a number of ancient savants are presumed to have lived at Massalia, often on the basis of no evidence at all. Indeed, these attributions are sometimes accepted unquestioningly even by modern scholars, and, unless one invokes pure local patriotism, it is hard to explain them otherwise than I have above: it is what you *expect* to have happened.

There is of course also another explanation, but one that I hesitate to

130. L'Envoi (I) – Marseille: the patriotic view, from Notre Dame de la Garde, with the Port of Marseille beyond.

224

La sardine de Marius qui a bouché le port de
MARSEILLE

131. L'Envoi (II) – Marseille: the view of traditional folklore – a local postcard celebrates the famous sardine of Marius that was so big it blocked the whole harbour.

mention even in conclusion. Marseille is a city with a versatile and fiery spirit that few can equal. On one side we can see the glorious days of 1792, when Rouget de Lisle's 'Song of the Army of the Rhine' rang out over the rooftops of Marseille; and Marseille, seizing upon it, made it its own, the most heart-wrenching and soul-stirring national anthem the world has ever known, the incomparable 'Marseillaise'. And, as the other side of the same coin, the wild stories of Marius and his gigantic sardine. Did Marius' ancient forebears share his talent for good-humoured self-exaggeration, and could this account for part of Massalia's ancient reputation? I question it, but yet feel that they may be more to Marius' tales than is generally believed; for I am happy to close this book with the testimony on Marius' sardine as provided by the camera – which, as we all know, cannot lie (Fig. 131).

Notes

1. Introduction

1. Dem. 32, Against Zenothemis; for details, see p. 252 n. 4 below).

2. *IG*² 9294-7, 9296a. This source is mentioned by Michel Bats, 'Commerce et politique massiliètes au IV et III siècles av. J C.', in the transactions of a conference *Velia et les Phocéens: un bilan dix ans après*, 261. This is published as a special issue of *Parola del Passato*, fasc. CCIV-VII (1982), under the title *I Focei dall'Anatolia all'Oceano* (ISSN 0031-2355, publ. at Naples). It contains much valuable and relevant material.

3. Views of Cicero: p. 253 n. 17 below. Effeminacy, Athen. *Deipn.* 12, 523, c. Tunics: *ibid.*: the Massaliots are compared with the Iberians, who also indulged in this deplorable perversion. It is also mentioned by Ps. Plutarch *Proverb. Alex.* 60 (*Corpus Paroimiograph. Graec.* 1, 330), quoting a proverb in current use at Alexandria ('*stolais poikilais kai poderesi chromenoi, kai dia tauten ten malakian aschemonountes*').

4. Suidas, s.v. '*Pleuseias es Massalian*' (= 'Go catch a boat to Massalia'); quoted also by Ps. Plutarch (n. 3 above).

5. Plaut. *Cas.* 963: 'Ubi tu es, qui colere mores Massiliensis postulas?' MacCary and Willcock, in their commentary to the *Casina* (Cambridge, 1976), *ad loc.*, note that 'the people of Marseilles had a reputation for effeminacy'.

6. The most famous 'histoire marseillaise', known to all Frenchmen, is about the time Marius went fishing and caught a fish so enormous that it blocked the entrance to Marseille harbour. In the end it appears that what he really caught was a sardine. See p. 225 above.

7. Both, for example, well represented in the Asterix comic books, where, however, Greeks are very few and far apart.

8. The commonest form of publication is as articles in the various learned journals, such as *Gallia*, *Revue des études ligures*, *Parola del Passato*, *Revue archéologique de Narbonnaise*, and the series of volumes *Études massaliètes* published by the Université de Provence. There is also the semi-professional, semi-popular *Dossiers de l'archéologie*. For further and more comprehensive details, see my Bibliography, p. 291 below. In all of these is published a veritable flood of valuable information and discussion (such as to enforce upon me a heartfelt apology for all the material that I have inadvertently omitted or passed over in this present study), yet it surely remains significant that, at the time of writing, there is not a single book (except the somewhat outdated, if excellent, M. Clerc, *Massalia*) in any language offering a comprehensive general view of Ancient Greek France.

2. Phocaea, the Mother City

1. Paus. 7, 3, 10; Herod. 1, 80; 146; Strabo 13, 3, 5; 4, 5; 14, 1, 3; 1, 38; Pliny *NH* 5, 119, 121. The fullest modern accounts are J. Keil, in *RE* 20, 1 (1941), 443-8;

226

Clerc, 1, 76-85; *PECS* 708-9; Ekrem Akurgal, *Ancient Civilizations and Ruins of Turkey* (6th ed., Istanbul, 1985), 116-18; Carl Roebuck, *Ionian Trade and Colonization* (New York, 1959; repr., Chicago, 1984), esp. 15-16 *et passim*; J-P. Morel, 'Phocée et ses colonies d'occident', in *Phocée et la fondation de Marseille* (publ. Musées de Marseille, Marseille, 1995; ISBN 2-907437-10-0), 19-29; biblio., *id.*, 63. The reader should also be warned that three of these references, the *PECS* entry, *Ancient Civilizations*, and the article 'La Grèce de l'est' in *Phocée et la fondation …* (31-40) are effectively reprints of the same material by the same author, Ekrem Akurgal – a thoroughly respected and reliable scholar, but the unwary should perhaps be cautioned that these are not three independent sources.

   2. So, specifically, Strabo 13, 1, 2; 14, 1, 2.

   3. Paus. 7, 3, 8. Alternatively, the original settlers may have come from mainland Greece (Pausanias suggests from Phocis, around Delphi, because of the resemblance in names, Phocis/Phocaea; unconvincing, though ancient writers are often attracted by such toponymic resemblances), the Teans and Erythraeans then arriving later as a second wave. Keil (n. 1 above), 444, also quotes alternative names for the kings: Abarneus, Teuthadeus and Perikleides.

   4. Herod. 1, 146: The league was also known as the Dodekapolis ('the 12 cities'), these being Miletos, Myos, Priene, Ephesos, Colophon, Teos, Lebedos, Erythrai, Clazomenai, Phocaea, Samos and Chios. The last two are Aegean islands, the others on the mainland: they may be located on Map Page 7, at the back of *PECS*, and Map Index p. 1012.

   5. The foundation was led by Miletos and encouraged by the Pharaoh Psammetichos I (664-610), and his successor Amasis (570-526). The city was divided up into separate residential quarters: one each for Miletos, Samos, and Aegina, and a fourth, the Helleneion, for all the others; Phocaea shared access to this last (*PECS* 609-10; Herod. 2, 178).

   6. n. 19 below; and p. 243 n. 47.

   7. Good summary of the situation and issues in Michel Gras, 'A propos de la "bataille d'Alalia" ', *Latomus* 31 (1972), 698-716 (esp. 703); Villard, 84, no. 8. See p. 140f. above for Alalia.

   8. Herod. 4, 152; Carl Roebuck (n. 1 above), 96, which see also for Tartessos in general.

   9. City walls: Herod. 1, 163. The dates of Arganthonios are remarkable – 670-550 BC; in other words, he lived to the age of 120. So as worked out by Roebuck (n. 1 above), 96 n. 52, and *PECS* 884; Anacreon (quoted by Strabo 3, 2, 14) goes one further, citing as a fate he would wish to avoid, 'being King of Tartessos for 150 years'. He does not specifically identify this with Arganthonios (through Roebuck, *loc. cit.*, does). Strabo, *loc. cit.*, adds that 'according to the historians', identity unspecified, when the Carthaginians invaded Tartessos (237 BC) they found there that the inhabitants had mangers for their horses and also casks all made of silver. This sounds as historically reliable a tradition as 'The streets of London are paved with gold'. The entire picture of the trade plied between Tartessos and Phocaea is discussed by Roebuck, 94-101.

   10. Herod. 1, 164.

   11. Herod. 6, 11-12. The rigour of his training methods provoked within a week a full-scale mutiny and he was thrown out, retiring with his three ships to Sicily where he settled and built up an established trade as a pirate, who, for old times' sake, never attacked Greeks. Lacking his leadership in the battle with the Persians, the undisciplined Greeks were soundly thrashed.

   12. Purple dye: Ov. *Met*. 6, 9. For the coins, see B.V. Head, *Historia Numorum* (rep. Spinks, London, 1963), 587-90. One of the commonest coin types was a seal, struck as a pun on the name of the issuing city (Gk. 'seal' = *phoka*, hence Phocaea:

'Sealtown'). Such a conceit was not uncommon in the ancient world, and is often reflected in choice of coin types (e.g., coins of Rhodes, = 'Rose', carried a picture of a rose). Hesychius, *s.v.* 'Phokaeis', says their electrum coinage was despised because the local electrum had a notably low gold content (electrum, found as a medium of currency only in Ionia, was a natural amalgam of gold and silver, the proportions subject to local variation).

13. Vitr. 7, praef. 12; Pausanias 7, 5, 4. The temple is also mentioned by Xen. *Hell.* 1, 3, 1 (who attributes the fire to lightning); Strabo 13, 1, 41 records the presence at Phocaea of a wooden cult statue (*xoanon*) of Athena, in a sitting position; presumably this was inside the temple, though Strabo does not actually say so; in which case one wonders how it survived the incendiarism of the Persians in 546.

14. See Livy 37, 21; 31-2.

15. Ekrem Akurgal, 'Les fouilles de Phocée', *Anatolia* 1 (1956), 4-11 (esp. p. 9) records the finding of the akroterion and an Ionic capital from the sixth-century archaic temple (drawn restoration in *Phocée et la fondation de Marseille* (n. 1 above), 39, and some polygonal house walls.

16. See p. 47 above.

17. Justin 43, 3 gives this as the reason why it became a seafaring state.

18. See n. 12 above. The Phocaea = *phoka*, 'seal', hypothesis is offered by Keil (n. 1 above), 444, and by others since.

19. Clerc, 1, 78, remarks that 'Située sur le promontoire qui sépare le golfe d'Elée du golfe de l'Hermos, en face du passage qui s'ouvre entre Lesbos et Chios, Phocée, on l'a remarqué bien des fois, offrait un aspect analogue à celui de sa future colonie Marseille.'

20. F. Sartiaux, 'Recherches sur le site de l'ancienne Phocée', *CRAI*, Janvier 1914, 6-18; *id.* 'Nouvelles recherches sur le site de Phocée', *CRAI*, Avril 1921, 119-29. See also E. Langoltz, *AA* 80 (1965), 883-91 (including Sartiaux's site plan); *AA* 84 (1969), 377-85. Photograph of stonecut footings for walls/stairways, *ibid.* abb. 9, p. 383. E. Langlotz, *Die Hellenisierung der Küsten des Mittelmeers durch die Stadte Phokaia* (Cologne, 1966).

21. Akurgal (*Phocée ...* n. 1 above), 34) notes of the excavation trench located on the isthmus, 'Comme on rencontre là une couche de sable à partir de 1,60 m., on peut en conclure que cette partie de l'isthme était encore occupée par le mer à l'époque romaine.' Fragments: n. 15 above. See also Paus. 2, 31, 6; 7, 5, 4; also 1, 1, 5.

22. Akurgal, *op. cit.*, 40. Which of these three different capitals came from the Temple of Athena? – 'C'est un problème difficile à resoudre.'

23. Herod. 1, 163; n. 9 above; Ömer Ozyigit (the excavator), *Phocée ...* (n. 1 above), 51: 'Dans la mesure où Hérodote a cité ces murs plusieurs fois, on les a appelés ainsi.' Excellent photography, *ibid*, and see my Figs. 8, 9.

24. i.e. it is heavily battered. The unwary reader is reminded that 'batter' is a technical term in architecture, meaning that the surface concerned slopes back away from the viewer; it has nothing to do with being beaten or smashed.

25. The emperor Claudius, who devoted some time to a study of the Etruscans, got the reputation of being an eccentric antiquarian. For an introduction to Etruria the reader may turn to any of the standard handbooks: Raymond Bloch, *The Etruscans* (London, 1958); N. Spivey and S. Stoddart, *Etruscan Italy* (London, 1990); Emiline Richardson, *The Etruscans* (Chicago, 1964); Sibylle von Cles-Reden, *The Buried People* (London, 1955). As an antiquarian study, George Dennis, *Cities and Cemeteries of Etruria* (London, 1883; repr. Everyman ed. London, n. d.), 2 vols., still has much to recommend it, especially for those with a romantic turn of mind.

26. Caere (Cerveteri) is not itself a port, being some 8 km inland from the coast and 22 km NW of Rome, but presumably had some sort of harbour dependency, like Ostia or the Piraeus. It is today much visited for its imposing cemetery of burial mounds and rock-cut tombs.

27. Maria Eugenia Aubet, *The Phoenicians and the West* (Cambridge, 1993; tr. from the Spanish, *Tiro y las Colonias Fenicas de Occidente* (ed. Bellaterra, 1987)), 134-9. By tradition the earliest foundations were Gadir, Lixus and Utica, supposedly founded just after the Trojan war around 1110 BC, and therefore before Carthage (Velleius Paterculus 1, 2, 3; 1, 8, 4; Strabo 1, 3, 2; see my p. 234 n. 39 below. Archaeology has not yet come up with any evidence earlier than the seventh century. Plans of Motya,Tharros, Sulcis, Gadir, and other colonies are printed in Aubet, figs. 39, 41, 46.

28. At the time of writing, Carthage has been undergoing excavation by an international consortium, but most of the material concerned belongs to the late period of Roman Carthage, refounded by Caesar in 49 on the ruins of the Punic city, and destined soon to become the capital of the province of Africa.

29. Sil. Ital. 1, 73-5; Justin 18, 2-6; Dion. Hal. 1, 74, 1; Curtius 4, 2, 10; Diod. Sic. 20, 14. The best summary of the foundation of Carthage and the development of the Phoenician trade in the West is Aubet (n. 27 above), 187-203; 332-3 (biblio. on Carthage; there is also a very full biblio. on Phoenicians and their trade in general: 317-44). See also E. Frèzouls, 'Une nouvelle hypothèse sur la fondation de Carthage', *BCH* 79 (1955), 153-76; S. Lancel, 'Fouilles françaises à Carthage. La Colline de Byrsa et l'occupation punique (VII siècle – 146 a. J.C.)', *CRAI* 1981, 156-93; F. Rakob, 'Deutsche Ausgrabungen in Karthago. Die punische Befunde', *RM* 91 (1984), 1-22; L.E. Strager, 'Excavations at Carthage. The Punic Project: first interim report', *Annual Amer. Sch. of Oriental Research* 43 (1978), 151-90; H.G. Neimeyer, *Das frühe Karthago und die phönizische Expansion in Mittelmeerraum* (Göttingen, 1989). S. Moscati, *I Fenici e Cartagine* (Turin, 1972); H.G. Niemeyer (ed.), *Phönizier im Westen* (Mainz, 1982) (esp. G. Ch. and C. Picard, 'Les navigations de Carthage vers l'ouest', 166-73). David Asheri, 'Carthaginians and Greeks', *CAH* 4, 739-90.

30. Aubet (n. 27 above), 197. Treaty, Polyb. 3, 23. Alalia, Herod. 1, 166.

31. See Aubet, 199; Diod. Sic. 20, 8, 3-4; 69, 5; livestock, Polyb. 12, 3, 3-4. This refers to the classic, Punic period of Carthaginian history. Originally, until the sixth/fifth century BC, Carthage paid the Libyans to work the land, themselves keeping the produce (Justin 19, 1, 3). Agricultural treatises: the best known was written by Magon, often quoted by Pliny (e.g. *NH* 18, 4, 22 (translation)).

32. Diod. Sic. 20, 14, 2; Polyb. 31, 12, 12; Arrian 2, 24, 5. Aubet (n. 27 above), 131, makes the point that this payment was probably not just a manifestation of religious reverence, but a sort of kickback from the year's commercial profits to induce either Tyre or its god to maintain an effective benevolence towards the operation of the trade routes to Tartessos and other attractive markets. Diod. Sic. 17, 40, 3, and 20, 14, 1-2, tells us how, when beseiged by Alexander, the Tyrians kept on optimistically, and vainly, expecting Carthage to step in and rescue them.

33. Even in staid and respectable Rome it was not unknown. The last recorded human sacrifice at Rome (of two Gauls and a Greek, buried alive by order of the Senate to fulfil a Sybilline oracle) was in the year of Cannae, 216 BC. Livy condemns it as a most un-Roman activity ('sacrum minime Romanum' – Livy 22, 57, 6).

34. Very full discussion of the origins and significance of the Tophet in Aubet (n. 27 above), 207-17. Diod. Sic. 20, 14, 4-6; Herod. 7, 167 (Hamilcar); Plut. *De superstitione* 13 (= *Moralia* 171 c). Though familiar in Semitic peoples, human sacrifice was generally frowned upon by the Hebrews (Jeremiah 7, 31; Ezekiel 16,

20, 23, 37 (but see also Exodus 22, 29); 2 Kings 3, 26-7; 16, 3; 23, 10; Jeremiah 19, 5; Leviticus 18, 21; 20, 1-5). The rite of sacrifice was called *molk* = Moloch, and, even at the risk of tasteless sensationalism (for sometimes such issues can only be fully understood by clearly spelling them out), we may note one resultant practice. Childless couples who still wished to sacrifice a child (presumably to please or propitiate the deity) could buy one from a poor mother, expressly for the purpose. The mother was expected to watch her baby being burned alive without weeping or showing signs of emotion (which, being of ill omen, would invalidate the ceremony): otherwise she did not get paid. So Plut. *Moralia* 171 d (*De superstitione*) (tr. F.C. Babbitt, Loeb Classical Library (Cambridge, Mass. / London, 1961), vol. 2, 493 n. *f*).

3. The Seaways to Massalia

1. For example, M. Cary, *The Geographic Background of Greek and Roman History* (Oxford, 1949), concentrates on land geography and ignores the sea entirely; nor is his general introduction to Mediterranean weather wholly satisfactory (p. 5).

2. I offer a simple example. In the nineteenth century, the era of the tea clippers, the standard route for a clipper sailing from London to Australia was to head SW till it reached mid-Atlantic (instead of coasting down W. Africa); thence the course ran due south down the middle of the S. Atlantic (and going nowhere near the Cape of Good Hope, the shortest and most natural route for steamers) almost to the latitude of the Falklands; there the vessel picked up the endless westerly gales, made a 90° alteration to port, and with the blast of the Roaring Forties dead astern went storming across the seas at hurricane speed, half-way round the world, until she made landfall with Australia in the Bass Strait, between Melbourne and Tasmania. The interested reader may wish to know that the log of the fastest run ever made over this route, by the record-breaking clipper *Thermoplyae*, has been published, and gives day-to-day positions, enabling one to trace the course of the voyage (W.S. Lindsay, *History of Merchant Shipping and Ancient Commerce* (London, 1876), vol. III, 613-17).

3. Herod. 1, 163, is very clear on the point: 'And they voyaged not in "round ships" [freighters] but pentekonters.'

4. On triremes: J.S. Morrison and J.F. Coates, *The Athenian Trireme* (Cambridge, 1986), *passim*. For more recent and detailed information, based on the sea trials of the replica *Olympias*, see Timothy Shaw (ed.), *The Trireme Project* (Oxbow Monographs, Oxford, 1993; ISBN 0-046897-58-1), also *passim*. For ancient ships and sailing in general the standard work is Lionel Casson, *Ships and Seamanship in the Ancient World* (Princeton, 1971), in which for merchant ships in general see 169-90; square-riggers, 239-43; pentekonters (limited details), 44, 58-9. See also A.M. Snodgrass, 'Heavy freight in Archaic Greece', in Peter Garnsey et al. (ed.), *Trade in the Ancient Economy* (London, 1983), 16-17.

5. It is not the purpose of this book to go into nautical technicalities, but the reader will find most of them clearly and conveniently explained in Peter Kemp (ed.), *The Oxford Companion to Ships and the Sea* (Oxford, 1976); see e.g. 'rig', 703-7. There is no entry under 'pentekonter'. 'Trireme' rates a brief yet comprehensive note, but it is illustrated with a wildly inaccurate eighteenth-century reconstruction – the reader must be cautioned against believing that the picture has anything whatever to do with reality. Of course, this does not apply to the text, which is excellent. See also Casson, *op. cit.* (n. 4 above), 271-2.

6. Though in her sea trials the *Olympias* was able easily to hold course through waves 1.0-1.5 m high (personal communication from Ford Weiskittel, the *Olympias'* American Rowing-Master).

7. H.A. Ormerod, *Piracy in the Ancient World* (Liverpool, 1924, repr. 1978; ISBN 0-85323-0447), 26-8. Ancient pirate ships were often so small and the crew so large that they sometimes evaded pursuit by landing and escaping overland, carrying their ship with them.

8. The assertion by Ekrem Akurgal, *Ancient Civilisations and Ruins of Turkey* (6th ed., Istanbul, 1985), 116 (repeated in his article 'La Grèce de l'est', in *Phocée et la fondation de Marseille* (ch. 2 n. 1 above), 32) that pentekonters were 'vessels capable of achieving great speed and carrying 500 passengers' cannot be checked since no source or reference is given, but should be viewed with extreme caution, and, indeed, skepticism – one wonders if it is a misprint. Even a trireme, jam-packed with human bodies, had space for only around 200 (J.S. Morrison and J.F. Coates (n. 4 above), 111). Carl Roebuck, *Ionian Trade and Colonisation* (New York, 1959; repr. Chicago, 1983), 32, ascribes the foundation of Cyrene to 'two pentekonters carrying perhaps two hundred people'.

9. Disputed at least with reference to Phoenician mariners, by Maria Eugenia Aubet (ch. 2 n. 27 above), 140-2 (141: 'not only could they face the hardships of the high seas but they must necessarily have travelled by night'). She bases this largely on known Phoenician trade routes to places like Ibiza, with no stopover by night possible because it was out in the open sea. Strabo 3, 2, 5 envisages open sea voyages, and François Lasserre (*Strabon, Geographie* 3-4, vol. 2 (ed. Budé, Paris, 1966), 189) assures us that 'des traversées en droite ligné de Gibraltar à Ostie ... se pratiquaient'. Most of these would refer to freighters, which had less need than the cramped crews of pentekonters to go ashore for the night. Nocturnal naviga-tion was by the stars, and evidently the Phoenicians were pioneers in it, the constellation of Ursa Minor (and hence the Pole Star) being first used by them. The classical world called it 'The Phoenician constellation' (Aubet, *op. cit.*, 142).

10. Lionel Casson, 'The feeding of trireme crews', *TAPA* 125 (1995), 261-9, esp. 264 (water). He thinks that two quarts per man daily should suffice, but notes that the volunteer oarsmen on the replica *Olympias* drank over one quart (= 1 litre) per man every *hour*.

11. The only estimate I know of is by Ferdinand Lallemand, *Le Journal de Bord de Pytheas* (ed. Franc-Empire, Paris, 1974). The book is fiction, a re-creation of the log of Pytheas' voyage from Massalia to the North Sea in a pentekonter, but Lallemand, writing 'après trois années de recherches archéologiques sous-marines avec l'équipe de la "Calypso" ' (i.e. Cousteau), has been forced by the format of his work to face and resolve in a manner as realistic as possible problems such as this. His reconstruction uses a pentekonter and crew of 53, which sails non-stop from Mainake (near Malaga (Spain); see p. 167 above) to Brest, in 12 days. To me this seems both a very optimistic estimate in terms of water consumption and improb-able in terms of ancient seafaring practice. Since the route inevitably involved hugging the west coast of Portugal and Spain as far as Cape Corunna, any pentekonter would surely have put in for one or two overnight stops along the way, for the territory was not particularly hostile. And the fresh-water tank alongside the harbour at Massalia (p. 85 above) underlines the importance of water supplies for shipping. Still, Lallemand's reconstruction remains the only one I know for a long-distance voyage by a pentekonter. C.F.C. Hawkes, *Pytheas: Europe and the Greek Explorers* (Eighth J.L. Myres Memorial Lecture; Oxford, 1975), 44, n. 90, says of Lallemand that 'the whole situation is imaginatively pictured, though with copious licence over detail'. As, of course, in such a work of fiction, it has to be.

12. J. Rougé, 'Routes et ports de la Mediterranée antique', *REL* 53 (1987), 151-70 (water, p. 154). Given the much smaller crew of a freighter and the greater space for storing adequate water supplies, one must not overestimate this factor. The article, however, is in general to be recommended.

13. March-November: Rougé (n. 12 above), 153. Hes. *WD* 663-77 limits it to 50 days. And even in summer fogs (commoner than in winter) could be a hazard. One can understand and sympathise with the comments of a knowledgeable and respected colleague of mine: 'When you read things like this you wonder how they ever got anywhere at all.'

14. The figures are from Aubet (ch. 2 n. 27 above), 142, whence also is drawn the map in Fig. 15.

15. Rounding Cape Malea (= Matapan) of course was famous for its own nautical perils. Odysseus was there driven off-course by the winds (Hom. *Od.* 9, 80), and *CIG* 3920 (= *SIG* Dittenberger, 3,1229), commemorating a certain Flavius Zeuxis who had successfully rounded Malea 72 times, tells its own story. The trouble with Malea is that it is on the edge of two weather systems, leading to abrupt changes as you go round it (Rougé (n. 12 above), 155).

16. I stress that this is only 'in theory', a theory from which actual practice often falls woefully short, even in what looks to the untutored eye as good (or at least ordinary) visibility. I have certainly stood in Western Sicily, including on Mt. Erice, in clear, sunny weather, and been unable to see any sign of the coast of Africa, which not only my own Fig. 15 but also all the standard guide books insist is visible. The distance is about 150 km. By comparison, the Straits of Dover are about 40 km wide, and though in good conditions one can indeed see the other side, in my experience it does not happen very often that, as the Channel steamer leaves the quay at Folkstone or Dover, one can look out between the enclosing break-waters and, on the horizon, already see Boulogne. Even less, to carry through the analogy with Sicily/Africa, can one, on sailing from Newhaven, in the distance see Dieppe (125 km) – normally it does not appear until one is at least three-quarters of the way across. Indeed, I have, like many other travellers, sailed on steamers through a lot of the areas marked white on Fig. 15 (e.g. Corfu-Brindisi, Nice-Corsica, and the whole length of the Adriatic) and been completely out of sight of land. One therefore must not rely too implicitly on the 'never out of sight of land' hypothesis. I expect that often what happened was that you sailed out, keeping some known landmark astern until it disappeared and then kept going on, holding what you thought was a straight course, relative to the sun or wind (and hoping that if it veered you would at least notice), until you raised your next landmark, somewhere ahead, and then corrected any error by steering for it.

17. *Instructions Nautiques* (Etat-major général de la Marine – Service Hydrographique, Paris) (in this chapter hereafter abbreviated to *IN*), no. 967, 21: 'L'atmosphère dans ce cas devient fréquement si obscure qu'au milieu de ce labyrinthe d'îles c'est à peine souvent, si l'on aperçoit la terre assez à temps pour pouvoir l'éviter.' In this sense the Aegean can only be called a nursery for mariners in so far as if you ever manage to graduate from it still alive, you are fully qualified to deal with anything anywhere.

18. Suggested by Ch. Bourdeaux, *Guide du yachtsman en Méditerranée (Marseille – St. Raphael)* (Paris, Editions 'Ecole', 1963). Hodge (n. 19 below), 84.

19. I have elsewhere published a fuller account, upon which my present remarks are largely based: A. Trevor Hodge, 'Massalia, meteorology and navigation', *The Ancient World* (publ. by Ares, Chicago) 7, 3 (1983), 67-88.

20. Compare Maria Eugenia Aubet, *The Phoenicians and the West* (Cambridge, 1993), 156, fig. 26. Her map shows essentially the same thing but is limited to the Mediterranean west of Sicily.

21. Contrary to popular belief, tides do exist in the Mediterranean, and real tides at that, caused by solar and lunar attraction and not simply water that has spilled in from high tides in the Atlantic. But the change in water level, though measurable, is minimal: some 26 cm at Marseille and in the Gulf of Lions. By comparison a south wind blowing in the same area can raise the sea level a full metre, up to two metres in the Gulf of Fos, at the south-east corner of the Rhône delta (*IN* (n. 17 above), 934, 14).

22. E.g. off the Camargue, Agde, and Cap de Creus (at the Spanish border). In the Gulf of Genoa the regular westbound current runs at about 4-6 miles a day (*IN* (n. 17 above), 922, 7). Of course, none of this applies to the well-known turbulent currents at places like Gibraltar, Messina, Chalcis, or Bosphoros/Hellespont.

23. My material on Mediterranean winds (including Figs. 11-14) is based on the work of the British Meteorological Office, as published in *Weather in the Mediterranean*[2] (London, H.M.S.O., 1962). This will be abbreviated in the present chapter to *WM*.

24. *WM* 32.

25. Land-sea breezes, caused by the different rates of heating and cooling of land and sea, result in a regular daily alternation of breezes blowing from sea to land by day (Beaufort Scale 4) and the reverse by night (Beaufort 2-3). This can be useful to ships entering or leaving port, but the effect does not usually extend more than 15 km or so from the coast. They are strong in the Levant and Egypt, being felt in Cairo, 140 km inland.

26. The chief exception is the Levanter, blowing as an easterly through the Straits of Gibraltar. It must also be noted that the winds indicated are not all blowing at once: the two arrows at Gibraltar do not mean that the winds there blow east and west simultaneously, only that they rarely blow north or south. Moreover, if a wind (such as the Mistral) is blowing very strongly and meets no contrary wind to stop it, it can go right across the Mediterranean and out the other side, there reversing the normal pattern.

27. Etesians: Dem. 4, 31; 8, 14. Arist. *Meteor.* 361b35; for presumed causes *De mundo* 4, 395a. Meltemi: A.R. Burn, *Persia and the Greeks* (London, 1962), 388.

28. *WM* 183.

29. Hor. *Odes* 3, 14, 14.

30. So Cicero's advice to Tiro, to sail with a cautious skipper, because 'solent nautae festinare quaestus sui causa – cautus sis, mi Tiro – mare magnum et difficile tibi restat – si poteris cum Mescinio – caute is solet navigare' – Cicero, *ad Fam.* 16, 9, 4. The next best thing, he adds, is to travel on the same ship as some VIP who can hold the skipper's natural rashness in check. This sounds less convincing. Landlubber VIPs who are in a hurry are surely more likely to put pressure on the skipper to sail, not understanding or accepting the dangers.

31. A further factor is that arriving in port must have been more dangerous than departing from it, for a captain can control his weather of departure by choosing his time of sailing, but may not be able to exercise a similar choice over his arrival. Statistically there ought here to be a correlation with the findings of underwater archaeology, with the approaches of a port showing a preponderance of incoming wrecks (identified by their cargoes) over outgoing. But I know of no such analysis having as yet been undertaken.

32. Lucian, *Navigium*, describes the arrival in the Peiraeus of an Alexandrian grain clipper bound from Alexandria to Puteoli that was driven by stress of weather up the wrong side of Greece altogether. See L. Casson, *TAPA* 81 (1950), 45ff.

33. *IN* 967, 20, *Routes maritimes: de Marseille ou de Toulon dans le Levant*, is worth quoting in full: Bonifacio/Messina is ruled out for sailing vessels
    à cause des calmes ou de brises folles qui règnent souvent dans l'Est de la
    Corse ou dans le détroit de Messine. Leur route consiste à passer dans le Sud

de la Sardaigne, surtout s'ils quittent la France avec des vents ou l'apparence des vents du NO. S'ils trouvent des vents de l'Est en débouchant dans le canal, entre la Sardaigne et la Tunisie, ils auront avantage à louvoyer le long de la côte d'Afrique où la mer sera moins dure que sur la côte de Sardaigne; ils auront, de plus, généralement, un courant favorable qui les portera dans l'Est. En hiver, il n'en est pas de même; les coups de vent du Nord sont très dangereux le long de la côte d'Afrique et un bâtiment devra s'en tenir à bonne distance.

This was written in the early years of the twentieth century, when sailing vessels were still common.

34. It is instructive to note that Scylax (*Periplus*, in *Geog. Graec. Minores*, ed. Müller (Paris, 1855; repr. Hildesheim, 1965) lists sailing times from Massalia to Carthage by three different routes. His figures are:

via Ostia, Rhegion, Lilybaeum	22 days
via Spain, Algeria	16 days
via Corsica, Sardinia (direct)	8 days

as summarised by J. Jehasse, 'La "Victoire à Cadméenne" d'Hérodote et la Corse', *REA* 64 (1962), 258, and are based on a 24-hour day with no allowance for overnight stops. Apparently no allowance is made for some voyages being made faster in one direction than the other. Thus the sailing time Gibraltar – Ampurias is listed as seven days; was Ampurias – Gibraltar (sailing with the current) less? We do not know.

35. Calms at Bonifacio: *IN* 967, 20; *IN* 922, 14. Clerc, 1, 83, makes the point that the Phocaean pentekonters were 'plus rapides et capables de suppléer à l'absence de brise favorable', which would answer some of the objections about Bonifacio calms. On the preferred route from the East to Toulon and Marseille, *IN* 967, 21, is again worth quoting:

En revenant de Port Said à Toulon, un bâtiment s'il recontre des vents d'Ouest frais dans le canal de Malte, devra passer par le détroit de Messine et dans l'Est de Corse. Pendant la mauvaise saison, cette route sera presque toujours préférable.

The short cut from Cap Corse across to Nice, or Antibes, and coastwise from there on, is urged by Jehasse (n. 34 above), 259, who believes that it is impossible to sail direct to Marseille because of winds and currents; this would partly account for the foundation of these cities.

36. Ampurias, in the fifth century, seems to have imported from Athens direct, without passing through the entrepot of Massalia (MC-L, 29; Villard, 117-18). Naturally this does not mean that the ship itself did not call at Massalia for purely navigational reasons – awaiting a wind, or taking on water –, only that the cargo was not actually unloaded there.

37. 'Drowning anyone bound for Gibraltar': Strabo 1, 19, quoting Eratosthenes. Nautical jungle: 'beluosi gurgitem Oceani' – Avienus, *Or. Marit.* 116-29, 408-15, quoting 'Himilco Poenus'. On the whole this scaremongering seems to have worked: Greek writers view the Ocean beyond Gibraltar as a *terra incognita* where nobody sensible goes (so Pindar, *Ol.* 3, 43-4; *Nem.* 3, 20-1), but without saying that it was the Carthaginians that stopped them. Carthaginians guarding the trick of navigating the Straits as a trade secret: the *locus classicus* is the account in Strabo 3, 5, 11, of a Carthaginian captain leading on to the rocks a Roman ship that was following him in an attempt to find the safe channel.

38. The Egyptian pharaoh Necho (who also achieved fame by starting the construction, finished by Darius, of a predecessor of the Suez Canal, linking the Red Sea and the Mediterranean), in the seventh century BC sent a squadron of ships manned by Phoenicians to circumnavigate Africa, travelling clockwise, from the Red Sea to Gibraltar. This they successfully did, taking three years on the voyage, via the Cape of Good Hope. See Herod. 4, 42, and the discussion in W.W. How and J. Wells, *Commentary on Herodotus* (Oxford, 1912), 1, 318. Later, in the early fifth century BC, the Carthaginian Hanno led an expedition from Carthage out through the Straits and down the cost of West Africa. He certainly got as far as Senegal, and perhaps even Cameroon, at the mouth of the Niger. His account of this voyage survives, and is available in English translation: Al. N. Oikonomides (ed.), *Hanno the Carthaginian: Periplus* (Ares Publ., Chicago, 1977; ISBN 0-89005-217-4). The editor believes that since Hanno's work on Africa is called the 'Circumnavigation', *Periplus*, he therefore must have circumnavigated it, right round to the Red Sea; the written description, he argues, only goes as far as Cameroon because the text is incomplete. This view has not won general acceptance, even though Pliny (*NH* 2, 67) says quite clearly that that is what Hanno did, and that his written account covers it: 'Hanno, Carthaginis potentia florente, circumvectus a Gadibus ad finem Arabiae navigationem eam prodidit scripto.' And Pliny repeats this in *NH* 5, 8, the implication being that part of Hanno's text was lost between Pliny's day and ours. For the argument, see Oikonomides, *op. cit.*, 13-16. The matter is also discussed at length by Jacques Ramin, *Le Périple d'Hannon / The Periplus of Hanno* (British Archaeological Reports, Supplementary Series, 3, Oxford, 1976), *passim*; he does not believe that Pliny can be taken literally: 'Il demeure que cet homme sérieux ne doute pas qu'Hannon n'ait affectué un voyage très lointain; c'est ce qu'il a voulu exprimer en donnant une précision apparamment absurde' (7).

39. Lixus was at the modern Larache, half-way between Rabat (Morocco) and Tangier (site summary and biblio., *PECS* 521). Gadir (*PECS* 341) was the classical Gades, modern Cadiz (Spain), located on a small offshore island now forming part of the mainland, and giving access to the rich territory of Tartessos (p. 8 above). Utica (*PECS* 949-50) was in Tunisia, between the modern Tunis and Bizerta, not far from Carthage. All three were supposedly founded 80-100 years after the Trojan war (i.e. around 1100 BC; Vellius Paterculus 1, 2, 3; 1, 8, 4; Strabo 1, 3, 2; Pliny, *NH* 19, 216; Pomponius Mela 3, 6, 46; Silius Italicus 3, 241-2; Ps. Arist. *De mirab. auscultat.* 134. Pliny *NH* 19, 63 also places the Garden of the Hesperides in the region of Lixus). The entire progress of Phoenician colonisation and its relationship to Atlantic trading is discussed by Maria Eugenia Aubet, *The Phoenicians and the West* (Cambridge, 1993; ISBN 0-521-41141-6; tr. from the Spanish *Tiro y las colonias fenicias de Occidente*), 135-7. See also her biblio., esp. 328-30.

40. Clerc, 1, 390.

41. Two months, etc. – Aubet (n. 39 above), 157. Her whole section on Sea Routes, 159-66, is of great value, and (162-3) particularly discusses 'The passage of the Straits of Gibraltar'. A possibly more detailed account is offered by M. Ponisch, 'La navigation antique dans le détroit de Gibraltar', in *Mélanges offert à Roger Dion* ('Litterature greco-romaine et géographie historique'), ed. R. Chevallier (Picard, Paris, 1974), 257-73. For my remarks on this topic I am much indebted to both of these sources.

42. Ponisch (n. 41 above), 265. For a brief summary on the causes of the currents, see Michael Grant, *The Ancient Mediterranean* (Penguin/Meridian, London, 1969), 4.

43. Aubet (n. 39 above), 163: Avienus, *Or. Marit.* 178-82. Aubet's thesis (*loc. cit.*) that Avienus, 365, describes how storm-bound seamen put in to a shrine of Melkart to pray for favourable winds, is not borne out by the text of Avienus, who is concerned only with shallow water while approaching the shrine, and does not mention praying for good sailing weather.

44. Paus. 10, 8; 10, 18 (dedication of spoils at Delphi); Thuc. 1, 13; 'quos saepe fuderunt, et pacem victis dederunt' – Justin 43, 5, 2. Strabo 4, 1, 5 assures us that Massalia was full of war memorials of naval victories over 'those unjustly disputing the sea', presumably thereby including the Carthaginians. Whether or not the memorials commemorated real victories, it at least shows what the Massaliots thought about it – or wanted to believe.

45. I therefore feel that I must dispute the judgement of Clerc (1, 404) who says the opposite: 'l'étain, qu'il fallait faire venir par terre, à travers toute la Gaule, à grands frais et à grande perte de temps.' Closer to the truth, I feel, is the thesis of Georges Vallet and F. Villard, 'Les Phocéens en Mediterranée occidentale à l'époque archaïque et la fondation d'Hyele', *P del P.*, fasc 108-10 (1966), 166-90: the Phocaeans deliberately abandoned Spain to Carthage as being more trouble than it was worth, 'préférant les routes les plus sures et plus profitables à travers la Gaule' (168). 30 days to cross Gaul: DS 5, 22; 38.

46. Aubet (n. 39 above), 145, offers calculations of sailing times between various ports, and estimates that Carthage to Gadir (Cadiz) would take seven days, and the Levant (Tyre) to Gadir three months. The first of these seems to me a little optimistic. The second, given the short sailing season, comes to one return trip per year, if that (return – six months, though the return trip would be quicker, enjoying favourable winds all the way).

47. The name was officially recognised (as 'maëstral: on prononce "mystral" ') by the Académie Française in 1798. Provençal, 'Mistrau'. Summary of the Mistral: H.M. Denham, *The Tyrrhenian Sea: A Sea-Guide to its Coasts and Islands* (London, 2nd ed., 1978), 26. For a further discussion, see p. 238 n. 15 below.

48. Papon, *Histoire de Provence* (Paris, 1777), 1, 341, tells us that in 1769-70 it blew for fourteen months on end and nobody could understand why. In winter it often blows for six, or even nine, days continuously, and 'à la vitesse de 60 à 90 km à l'heure. En hiver, il n'est pas rare de le voir depasser le 100' (Bourdeaux (n. 18 above), 12).

49. *WM* (n. 23 above), 73: peak, 10 am (12 in winter); Bourdeaux (n. 18 above), 11: 'entre midi et 14 h., et retombera le soir vers 17 h.' This in spite of Homer, *Od.* 12, 286-7.

50. Strabo 4, 185 (= Poseidonios) says they do not, a puzzling statement that is demonstrably out of touch with reality. See my note (n. 19 above), 81 n. 29.

51. East wind: Bourdeaux (n. 18 above), 12. *Le Poulain, ibid.* Sailing with the wind, *id.*, 11: 'Vous n'attendrez jamais longtemps pour trouver le *vent portant* qui vous convient [compare conditions at Gibraltar (above), which often enforce a long wait], permettant de longues courses, sans avoir à lutter "contre" la mer ... La formule, dans cette region, consiste à faire le "Route du Vent".' Difficulty of leaving Marseille during a Mistral: 'Avec les vents de N-O frais, la sortie est dangereuse même pour un grand vapeur' – *IN* (n. 17 above), 934, 117. The recommended procedure is to point her at the middle of the channel, ring down for full steam ahead, and rush it. One feels inclined to add: 'and hope for the best', but the French pilot does not actually say so. See also p. 247 below, n. 26.

52. 'JUIN, est certainement le meilleur mois pour naviguer. Les journées sont les plus longues, nuits courtes. Pas de coups de temps.

JUILLET, la première quinzaine est, en général, très belle aussi. Les premier coups de Mistral se situent parfois ... vers le 14 juillet.

AOÛT est en général tourmenté, avec des alternances de grands calmes et de coups de vent. Surtout de Mistral parfois brutal et de Ponant (S-O), plutôt sur la côte de l'Esterel ... Ce sont les grands chaleurs qui, provoquant l'évaporation rapide des surfaces marines, produisent de forts courants atmosphériques.

FIN SEPTEMBRE, au moment des equinoxes, il faut prendre garde et de préférence relâcher dans des ports sûrs.

OCTOBRE, est un très beau mois pour naviguer … mais les jours commencent à être bien courts.' – Bourdeaux (n. 18 above).

53. For further discussion of the facts and arguments raised in this chapter the interested reader is referred to my Ancient World article (n. 19 above), much of which repeats the present text but also offers some expansion of it.

4. The Topography of the Region

1. It will be helpful to follow this, and other sections of my book, on a good map of France. France is fortunate, as few other countries are, in having the famous Michelin series, which are quite adequate for our purposes. Not always stocked by university libraries because they are considered primarily tourist material, they will be found readily available at any good bookstore or map shop. The general map of France is to a scale of 1:1,000,000 (1 cm: 10 km), and for closer study of our area the regional maps at 1:200,00 (1 cm: 2 km) will be found useful. The relevant sheets are Nos 240, 'Languedoc, Roussillon', and 245, 'Provence, Côte d'Azur'. The Guide Bleu 'Provence, Côte d'Azur' (Hachette, Paris) can also be consulted with profit. An excellent summary and analysis of the general topography of the region is A. Rivet, *Gallia Narbonensis* (London, 1988), 3-9 (very extensive bibliographies).

2. For convenience of reference I shall call the coastline east of the Rhône the Côte d'Azur, and that west of the Rhône, Lauguedoc. Though both of these are accepted names in modern French geography and administration, their limits are not as I have just described. Nobody thinks of Marseille as being on the Côte d'Azur which has its hazy beginnings somewhere east of Toulon, nor of Nîmes as being in Languedoc. But 'Provence' will not work either, for it does not extend far enough on either side (Nice is not in Provence), and the Côte d'Azur / Languedoc terminology best fits the ancient coastline, as I have analysed it, even though it is, strictly speaking, inaccurate.

3. Rivet (n. 1 above), 8-9.

4. The passes rise to an average of 1,000-1,200 m. As one is starting from a very low level, the Languedoc plain or the Rhône valley, this means a substantial climb in a short distance. Two examples will give the picture. The road from Montélimar, in the Rhône valley to Le Puy, in the Massif Central, runs up the valley of the Ardèche. The climb starts at Aubenas (elev. 300 m) and goes over the top of the Col de la Chavade at an altitude of 1,266 m = a climb of 966 m in 40 km. For the route from Nîmes up to Florac, in the Cevennes, the equivalent figures give a rise from Alès (elevation 140 m) at the bottom up to the Col de Jalcreste (833 m), a 693 m climb in 48 km. A comparison of these two little known passes with the two most famous passes in the Swiss Alps is illuminating. From Brig (elev. 681 m) the climb up the Simplon Pass (2,005 m) is 1,324 m, not all that much more than the climb up the Col de la Chavade; while from Andermatt (elev. 1,438 m) the ascent to the St. Gotthard Pass (2,108 m) is no more than 670 m. These figures can give no more than a rough outline, but they do make clear the general picture. The Greeks arriving on the Languedoc coast were faced, a short distance inland, with a natural barrier of formidable proportions.

5. The proximity of the headwaters of the Loire to the Rhône is noted by Strabo 4, 1, 14. There is, of course, no possibility of transshipment here since the Rhône is down in the valley and the Loire a tiny stream up in the mountains.

6. Strabo 4, 1, 2.

7. *HMG* 200-1, nn. 83-4, w. biblio. Parts of this prehistoric track-system were taken over by the Romans and rebuilt as roads, where it coincided with their different needs (i.e., military, and linking towns which did not exist in Gaulish days). The Roman road system converged on Lyon (Lugdunum), the Capital of the

Three Gauls, while the old salt and tin tracks slanted across diagonally from the Lower Rhône to Nantes and Brittany, and also east over the Alpine passes to the Po valley. Indeed, these prehistoric trade routes formed a basis for internal French communications that remained unchanged right up to the modernisation of the French road system in the eighteenth century. For speeds over this network, see p. 31 above.

8. Strabo 4, 1, 14.

9. *Utri* (animal skins inflated or stuffed with straw and supporting a wooden raft) were a common form of water transport in many civilisations. Picture in Henry Hodges, *Technology in the Ancient World* (Penguin, Harmondsworth, 1970), fig. 168, p. 152. Arles *utricularii*: L.A. Constans, *Arles Antique* (Paris, 1921), 191-4; *CIL* XII 731; 4107; 982; 3316 , 3351 (Nîmes); cf. XIII 1954, 1960, 2009 (Lyon).

10. See also p. 160 above.

11. Among ancient sources Timaios gave it five mouths, Artemidoros and Pliny three, and Polybios two (Strabo 4, 1, 8; *q.v.* also for difficulties of navigation therein).

12. G. Denizot, 'Le rivage de Languedoc en temps des Ligures', *REL* 25 (1959), 23-86; Fossae Marianae, p. 51. In view of modern development and frequent changes in course of the river it is almost pointless to look for these names on a modern map. My Fig. 27 is based on Denizot's (p. 49) reconstruction of the ancient topography. See pp. 56-69.

13. 'L'idée d'une progression graduelle de la côte et d'un atterrissement concomitant doit être complètement abandonnée': Denizot, n. 12 above, 42. For a detailed account of the various changes involved (often very complex), see this article.

14. It must also be made clear that the popularly accepted image of the Camargue, an endless expanse of swampy salt pans and mud flats roamed by flamingoes, bulls and wild horses, is very misleading. While it is accurate so far as it goes, the Camargue is not all like this, and this traditional picture holds good for only a strip some 8 or 9 km deep stretching along the coast and around the Étang de Vaccarès. From Arles, at the head of the delta, to S.S. Maries on the coast is 38 km, and for 30 km one is driving through cultivated fields and farmland. This is doubtless partly because through most of the area the Rhône runs between a pair of high earthen embankments which prevent flooding. They much resemble the levees on the Mississippi and one is not really surprised to find a small settlement (near Salins de Giraud) called La Louisiane.

15. In the myth, Heracles ran out of ammunition and Zeus, his ally, rained stones from the clouds to resupply him, evidently omitting to sweep up afterwards. In Aesch. *Prometheus Unbound* (Nauck, frag. 199), quoted in Strabo 4, 1, 7, Prometheus foretells the story of Heracles. It is noteworthy that this detail of distant Massaliot topography was evidently familiar to an Athenian fifth-century audience (or at least to Aeschylus) who had never been there. The ferocity of the Mistral, still to-day emphasised by the Guide Bleu ('le mistral, qui oppresse, fustige et paralyse le voyageur' – Guide Bleu *Provence – Côte d'Azur* (Paris, 1971), 28), was such that vehicles and people were blown off the roadway, and sometimes the clothes off people. See A. Trevor Hodge, 'Massalia, meteorology and navigation', *Anc. World* 7 (1983), 67-88. Strabo 4, 1, 7, Pliny *NH* 2, 46, 121. Pliny (*NH* 21, 31, 57) adds that nothing grows in La Crau except thyme, which however sheep much enjoy. For the Mistral blowing down houses, Sen. *QN* 5, 17, 5.

16. So Ternaux, 18, n. 40: 'sed omnia ingentium hujus portus laudum plena'. Strabo 4, 1, 10, basing himself on Poseidonios, says it has the only good harbour on the whole coast. But see p. 74 above.

17. The Romans, on the other hand, preferred artificial harbours, basins formed by excavation on land otherwise flat (Ostia, Fréjus, even Carthage). Plin. *Ep.* 6, 31;

Vitruvius, 5, 12, 2, gives instructions on how to build one. K. Lehman-Harleben, *Die antiken Hafenanlagen des Mittelmeers*, Kilio, Beiheft 14, Leipzig 1923. See also Rougé, n. 20 below, p. 158, and John Peter Oleson, 'The technology of Roman harbours', *International Journal of Nautical Archaeology* 17, 2 (1988), 147-57; D.J. Blackman, 'Ancient harbours in the Mediterranean', *IJNA* 11 (1982), 79-104, 185-211.

18. There are six of them between Marseille and Cassis – The Calanque de Port-Miou, Port-Pin, d'en Veau de Surgiton, de Morgiou, and de Sormiou (counting from east to west), and a further two small ones west of Marseille, near Carry-le-Rouet.

19. See also p. 173 above.

20. The commonly held view that ancient ships always stopped for the night at some convenient beach and did not sail in the dark (as urged by Lefebvre des Noettes, *De la marine antique à la marine moderne* (Paris, 1935)), is strongly and convincingly challenged by J. Rougé, 'Routes et ports de la Méditerranée antique', *REL* 53 (1987), 151-70. He argues that (159) quite a lot of direct deep-sea routes were in use, notably N-S, across the Mediterranean to Africa, where the winds were helpful. It was E-W voyages that caused trouble (168). But, as Rougé recognises, coasting traffic, carrying short-distance cargoes, is a different matter, governed mostly by the need to trade rather than the sailing capacities of the ships. We may also note that coasting is in some ways a more inherently dangerous trade than deep water sailing. Rocky coasts paradoxically provide both dangers (in bad weather) and the necessary refuge from them. Deep-sea vessels, caught in the open, can always handle the storm by running before it, but to do this they need sea-room.

21. Rougé, n. 20 above, 157, lists ports that are 'aberrant au point de vue des conditions maritimes', and Strabo 17, 1, 6 points out the weaknesses of Alexandria: it is hard to enter ('*ouk eueisbolon*') and, the coast being low-lying and beset with shallows, the entrance was hard to find. This was why the famous Pharos was build to mark it, more or less in the same way and for the same reasons that the Massaliots had to build towers to mark the entrances to the Rhône.

22. Second century BC, based on foundations of fourth-third century. See p. 158 above.

23. For ancient views on the topography of Provence, see Strabo 4, 1, 3; commentary, A. Dirkzwager, *Strabo über Gallia Narbonensis* (Leiden, 1975), 30-41. Essentially, Strabo saw the area as a parallelogram. He also thought that the Alps began at Massalia, evidently considering the various coastal massifs, such as the Maures and the Esterel, part of them. They are in fact separated from them by the Aix-Fréjus valley previously mentioned.

24. Tenney Frank, *An Economic Survey of Ancient Rome* (Baltimore, 1937; repr. Paterson, NJ, 1959), 3, 578ff. Gaul, in Roman times, was self-sufficient in grain and had plenty for export. The Narbonnaise was one of the two great grain-producing areas (the other being Aquitania, which exported via Narbonne and thence by sea to Italy). Arles (Frank, 477) even had an agency at Beirut and evidently exported grain to Syria (478 n. 55; *CIL* III 14165a). For Odysseus, Hom. *Od.* 9, 133.

25. No olives north of Avignon, Strabo 4, 1, 2; in 1,4 he stresses olives and vines as the principal Massaliot crops. Justin 43, 4. 'Gel des oliviers', *Guide Bleu* (n. 13 above), 29. Olives and olive oil were not used by the native Gauls or Celts, in spite of their ready availability by trade from Massalia. Evidently they just didn't like the taste; so Poseidonius, *ap*. Athen. 4, 152, who says it was because they weren't used to it, but they must have been, to start with, just as unused to the taste of wine, and the Celts plainly had no difficulty adapting to that.

26. We may note as bibliography the following: G. Curtel, *La vigne et le vin chez* *les Romains* (Paris, 1903); R. Billiard, *La vigne dans l'antiquité* (Lyon, 1913); H. Jeanmaire, *Dionysos* (Paris, 1951); E. Thévenot, 'Les importations vinaires en pays bourguignons avant le développement de la viticulture', *RAE* 1953, 234-9; J. André, *La vigne et le vin en Provence dans l'antiquité* (Mélanges Bénévent, 361-8; Gap, 1954); Roger Dion, *Histoire de la vigne et du vin en France* (Paris, 1959) (recommended); A Tschernia, *Le vin de l'Italie romaine: essai d'histoire économique d'après les amphores* (École française de Rome; Rome, 1986); M-C. Amouretti, 'La viticulture antique: contraintes et choix techniques', *REA* 90 (1988), 5-18. A rare and valued study of a much neglected topic is also Pierre Villard, *Recherches sur l'ivresse dans le monde grec* (Thèse d'Etat, Université de Provence, Aix-en-Provence, 1988). The general question of wines is considered by Pliny, *NH* 14, 34, 29-5; 122, who (68f.) ranks the various vintages in order of preference. The wine trade and other related aspects will be dealt with in more detail when we turn our attention to Massalia (p. 117f. below). Here we are concerned only with agriculture in Provence. Greeks importing vines – Dion (above), 89.

27. 'Le martyre de Saint Baccus', A. Jubinal, *Recueil de contes ...* (Paris, 1839-42), I, 251; as quoted by Dion (n. 26 above), 76.

28. As of course is demonstrated by the pre-eminent position held by French wines ever since. But a caveat here is in order. We must not look at the regions of modern France most famed for their wines and assume from that that the same situation held good in antiquity. Provence, for example, though it does produce some reasonable wines – practically anywhere in France does – is not one of the great areas, like Burgundy or Bordeaux; but this is barely relevant for antiquity. It is not so much that climates or the soil has changed, but tastes have. What ancient wine actually tasted like has been much discussed but, naturally, cannot be proved. It was probably more rich and syrupy than ours (and, of course, in Greece was normally watered), and, in Gaul at least, often flavoured with herbal additives, a practice that we accept in liqueurs but not usually in wine. This alone is enough to tell us that modern preferences are not a reliable guide to what the ancients saw as quality in their wines.

29. Dion (n. 26 above), 89-91, on Greek colonies: 'ces franges Hellénisées étaient par excellence le domaine de Dionysos'. cf. Cic., *Rep.* 2, 4, 9. For the economics of the wine trade with the Celts, see p. 211f. above. For my use of the names Celts/Gauls see p. 195 above.

30. Full listing and commentary on all these herbs in *HMG* 198-9. Dioscorides I, 2, 9, 103; III, 25, 33, 108, 122; IV, 148; Galen 5, 5. Hellebore: Theophr. *HP* 9, 10, 3; Pliny *NH* 25, 25, 61 (Gauls' arrows). Ouzo, pastis, *HMG loc. cit.* Absinthe, Papon, *Hist. of Provence* 147; Dioscorides III, 23; V, 49; Pliny 14, 109; Columella 12, 35. Nard, Dioscorides I, 7; V, 59; Galen 8, 13; Benoit 60, 221.

31. At a later date, wood was exported from Gaul in bulk to heat the great public baths at Rome (A. Grenier, *ap.* Tenney Frank, *Economic Survey of the Roman Empire* (n. 24 above), 580). It does not look as if there was too much available close to Massalia, and when Caesar needed timber for his siege engines he had to get it from the forests of St. Baume (Clerc 2, 23ff.; see also Lucan 3, 339-452).

32. *HMG* 199ff., and esp. p. 201, n. 84 (biblio.); F. Benoit, *REL* 25 (1959), 87-110; M. Rostovtzeff, *Social and Economic History of the Roman World*, 690 n. (use of salt in *garum*); R. Busquet, *Histoire du commerce de Marseille* (Marseille, 1949) 1, 36; for ancient texts, see Pliny *NH* 2, 233; 31, 81 (the main source); 34, 125. The technique is to admit salt water to the pans, and then add fresh water. Pliny thinks that it also helps if the moon is shining. Rutil. Numantius 1, 475-84. The salt trade is somewhat neglected in ancient sources, and what we have are largely of Roman date, nor is there any archaeological evidence. Salt travelled in sacks and left no trace. But then, there is no ancient literary evidence for a trade in ceramics, yet we know from archaeology that it existed, so the absence of literary reference to the salt traffic proves nothing.

33. The chief salins (salt pans) in the area today are in the Camargue (salins de Giraud, Aigues-Mortes), Étang de Berre (Berre, Istres, Vitrolles, St. Blaise), Six Fours/LeBrusc (anc. Tauroentum, near Sanary), Hyères/Giens, and St. Tropez (Cap des Salins), Narbonne, Agde, Port Vendres. Ports founded alongside salt pans include Olbia, Tauroeuntum, Fos, Agde, Narbo, and Port Vendres. (Benoit (n. 32 above), 93; *HMG* 90, fig. 7 (map).)

34. Herod. 5, 9-10; Clerc 154.

35. We do not know whether the Greek colonists operated the salt pans privately or as a state-owned monopoly. In Roman Italy and some cities in Greece it was the latter (Benoit, n. 32 above, 95).

36. Eating fish fresh – terracotta grills for grilling fish have been found locally (at Martigues and St. Blaise): La Grand, *Gallia* 16 (1958), 426, fig. 22; 17 (1959), 195, figs. 4, 5 and pl. IX, 1. Cargoes of salt fish shipped in amphorae: *Gallia* 14 (1956), 29.10; 16 (1958), 6; 17 (1959), 451. Good fishing in lagoons, Benoit (n. 32 above), 99-100. Clerc, 285. 'All the fish they want' is reported by Ps. Aristot., *De auscult. mirab.* 89 (he is evidently talking about Vaccarès; Livy 42, 2, may have this in mind when he tells of a prodigy, the Gauls ploughing up fish embedded in the earth). The reason that the murky waters make for good fishing is that the fish get blinded by the excessive saltiness and dirt of the half-evaporated water and cannot see the trident coming, while the poor visibility does not inhibit the fisherman, who keeps on thrusting at random (Benoit, *op. cit.*, 101). Gauls feeding fish to horses: Aelian 15, 15.

37. Milo's mullets: Diod. Sic. 40, 54,2; it is surprising that this remark of Milo's has often been taken seriously at face value, indicating that Milo did not mind his exile. Diodorus specifically rules this out, saying Milo is being sarcastic. I am sure this is right, particularly since Cicero had proved a broken reed in the trial that led to his exile. It is like a criminal convicted in the absence of his lawyer then sending him a postcard from Dartmoor 'Having wonderful time, wish you were here'. Oysters: Strabo 4, 1, 8; *HMG* 208, n. 159; Tunnies: Strabo 3, 2, 7; Polyb. 34 *ap*. Athen. 7, 302c; Aelian 13, 6. Benoit (n. 32 above), 99 incorrectly quotes Oppian, *Halieut.* 3, 546-54, to the effect that the Massaliots built fishing boats with a spiked ram that caught the fish by ramming it and bodily spearing it, as on a spit. The prospects of a boat ramming a fish are not good, and what Oppian says is that these boats were designed to hunt swordfish (not the tunny), and that it worked by deceiving the swordfish into thinking that the boat was another swordfish; it was then killed with a trident in the usual way. All this is correctly reported and quoted at length by Clerc, 286. Tunnies at Antipolis, Martial 4, 89; 13, 103.

38. Gold: F. Benoit, 'L'economie de la Provence – Le grenat et les mines des Maures', *REL* 26 (1960), 221-32: esp. 227; 226, n. 4, and 228, n. 3, for biblio.; *HMG* 192; a brief summary is listed in Oliver Davies, *Roman Mines in Europe* (Oxford, 1935), 77-8; Tenney Frank, *Economic History of the Roman Empire*, 2, 969 (written by A. Grenier). Lead: *HMG* 193. Lead was mined in profusion in the ancient world (often as a by-product of mining silver for currency), especially in Spain and Britain: see A. Trevor Hodge, *Roman Aqueducts and Water Supply* (London, 1992), 466 n. 13. Iron was found at Six-Fours, just west of Toulon. See also J-P. Morel, 'Les Phocéens en occident', *P del P*, 1966, 408-9 ('Les resources de la Gaule et les causes de la fondation de Marseille').

39. The question of tin in antiquity could by itself fill a whole book. The ancient sources are listed and translated in Villard 143-58; modern (i.e., up to 1960) commentaries, 148-61. The chief references to the Scillies as the source of tin are Strabo 2, 5, 15; 3, 5, 11; Diod. 5, 2; 5, 38. Pliny, *NH* 34, 47 adds that it is supposed to have been exported to the mainland in curraghs, or coracles (? – 'des barques d'osier couvertes de peaux cousues' – Villard 144). Diod. 5, 22 adds that the ore was smelted in the islands and exported in the form of ingots the size of knuckle-bones, but Ramin (below) suspends judgement on this. The identification of the Scillies with the 'Katterides Islands' of the Greek texts seems to be safely established. Avienus, *Or. Mar.* 94-116. The British (Cornish) sources are mentioned by Caesar (*BG* 3, 8; 4, 21; 5, 12). Tin also came from Spain, from the region around Gades known as Tartessos (Avienus, *Or. Mar.* 259-61; 291-3; see Villard 146; Ps. Scymnos, 164-6). This has sometimes been identified as the Tarshish of the Bible (Ezekiel 27, 12; Jonah 1, 3). Modern commentaries are probably led by *HMG* 193-5. We may also note Villard 137-61; P. Amandry, 'Vix et la route d'Étain', in *Hommage à J. Carcopino* (Paris, 1977), 13-19; Clerc, 1, 59-63; J.E. Dayton, 'The problem of tin in the ancient world', *World Archaeology*, June 1971, 49-70; J. Heurgon, *Rome et la Mediterranée occidentale jusqu'aux guerres puniques* (Paris, 1969), 505-6; Jean Gagé, 'Gades, l'Inde, et les navigations atlantiques dans l'antiquité', *Rev. Hist.* 1951, 189-216; R.J. Forbes, *Studies in Ancient Technology* (Brill, Leiden, 1964), 9, 134-80, esp. 140-8; J.D. Mulhy, *Copper and Tin* (New Haven, 1973); Jacques Ramin, *Le problème des Cassitérides* (w. full biblio; Paris, 1965), esp. pp. 91-5; R. Dion, 'Le problème des Kassitérides', *Latomus* 11 (1952), 306ff.

It would seem that the Bronze Age also derived its tin from Anatolia and Assyria, a source almost passed over without mention in most general histories of the ancient world, which concentrate their attention entirely on Cornwall and Brittany – a source surely much more improbable in strict terms of geography and transport, at this very early period. See K. Aslihan Yener, Hadi Özbal, Ergun Kaptan, *et al.*, 'Kestel: an Early Bronze Age source of tin ore in the Taurus Mountain, Turkey', *Science* 244 (14 April 1989), 200-3. *Science* is published by the American Association for the Advancement of Science. Kestel is located near Nigde, in South Central Turkey. The mine is dated by pottery and radiocarbon to the third millennium BC, and 'from one chamber some four or five thousand tons of ore had been removed, which, if the tin content was 2-3% tin, as is standard, was a lot of tin'. The tin (*anaku* in Akkadian tablets) was transshipped through Assur in N. Mesopotamia. Biblio on p. 203. See also D. Muhly, *AJA* 89 (1985), 275f.; R.D. Penhalurick, *Tin in Antiquity* (Institute of Metals, London, 1987); K. Branigan, *Aegean Metalwork of the Early and Middle Bronze Ages* (Oxford, 1974). Of an earlier date, but offering valuable insights into the topic is Llyn Willies, 'Kestel tin: Early Bronze Age mining in Turkey', *HMS News* (Journal of the Historical Metallurgical Society, Britain), 22 (Winter, 1922) 3ff. There is also an interesting article by Brian Earl in the same issue, reporting on an experimental tin smelting *in situ*.

40. There were three chief tin routes from Cornwall (or the Scillies) across France to the Mediterranean. One crossed the Channel from the Isle of Wight (Gk. Ictis, Lat. Vectis) to around Le Havre (a sail of one day – Strabo 4, 1, 14), thence by the Seine to the headwaters of the Saône (anc. Arar) around Chaumont or Langres, and down the Saône and the Rhône to Massalia. Of particular significance here is the finding of the Vix crater (Mont Lassois) near Chatillon-sur-Seine (R. Joffroy, 'Le trésor de Vix', *Mon. Piot* 48 (1954), 1-68; R. Joffroy, *Vix et ses trésors* (Paris, 1979); Anthony King, *Roman Gaul and Germany* (Berkeley, 1990), 14; *HMG* 194 n. 26, for Vix and the tin route) illustrating the importance of this trade route (though suggestions have been made that the crater was perhaps instead imported via the Adriatic and over the Alpine passes). A possible variant of this route crosses at the Straits of Dover, thence heading directly south to the Saone, but this seems to be less used or at least less well attested. The second route is from Cornwall across to Brittany, thence via Nantes (anc. Corbilo; Strabo 4, 2, 1) and up the Loire to Lyon and the Rhône, or possibly round the other side of the Massif Central to reach the sea at Narbonne. This, of course, will serve tin traffic originating from Brittany as well as from Cornwall. The third route is by sea down the Bay of Biscay to Bordeaux, up the Garonne to Toulouse, across the 'Isthmus' joining France and Spain, and down the Aude to Narbonne. This route, of course, does not pass through Massalia. The other two do. (See *HMG* 27 (map) and my Fig. 38.) A further possibility was to take the tin by sea all the way, round by Gibraltar. This meant passing the native Spanish tin mines of Tartessos (around Huelva and Seville), which sometimes led to the mistaken impression that that is where the tin had come from, when the reality it originated in Cornwall (Clerc, 1, 85; *HMG* 61). Tartessos, of course, did quite genuinely also produce tin of its own. This route, possibly previously used by the Greeks, was monopolised by the Phoenicians after the foundation of Carthage (trad. 814 BC) and may explain why they chose to settle the mountainous Western half of Sicily, leaving the more fertile remainder for the Greeks (who had not yet arrived to lay claim) – it was to hold the tin route across to Tartessos, via Sardinia and S. Spain (Amandry (n. 39 above), 16). Tartessos itself (in spite of its Greek-sounding name) has not been reliably identified, but is thought (Clerc, *loc. cit.*) to have been a city on an island at the mouth of the R. Guadalquivir. Full discussion and references in *PECS* 884. The region in general was known as Turdetania.

41. Ternaux, 80.

42. Basalt millstones: *HMG* 122. There are some in the museum at Agde, and in the museum at Toulon. F. Benoit, 'L'economie littoral de la Narbonnaise à l'epoque antique – le commerce du sel et les pecheurs', *REL* 25 (1959), 87-100; esp. 87-8, see also Owen Williams-Thorpe, 'Provenance and archaeology of Roman millstones from the Mediteraean area', *Journal of Archaeological Science* (1988), 15, 253-305. Coral: Pliny *NH* 32, 21; Benoit, *loc. cit.;* Clerc, 1, 287; Benoit, *REL* 20 (1956), 'Les relations de Marseille grecque', 26. Once the coral trade got started it was exported through Massalia and Alexandria, to as far away as India.

43. For the garnet, see Theophr. *De lapid.* 3, 48; 6, 34; Pliny, *NH* 37, 92 (*carbunculi*). The local working and cutting is attested by references to *'lapidarii Almanticenses'* at Arles and Cimiez (Nice) in *CIL* 12, 732; 5, 7869. The name comes from Albanda, in Caria, the chief source of production. Benoit, 1960 (n. 38 above), 221-32; Michel-Levy, 'Le grenat des Marseillais', *REA* 1907, 287 (biblio.).

44. Strabo 3, 5; 3, 144. The plague of rabbits originated in Turdetania, SW Spain, and spread eastwards. Some time between 121 and 87, the inhabitants of the Balearics sent a delegation to Rome, asking for aid in resettling on new lands somewhere else, since the rabbits were chasing them out of house and home, uprooting the trees and overturning the houses. The Turditanians learned how to control the pest by sending muzzled ferrets down the burrows, but knowledge of this had evidently not spread to the Balearics, and the rabbits themselves, though spread as far east as Massalia, evidently never got any further. Sceptics inclined to scout this tale of lapine ferocity are referred to the text of Strabo, and to François Laserre, *Strabon, Géographie* (Budé ed.; Paris, 1966), 189.

45. Diod. 5, 39, 1; Cic. *De leg. agr.* 2, 35 ('hillbillies' – 'montani duri et agrestes'); Strabo 4, 1, 5.

46. Justin 43, 3, 7. Gregory of Tours 1, 92 ('locus amoenissimus'), quoted by N. Lamboglia, 'Prata Liguriae', *REL* 25 (1959), 5 (*q.v.*).

47. Justin 43, 3, 7: 'Phocaeenses exiguitate ac macie terrae coacti, studiosius mare, quam terras, exercuere: piscando, mercando, plerumque etiam latrocinio maris, quod illis temporibus gloriae habebatur, vitam tolerabant.'

5. The City of Massalia

1. So Michael Grant, who, writing as late as 1969, could say of Massalia that 'like early Montreal and then Winnipeg, it lay on the very outskirts of a barbarous world, with no civilisation to its north' (*The Ancient Mediterranean* (London, 1969), 172). This judgement has been received by my colleagues in Montreal with interest, and in Winnipeg with tolerant amusement; I have not yet dared to show it to anyone in Calgary or Vancouver. But Grant's main point is probably right. A premier of Alberta, the Rt. Hon. Ralph Klein, once remarked of the city of Edmonton: 'It's not the end of the world, but you can see it from there.' That is probably how Athenians privately felt about Massalia.

2. Today the Vieux Port. Nautically, it was not perfect – its access channel was, and is, exposed to the contrary blasts of the Mistral (see p. 236 n. 51 above). But all things considered, it was still an exceptionally good harbour.

3. So the chief authorities on Alalia, J. and L. Jehasse, *Aléria Antique* (1991: a locally-sold guidebook, published by 'Les Amis d'Aléria', no place of publication or ISBN number given), 23-4: 'La principale installation portuaire semble être à Sainte-Agathe, dont le nom grec, signifiant le "bon port" se retrouve à Agde, Agay, peut-être Ajaccio.' This is very thin evidence indeed, particularly since Agathe does not, in Greek, mean a 'bon port', just 'bonne', applying to any feminine singular noun, including the Christian saint of that name. No one ever suggested that Santa Agata di Militello, a major railway station on the line from Messina to Palermo, must therefore have been a Greek port. At Agde (p. 158 above) the missing noun was Tyche, *Agathe Tyche*, 'Good luck', being the name of the town. That it was a port was, linguistically speaking, purely coincidental. For J. and L. Jehasse on Alalia, see also p. 305 (biblio.).

4. Corsica plays little part in the story of ancient history and so is probably unfamiliar to many readers with classical interests; and within Corsica Bonifacio is itself somewhat off the beaten track, located at the southern extremity of the island, facing Sardinia across a narrow strait. The quickest and easiest way of confirming my statements is probably to look at the town plan in the Guide Bleu or the green Guide Michelin. The similarity to Marseille will be immediately evident.

5. Benoit (*HMG* 191, following J. Bérard , *Rev. Arch.* 1 (1950), 187) differentiates between colonies which were trade-based (founded by Ionian states) and those which were purely agricultural (founded by Chalcis and Corinth).

6. Thuc. I, 13; Strabo 4, 1, 4 (based on Posidonios); Paus. 10, 8; Livy 5, 34; also Plut. *Solon*, 2, 3; Justin 43, 7-8; Hyginus, *ap.* Aul. Gell. 10, 16, 4; Timagenes, *ap.* Amm. Marcel. 15, 9; Aristotle, *ap.* Athen. 13, 576a. The statement by the scholiast to Thuc. 1, 13, that the city of Massalia is in Africa need not here detain us; he has confused it with the Libyan tribe of the Massylii.

7. The 600 BC dating is made clear by internal cross-reference in the various authors using it. Livy (5, 34) ascribes the foundation to 'the reign of Tarquinius Priscus', which by orthodox Roman annalistic chronology, puts it between 616 and 578. Justin 43, 3 dates it to 'temporibus Tarquinii regis', the Livy passage making it plain that the Rex Tarquinius concerned is Priscus, not Superbus. The late writer Timaeus (*ap.* Ps. Scymnos 211-14, = *F. Gr. Hist.* 3B, 622, frag. 71) puts it 120 years before Salamis, or in 600-599.

8. n. 7 above. The fall of Phocaea is dated because it is known to have occurred after Cyrus took Sardis (c. 546) and before the conquest of Babylon (autumn, 539), which puts it around 544.

9. The whole question is fully discussed by Francois Villard, *La ceramique grecque de Marseille* (Paris, 1960) (= 'Villard') 76-81 ('La date de fondation de

244

Marseille'), basing himself on the seminal study by J. Brunel, 'Marseille et les fugitifs de Phocée', *REA* 50 (1948), 2-26. Villard (80) is explicit: 'la date de 600 que donne une partie de la tradition littéraire concorde parfaitement avec la date de la plus ancienne ceramique recueillie sur le site'. His conclusion is accepted by MC-L, 10.

10. On Thucydides see the discussion by A.W. Gomme, *Historical Commentary on Thucydides I* (Oxford, 1945), 124; on Herodotus, How and Wells, *A Commentary on Herodotus I* (Oxford, 1912), 128-9. The 600 BC foundation date was municipally sanctified in 1899 with processions through the streets of Marseille celebrating its 2,500th anniversary: the principal float carried an attractive young Marseillaise enacting the role of Gyptis (see p. 65 above and n. 11 below).

11. Strabo 4, 1, 4. He is here following Posidonios, who in turn is following Arisotle's now-lost *Constitution of Massalia* (= Athen. 13, 576a). Like so many of the works attributed to Aristotle, this may well have been written by one of his students, but must nevertheless be respected as a reasonably reliable source. Justin 43, 3-4. Justin is himself unreliable, but this means only that there is good in him as well as bad, and the good can be valuable whenever we can be sure that he is in fact repeating a reliable source. In this matter he is known to be repeating Pompeius Trogus, who lived at Vaison-la-Romaine and would accordingly be familiar with preserved local traditions. We may therefore be reasonably sure that the Protis-Gyptis story was firmly embedded in local folklore, for what that is worth. For the way Gyptis signalled her choice, by offering a cup of water to the chosen suitor, compare Pindar, *Ol.* 8, 1-6. The scene was recreated in a poster advertising the 1899 Anniversary celebration and now reproduced in the catalogue of *Le Musée d'Histoire de Marseille: L'Antiquité* (Marseille, 1988), 29, fig. 139. The accompanying text comments 'A noter l'aspect gaulois des Ligures', who all have long, drooping, Asterix-type moustaches. Gyptis wears a head-dress copying the highly individualistic, not to say bizarre, accoutrement modelled by La Dame d'Elche; it consists of a pair of circular ruffs worn over the ears, like a pair of enormous radio headphones or ear-muffs. This statue, found at Elche (in Alicante, Spain), is now in the National Archaeological Museum at Madrid, and is most conveniently illustrated in Paul MacKendrick, *The Iberian Stones Speak* (New York, 1969), 79, and in S.J. Keay, *Roman Spain* (Berkeley, 1988), 20. At the time of the Marseille celebration it had been discovered only two years before and so was very much present in the mind of the poster artist, but it has no logical connection with Gyptis or Massalia that is discernible. Elche was a Phoenician site, so that may be where the fashion came from; the Museum catalogue sees it as Oriental. Justin also from time to time incorporates smatterings from Timaeus, who came from Tauromenion, the modern Taormina, in Sicily; his history emphasised the role of Greek colonists. Foundation myths: these were plentiful and often featured an imaginary hero whose name was retroactively formed from the name of the city, thereby explaining where it came from. A good example is Taras (later Taranto), so called because it was founded by Taras, who arrived there on the back of a dolphin. This proclivity was not restricted to Greeks. Romans indulged themselves with not one but two mythical founders Aeneas and Romulus ('hence the name Rome') and were then hard put to it to reconcile the two (since they supposedly lived 300 years apart). The conundrum was only resolved in the first century AD, by the ingenuity of Virgil, who provided two separate cities, Alba Longa and Rome, for them to found.

12. For a full discussion of these foundation myths, see Clerc, 1, 115-31, esp. 126-30; MC-L, 10-12. The names of the protagonists sometimes vary: Protis sometimes becomes Euxenos, and Gyptis, Petta. It is also interesting to observe that in modern Marseillais folklore it is Gyptis, the local native, not Protis, the alien import, who is honoured as having founded the city. On the other hand, half-way down the great monumental stairway outside the Gare St. Charles, the main Marseille railway station, is a large sculpture group entitled 'Marseille, Colonie Grecque'. It shows a woman, of unmistakably Hellenic appearance and wearing a Doric chiton, arriving on the bows of a Greek oared ship accompanied by two children (and a pair of dolphins, whose quizzically cynical expression seems to reflect a spirit of scepticism about the whole enterprise): Fig. 39.

13. This is not complete fantasy. June: the sailing season began around 27 May, and it would have taken the fleet at least a month to get to Massalia. They would naturally have wanted to get there as soon as possible so as to settle in and get crops planted well before the winter (sailing season: Lionel Casson, *Ships and Seamanship in the Ancient World* (Princeton, 1971), 270-2; sailing time Phocaea-Massalia, *id*. 289). Favourable breeze: the entrance channel, the Goulet, to the Lakydon is angled towards the NW, so that the Mistral, the prevailing wind (p. 33 above) of Massalia, is directly behind a ship entering it. Long pull: from Phocaea to Massalia the route is against the prevailing winds (Casson, *op. cit.,* 290 n. 86). Normally freighters and transports would simply await the relatively fewer occasions when the wind was easterly, and then sail on that. But the Phocaeans are known always to have used pentekonters for these voyages, which being oar-powered vessels, would simply row ahead through contrary winds: that's what the oars were there for (pentekonters: Herod. 1, 163). Welcoming Celts, smiling migrants, 'just like home': see pp. 12 and 228 n. 19 above.

14. See p. 243 n. 46 above.

15. Strabo 4, 1, 4 ('theatroeides'). Vitruvius (2, 8, 11) says something the same of Halicarnassus; Wycherley (n. 35, below), 25, points out that this 'was a form which a seaside town might naturally tend to take'. Caesar, *BC* 2, 1: 'Massilia fere ex tribus oppidi partibus mari adluitur; reliqua quarta est quae aditum habet a terra.' So also Avienus, *Or. Mar.* 704-11 ('civitas paene insula est').' Pomponius Mela 2, 5 adds that 'Massalia is in its harbour', 'Lacydon, Massiliensium portus, et in eo ipsa Massilia'. He apparently means that the city is a peninsula projecting into the Lakydon. This is, in a way, true, given that the northern shore of the harbour was much more curved than now, particularly since it then extended into the 'horn of the harbour', no longer existing. See Fig. 42. See also F. Benoit, 'L'évolution topographique de Marseille', *Latomus* 31 (1972), 54-70.

16. Clerc, 2, 166.

17. See Ternaux (p. 238 n. 16 above). The fullest discussion of the Lakydon remains that of Clerc, 2, 164-87; brief survey, MC-L, 107-9. The spring Lakydon: Pol Trousset, 'L'eau à Marseille dans l'antiquité', *Doss. Arch.* 154 (Nov. 1990), 34-5. The identification of the name and the spring was first made by Camille Jullian, 'Le port du Lacydon et le ruisseau sacré des Marseillais', *Provincia* 1 (1921), 1-6.

18. The maximum depth of the Vieux Port today is 6 m, making it unsuitable for large modern vessels. The advancing coastline has also had the result that the eastern quay of the Vieux Port, at the foot of the Canebière, is in fact the middle of the ancient Lakydon. It carries, cemented into the sidewalk, a brass plaque commemorating the arrival of the Phocaeans and insisting that it was at this very spot, 'Ici!' that they stepped ashore. Had they tried to do so, the foundation of Massalia would have been inaugurated with a resounding splash, the location being still some 100 m out from the ancient shoreline. See Figs. 47, 48.

19. This subterranean marsh apparently extends inland as far as the intersection of the Canebière and the Cours Belsunce. Clerc, 2, 169, records that some of the houses near the lower (i.e. south) end of the rue de la République (in the Place Victor Gelu) have their cellars permanently flooded by water seeping in from the harbour and have to be constantly pumped out, 'non seulement pour les assécher quelque peu, mais pour détruire les myriades de moustiques qui infestent ces maisons'. This does not paint an attractive picture of the situation in antiquity.

20. Clerc, 2, 276.

21. Wooden piling: Editions Edisud, *Naissance d'une ville: Marseille* (Aix-en-Provence, 1979), 66; MC-L, 107; F. Benoit, *Gallia* 6 (1948), 208, and R. Lantier, *ibid.*, 448ff. Oysters: MC-L, *loc. cit.* For the early development of the 'horn', M. Euzennat, 'Ancient Marseille in the light of recent excavations', *AJA* 84 (1980) 135, ill. 2.

22. Clerc, 2, 184-6. Strabo 4, 1, 5 mentions the ship-sheds (*neosoikoi*) and armoury. Zea ship-sheds: J.S. Morrison and R.T. Williams, *Greek Oared Ships* (Cambridge, 1968), 181-9. Philo's arsenal: W.B. Dinsmoor, *The Architecture of Ancient Greece 3* (London, 1950), 241-2.

23. Clerc, 2, 156, quoting Grosson.

24. Euzennat, *op. cit.* (n. 21 above), 138, quoting supporting evidence from Cosa. Antibes: Jean-Pierre Violino, 'Antibes et sa vocation maritime à l'époque romaine', in *L'exploitation de la mer de l'antiquité à nos jours* (Vième rencontres internationales d'archéologie et d'histoire d'Antibes (Editions APDCA, Juan-les-Pins, 1986; ISBN 2-904110-07-0), 58. The figure of 25-40 cm below present level is, more or less, confirmed for the Roman quay (there is a lot of variation at different periods) by R. Guery, Paolo Pirazzoi, and Pol Trousset, 'Les variations du niveau de la mer depuis l'antiquité à Marseille et à la Couronne', *Doss. Arch.* 50 (fev. 1981), 8-17, which is probably the best and fullest study of the question. Indeed, this whole issue, entitled *Ports et villes engloutis*, can be highly recommended.

25. 'Water level uniform': it is however quite possible for one part of the sea to be higher than another. Tides, not normally a serious factor in the Mediterranean, can cause a change in level of 20-60 cm. Winds are a more serious consideration, for a strong Scirocco, blowing north across the Mediterranean from North Africa, can cause a rise of a full metre in the sea level of the Gulf of Lions and up to 2 m in the Gulf of Fos. See Hodge (p. 232 n. 19 above), 74; Violino, *op. cit.* (n. 24 above), 58. Moreover, the sea level in the Mediterranean is itself always lower than the two bodies of water connecting with it, the Black Sea and the Atlantic. This is caused by the climate, which produces a greater rate of evaporation in the Mediterranean, resulting in turn in a constant incoming current through the Bosphoros and the Straits of Gibraltar to replace the water evaporated. Proof of the land/water level having been affected in antiquity by land movements comes from Crete. Roman-date *vivaria* (fish-ponds, originally built exactly at sea level, and communicating with it), have been found at both ends of the island. That at the East end, at Mochlos, is high and dry, while that at the west end, at Falsarna, is totally submerged, showing that the island has tipped like a see-saw, the east end rising and the west end subsiding. (See N.C. Fleming and P.A. Pirazzoli, 'Archéologie des côtes de la Crète', *Doss. Arch.* (n. 24 above), 66-81.) The point is worth emphasising, because it is often assumed that where one finds ruins submerged (which is common enough), it is the sea that has risen; this is misleading, for it can then lead to the inference that there was a general rise in the sea since antiquity, applying equally to other locations where there is otherwise no evidence for it.

26. Hodge (p. 232 n. 19 above), 84. *Instructions Nautiques* (see p. 236 n. 51 above). I have preferred to refer to an old edition, published in 1913, since it was written at a time when sailing vessels were still common, and is so more in harmony with the needs of seafaring in antiquity. Perhaps I should add that I have watched a yacht tacking to within a few feet of the rocks as she beat her way through the Goulet in the teeth of a strong breeze, and her convolutions made me glad I was on the dry land by the Fort St. Jean, and not aboard her.

27. Hodge (p. 232 n. 19 above), 69; also my p. 233 n. 25 above.

28. *Weather in the Mediterranean* (p. 233 n. 23 above), 73. The Mistral is also a seasonal wind, beginning its most vigorous period around 14 July and lasting till mid-September, though it does continue to manifest itself on a less ferocious scale throughout the year. Hodge (see p. 232 n. 19 above), 83, 85.

29. Stephanos of Byzantium, quoting Timaeus, derives it from the Greek *massai, halieus!*, 'Tie up here, fisherman', referring it to some event during the arrival of the Phocaean fleet. This is saved from downright ridicule only by the striking parallel of Haulbowline Island, in Southern Ireland. A bowline is a knot commonly used by sailors. Haulbowline is a small islet prominently situated just off the harbour of Cobh (formerly Queenstown), near Cork, Ireland, once a regular port of call for transatlantic liners. As the source for a toponym, 'Haul on the bowline!' can hardly be less improbable than 'Tie up here, fisherman!', but in Ireland it seems to have worked. Another proposal, recalling that *mas* is a Celtic word meaning villa or farm (still much used today, especially by real estate agents) and that the local Ligurian tribe were the Salyii, sees in Massalia the *Mas* of the *Salyii*. Variant Greek spellings are Massylia, Mattalia, and Messalia (so Thucydides). Full discussion of all these in Ternaux, 9 n. 20.

30. M. Euzennat (n. 21 above), 139, and his n. 17 (biblio.), thinks that 'the ancient dell of the Joliette' was included, and he may well be right. No one can really tell, and my dotted line is taken from the most recent French publications.

31. Strabo (4, 1, 4) says that 'the entire city is walled' (*teteichistai ... he polis sympasa*), Benoit (n. 15 above), 55 maintains that the 'ville basse ou marine était dépourvue de remparts', being sufficiently defended by fortifications on the Goulet.

32. On this basis, the archaic wall ran along the more modern rue Négrel (now obliterated by redevelopment: it was around the rue du Cheval, just off the Place Carnot, half-way up the rue de la République), where a section of foundations to carry a mud-brick wall, with a ditch along its outer face (filled in during a fifth-century expansion of the city) was excavated by Benoit (F. Benoit, *Gallia* 8 (1950), 117, and 24 (1966), 19; filling the ditch, *id.*, 6 (1948), 208; *AJA* 53 (1949), 238-9; R. Lantier, *Gallia* 6 (1948), 448f.; dating, Villard 45 n. 5). MC-L, 105-7. The section of Hellenistic wall on the other side of the hill, 'permettant pour la première fois, d'affirmer que cette butte se trouvait bien à l'intérieur du perimetre de la Ville' is attested in the catalogue of the Musée d'Histoire de Marseille (n. 11 above), 31, and published in *Gallia* 44 (1986), 419.

33. 50 ha – MC-L, 107; 50 ha, 50,000 inhabitants, Catalogue of Musée (n. 11 above), 32. Strabo 4, 1, 4, calls it a city 'of considerable size' (*megethos echousa axiologon*), and Ps. Skymos 'very large' (*Geogr. Graec. Minores*, ed. Müller (Paris, 1855), 212).

34. Caesar's siege – p. 107 above. Nero, see F. Benoit, *RA* 1 (1956), 43. Villard, 3 n. 3. 'Population indocile' – *Guide Bleu, Provence / Côte d'Azur* (Hachette, Paris, 1971), 360. The trouble was that a lot of the buildings in the Old City had connections at cellar level that facilitated clandestine movement by the Resistance.

35. This 'Hippodamian' type of plan was once thought to have originated only in the fourth century BC (so, R.E. Wycherley, *How the Greeks Built Cities* (London, 1962), 18ff., but it has now been found in many Greek cities of earlier date (e.g. Metaponto: *N.Sc.* 20 (1966), 139-40, and tav. II). Route of main street and excavations, Musée de Marseille catalogue (n. 11 above), 32.

36. Excavations of houses: Lucien-François Gantès, 'Massalia retrouvée', *Doss. Arch.* 154 (Nov. 1990), 14-21. Potters quarter: *Gallia* 44 (1986), 418-423. Olynthus: Wycherley (n. 35 above), 24; 187-92. General discussion, MC-L, 187-9.

37. Or his source: Vitr. 2, 1, 5. We have no reason to believe Vitruvius himself ever went anywhere near Massalia. And there is no telling what date the source was, and hence to what period these thatched roofs belong. Ternaux, 19, believes that 'Aedificia privata angusta admodum erant et misera structura' and suggests that the city may also have included native Gallic huts, round structures of wattle and daub (Strabo 4, 4, 3). It is possible, but this can hardly have formed a significant component in Massaliot architecture.

38. H. Rolland, *Gallia* 5 (1947), 155; Rolland excavated the theatre in 1945. F. Benoit, *Gallia* 24 (1966), 1-12, made the Roman identification.

39. Butte des Moulins as Acropolis: MC-L, 108. Stadium inscription: Musée d'Histoire de Marseille inv. no. 83.5.2; catalogue (n. 11 above), no. 202, p. 33. Clerc, 2, 279-80. He sees no particular significance in where the block was found – since it was re-used it could have come from anywhere, and so cannot be said to support the placing of the stadium at the cathedral site. But for rough, re-use work (and the Christian cross is engraved on the block, says Clerc, 'assez grossièrement'), stones are not usually moved very far from their original position. They are too heavy, and one looks for something close at hand. Bringing it from the quarry for official use in monumental construction is, of course, quite a different story. But Clerc is correct in pointing out that often the stadium was outside the city, though he overstates. It was outside in Athens, but he added, 'et partout' goes too far. From the style of the lettering he tentatively dates it to the second century AD. I should perhaps remind the reader that Greek continued in use in Massalia while it formed part of the Roman Empire after 49 BC, and hence the fact that the inscription is in Greek does not mean that it dates to the independent Greek Massalia that is the subject of our study.

40. Benoit records that a few paving stones from it have been found (Benoit (n. 15 above), 69).

41. Strabo 4, 1, 4. A statuette of the unmistakable multi-breasted Artemis of Ephesos (I hesitate to call her 'polymastic'), of the third-second centuries BC, is now in the Marseille museum (inv. no. 83.5.18; catalogue, no. 223, p. 44; W. Froehner, *Catalogue des antiquités grecques et romaines au Musée de Marseille* (Paris, 1897), no. 101). The Treasury of Massalia at Delphi is fully published in *Fouilles de Delphes* (n. 59 below); it is noteworthy chiefly for its palmette-decorated capitals, which do not fit into any of the established orders. John Boardman, *The Greeks Overseas* (Harmondsworth, 1964), 225, sees Phocaean influence in their design. The Treasury was probably dedicated as a thank-offering after the Battle of Alalia (cf. Justin 43, 5; Diod. 14, 93). Athena on coins: Claude Brenot, 'La monnaie de Marseille', *Doss. Arch.* 154 (Nov. 1990), 89, fig. 4. There was also at Massalia (as at Phocaea) an ancient and highly respected *xoanon* (primitive wooden statue) of Athena (Strabo 13, 1, 41.)

42. Ionic capital: F. Benoit, 'Le chapiteau ionique de Marseille', *RA*, 1 (1954), 17-43; G. Daux, *BCH* 82 (1958), 363 (who dates it to the fifth century); R. Martin, *REA* 61 (1959), 75-6 (who detects Halicarnassian/Phocaean overtones); *HMG* 40. Full biblio. in J.P. Morel, *P del P* 21 (1966), 404 n. 82. Illustration, MC-L, 160; catalogue of *Musée de Marseille* (n. 11 above), no. 203 (inv. 85.5.3), p. 33. Given the size of the capital – it is 1.80 m wide – the temple must have been a large one to remain in scale. The width of the Ionic capitals in the Propylaia at Athens is about 1.65.

43. The Docks, MC-L, 107; F. Benoit, *CRAI* (1947), 583; *Gallia* 6 (1948), 208; 18 (1960), 286-8. The fragment of the ship was uncovered during the works building the rue de la République, then the rue Impériale, and was for long known, for no good reason, as 'The Galley of Caesar'.

44. Like the Bourse site, excavation at the Place Jules Verne was a hurried rescue operation, triggered by a project for the construction of a car park. The excavation, by Antoinette Hesnard, was limited to one year (1992-93) and is briefly described by Paul G. Bahn in *Archaeology* 47.3 (May/June 1994), 15. Roger Guery 47.3 (May/June 1994), 15. Roger Guery (*Préactes*, p. 252 n. 3 below), 19, stresses that nearly all of our evidence for harbour works dates to the Roman period, and 'les données archéologiques concernant le port grec sont des plus précaires'.

45. Plan and axonometric reconstruction in *Doss. d'Arch.* 154 (Nov. 1990), 40-1; 'neuf grottes': quoted, *loc. cit.*, from Ruffi, *Histoire de la ville de Marseille* (1696). G. Bertucchi and F. Salviat, 'Un monument méconnu de Massalia: Les caves de "Saint Sauveur", citernes-fontaines de la cité antique', *Archéologie du midi méde-terranéen* 3 (1981), 8-17. An early publication by Grosson, *Recueil des antiquités et monuments marseillais qui peuvent intéresser l'histoire et les arts* (1773), gives a plan and records the presence of an aqueduct 'de construction antique' but it was more probably just a supply channel bringing water in from the catchment area. Workmanship: the stone is the pinkish limestone from La Couronne used for the Hellenistic city walls and carries similar mason's marks. The second century BC dating is confirmed by pottery finds in the fill behind the back wall of the complex.

46. Pliny, *NH* 29, 9, tells how a certain Crinas, a wealthy physician of Massilia who also became famous at Rome, rebuilt, at his own considerable expense, the walls of his native city. Crinas lived during the reign of Nero and the walls in the Bourse site are dated to the second century BC, two and a half centuries earlier, so there is no question of this being the real wall built by Crinas. However, the identification was made during earlier and very limited excavations (around 1913) which found fragments of the wall, and the name, though inaccurate, has stuck. For a detailed account of these early excavations, see Clerc, 2, 281-7. Grand Rue: the spelling is correct, being an archaic form of French, which is retained in a few set phrases. It is sometimes written Grand'Rue.

47. So on the analogy of the well-preserved towers on the circuit wall of Messene. The artillery (firing through square windows), being a long-range weapon, was put upstairs so that it could outrange the artillery of a besieging force, which was obliged to fire from ground level. Archers, who could fire much more rapidly but had a shorter range, used arrow slits and loopholes. They too, of course, could profit from the extra range given by height, and often did, in towers that did not carry artillery; but where you had archers and artillery you could not put them both on the top floor, for they would get in each other's way, and in the context of Hellenistic military science it was the artillery that was considered most impor-tant and hence got the preference. We may therefore presume that the Massalia towers accommodated artillery on top and archers below. E.W. Marsden, *Greek and Roman Artillery: Historical Development* (Oxford, 1969), 126-39.

48. Archaeology, however, has profited from it all. One of the hulks, rescued from the mud, is now preserved in the Musée de Marseille, a priceless relic of marine history. Euzennat (n. 21 above), pl. 24, fig. 13. This whole Euzennat article (pp. 133-40), though brief and intended only as an introductory survey, is for most readers of this book the best and most readily accessible account of the Bourse excavations; it is almost the only one in English. The excavation reports (there has as yet been no definitive site publication) are in *Gallia* 26 (1969), 423-30 (Euzen-nat); 30 (1972), 520-4 (Salviat); 32 (1974), 512-16 (Salviat); 35 (1977), 520-5 (Salviat); and in *CRAI* (1968), 154f. (Euzennat-Salviat); (1974), 529-52 (Euzennat). The wrecked ship is published by P.M. Duval, *CRAI* (1975), 49-50, and by F. Salviat, *Gallia* 35 (1977), 522, and fig. 12.

49. Three *sestertii* of Vespasian were found in the lower courses of the quay (Euzennat (n. 21 above), 136). Avienus, *Or. Mar.* 696ff, enthusiastically celebrates the artificial improvements made to the Port of Massilia by harbour construction – 'sic omne aequor caespiti infudit manus', 'So has the hand of man brought the deep sea into the countryside'.

50. Compare the very shallow cisterns used in irrigation in the Maghreb: A. Trevor Hodge, *Roman Aqueducts and Water Supply* (London, 1992), 63-5.

51. The evidence is not clear. Wooden fragments of a wheel have been found, and are exhibited in the Museum, but was it a water-lifting wheel or an ordinary water-wheel, turned by the current and used to drive machinery (Fr. *roue éléva-trice, roue motrice?*) The Museum catalogue (n. 11 above), 106, describes it as a water-wheel driving a flour mill. Pol Trousset, 'L'eau à Marseille dans l'antiquité' (*Doss. Arch.* 154 (Nov. 1990)), 37, also sees it as a water-wheel, of late (fifth century AD) date and located on a nearby conduit to provide the water to turn it, but he also suggests a second wheel, for water-lifting, of which apparently no fragment survives but which is attested to by 'une mortaise creusée dans la paroi ouest' of the reservoir. The original brochure to the excavations, *Les découvertes archéolo-giques de la Bourse à Marseille* (Marseille, 1968) describes a drawing of the preserved fragments of the wheel as (fig. 40), 'segment d'une roue élévatrice d'eau', but (p. 41) says it was found in situ not in the reservoir but in the conduit. For a fine illustration of the reservoir, see Trousset, *op. cit.*, 30-1.

52. Importance of wells: Hodge (*op. cit.*, n. 50, above), 49; 57. St. Laurent aqueduct, (discovered in 1987): Manuel Moliner, in *Doss. Arch.* 154 (Nov. 1990), 42-3. See also Trousset, *ibid.*, 38. The whole of this article (n. 50 above) is recommended reading.

53. L.F. Gantès, 'La topographie de Marseille grecque: bilan de recherches (1829-1990)', in *Préactes* (p. 252 n. 3 below), 11-13.

54. Although easily accessible, it is so little published that a travel note may assist the visitor. Rail services are by local trains from Marseille to Miramas, via the l'Estaque line; La Couronne – Carro station is 1 km from the sea. By road La Couronne is (at time of writing) a dead-end, the terminus of the D9 super-highway, which however may be in the future extended towards Martigues. The quarries are mentioned by Strabo (4, 1, 6; '100 stades from Massalia city'). The Budé editor, François Lasserre (Strabon, *Géographie*, t.2 (Paris, 1966), 206), derives the names of both Carro and Carry-le-Rouet from their quarries. For another view, see *HMG*, 100 n. 9. See also R. Bedon, *Les carrières et les carriers de la Gaule romaine* (Paris, 1984).

55. The remains of one such barge were found in the harbour of Carry-le-Rouet (Henry Tréziny, in *Doss. Arch.* 154 (Nov. 1990), 25).

56. One must exercise caution in statements about ruts. One often finds references to ruts in a stone roadway (especially passing between the *pondera*, stepping stones, in the streets of Pompeii) as having been 'worn by the wheels of chariots'. Chariots were seldom used except in ceremonial processions and were in any case a very light vehicle – they had to be, to give military speed and man-oeuvrability – which simply would not wear ruts in stone. Heavily laden carts would, but even so I suspect that a lot of so-called ruts were deliberately cut, though perhaps worn by use afterwards. Their positioning and spacing seems to me too regular to be haphazard. One of the very few publications on this (general) feature is M.E. Caillemer, *Notes sur les railways ou chemins à rainures dans l'antiquité grecque* (Paris, 1869); it is fairly skimpy.

57. Ancient use of the quarries dates back to the sixth century BC (*HMG*, 66).

58. There is, for example, a double track line down the west side of the plateau. From the quarry to the ship loading dock is about 400 m, and, given the time it would take to cut a cartload of stone and the fact that for such a distance the cart could not have taken much more than a quarter of an hour on the trip, I was puzzled why a double track was required. I then discovered the difference in gauge. The western track is wider gauge than the eastern one and so they were not parts of the same system. Both tracks came together in a Y-junction at the loading area and the wide-gauge one also has a branch line or siding half-way along it. One cannot tell just by looking which track is older, though relative dating may be possible by drilling, to see how far surface weathering has penetrated into the stone exposed by cutting the grooves. This whole site is urgently calling out for a systematic study.

59. The capitals are given two rows of leaves, one above the other, in W.B. Dinsmoor, *Architecture of Ancient Greece*[3] (London, 1952), 139-40, and 138 (fig. 50); and *AJA* (1923), 164-73. This is because there are difficulties over reconstructing the correct height for the shaft of the column to give it the right proportions relative to its known lower diameter. The French authorities at Delphi now opt for a single row. See J.F. Bommelaer, *Guide de Delphes* (publ. École française d'Athènes: Paris, 1991: ISBN 2-86958-037-1), 62-3. The site publication is by G. Daux, *Fouilles de Delphes* 2 (Paris, 1923), 'Les deux trésors'. Aeolic capitals: one must not confuse this with the 'Proto-Ionic' capitals referred to in some publications as 'Aeolic'. For classification see Dinsmoor, *op. cit.*, 387, and plate XXXIII.

60. Diod. 14, 93.

61. Paus. 10, 8, 6-8. The current state of the problem is summed up by Bommelaer (n. 59 above), 51: 'après plus de trente études, l'accord ne s'est realisé ni sur cette question ni sur celle de savoir quel édifice Pausanias a omis.'

6. The History of Massalia

1. Justin 43, 4. Clerc, 1, 146-51. Some of the infiltrators entered the city hiding under heaps of greenery on decorated carts. It is impossible to read the whole story without being reminded of the Trojan Horse, and wondering whether, in the field of Greek literature, the Hellenisation of the Ligurians had not progressed further than the Massaliots would perhaps, on reflection, have wished.

2 'Magna illis cum Liguribus, magna cum Gallis fuere bella' (Justin 43, 4-5). The Massaliots responded to the attempted assault by redoubling guards and putting the city on to a permanent war footing – 'veluti bellum habeant, sic urbem pacis temporibus custodire'. Clerc (151) comments on the difference with Ampurias, where, in similar circumstances Greeks and natives seem to have settled down to live together amicably in an open and united city (Strabo 3, 4, 8).

3. 'Les données historographiques suivies et bien datées n'apparaissent guère avant –200' – Claire et Roger Rougemont, 'Marseille grecque: les textes antiques', in *Marseille grecque: Marseille et la Gaule; Préactes d'un Colloque international d'histoire et d'archéologie, Marseille, 18-24 novembre 1990*. They stress that 'la masse des textes date de l'époque impériale', and even when incorporating earlier material and sources, deal essentially with Hellenistic Massalia, in the period betwen the Hannibalic War and the siege of Julius Caesar.

4. Zenothemis and Hegestratos. We know about them only because the speech against them was written by Demosthenes (*Orat.* 32) and so preserved among his works (A.T. Murray, *Demosthenes* (Loeb Classical Library, London 1936), 179-97). It is much referred to as a valuable source of information on marine insurance and shipping contracts. The two protagonists were Massaliots who owned and operated a ship chartered to bring a cargo of grain from Syracuse to Athens; they heavily insured the cargo (which they did not own) and then sought to recoup by scuttling the ship. Full account in Lionel Casson, *The Ancient Mariners* (New York, 1959), 116-18. The episode is sometimes quoted to show the extent of Massaliot trading. For this, so isolated a case is weak evidence; it is better than nothing, but not much.

5. Herod. 1, 166; J. Jehasse, 'Victoire à la Cadméenne d'Hérodote et la Corse', *REA* (1962), 241-86; *HMG* 41-2; Clerc, 1, 133-4.

6. The Phocaeans fought with sixty ships, the Etruscans and Carthaginians with sixty each. The Phocaeans lost forty in the battle, and the remaining twenty were left unserviceable, their rams broken. Herod. 1, 166. For a fuller account of Alalia, see p. 140f. above. For some of its economic results, M. Gras, *Latomus* 31 (1972), 678-716.

7. Similar stories of divine intervention are often invoked to cover up distasteful historical truths. During the Persian invasion of Greece in 480 the invading Persians were supposed to have been chased away from Delphi by the intervention of various supernatural figures; this is generally taken as an excuse to cover up a tame surrender of the shrine. For Catumandus, see Justin 43, 5.

8. Justin 43, 5, 8. No mention in Diod. 14, 116.

9. The link evidently worked both ways. J-P. Morel (*P del P* (1966), 402 n. 82) records the existence at Phocaea of a 'priest of Massalia'.

10. See p. 91 above.

11. Diod. 17, 113; Justin 12, 13. Arrian 7, 2, 3, our best source for anything connected with Alexander, only says that the embassy was composed of Greeks, not mentioning Massalia. But their inclusion does seem reasonable.

12. For a full bibliography, see Morel (n. 9 above), (1966), 411 n. 99 (on 'Le "domaine" de Marseille'): also Villard, 107-11 ('il ne faut ni réduire à l'excès le domaine terrestre de Marseille ni non plus en exagérer l'importance' – p. 111). On 16 March 1985, a round-table discussion on 'Le territoire de Marseille grecque' took place at Aix-en-Provence, and its transactions were published as *Études massaliètes* 1 (publ. as *Travaux du Centre Camille Jullian*, CNRS, Université de Provence à Aix, ed. Michel Bats and Henri Tréziny). This is the fullest discussion of the subject, though many of the twelve contributions zero in on specific local points (such as whether individual Celtic *oppida* were included within the Massaliot 'territoire'). Particularly recommended as overviews of the topic are the chapters by H. Tréziny, 'Cité et territoire: quelques problèmes', pp. 7-15; M. Bats, 'Le territoire de Marseille grecque: réflexions et problèmes', pp. 17-42; and J.-P. Morel, 'A la recherche d'un territoire: le cas de Marseille', pp. 161-78. Aristotle, *De mirab. auscult.* 89.

13. *HMG* 191, following J. Bérard (*RA*, 1950, 187), maintains that Phocaean colonies were founded for commercial reasons, while those founded by Corinth and Chalcis were purely agricultural.

14. Frioul Islands: *HMG* 101 n. 23. Lerins: Strabo 4, 1, 10. He also identifies a series of islands, the Stoechades, as being farmed by the Massaliots, which may be the Hyères Islands (Porquerolles), just east of Toulon. Ampurias: *PECS* 303; the island was called Palaiopolis,and eventually was linked to the mainland.

15. e.g. the *oppidum* of the Baou de Saint-Marcel, at the mouth of the Huveaune Valley and only 7 km from the Lakydon. For Celtic *oppida*, see p. 135ff. above.

16. Justin 43, 5: '[Carthaginenses] saepe fuderunt, et pacem victis dederunt' ('they didn't hit them when they were down'); Strabo 4, 1, 4-5.

17. Justin 43, 5: 'Cum Romanis prope ab in initio conditae urbis foedus summa fide custodierunt, auxiliisque, in omnibus bellis, industrie socios iuverunt.' Amm. Marcel. 15, 11: 'Massilia ... cuius societate et viribus in discriminibus arduis fultam aliquoties legimus Romam.' So also Strabo 4, 1, 5; Polyb. 3, 95. For the various effusions of Cicero I cannot here do better than reproduce Clerc's note (Clerc, 2, 2, nn. 2, 3, 5): *De off.* 2, 8, 28: 'Massiliam ... sine qua nunquam imperatores ex transalpinis bellis triumpharunt'; *Phil.* 2, 37, 93: 'Massiliensibus

... quibus rem publicam populi Romani caram esse sentiebat'. 8, 6, 18: 'Massilia, sine qua nunquam ex transalpinis gentibus maiores nostri triumpharunt'; *Pro Font.* 1, 3: 'Massilia ... fortissimorum fidelissimorumque sociorum, qui Gallicorum bellorum pericula populo romano [copiis armisque?] compsensarunt'. Likewise Val. Max. 2, 6, 7: 'Massilienses ... caritate populi romani praecipue conspicui'. Clerc's comment, 2, 2.

18. p. 5 above.

19. Massaliot attitudes: Livy 21, 20; 25-6; 26, 19. Polyb. 3, 96. Ligurians: Ternaux, 25 n. 63.

20. Hannibal's crossing: Polyb. 3, 41. He crossed the Rhône 'where the stream is single, at a distance of about four days' march from his camp on the coast'. For the location, see F.W. Walbank, *Commentary to Polybius* (Oxford, 1957), 1, 377-8. The question is whether Hannibal made the crossing above the confluence with the Durance (i.e. Avignon) so that the Durance would protect his flank from Scipio. It is complicated by the possibility that the Durance has changed its course since antiquity. But Tarascon seems to be the most likely answer. Hannibal assembled his fleet for the crossing in only two days, which certainly implies that neither the Massaliots nor anybody else did much to stop him (Polyb., *loc. cit.*). Dugouts are *monoxyla*.

21. Hasdrubal: Livy 27, 36; Support: Polyb. 3, 96.

22. Livy 37, 54; 40, 18. Apart from the Veneti, who caused trouble during Caesar's conquest with their fleet of heavy, ocean-going ships, the Gauls seem not to have shone as a nautical race. It is not easy to see where they could have got naval assistance from, at this late date. Perhaps Livy was simply speaking loosely and we should not read too much into him on the strength of a single word.

23. Polyb. *Excerpt. Legat.* 131, 134; Livy, *Epit.* 47. Ternaux 26, n. 68.

24. Livy, *Epit.* 40; Florus 3, 2, 3.

25. Narbonese Gaul: The names of the various parts of Gaul are highly confused and confusing. The region closest to Rome was Cisalpine Gaul, which covered the Po basin (including modern Milan and Turin), and to our way of thinking is not part of Gaul at all – certainly not of France. Transalpine Gaul, 'Gaul Beyond the Alps' is also misleading, for, translated as 'Gaul Across the Alps' it evokes in our minds visions of modern France, the scene of Caesar's campaigns, accessible from Italy by passage over the great Alpine passes like the Mont Cenis and the St. Bernard. In fact it originally referred to Provence, and the Alps referred to seem to have been the Maritime Alps, which, though passes existed, most travellers simply by-passed by sea instead of climbing over them (hence my translation 'Beyond' rather than 'Across'). This Transalpine Gaul was eventually organised as a Roman province which, with the foundation of the *colonia* of Narbo (Narbonne) in 118 (so Velleius Paterculus: date disputed – see Rivet (ch. 4, p. 237 n. 1 above), 44) took its name from the new colony and became Narbonese Gaul. Further Roman excursions from Narbonese Gaul led to involvement in the bulk of mainland France, which was thus in turn often loosely referred to as Transalpine Gaul, though that is not what the term meant originally. This whole region was also known by the questionably courteous title of Gallia Comata, 'Hairy Gaul', evidently reflecting the appearance of its inhabitants. Eventually, in the Imperial era, this region was then subdivided into Gallia Belgica, Gallia Lugdunensis, and Aquitania, which, with a kind of joint capital at Lugdunum (Lyon), were generally known as 'The Three Gauls', Cisalpine and Narbonese Gaul not being counted. There were other Gauls as well. Their migrations in the third century took them as far as Turkey, where many of them settled permanently in Anatolia, giving to it their name, Galatia ('Galatai' being 'Gauls' in Greek); so that St. Paul's Epistle to the Galatians is, with both historical and linguistic accuracy, actually addressed 'To The Gauls'.

26. The siege of Entremont is attested by the excavation on the site of large quantities of missiles from Roman artillery. The same is also true of other Celtic *oppida* in the area.

27. Fuller exposition and sources, Rivet (ch. 4, p. 237 n. 1 above), 44-7. The chief tribes involved seem to have been the Cimbri and the Teutones. Inundation: Strabo 7, 2, 1-3 and Florus 1, 37 (III, 3) mention the inundation but do not believe it; Rivet, *loc. cit.,* does. Barbarian hordes: Marius at first declined battle, and when the enemy scornfully staged a march-past in front of his camp, it took them (Plutarch says) six days to do it. 100,000 killed: Plut. *Marius* 21, 2; fertilised fields, *id.*, 15.

28. Orosius 5, 16, 9.

29. Fossae Marianae – see pp. 43, 148 above. The only real evidence is literary, Strabo 4, 1, 7. This no doubt made Marius popular at Massalia and to this day the stereotype Marseillais is always called Marius; Rivet's note (p. 53 n. 73) 'When the widespread local practice of giving boys the Christian name of Marius developed is not quite clear' must be admired for its even-handed blend of perceptiveness and academic reticence.

30. Herod. 2, 158; How and Wells, *Commentary to Herodotus* (Oxford, 1912) 1, 245-6. It was built by Sethos I (1326-1300 BC) and continued in desultory use till the eighth century AD.

31. Cicero, *Pro Fonteio*, tr. N.H. Watts (Loeb Edition, London, 1931). Rivet (69, n. 26) recommends the commentary in G. Clemente, *I Romani nella Gallia meridionale* (1974).

32. Strabo 4, 1, 5; Florus, 3, 2.

33. Caes. *BC* 1, 34-6; 56-8; 2, 1-16. Lucan, *Phars.* 3, 300-74. Vell. Pat. 2, 50. Dio Cass. 41,19. Rivet, 65-6.

34. Clerc, 2, 78, n. 2. The Massaliot naval commander was Parmenon, whose performance in his first battle led him to being replaced (Clerc, 2, 123 n. 1).

35. Ships' tackle: Caesar, *BC* 1, 58, 'neque dum etiam vocabulis armamentorum cognitis'. The mind frankly boggles at the skilled Massaliot sailors being confronted, let alone beaten, by ships commanded on a basis of 'Hey, you! That rope over there, give it a good pull, till I tell you to stop – no, not that, the *other* one!'; but beaten they evidently were. Of course, Caesar is a master of soft-sell propaganda and adept at playing up his own success over difficulties, but to me at least the bit about ignorance of the technical terms for the rigging sounds both unusual and realistic enough to carry the ring of truth. It doesn't sound like an invention, particularly since Caesar did not need excuses, since he won the battle. All this makes the Massaliot defeat even more incredible. On Lucan's account vs. Caesar's, see Clerc, 2, 113.

36. Hermon: Scholiast to Lucan 3, 524. Caes. *BC* 2, 7: 'Nasidianae naves nulli usui fuerant.'

37. Pompey: Plut. *Pomp.* 64. Actium: Florus 21, 25. Clerc, 2, 126-7, not unjustly lambasts 'l'abominable défection de la flotte pompéienne', pointing out that if Pompey had send a squadron of fifty ships, even after Tauroentum, it could not have failed to smash ('écraser') Brutus' makeshift force and save Massalia, a faithful Pompeian ally that Pompey let fall entirely by default. He could easily have spared 50 ships out of 500, especially since he had complete command of the sea (Caesar, effectively, had no navy) and this fleet yet spent the entire war doing nothing.

38. Strabo 4, 1, 5.

39. So Clerc, 2, 29 (following Camille Jullian, *Histoire de la Gaule* (Paris, 1908), 1, 519).

40. Clerc, 2, 29; 2, 2.

41. When I consider the history of the Massaliot navy, I find naturally coming into my mind a Northern Ireland proverb: 'Once you get the reputation of being an early riser you can lie in bed all day.'

42. *IG* 14, 2445, records the achievements of a certain Kleudemos who was an *ephebe geraiteros* (= in his senior year. The term is also known from Chios, where *ephebes* were classed as 'younger, middle, older (*presbyteroi)'*, Chios evidently having a three-year length of service). Kleudemos, after graduating as the leading cadet of his year, went on to serve twice as gymnasiarch, so that this inscription may also be evidence for the existence of liturgies at Massalia, depending on what the office of gymnasiarch involved (the responsibilities vary from city to city, being sometimes a financial backer and sometimes an Honorary President of the Games). See Clerc, 1, 448. *IG* 14, 2444, from St. Gilles (in the Camargue), commemorates a parallel case, a senior *ephebe* who served as *gymnasiarch* (?) and *choregos*.

43. Polyb. 3, 41, 8; Livy 21, 26, 5; Caesar, *BC* 1, 34. The Carthaginians seem to have followed the same principle, relying extensively on 'barbarian' mercenaries, no doubt for the same reason – the smallness of their domestic population.

44. Strabo 4, 6, 4; G. Barruol, 'Le territoire des Albiques', *REL* 24 (1958), 228-56; see also G. Barruol, *Les peuples préromains du sud-est de la Gaule (RAN* suppl. 1).

45. Strabo 14, 2, 5; 12, 8, 2. Clerc, 1, 446.

46. Strabo 4, 1, 5. He compares the arrangements with Cyzicus, where this tripartite division of military stores was evidently the rule. When the siege actually began, it was found that half of the grain in store had been there so long it had turned mouldy and proved inedible (Caesar, *BC* 2, 22, 1).

47. The siege is described in detail by Caesar (*BC* 2, 1-22), and, more poetically, by Lucan, *Phars.* 3, 298-762. Clerc, 2, 128-55.

48. Caesar, of course, says that it was the Massaliots who broke the truce, Dio (DC 41, 25, 2) that it was the Romans. Clerc inclines to the view that it was an unauthorised attack, against orders, by the Roman soldiery, who saw in the truce all their keenly awaited chances of looting go down the drain. See also Cic., *De off.* 1, 10, 33.

49. n. 46 above. Clerc, 2, 146 n. 1, quotes an authority of his day on the storage of grain: three years storage is the limit. There has been much discussion of when the Massaliots had stockpiled their grain if half of it had already gone bad by the start of the siege.

50. Strabo 4, 1, 5. DC 41, 25.

51. Dio (*loc. cit.* above) implies that the terms of Caesar's peace treaty were phased in over a period, only the disarmament and confiscation of the treasury taking effect immediately. Cicero: *Phil.* 8, 6, 18.

52. One is naturally sceptical of this in view of the small size of the Massaliot navy, as discussed above, but what was a very inadequate force in terms of superpower politics may yet have been very effective locally, for there is little record of any of the other cities in the area having had a navy at all. One thinks of the Victorian tradition in the far-flung reaches of the British Empire, accustomed to remedy all sorts of imperial dysfunctions with the prescription 'Send a gunboat!' A gunboat was almost the smallest warship in service, a veritable pip-squeak in any serious navy, but evidently very effective if there was nothing else at all in sight. So may a minuscule Massaliot navy have proved perfectly adequate for the protection of Massaliot trade, until the arrival of Caesar and Pompey lifted naval operations on to a completely different level.

7. Massalia – Politics and Economics

1. Arist. *Pol*. 3, 6 (on which the note *ad loc*. by Jean Aubonnet, Aristotle *Politique*, t.2 (Budé edition, Paris, 1971), 235); here Aristotle uses *demokratia* to mean the bad form (like ochlocracy), a perversion of what we would call 'democracy', his *politeia*. See also *Pol*. 5, 7, for his comments on aristocracy and oligarchy, and n. 5 below.

2. It is clearly put by Clavel-Leveque, 93: 'Marseille reste jusqu' à la fin dominée par une oligarchie qui conserve la totalité des pouvoirs et donne à la constitution, comme au choix de la politique extérieure, une orientation spécific dans le sens bien compris des intérêts d'un Etat dont le caractère des classes est patent.' The 'specified orientation of foreign policy' was the alliance with Rome.

3. Timocracy, Arist. *Eth. Nic*. 8, 10, 1. Xenophon (*Mem*. 4, 6, 12) anticipates modern usage by calling it plutocracy (*ploutokratia*).

4. Athen. *Deipn*. 13, 576A. Some of the names are changed, e.g., Protis becomes Euxenos, and Gyptis Aristoxene, with the name Protis now carried by their son. Strabo 4, 1, 4. The ancient sources (and the Massaliot constitution) are fully discussed by Clerc, 1, 424-34, and by E. Lepore, *Strutture della Colonizazione focea in Occidente (P del P*, 1970), 41-54.

5. Strabo 4, 1, 5, probably based on Aristotle's 'Constitution of Massalia', now lost. The name *Timouchoi* is ambiguous, for its Greek root, *time* can mean either honour or financial wealth. The word could thus mean either the rich or men holding a high position. The distinction is not really important, for at Massalia the two probably came to the same thing. Likewise timocracy could mean a state run either by the wealthy or the honourable (LSJ quote both). In common modern usage it means the first, and is often applied to the constitution of Athens as introduced by Solon. See n. 18 below. Arist. *Pol*. 5, 5, 2 (1305b) comments on the six-hundred limit on the *timouchoi*. General discussion, MC-L, 120-1; significance of the figure 600, 124 n. 31.

6. Clerc, 1, 431; MC-L, 123 n. 10; Lepore (n. 4 above) 47 n. 56. The name *timouchoi* was also used for magistrates at Messenia (Suidas, *s.v.*), Teos (*BCH* 4 (1880), 115, 1.61) and Naucratis (Athen. *Deipn*. 4, 149 F; since Athenaeus actually came from Naucratis we may assume that here the author of this academic rag-bag of trivia for once personally knew what he was talking about). Naucratis being a colony founded by Miletos, and Miletos and Phocaea both being in Ionia, it is possible that the term is of Ionian origin, imported into Massalia from their mother city. There is also epigraphical evidence for the existence at Chios of a board of fifteen, forming an executive committee reporting to the Council (*IGA* 381).

7. Clerc, 1, 426; MC-L, 11 Lepore (n. 4 above), 46.

8. The fifteen as judges: Clerc, 1, 435: as generals, 433; Ionian laws: Strabo 4, 1, 5. Valerius Maximus (2, 9, 8) notes of one law that it was 'non in Gallia ortum', implying that most of the others were, but this seems unreliable.

9. Athen. *Deipn*. 10, 33, 429; Aelian, *VH* 2.38. 'Nam quae est affectuum muliebrium, eorumque Baccho incitatorum, impotentia!' – Ternaux, 49. Clerc, 1, 440, notes that in Aristoph. *Thesm*. secret drinking was satirised as endemic to the women of Athens, but, himself a Marseillais, insists that 'rien ne nous authorise à faire aux femmes de Marseille le même reproche', and that the object of the law must have been merely to enforce a simple and austere lifestyle. He does not explain why men should be exempted. See also A. Tschernia (n. 30 below), 60; Polybius, 7, 11a, 4 (*ap*. Athen. *Deipn*. 10, 440e-441) mentions the prohibition as still being enforced at Rome in his day, but Pliny (*NH* 14, 90) notes that the last case of divorce on such grounds dates to 194 BC. T.J. Dunababin, *The Western Greeks* (Oxford, 1948), 186-7 discusses several parallel cases of wine being forbidden to women, or perhaps refused by them, citing an interesting one, from modern Crete, where it seems to be linked to pride in the maintenance of a local identity. Compare Caesar's report on the Nervii, p. 212 above.

10. Val. Max. 2, 6, 7. He adds (8) that a similar custom obtained on Ceos. To an academic the whole procedure sounds uncomfortably like an application to a granting authority for a subvention towards a sabbatical, and I would not be surprised to hear that the Massaliots had a standing committee with quarterly deadlines for considering applications. Clerc, 1, 436.

11. Val. Max., *loc. cit.* (n. 10 above): 'index in minimis quoque rebus omnia antiquae consuetudinis monumenta servandi' – i.e. it shows how 'they maintained the good old traditions even in the most trivial matters' – such as killing people.

12. 'ne talis spectandi consuetudo etiam imitandi licentiam sumat' – Val. Max., *loc. cit.*

13. 'Omnibus autem, qui per aliquam religionis simulationem alimenta inertiae quaerunt, clausas portas habet, et mendacem et focosam superstitionem submovendam esse existimans' – Val. Max., *loc. cit.*

14. Justin 43, 11, 12.

15. It has been suggested (C. Ebel, *Transalpine Gaul* (Leiden, 1976), 30) that the various restrictions on women were aimed at 'controlling the vivacity of Celtic wives' (the description is Rankin's (p. 286 n. 6 below), 43) or at retarding the rate of intermarriage. Limit on dowries, Strabo 4, 1, 5.

16. Val. Max., *loc. cit.*

17. A.H.M. Jones, *Athenian Democracy* (Oxford, 1964), 81, estimates that 60% of the population of Athens consisted of poor landowners, without even counting the rich ones.

18. Plut. *Solon*, 2, specifies that Massalia was founded (and presumably run) by merchants. The interpretation of Massalia as a city of merchant princes is clearly argued by Clavel-Leveque ('la république marchande qu'est Marseille' – p. 95; 'L'import-export pratiqué par les riches qui dominaient l'État' – 102). Doubts about merchant princes and trade guilds, J. Hasebroek, *Trade and Politics in Ancient Greece* (New York, 1965), 30, 101-2. M.I. Finley, *The Ancient Economy* (Berkeley, 1973), 137-8, emphasises the absence of trade guilds but (131), while recognising the political pre-eminence of farmers at the expense of traders and craftsmen, specifically names Massalia as an exception, basing himself on the article by Lepore (n. 4 above).

19. But see (p. 106 above) my doubts on the effective strength of the Massaliot navy.

20. 'Si Massilienses, nostri clientes, per selectos et principes cives summa iustitia reguntur, inest tamen in ea condicione populi similitudo quaedam servitutis' – Cic., *De rep.* 1, 27. He continues: 'In optimatium dominatu vix particeps libertatis potest esse multitudo, cum omni consilio communi ac potestate careat.' The impotence of the *demos* is repeated by MC-L, 119.

21. The Persian invasion of 480 is often cited as an example of national unity achieved in the face of an external threat. Cynics, however, have often pointed out that it was indeed an unusual and striking demonstration of national cohesion in that it had almost half the Greeks fighting on the same side.

22. For a general account of ancient slavery and attitudes to it, see Keith Bradley, *Slaves and Masters in the Roman Empire* (Brussels, 1984) *passim*. To those unfamiliar with this aspect of antiquity it should perhaps be emphasised that the coming of Christianity made no difference at all. Christians, and Christian clerics, owned slaves just like anybody else, and in all the well-known Bible stories dealing with 'servants', these are not paid servants in our sense, but slaves

– the text of the original Greek makes it quite clear, using the word 'doulos', slave, bowdlerised to 'servant' by the King James translation.

23. Diod. 5, 26. As a free translation 'They swap the barmaid for the bottle' lacks accuracy but perhaps preserves the spirit of the original. The Scythians supposedly went even further, selling their own children into slavery to get wine (*HMG* 202).

24. I must here cheerfully acknowledge my debt to the work of Dr. A. Tschernia, of the Centre Camille Jullian, Aix-en-Provence.

25. A. Tschernia (n. 34 below), 98.

26. Diod. 5, 26, on drunken excesses of Gauls: they either get fighting drunk or pass out under the table. 'Gold mine': he specifically links the Gaul's *philoinia* and the traders *philarguria*. Benoit: *HMG* 191. See also Michael Dietler, 'Commerce du vin et contacts culturels en Gaule', in *Marseille grecque et la Gaule* (*EM* 3, A.D.A.M. éditions, Lattes (France), 1992; ISBN 2-908774-03-8), 401-10, esp. 402, 'l'Hellénisation et la soif celtique'. The whole question of ancient wine is very well treated in Roger Dion, *Histoire de la vigne et du vin en France* (Paris, 1959). See also J. André, 'La vigne et le vin en Provence dans l'antiquité' in *Mélanges Bénévent* (Gap, 1954), 361-8.

27. Diodorus, *loc. cit.*; wine-skins: Dion (n. 26 above) 84-5. In nineteenth-century France wine-skins were still in use for transporting wine in mountainous regions. Wineskins were, in all probability, of two different types. There was the small, personal wineskin, replaced by our bottle or flask, and carried on a trip, as it still is by hikers and skiers. Thus Odysseus, before disembarking on the island of the Cyclops, fills up his wineskin from the amphoras stored on board ship (Hom. *Od.* 9, 196; 204-12). Second, there is a large wineskin, made from the whole skin of a large animal, used for transporting wine in bulk. Full of wine, this must have been a very heavy and unwieldy mass to handle – one can only admire the effortless aplomb with which satyrs regularly manipulate it in vase-paintings – but, unlike amphoras, the container was itself light and not only eliminated a useless deadweight to be transported for the sake of its contents, but when empty could easily be folded and packed for return and reuse. But see A. Tschernia, *EM* 3, 475; Ch. Goudineau, *Trade in the Ancient Economy* (n. 34 below), 80, denies the widespread use of goatskins: 'all that is false'. An alternative for overland transport was to transfer the wine to casks, often thought to be a Gallic invention (or at least speciality). The casks were then frequently transported by carts or even ships, as we know from various representations in plaques and reliefs. The best known are the 'tank-wagon' from Langres (shown in K.D. White, *Greek and Roman Technology* (London, 1984), 133, fig. 132), and the Moselle wine-barge, now in the Landes museum, Trier (F. Kretzschmer, *La technique romaine* (Brussels, 1966), 87, fig. 143; see also 77, fig. 128). See also Benoit, *HMG* 202 n. 94: 'Marchandise pondéreuse et fluide à la fois, le vin ne peut être transporté en quantité importante que par voie d'eau'.

28. See Lucien-François Gantès, 'L'apport des fouilles récentes à l'étude quantitative de l'économie Massaliète', *EM* 3, 171-8, esp. table 2 (graph of relative frequency of finds), 175. Amphorae of other types, such as Punic or Iberian, have been found as well, but not in such numbers as seriously to upset the general picture here outlined. There is also the possibility that some of the amphorae found did not contain wine but olive oil, or even dry goods, such as grain; in Spain they even exported tuna in them (B.B. Shefton, *ibid.*, 466). But in most of them it seems to have been wine (*HMG* 191). Wine imports were also accompanied by the import of fine pottery, figured cylixes, kraters, and the like, destined not for the transport but the drinking of wine. See p. 124 below. The influx of Italian wine seems not to have been a case of cut-throat competition, but to start with at least a joint

259

Italic-Massaliot enterprise under the protective treaty of friendship between Massalia and Rome, with Massaliot merchants co-operating. MC-L, 55.

29. Toulouse: thousands of Italic amphorae, or fragments of them, have been found, and it is estimated that the total figure for those having existed may run into millions (lecture by A. Tschernia at Univ. of Provence at Aix, 10 January 1980). Toulouse may have been a trans-shipment centre. It is certainly unlikely that all this wine was drunk locally; even a Celtic thirst has its limits, set by physical cubic capacity if by nothing else.

30. For a full account of the use of *dolia* in shipping wine, see A. Tschernia, *Le vin de l'Italie romanine* (Ecole Française de Rome; Paris/Rome, 1986), 138-9. The *dolia* were apparently a permanent fixture on the ship, and 'faisaient des ces navires des sortes de bateaux-citernes'. It is understandable that they must have formed such an enormous dead-weight, especially when full, that one would not have wanted to move them by unloading, but emptying the wine out of them once its level got down towards the bottom of the *dolium* much have presented a real problem. Since it also effectively turned the ship into a tanker this must also have increased costs, by restricting the nature of any return cargo it could carry from Gaul to Campania. Modern tankers, it will be remembered, spend half their life sailing empty. An empty *dolium* weighed one-third as much as the wine it could contain, while fully a half (or even more) of the weight of a full amphora was that of the container (p. 139).

31. Antoinette Hesnard, 'Marseille et la mer', in *Doss. Arch.* 154 (Nov. 1990), 56, photo 2. Tschernia (n. 30 above), 140.

32. L. Casson, *Ships and Seamanship in the Ancient World* (Princeton, 1971), 172 n. 25, quoting N. Lamboglia, 'Il relevamento totale della nave romana di Albegna', *Rivista di Studi Liguri* 27 (1961), 213-20. This ship, though rather large, was apparently in no way exceptional, being about one-third the size of the Alexandria-Rome grain clippers (Casson, *loc. cit.*). On shipwrecks in general in the area, see Luc Long *et al.*, 'Les épaves archaïques de la Pointe Lequin (Porquerolles, Hyères, Var)', in *EM* 3, 199-234 (esp. e.g., fig. 50 (230, map)); and Antoinette Hesnard, 'Nouvelles recherches sur les épaves préromaines en baie de Marseille', *ibid.*, 235-43. Both articles have extensive bibliographies.

33. Another (very rough) estimate by Tschernia (n. 34), 86, is 12,000,000-15,000,000 litres.

34. A. Tschernia, 'Italian wine in Gaul', in *Trade in the Ancient Economy*, ed. Peter Garnsey *et al.* (London, 1983), 87-104, esp. 92.

35. Abbé Audibert, *Dissertation sur les origines de Toulouse* (Avignon and Toulouse, 1764), 3, quoted by Tschernia (n. 34 above), 90. Châlon; *loc. cit.* Tschernia (p. 113) offers illuminating comparisons on the volume of consumption. Mediaeval Siena averaged 419 litres of wine per person per year, while he estimates total consumption at Rome around 1,450,000-1,800,000 h.l. – three times the per capita consumption of eighteenth-century Paris.

36. MC-L, 56. For regulation of the traffic by taxes, see Cicero, *Pro Fonteio* 19-20, and Tschernia (n. 34 above), 93; also Cic. *De rep.* 3, 9, 16.

37. Tschernia (n. 34 above), 99, well equates the Celtic use of wine to the tribal ceremony known to anthropologists as potlatch. The connection between wine and local cultures, particularly its role in reinforcing the hierarchy, is discussed by Michael Dietler, 'Commerce du vin et contacts culturels en Gaule au premier âge du fer', *EM* 3, 401-10.

38. One thinks of a Roman parallel. Members of the Senatorial Order were forbidden to engage in trade and were supposed to make their money out of their landed estates. But they were allowed to get into the trade of brick-making, since that was originally part of the work carried out on farms and therefore counted as agriculture; and hence was a respectable job fit for gentlemen.

39. An alternative explanation is offered by Christian Goudineau, that Massalia may have been founded, as Plutarch (n. 18 above) says, as a trading city run by its merchants, but by the first century BC the commercial element had faded, leaving the city as an orthodox Greek *polis* which then became 'of minor importance' when Caesar stripped it of most of its territory ('Marseilles, Rome, and Gaul' in *Trade in the Ancient Economy* (n. 34 above), 76-86, esp. 86).

40. See Guy Bertucchi, 'Les amphores et le vin de Marseille, VI s. av. J.-C. – II s. ap. J.-C.': 25 supplement to *RAN* Edn. du CNRS, Paris, 1992 (esp. 193-209, for ancient sources on Massaliot wine).

41. As previously noted, the first automatic reaction of Greek travellers in a foreign land was to look and see if it would be good for growing vines; Hom. *Od.* 9, 133. Ionian imports: MC-L, 47. The references are conveniently assembled in her n. 309, p. 74. There is a map of Rhodian amphora finds in the Gulf of Lion in M. Labrousse, *RAN* 1971, 43, fig. 7.

42. Pliny *NH* 14, 68: 'Inter Pyrenaeum Alpesque [palmam habet].' Athenaeus 1, 27, C: '*ho Massalietes kalos; oligos de gignetai.*' Martial 3, 82; 10, 36; 13, 123. The point about the smoky taste is that genuinely old wines did taste smoky, having acquired the taste from the pitch sealing the jar, but it was also a way of artificially giving the wine an appearance of age. Martial evidently thought the Massaliots overdid it. Columella 1, 6, 20, describes the process, maintaining that the smoke treatment, if not carried to excess, actually does age the wine.

43. *Vinum silatum* was made from the herb *seseli*, which was probably the same thing as *silphium*. For the question of herbal wines, see *HMG* 198-9; Clerc, 1, 283-4. An amphora found at St. Blaise actually carries the inscription 'myrrh wine', *oinos myresikos* (H. Rolland, *Saint-Blaise* 1, 145, and fig. 163). Dion (n. 26 above), 49, theorises that tastes and fashions in drinks tend to originate in seaports and to spread following the sea-routes, not just because sailors were hard drinkers, but because major vineyards needed convenient transport for their exports, and without it did not become major. As an example of 'wine cities' in Iberia he quotes Alicante, Malaga, Jerez and Oporto, all seaports; also Madiera. Benoit (*loc. cit.*) goes further, seeing in the seseli-flavoured *vinum silatum* the ancestor not only of 'fenioueto', celebrated by the Provençal poet Frederic Mistral as a traditional Christmas-time liqueur at Aix-en-Provence (F. Mistral, *Trésor du félibrige*) but also of both pastis and ouzo, 'liqueur des ports méditerranéens de l'Orient à l'Occident de la Méditerranée'. The resemblance in taste between ouzo and pastis is undeniable, but neither can have taken its definitive form before the arrival of distilled spirits in the late Middle Ages or thereabouts, and this time-lag of over a millennium makes it hard to say that both were derived from Massaliot flavouring of wines (which Benoit explicitly does say, even for ouzo). The flavouring agent may have remained the same but in wine would taste very different from spirits, and in any case the Greeks may have taken to giving ouzo its distinctive aniseed flavour on their own, quite independently of what the French were doing to pastis in Marseille. Certainly there must be quarters outside the academic world where the suggestion that the national drink of Greece was invented in France would not be welcomed with enthusiasm.

44. *HMG* 197 n. 40; Villard, 134 n. 1. See also G. Barruol, *Les peuples préromains du sud-est de la Gaule* (*RAN* Supplement 1; Paris, 1975), 93.

45. *apsinthetes* (Dioscorides 5, 49). Pliny *NH* 14, 109. Columella 12, 35, includes it in a list of flavoured wines: 'vinum absenthiten et hysopiten et habrotoniten et thymiten et marathiten et glechoniten sic condire oportet ... idque mox tussientibus per hiemem recte datur.' For a full discussion of ancient absinthe see Apicius,

1, 3, and J. André's note *ad loc.* (J. André, *Apicius, l'Art Culinaire* (Paris, 1965), 29-30.

46. The process sounds impractical, but a modern authority on viticulture is quite clear on the point that it does work: 'La vigne peut effectivement prendre certaines odeurs des plantes voisines' – H. Isnard, *La vigne en Algérie* (Gap, 1955), vol. 2, 183 (quoted by J. André, Pliny *NH* 14 (Paris, 1958; Budé edition), 132 n. 2, *ad* ch. 109).

47. Dion (above n. 26), 1: 'L'homme, en effet, aime le vin comme l'ami qu'il a choisi; par préférence, non par obligation.' This diversity of local tastes also makes it risky to assume that regions today famous for producing fine wines (especially in France) must have produced equally great wines in antiquity. Geology and the climate may have been the same, but taste was not, and for this or other reasons French wines remained in Classical times a regional product for local consumption and were little exported.

48. Therapeutic qualities: *seseli*, just mentioned as the putative ancestor of ouzo, is recommended by Pliny *NH* 20, 36, for convulsions and liver complaints, and when eaten by animals is a purgative (*NH* 8, 112; the same story is found in Cicero, *ND* 2, 50, 127). Absinthe, which grows on the lower slopes of the Alps, is used to induce perspiration and as a cough cure: coughs, n. 45 above); 'puissant sudorifique', Papon, *Histoire de Provence* (Paris, 1777), 1, 147. Herbs in general, *HMG* 198. Sometimes even the climate must have helped. In the winter rigours of Northern Gaul no doubt sufferers from coughs and sneezes often had pressed upon them steaming cups of *Côtes du Lacydon, appellation controllée*, fragrant with heaven knows what herbal infusion, with the vague but comforting assurance that 'It'll do you good'; as it surely often did, psychologically if not otherwise.

49. Coastal finds: *HMG* 199, n. 72. *Oppida*: *HMG* 184-6 for full listings. MC-L, 45, notes that from the fourth century on Massalia had a monopoly of trade with the *oppida* ('Marseille, seule à même de commercer avec les *oppida* indigènes'), though this includes also wine imported from overseas and not made in Massalia. Shipwrecks: Patrice Pomey and Luc Long, *Les premiers échanges maritimes du Midi de la Gaule du Vie au IIIe s. av. J.-C., EM* 3, 189-98 (with biblio.). M. Bats (ed.), *Les amphores de Marseille grecque: chronologie et diffusion (VI-I s. av. J.-C.),* Actes de la table ronde de Lattes, 11 mars 1989 (*EM* 2, Aix-en-Provence, 1990, esp. (P. Arcelin), 191-205 (extensive biblio.)). Also, M. Py, *La diffusion des amphores massaliètes sur le littoral du Languedoc oriental, ibid.* 73-86. This whole volume of *Etudes massaliètes 2* is worth studying on the subject. See also C. Goudineau, 'Marseille, Rome and Gaul', in *Trade in the Ancient Economy* (n. 34 above), 80-2. He denies the relevance of shipwrecks as evidence for the distribution of Massaliot wine (80): 'For us, it has no value, since Marseilles did not need boats to distribute her wine in Gaul.' This overlooks the transport of wine both by river boats (p. 41 above) and along the littoral by coasting vessels. Many cities, especially around Nice, Antibes and the Esterel, must have depended largely on seaborne supplies, there being, at this period, no coastal road adequate for heavy freight. One must be careful in the interpretation of the distribution of find spots. An abundance of amphorae of some given type in a certain region may indeed be evidence of ancient trade patterns, but may reflect nothing more than assiduous local excavation. A. Tschernia well describes and illustrates the perils of such an approach by reproducing a map in which the recorded find-spots of Dressel I amphorae show an intense concentration in Brittany. This is solely because this area was intensively studied by one archaeologist, P. Galliou, and 'it would be absurd to conclude that Italian wine was exported to Brittany in particular' (Tschernia (n. 34 above), 88-9).

50. The standard work here is François Villard, *La céramique grecque de*

Marseille (VIe-IVe siècle) (Bibliothèque des Ecoles d'Athènes et de Rome; Paris, 1960) (abbrev. Villard), 13-137. *HMG* 137-90. Clerc, 1, 204-10, 307-14, deals with ceramic imports as evidence for trade with Greece and Ionia. See also Pierre Rouillard, *La place de Marseille dans le commerce des vases attiques à figures rouges en Méditerranée occidentale (Ve-IVe s. av. J.-C.)*, *EM* 3, 179-87.

51. Celtic fondness for unmixed wine: Poseidonios *ap.* Athen. *Deipn.* 4, 152; MC-L, 52. Vix krater, p. 214 above. Shipwreck, Luc Long *et al.*, 'Les épaves archaïques de la pointe Lequin', *EM* 3, 205, tabl. II. The wreck, Épave IA, is located at the Porquerolles (Iles d'Hyères).

52. *HMG* 168-79 for the spread up the Rhône valley. MC-L, 16 for proportions of vases imported from the various sources to Marseille c. 600 BC. F. Villard, 'La céramique archaïque de Marseille', *EM3*, 164-70.

53. MC-L, 26: 'Dans un tel système d'échanges, le troc est la règle essentielle: c'est sur lui que repose la plus grande partie des mouvements de marchandises.'

54. Poseidonios *ap.* Strabo 3, 2, 9.

55. This of course does not mean that tetradrachms were in wide daily use, just that, being the largest and finest coins struck (apart from the quite exceptional and very rare Attic decadrachms), they are the ones the museums select for exhibition. The point is that while we have whole ranges of tetradrachms from other quite small cities, Massalia produced none.

56. MC-L, 27; Clerc, 1, 198-203. The coin-types come from Phocaea, Aegina, Mitylene, Cyzicus, Lampsacus, Clazomenai, and Velia. Some of these may have been actually struck in Massalia, not imported. Auriol: A.E. Furtwangler, *Monnaies grecques en Gaule. Le tresor d'Auriol et le monnayage de Massalia 525/520 – 460 av. J.-C.* (Fribourg, Office du Livre, 1978). The technique of minting coins and the use of the incuse punch is well illustrated in Charles Seltman, *Greek Coins* (London, 1933), 21.

57. Full account by Claude Brenot, 'Le monnayage de Marseille au Ve s. av. J.-C.', *EM* 3, 245-53. The reader may find more readily available Claude Brenot, 'La monnaie de Marseille', *Doss. Arch.* 154 (Nov. 90), 88-93, an excellent summary of the whole topic. MC-L, 41-3, and, esp., 95-103.

58. MC-L, 98. There has been a good deal of discussion of the various problems raised by these light drachmae, notably on how the actual weights of the various coins, at Massalia and elsewhere, are to be reconciled, discussed by MC-L, 100-1; also Brenot (*Doss. Arch.*, n. 57 above), 91. Heavy drachmae, *id.* 90; MC-L, 99-100.

59. For this last century and the influence of Roman currency on Massaliot bronze ('Aligné sur le monnayage de bronze de Rome, le monnayage de Marseille en suit par voie de conséquence, la chronologie') see Brenot (*Doss. Arch.,* n. 57 above), 93. MC-L, 103.

60. So MC-L, 41. Britain: her p. 70 n. 237. Full biblio in her p. 70 n. 236.

61. MC-L, 102.

62. Hence the remarks of Furtwangler on the parallel if less pronounced case of the large small-denomination coinage of Phocaia: 'N'est-ce point un des secrets de la pénétration phocéenne que d'avoir suivi une politique monétaire basée sur la diffusion de monnaies de petit module là où les fortes concentrations de capitaux n'étaient pas nécessaires?' (quoted in MC-L, 102). The same argument explains Massalia's decision to expand their currency downward, as it were, into bronze pieces rather that upwards into tetradrachms: 'Ce monnayage de bronze était destiné à servir aux besoins des petites transactions locales en ville et dans la *chora*, comme à servir aux colporteurs et aux patrons – caboteurs dans leurs rapports avec leurs indigènes.' – MC-L, 103.

63 For some fine examples, see David C. Young, *The Myth of Greek Amateur Athletics* (Chicago, 1984), 124 n. 15. The modern scholar Stephen Miller, *Arete*

(Chicago, 1979), iii (quoted by Young *ibid.*) 'equates the wages of a skilled work-man with $8 per day [1979]'. This works out at one-third of the legal minimum wage ('so far below the official poverty level that no graduate teaching assistant receives so little [to say nothing of the unemployed]'). The correct official union wage per day, 'at this same period', as attested by 'the Santa Barbara Carpenters Local Union No. 1062' is $101. $8, when the real figure is $101! *Caveat lector.* Erechtheion inscriptions: *IG*² 1, 372-4 (e.g. 373, 1, 65-7).

8. Cultural Massalia

1. Clerc, 2, 313.

2. Architecture, p. 79; support, p. 255 n. 33.

3. Cic. *Pro Font.* 5, 13 ('staunchest allies'); *Phil.* 8, 6 ('Gaul'); *De off.* 2, 8, 28 ('triumphs'). The first two references can be partly discounted, for Cicero was there speaking as a trial lawyer, but in the *De officiis* he presumably wrote what he really thought. See also p. 253 n. 17 above.

4. 'At the ends of the earth, encircled by tribes of Gauls, they are washed by the waves of barbarism' ('cum in ultimis terris cincta Gallorum gentibus barbariae fluctibus adluatur') – Cic. *Pro Flac.* 63. His climax is the observation that Massalia's aristocratic administration is more easily admired than imitated.

5. 'Fair dealing' = *fides*; 'self-control' = *disciplina*; 'responsibility' = *gravitas*. These Latin abstracts are notoriously difficult to translate, but the definitions will give some idea of what is meant. For the qualities themselves, see Cic. *Pro Font.* 5, 13; *Pro Flac.* 63; Valerius Maximus (2, 6, 7) also praises Massalia's 'disciplinae gravitas, prisci moris observantia ("respect for tradition"), severitatis custodia'. See also Tac. *Agr.* 4: 'locum Graeca comitate et provinciali parsimonia mixtum ac bene compositum' ('a fine blend of Greek sophistication and a thrifty peasantry'). Expatriate Romans at Massalia: the best known is Milo, in exile (DC, 40, 54, 2), but Catiline also wrote to the Senate that, to avoid civil dissension, he was emigrating there (Sallust, *Cat.* 34). He did not go, but his letter suggests it was a common destination. Strabo (a writer of imperial date) 4, 1, 5, maintains that in his day 'all the most illustrious Romans' went there to study, instead of Athens. Cic. *Pro Font.*, pictures it as a centre of heavy Roman immigration and a leisure resort: 'Gallia plena civium Romanorum'. They also often sent their children there to get a Greek education.

6. Clerc, 2, 29-30. Roman expeditions against brigands, Florus 1, 19. 'Dès la fin du seconde siècle Marseille semblait avoir considérablement négligé sa marine de guerre, au point de ne plus pouvour faire la police de ses rivages' – Clerc, 2, 53. The dockyards and harbour installations were still there to impress Strabo (4, 1, 5), but when the war with Caesar came the fleet was not ready and they had to try to rebuild it in a hurry ('classem reficiebant' – Caesar, *BC* 1, 34-5). Clerc (2, 2) sums it all up very well (p. 106 above).

7. G. Nenci, 'Le Relazioni con Marsiglia nella Politica Estera Romana', *REL* 24 (1958), 24-97, esp. 25-47. 'L'attegiamento ciceroniano verso Marsiglia è dunque caratteristico' (31). He argues that, roughly speaking, Cicero vociferously praised Massalia until it fell to Caesar, then kept quiet until Caesar himself fell, where-upon he opened up again and 'Marsiglia è oggetto di continui rifermenti ciceroniani'.

8. Only its extreme relevance emboldens me here to remind the reader of the familiar and famous critique of Virgil, *Aen.* 6, 847-53 ('Excudent alii ...'). That hits the nail on the head.

9. Cato: John Scarborough, *Roman Medicine* (London, 1969), 52-65 ('Cato and the medical encyclopaedists'). On Greek names of professionals, it may not be too

trivial to recount what put the idea into my head. I was once looking for a ladies' hairdresser for my wife, and searching through the appropriate listings in the Yellow Pages of the Ottawa phone book was much struck by the vast number of names claiming an origin in some accepted centre of sophistication, usually in Europe. There were 'Antoine of Paris', 'Luigi of Rome', Adolphus of Munich', even 'Louise of New York'. 'Greg of Calgary' and 'Joe of Kansas' were signally absent. The principle is of course familiar from actors' use of stage names designed to project an image, and made me wonder if another identity sometimes lay concealed under the 'Apollodorus of Rhodes' sobriquet. What good Roman, after all, would want to employ as a doctor 'Eskingorix of Lugdunum', or even 'Gaius Sidius of Puteoli'?

10. The best discussion of Pytheas is in Clerc, 1, 399-423, with biblio. (399 n. 2) up to Clerc's date of writing (1926). Christina Horst Roseman, *Pytheas of Massalia* (Ares, Chicago, 1994) is recommended though it is unfortunate that she is evidently unaware of the account of Clerc (which is not readily accessible in N. America). She prints a full text and commentary of the surviving fragments of Pytheas' account, and a nine-page biblio. (161-8). Pytheas' text (it survives only in 28 fragments) is also published by H.J. Mette, *Pytheas von Massalia* (Berlin, 1952). See also C.F.C. Hawkes, *Pytheas: Europe and the Greek Explorers* (Oxford, 1975), and F. Gisinger, 'Pytheas von Massalia', *RE* 24 (1963), 314-66; see also Lallemand (p. 231 n. 11 above).

11. Clerc, 401. Polybius seems to have been motivated by professional jealousy, for, having himself between 150 and 146 embarked on a voyage beyond the Straits of Gibraltar, he wanted to represent it as the first time anyone had been there (Polyb. bk. 34; F.W. Walbank, *Polybius* (Berkeley, 1972), 127). He even tried to prove that Odysseus had not got that far either. Strabo 'a eu en Polybe une confiance aveugle' (Clerc), and his understanding of Northern Europe ran counter to Pytheas' personal observations there.

12. Attested by Strabo 2, 4, 2.

13. The error is much less if, as has been suggested, Pytheas' figure is really 43° 18′25″, giving an error of a mere 3.5 km. (Clerc, 1, 403 n. 3).

14. Tides, Clerc 1, 403. The existence of tides in the Ocean was known, but they were wrongly thought to be caused by winds. North Pole: Clerc *ibid*; Roseman (n. 10 above), 118-19, and fig. 7. There are two factors involved. One is that the location of the celestial North Pole has moved since Pytheas' day, because of the phenomenon known as the Precession of the Equinoxes, and was not then near what we know nowadays as the Pole Star. The other is that in the fourth century BC there was no star at all at the North Pole, which could be located only in the middle of an empty space between one star of Ursa Minor and the constellation Draco (p. 231 n. 9).

15. Strabo 2, 4, 2 (Eratosthenes); 2, 1, 18 (Hipparchus). For the reputation and achievements of Eratosthenes and Hipparchus see Benjamin Farrington, *Greek Science* (Penguin ed., Harmondsworth, 1901), 222, 232ff.). He seems also to have been for long honoured in Massalia, where what was claimed to be his original gnomon was kept on public display. Canadian readers will inevitably think of the astrolabe (a surveying instrument) of Samuel de Champlain, the seventeenth-century explorer of Canada, which is now preserved in honour in the Museum of Civilisation in Ottawa/Hull. The authenticity of this astrolabe has often been challenged, which may possibly offer a further parallel with Pytheas' gnomon in Massalia.

16. Roseman (n. 10 above), 149-50; three years, 155. Hawkes (n. 10 above) 40, 44, suggests a political deal between Massalia and Carthage to permit his passage. The possibility that he actually travelled on a Phoenician ship is rejected by Clerc,

1, 404, who believes it was a semi-official, semi-private venture, and that he had to call at Cadiz to top up supplies, thereby necessitating Carthaginian co-operation. Hawkes (n. 10 above), 44 on 325 as Pytheas' date.

17. Probably called Mona (hence the modern name, Man – it has nothing to do with men!), and referred to by other writers (Tac. *Agr.* 14; Pliny *NH* 2, 186-7; 4, 103 (who also mentions a 'Monapia'); Caesar *BG* 5, 13). There is also some debate whether some of these 'Monas' may instead be Anglesey. Hawkes (n. 10 above), 35, raises the interesting point that Mona may be a rendering of *monè*, which in Greek means 'alone', a good description of the Isle of Man (but certainly not Anglesey, which some might think hardly rates as an island at all, being so close to the mainland, and connected to it by bridges across the Menai Strait). Pytheas evidently referred to the Britons as 'Albions' and the Irish as 'Ierni', thus establishing a very early existence for the names Albion and Hibernia (Avienus, *Or. Mar.* 111-12). The commentator J.P. Murphy (Avienus, *Or. Mar.* (Ares, Chicago, 1977), 52) thinks that '*Albiones* is a pre-Celtic name, probably Ligurian', while *Ierne*, Ireland is a transliteration of the Greek appellation 'Iere Nesos', Holy Island. No one seems to have suggested any parallel with the modern Holy Island, the small island off the coast of Anglesey, nowadays known chiefly as the location of the Irish ferry port, Holyhead.

18. Pliny, *NH* 2, 186-7 (six days). Iceland/Norway: Roseman (n. 10 above), 156-8. Hawkes (n. 10 above), 35: 'So Thule as Iceland seems to me clear.' Clerc, 1, 414(esp. nn. 3-4)-16, opts for Norway, bringing Pytheas as far north as Tromsø, north of the Arctic Circle.

19. Pliny, *NH* 4, 104. The midnight sun in particular has caused much astronomical calculation of latitudes (Roseman (n. 10 above), 141); it implies a latitude of around 66°N, which would be acceptable for both Tromsø and N. Iceland (map in Hawkes (n. 10 above), 30, showing also the limits of drift ice). The trip to Iceland may perhaps not have been quite so hair-raising a shot in the dark as one often thinks. First, even Europeans think of Iceland as impossibly remote: in fact, the distance from Scotland to Iceland is much less than that from Marseille to Gibraltar, which we often think of as quite close together. Second, Roseman (107) notes that in polar latitudes, because of increased refraction, visibility can be extended to distances we would consider incredible, so that 'there are attested sightings of Iceland from ocean positions several hundred kilometres to the west, and from the Faroes some 386.24 km to the east'. It must also be remembered that such concepts as latitude, the tropics, and the Arctic Circle were the creation (or discovery) of Greek astronomers, and familiar to ancient writers (see Strabo 2, 5, 8.)

20. Hawkes (n. 10 above), 10-12. Roseman (n. 10 above), 85-7. All this region Pytheas, surprisingly to us, calls 'Scythia'. See Clerc, 1, 412-13.

21. Kantion – Hawkes (n. 10 above), 32. Clerc, 1, 409. Did he, for example, follow the Channel from Cornwall east to Kent, returning to make the trip up through the Irish Sea (so Clerc) or did he return from Jutland to the Orkneys and thence down the East Coast of Britain to Kent, and on to Brittany by the Channel (so Hawkes)?

22. Euthymenes: Athen. *Deip.* 11, 87; Plut. *De placitis philosph.* 4, 1; Lydus, *De mensibus* 4, 106; Sen. *Quaest. Natur.* 4, 1. Again, the best account is in Clerc (1, 393-9). Roseman (n. 10 above), 81 n. 79, quotes P. Fabre, 'Les Massaliotes et l'Atlantique', *107me congrès national de sociétés savantes d'archéologie* (Brest, 1982), 29, as dating Euthymenes to the sixth-fifth century BC. *RE* 6, 1 (1907), 1509-11 (F. Jacoby).

23. To the theory-bound minds of many ancient savants symmetry was a great virtue, and it was therefore attractive to believe in an east-west oriented Nile south of the Mediterranean to balance the undoubtedly east-west oriented Danube north of it. To an ancient mind there was therefore nothing inherently unlikely about the Nile turning up somewhere in Mali or E. Mauritania.

24. p. 235 n. 38.

25. Clerc, 1, 390f. See p. 235 n. 38 above for short biblio. Connoisseurs of the exotic in travellers' tales will appreciate Hanno's account of how in the tropics of Africa he encountered wild, hairy women, known locally as gorillas; they caught and killed three of them, skinned then, and took the skins back to Carthage (Hanno, *Periplus* 18).

26. Both are mentioned together by Pliny, *NH* 2, 169, who specifies 'ad Europae noscenda missus eodem tempore Himilco'. Otherwise Himilco is scarcely anywhere mentioned.

27. Pliny, *NH* 7, 56, 197. MC-L, 69 n. 208 – 'le mystère reste entier à son suject'. Benoit (*HMG* 61 n. 68) is equally sceptical – 'il n'y a aucune raison d'identifier le navigateur Midacritus ... avec un marseillais du VIe siècle'. Villard (158) quotes, only to reject, the theory that the name is a misspelling for *Midas Phryx*, 'the Phyrgian Midas'.

28. Clerc, 1, 462.

29. Clerc, 2, 314, is scathing: 'Toute fois, ce titre "L'Université" peut paraître quelque peu ambitieux. En fait, le plupart des historiens de Marseille ont grossi démesurément le rôle joué par Marseille à ce point de vue, et attribué à ses écoles la formation de quantité d'orateurs et de littérateurs connus, originaires de la Gaule romaine, mais dont rien absolument indique qu'ils aient jamais séjourné à Marseille.' The reader so interested may find an impressive list of names in [Mgr.] Paulin Scolardi, *Marseille la Grecque* (Marseille, 1975), 184-5.

30. Greek inscriptions found in France are conveniently reproduced in *IG* XIV, Suppl. (repr. Ares, Chicago, 1978). Those from Massalia itself are nos. 2432-66 (pp. 8-29). Some are quite late, showing that Greek continued in use long after the Roman conquest: no. 2462 is of Christian date and content. Of equal significance is the common appearance of familiar Latin names such as Flavius, Titus, Gemellos, or Fulvius, in Greek script (as of course was also common in the Eastern half of the Empire).

31. Ch. Rostaign, *Essai sur la toponymie de la Provence* (Paris, 1950), esp. 307-15, *HMG* 20-4, including extensive and interesting biblio. in the notes (see 20 n. 3); MC-L, 13 n. 9 ('si obscur qu'il soit, le nom de Massalia est ligure'), follows the thesis that 'Massalia' was the Ligurian name of one of two streams flowing into the Vieux Port, the name of the other being 'Lakydon', so that between them they gave their names both to the Greek city and its port.

32. So W. v. Wartburg, *Evolution et structure de la langue française* (Paris, 1934), 10. He maintains (9) that 'on a tort de nier toute influence du grec sur les parlers du Midi'. For the Greek (Agde, Antibes, Nice, etc.), and sometimes Ligurian (Arles, Cimiez, Marseille, etc.) origins of place-names, see A. Dauzat, *Les noms de lieux* (Paris, 1937), 92-4.

33. Strabo 4, 1, 5. 'University of Marseille' – see Clerc, 2, 313-29.

34. It is also possible that some of those who went to Massilia ostensibly for an education were in reality exiled there. This is what Augustus arranged for L. Antonius, the young son of Iullus Antonius (himself the son of the Triumvir, Antony, and executed by Augustus), who in 2 AD found himself packed off to Massilia to, as it turned out, spend the rest of his life as a student there ('Hunc admodum adolescentulum ... seposuit Augustus in civitatem Massiliensem, ubi specie studiorum nomen exsilii tegeretur' – Tac. *Ann.* 4, 44). He was in theory still a student when he died there some 23 years later, which must set a record for completing the curriculum: one cannot disagree with Clerc's (2, 316) verdict 'il fut sans doute le doyen des étudiants de son temps'. Among other Roman exiles at Massalia we have already (p. 241 n. 37 above) noted the most familiar, Milo.

35. Sen. *Controversiae* 2, 5, 13: 'reus veneficii fuit et a Pollione Asinio defensus, damnatus Massiliae docuit.' He is mentioned in Hor. *Ep.* 1, 5, 8-9. Clerc. 2, 316.

36. Sen., *op. cit.* (n. 35 above), 2, *praefatio*, 10; 2, 6, 12. *RE*, s.v. *Agroitas*. Several other names are known to us, though their connection with Massalia is often little-known or very flimsy. For example, Philon and Artemidoros (they were brothers, and rhetoricians) moved from Cilicia to establish themselves at Baeterrae (Béziers) (Clerc, 2, 316 n. 1).

37. Varro, *ap.* Isid. Orig. 15, 1. Sicilians also were reputedly trilingual (Latin, Greek, Punic: App. *Met*, 11, p. 259), and in the East learned Jews naturally spoke Latin, Greek and Hebrew.

38. Pliny, *NH* 29, 5; 9. Clerc, 2, 326-8.

39. Pliny, *NH* 29, 10: 'repente civitatem Charmis ex eadem Massilia invasit, damnatis non solum prioribus medicis, verum et balineis: frigidaque etiam hibernis algoribus Ianuarii persuasit. Mersit aegros in lacus. Videbamus senes consulares usque in ostentationem rigentes.' See also Quint. *Inst. Or.* 2, 4 (L. Plotius).

40. Clerc, 2, 328.

41. *CIL* 12, 3343; 4485-9. One of them (3341) particularly attracts our attention, for the name (?) is, in Greek, *Hedone*. One wonders about the clientele attracted by a woman doctor working under such a name (= 'Miss Pleasure').

42. Clerc, 2, 336: 'A l'université de Marseille il aura manqué quelque chose, une École des Beaux-Arts.'

43. Clerc, 1, 283: 'les jambons et saucissons dits d'Arles et de Tarascon remonteraient au temps de la colonie grecque, et sans doute plus haut encore'. His n. 2, *ad loc.* insists that Marseille, in his day, was still 'infesté de porcheries'. The term 'saucissons' is not easily translated into English. It means not sausages, such as one fries in the pan, but sausages such as salami, already cooked, that are cut into slices. Olives, etc., p. 51 above. Fish, 55. Milo, 241 n. 37.

9. The Greeks in Provence and Languedoc

1. Phocaean = Greek. An interesting parallel is the way that the Romans becoming familiar with a minor tribe called the Graii, not only eventually extended that name to cover the whole race, from which they came, calling them 'Greeks', not 'Hellenes', but successfully bequeathed this linguistic misnomer to all subsequent Romance languages. Castellum Massiliensium: so, for example, is Tauroentum described in Caesar (*BC* 2, 4). In fact next to nothing is known about Tauroentum. Lenthéric (114-16) gives full reign to his most scathing eloquence on the subject, and even its location is far from certain (see p. 172 above).

2. The most useful of these sources is of course Strabo 4, who not only lists the various sites and cities, but includes also a lot of material on their history and other valuable topics. He is most conveniently referred to in either of the two bilingual editions, the Loeb (English) or the Budé (French). The Budé has the added advantage of having short explanatory notes. Other sources are Avienus, *Ora Maritima*, ed. J.P. Murphy (repr. Ares Press, Chicago, 1977). Though apparently a marine coastal itinerary it is in fact an adaptation of a road-based one, following the Via Domitia ('la route suivie n'est pas maritime, comme on l'a toujours supposé, mais terrestre': D. Ugolini, Ch. Olive, 'Béziers et les côtes languedociennes dans l'*Ora Maritima* d'Avienus', *RAN* 20 (1987), 143-54 (esp. 152)); Pomponius Mela, *Chorographie* (ed. A. Silberman, Paris, 1988 (Budé series)), esp. 2, 5, 74-84 (inc. Silberman's notes *ad loc.*); Pliny, *NH* 3, 32-7; Ptolemy,

Geog. 2, 10, 1-20; Skylax; and (Ps.) Skymnos. Skylax and Skymnos are most conveniently to be found in Karl Müller, *Geographi Graeci Minores* (repr. Hildesheim, 1965), 1, 15-96 (esp. 15-59); 196-237 (esp. 200-4). Also useful is Stephanus of Byzantium (Stephan von Byzanz, *Ethnika*, ed. Augustus Meineke, repr. Graz, 1958): cities are listed alphabetically. The most helpful modern source is James Bromwich, *The Roman Remains of Southern France* (Routledge, London, 1993). This is a guidebook, not a scholarly study, giving opening times of museums and directions for road access to sites. It is exceptionally comprehensive and the author personally visited all sites and monuments listed.

3. See p. 178 above.

4. The chief pitfall here is *rhabillages*. A *rhabillage* is an original native name, probably meaning something in native language, but taken over by later settlers and adapted ('re-dressed', *rehabillé*) by them to form a known and familiar word in their own language, a word that happens by chance to resemble it but has otherwise no logical connection with it at all. This then becomes highly misleading if in its new form and in the new language it does carry a meaning that is both recognisable and, also, in the circumstances, plausible. It just also happens to be quite wrong. A modern example will make the point. The city of Bordeaux is a port on a large estuary, so what more natural than that is name should make sense, in French – 'Bord des Eaux', 'Waterside'? In fact it is derived from its Latin name in Roman times, 'Burdigala', which probably itself came from a Celtic original; and Heaven only knows what that meant. Although perhaps commonest in place-names, *rhabillages* are also found elsewhere in language (see p. 135 above). The reader must differentiate clearly between loan-words, foreign words that become embedded in a language but retain their original form and original meaning, and *rhabillages*, where the word is changed to a more familiar form and so loses its real meaning.

5. One further exception should be noted: Glanum, which is a sort of Greco-Roman hybrid, is also an open site. So are most of the Ligurian native sites, the *oppida*, such as Entremount, Ensérune, Ambrussum, Nages. Once abandoned they were not reoccupied, thus leaving the field clear for subsequent excavation. See pp. 197-208 above.

6. See p. 172 above; *HMG* 104 for differing locations.

7. Biblio. on Aleria: *PECS* 29-30; J. Jehasse, 'Les fouilles d'Aléria: le plateau et ses problèmes', *Gallia* 21 (1963), 77-109; *id.*, *Gallia* 36, 461-69; *id.*, *Gallia* 40, 428-35; J. and L. Jehasse, *Aléria antique* (Lyon, 1982; 2nd ed., 1991).

8. Cyrnos was the Greek name for the island; it was called Corsica by the Romans, and, apparently, the native population. As 'Cyrnos' it was supposedly named after a son of Heracles of that name, who seems to be attested, among other sources, by a graffito 'Cyrnu' at Pompeii (*CIL* 4, 1424). See Herod. 7, 165; Lykos of Rhegion, *ap.* Athen. 2, 47a; Strabo 5, 2, 7; Diod. Sic. 5, 13; Virg. *Ecl.* 9, 30, and Servius, *Comm. ad loc.* The Corsi, as applied to the native inhabitants, is first used by L Calpurnius Piso (231 BC), *ap.* Pliny, *NH* 15, 126, and then comes into general use (e.g., Livy 22, 16, 4; 40, 19, 6-7; 40, 34, 12; 42, 7, 1-2). They were thought to be of Etruscan, or even Libyan extraction (Paus. 10, 17, 8-11; Ptolemy 3, 3, 6; Pliny *NH* 3, 85; Dionys. Perieg. 457-60). Strabo (*loc. cit.*) gives the names of four tribes, the Blesinoi, Enikoniai, and Ouapanes: the fourth name, Charax, seems more likely to be in reality a place-name. The name Corsi, though applied by the Romans to the population of the whole island, seems to have originated in the area around Aleria (below). For an overall view of Corsica in antiquity, see O.J. Jehasse, *Corsica Classica* (ed. La Marge, Ajaccio, 1986; ISBN 2-7363-0005-X), esp. 67 ('Le nom de l'île') and 118-21 ('Les noms de peuples'); Corsi/Aleria, 119.

9. H.M. Denham, *The Tyrrhenian Sea: A Sea-Guide to its Coasts and Islands*

(London, 1978), 57-8, summarises: 'For the first 20 miles (i.e. starting from the south) the coast is mountainous and wooded and a yacht is warned against the strong squalls that sweep down especially during fresh west and north-west winds, when it is advisable to stand four or five miles off the coast. Thereafter the mountains begin to recede from the coast, which becomes low, flat and uninteresting with lagoons and blocked river mouths.'

10. The arable land around Aleria was a rarity (Theophr. *HP* 5, 8), and though the major industry of Corsica was agriculture, this usually meant the rearing of cattle, sheep and goats (Polyb. 12, 3, 7 (transhumance); DS, 5, 14). On metals, 'il est curieux de constater qu'en ce domaine aucun de nos textes n'évoque la présence de minerai en Corse. Pourtant l'île recèle une grande variété de minerais: on trouve de l'anthracite à Osani, du manganèse à Valle d'Alisgiani, du plomb à Castifau, de l'antimoine à Luri et à Meria, dans le Cap Corse, du cuivre à Linguizette et à Vezzani, dans les environs d'Aleria, à Ponte-Leccia, et à Castifau, enfin du fer un peu partout' (P. Simi, *Précis de géographie de la Corse* (Bastia, 1981), 158, as quoted by O. Jehasse (n. 8 above), 137). The reference to the existence of copper close to Aleria is particularly interesting. Beekeeping was important enough for Virgil to devote the whole final book to the *Georgics* to it. Swarms of bees were endemic in ancient Corsica, both in their wild state (i.e. living in trees) and domesticated in beehives (M.J. Battesti, 'Etude biométrique de colonies d'abeilles corses', *Bulletin de la Société des sciences historiques et naturelles de la Corse*, 1983, 73-98; DS 5, 14). Corsican honey was produced in great quantities, and in the archaic period was exported by the aboriginals (and possibly also by Phocaean settlements such as Aleria) to the Etruscans as a form of tribute (DS 5, 13), but 'it was considered inferior and even poisonous' (R.J. Forbes, *Studies in Ancient Technology* 5 (Leiden, 1966), 91; Martial 9, 26, 4; 11, 42, 4). The bitter taste of Corsican (as also Sardinian) honey evidently came from the local vegetation on which the bees fed: see Virg. *Ecl.* 7, 41; 9, 30; Hor. *AP* 375; Ovid, *Am.* 1, 13, 9; Plin. *NH* 30, 4, 10 ('*asperrimum*'); Dioscorides 2, 102. Lykos of Rhegion (*ap.* Athen. 2, 47a) ascribes to Corsican honey the extraordinary longevity of the local inhabitants who ate it. For the role of honey in general in the ancient world, see Forbes, *op. cit.*, 80-101; also J. André, *L'alimentation et la cuisine à Rome* (Paris, 1981), 186-7. Good honey was a commodity much prized. The best summary of the economics of Corsica is by O. Jehasse (n. 8 above), ch. 8, 'L'economie', 133-44.

11. Local authorities, keen to promote the importance of Aleria, tend to magnify the attractions of the Tavignano: 'Le Tavignano est un veritable fleuve, de plus de 20 metres de large, qui, même en periode de basses eaux, garde une profondeur supérieure à 2 mètres' – J. and L. Jehasse (n. 7 above), 14. Two metres draught may be acceptable for river boats but is surely too little for deep-sea craft, particularly if there may also be occasional sandbars. And in France normally only four rivers are accorded the dignity of being called a 'fleuve': the Seine, Rhône, Loire and Garonne – the Tavignano is very far indeed from being in this league. A further disadvantage is that the river flows from west to east, and this is, roughly, the same direction as the prevailing winds. While this would make it plain sailing for traffic outward bound, with wind and current behind them, incoming vessels would find it hard going struggling up-river in the teeth of both. Navigation is always facilitated by having wind and current in opposite directions, for the sails, once hoisted and filled by a good breeze, will usually be enough to overcome a current unless it is very strong, while if one wants to go in the other direction it suffices simply to let the ship be carried along by the current, under bare poles.

12. I am not quite sure how valid, nor how relevant, the comparison may be, but when I visited the site it reminded me of Tiryns – about the same height, about the same distance from the sea, and in the same order of size. To readers who may

270

perhaps be more familiar with Greek sites, I offer this impression for what it is worth.

13. Attic vases: 'They are all exceptional works which are not found in such abundance except on the largest Etruscan sites' – C. Goudineau, *PECS* 29. The necropolis site is Casabianda, about 1 km south of the ancient city, on an extension of the escarpment. Cosmopolitan mélange: 'Imaginons donc une ville corse, hellénisée, étruscisée, punicisée, en rapports avec tout le bassin méditerranéen occidental' – J. and L. Jehasse, *op. cit.* (n. 7 above), 18.

14. Scipio's conquest is commemorated in his preserved epitaph (*CIL* 1, 32: 'Hec cepit Corsica[m] Aleria[m]que urbem'). Augustus eventually became a patron of Aleria (*CIL* 10, 8035: 'C.C.V.P.R.' = 'Colonis Coloniae Veneriae Iuliae Pacensis Restitutae').

15. So C. Goudineau, *PECS* 30; some of the smaller rooms in this complex have nevertheless tentatively been identified as shops (?), which would argue some form of public access.

16. DS 5, 14. Jehasse, the chief authority on Aleria, suggests that while Nikaia may be another and quite separate city, it may be a new name by the new, multiracial Aleria after the Battle of Alalia (Jehasse, n. 8 above), 124-5. Diodorus (5, 13) also mentions a city Kalaris, founded by the Phocaeans, which is evidently Alalia (Aleria), perhaps reflecting a minor change in site. He further refers to a 'Limen Syrakosion' on the east coast, which was probably Porto Vecchio. Ptolemy (3, 2, 1-7) lists no fewer than 32 towns or cities in Corsica, but most of them remain mere names, and are in any case of post-Greek date. Certainly one feels that there must have been something at Bastia (a natural port of call for shipping rounding Cap Corse en route from Italy to Massalia), Bonifacio (controlling the straits) and Ajaccio (for its harbour and easy land access to the interior, up the route of the modern railway and highway N 193 to the Col de Vizzanova).

17. Avienus 701; Pliny, *NH* 3, 34. Strabo (4, 1, 8) called it Stomalimne, which the Budé editor, François Lasserre (*Strabon, Geographie* (Paris, 1966), 2, p. 207) identifies with the Étang de l'Estomac, presumably on the strength of the name. The Étang de l'Estomac may be a rhabillage with no connection with the word 'estomac'. The étang itself has been obliterated by the development of the Port of Fos.

18. Pomponius Mela 2, 5, 78; Pliny, *loc. cit.*; Ptolemy, *Geog.* 2, 10, 8. Heraclea: Bouloumié (n. 19 below).

19. The paved road was on the bed of the Étang de Lavalduc, revealed when in the 1960s, the lake was drained. Previously it had been suggested that in antiquity the lake communicated directly with the sea, making Saint Blaise a port. Both coastline and water level in the lakes seem to have changed since antiquity, and the modern commercial development of Fos makes, any evaluation of the situation very difficult. See Bernard Bouloumié, *St. Blaise* (Marseille, éditions Provence, 1980; ISBN 2-903350-07-8), 10-12; also Bernard Bouloumié, *Saint-Blaise: l'habitat protohistorique; les céramiques grecques* (Travaux du Centre Camille-Jullian, 13; Publ. Univ. of Provence, 1992; ISBN 2-85399-295-0), 12-13. Heraclea as ancient name: *op. cit.*, 17. See also Bernard Bouloumié, 'Saint-Blaise, oppidum du sel', *Doss. Arch.* 84 (1984), 6-96. Detailed site plan in Bouloumié, *Gallia* 37 (1979), 234-5.

20. So Bouloumié (1992) (n. 19 above), 272, on the basis of trading patterns based on pottery evidence.

21. It was not, after all, on the sea coast, but this is an argument of questionable validity; neither was Athens.

22. See H. Rolland, 'Fouilles de Saint-Blaise', suppl. 3 to *Gallia* (1951); suppl. 7 (1956). Henri Tréziny, 'Rémarques sur la fonction du rempart hellenistique de

Saint-Blaise' (*EM* 1 (Travaux du Centre Camille Jullian, publ. Université de Provence, 1986; ISBN 2-85399-157-1), 145-51).

23. There is no trace of such rounded crenellations being used anywhere in the Carthaginian homeland of North Africa, but they occur in overseas Carthaginian colonies, notably Motya (West Sicily). Two more such crenellation-blocks have been found at Glanum but nowhere else in the Greek world. H. Tréziny, 'Sur quelques problèmes d'architecture et d'urbanisme en Gaule méridionale', *EM* 3, 337-49: 'Les fortifications de Saint-Blaise', 342-4, for full discussion.

24. Bouloumié (1980) (n. 19 above), 42.

25. G. Denizot, 'Le rivage de Provence et de Languedoc au temps des Ligures: II. Les bouches du Rhône et la côte Languedocienne', *REL* 25 (1959), 23-86, inveighs against the local fondness for attributing anything even remotely old to Marius (23): thus (30-1) 'Les Arcades' alongside the railway are not ancient, and (33) local tales of a submerged city in the sea off Fos are pure myth. See also B. Liou, 'Les découvertes archéologiques du Golfe de Fos et les traces du littoral antique', in *Déplacements des lignes de rivage en Méditerranée* (Colloques du CNRS, Aix-en-Provence, 1985) (Paris, 1987). Bernard Liou and Jean-Marie Gassend, 'L'épave *Saint-Gervais* 3 à Fos-sur-mer (milieu du IIème siècle ap. J-C.). Inscriptions peintes sur amphores de Bétique. Vestiges de la coque', *Archaeonautica* 10 (1990), 157ff.; pp. 219-59 for the ship.

26. Strabo 4, 1, 8; the Budé editor, François Lasserre (*Strabon, Geographie*, t.2 (Paris, 1966), 207) records the discovery of the 'extrémité maritime' of the canal now underwater, off Fos ('Voir P. Diolé, *Promenades d'archéologie sous-marine* (Paris, 1952), 123ff.'); Plut. *Marius* 15; Pomponius Mela 2, 79; Pliny, *NH*, 3, 34. The name is also indicated on the map of the Peutinger Table, but the accompanying 'cartography' gives no intelligible clue to the actual course of the canal. Clerc, 2, 54. Michel Bellet, in *L'archéologie des rives de l'Étang de Berre* (ed. Édisiud, Aix-en-Provence, 1979: ISBN 2-85744-045-6), 48, is concisely scathing: 'On a beaucoup écrit sur ce canal et on a écrit n'importe quoi'. See p. 102 above.

27. To many this canal will be unwittingly familiar, for it is the one spanned by a wooden drawbridge a kilometre or so south of Arles and featuring in a well-known painting by Van Gogh.

28. The mouth of the Old Rhône is marked, the 'Vieux Rhône', on the 1:200,000 Michelin map, Pli 245 (Provence, Côte d'Azur); also Pli 93 (Marseille-Lyon). It is near the Faraman lighthouse, a local landmark. Its course may be traced along the 'Canal du Japon ou Bras de Fer', where it crosses the present river to loop around through the marshes on the far side (the Boucle d'Escale), rejoining the main stream at La Porcelette. All this may be more easily followed on the larger scale 1:100,000 map of the Institut Géographique National, Pli 66 (Avignon, Montpellier), which marks the loop through the 'Marais de l'Escale', but this map is liable to be less readily available to most readers outside of France (where, however, it is common). The most careful and convincing reconstruction, which I here follow, is that of G. Denizot (n. 25 above), 31; 51-2. He suggests (51), that the coastal terminus of the canal was not at Fos proper but ran into the (now obliterated) Étang Galéjon, 5 km to the west, which communicated with the sea.

29. Strabo, Plutarch and Mela (n. 26 above), all state that Marius *diverted* part of the river into the canal, implying a current through it. For canals in the ancient world, see K.D. White, *Greek and Roman Technology* (London, 1984), 110-12, and N.A.F. Smith, 'Roman canals', *Trans. Newcomen Soc.* 49 (1977-78), 75-80. In the article on 'Fossae' in *RE* 7.1, 74-6, some twelve such *fossae* (including the Marianae) are listed, some of which may be natural waterways.

30. So located by Denizot (n. 25 above), 50, following E. Bernard and Gautier-Descottes.

31. Peutinger Table: Konrad Miller, *Die Peutingersche Tafel* (Stuttgart, 1962). Antonine Itinerary: G. Denizot, 'Le rivage de Provence et Languedoc aut temps des Ligures: I. La côte rocheuse Provençale', *REL* 23 (1957), 47. Denizot (n. 25 above), 50. Cf. Amm. Marcel. 14, 11, 18, who locates it as around 18 miles from Arles.

32. Lattes is published in successive volumes of the site publĩcation *Lattara*, ed. Michel Py, and produced by the *Association pour la recherche archéologique en Languedoc oriental*, Route de Pérols, F34970 Lattes. Up to 1992 five volumes have appeared (ISSN 0996-6900) (site location in vol. 1 (1988) 15-56, with biblio.). See also M. Py and Dominique Garcia, Bilan des recherches archéologiques sur la ville portuaire de *Lattara* (Lattes, Mérault)', *Gallia* 50 (1993), 1-93 (with biblio.). Also J. Arnal, R. Majurel, and H. Prades, *Le port de Lattera* (Bordighera/Montpellier, 1974).

33. Pliny *NH* 3, 4; Ptolemy 2, 10, 18. Coins: Clerc, 1 379f.; Cl. Brenot, 'La "drachme" de Glanum', *Doss. Arch* 140 (juillet – août 1989), 75; G. Barruol, *Les peuples preromains du sud-est de la Gaule* (suppl. to *RAN*; Paris, 1969), 200; A Roth Congès, 'Le centre monumental de Glanon', *EM* 3, 351-67 (esp., for coins, 353). General account of the site: J.C. Bessac and N. Lambert *et al.*, 'Glanum', *Doss. Arch*. 140 (1989), 2-83.

34. François Salviat, *Glanum et les antiques* (Guides Archéologiques de la France, no. 19; Paris, 1990; ISBN 2-11-081042-4), 17-18. The view is not uncommon, and is echoed in the interpretative texts hung up in the Glanum Museum on the site (not to be confused with the Musée de l'Hôtel de Sade in St. Rémy, where most of the sculpture and small finds are). The Peutinger Table (n. 31 above) shows Glanum as a stop on the direct route from Cavaillon to Arles (not Tarascon) and also on that from Aix – in other words, it is the basis for Salviat's description. We must remember that, in terms of long distance traffic, the via Julia (Ventimiglia) did not exist at the period when Glanum was founded (being built by Augustus) and hence cannot have been a factor in the choice of site. A milestone has been discovered at Mont Gaussier, overlooking the site, establishing that the Aix-Rhône road ran through Glanum (H. Rolland, 'Un nouveau milliare de l'itinéraire de Peutinger', *CRAI*, 1962, 676-80; see also R. Chevallier, *Roman Roads* (London, 1976), 46.

35. The Rev. Thomas Gaisford (1779-1885) used the phrase in a sermon preached in the Cathedral, Oxford, on Christmas Day. 'Considerable emolument' was what he said you might expect to get from your job if you first took a degree in Classics. The phrase is memorable and often quoted (in speeches and newspaper articles) because it is almost the only thing listed under Classics in the *Oxford Dictionary of Quotations*.

36. This is pretty well the analysis offered by C. Goudineau, *PECS* 356: 'Situated close to the two roads leading from the Rhône to Italy and linked to them, Glanum ... owed its prosperity both to its position and to the religious character of the site.'

37. For fuller consideration, see A. Roth Congès (n. 33 above), esp. the discussion that followed presentation of her paper (*EM* 3, 472-3). H. Tréziny offers the, to me, reasonable objection that there are no other defence works at Glanum, and this small section of wall 'ne peut jouer ce role'. This he thinks self-evident (I do too), but it is not accepted by Roth. Roth's reply leans heavily on the hypothetical: the absence of a second wall blocking the other end of the gorge 'n'est pas de tout certain', and the short existing wall 'devait monter assez haut, et faisait peut-être le tour de la ville' – even though the town is completely on the wrong side of it. And, in spite of resemblances in the masonry techniques with the walls of Saint Blaise, it is surely misleading to refer to this small and limited crosswall as a 'rempart', which summons up to the reader something much longer, comprehensive, defensible, and grandiose.

38. See pp. 197, 202, 205 above.

39. Goodineau, *loc. cit.* (n. 36 above).

40. H. Rolland, *Fouilles de Glanum* (*Gallia*, Suppl. I, 1946), 20; see also H. Rolland, *Les fouilles de Glanum* 1947-56 (*Gallia*, suppl. XI, 1958). A. Roth Congès, 'Le Centre Monumental de Glanon', *EM* 3, 351-67, and discussion, 472-3. This is a very full discussion of the issue, with extensive bibliography. She sees Glanon in the period preceding the eventual Roman takeover as a 'vitrine et refuge de la civilisation salyenne', becoming even the 'dernier bastion de la résistance salyenne' (363). For objections, see n. 37 above. This forms part of a larger issue, her conviction that the Ligurians (Salyii) formed a much more sophisticated culture than is generally suspected by those who tend to dismiss them as 'uncivilised natives', and had a great ability to receive and adopt features of other civilisations without themselves becoming part of them: 'les capacités d'assimilation culturelle autonome (et pas seulement d'acculturation) d'un monde indigène enrichi, dynamique, conscient de son identité mais également de son aptitude à maîtriser les innovations extérieures, et certainement désireux d'en faire étalage à une époque où son indépendance est dangereusement menacée' (362). See also P. Arcelin, 'Le territoire de Marseille grecque dans son contexte indigène', *EM* 1, 43-104, esp. 67-8; M. Bats, 'Le territoire de Marseille grecque', *EM* 1, 17-42, esp. 30. The issues are complex, often confused. For further discussion, Pierre Gros, 'Nature et signification de l'hellénisme glanique', *EM* 3, 373-4. See also p. 215ff. above.

41. For discussion of the origins of the name Glanum, see the editorial comments of Otto Hirschfeld, *CIL* 12, 125.

42. Sanctuaries are not usually fortified, but if this gate was not intended to protect the sanctuary, what else *was* it protecting?

43. Roth, *EM* 3 (n. 33 above), 361; H. Tréziny, 'Remarques sur la fonction du rempart hellénistique de Saint-Blaise', *EM* 1, 145-51, esp. 147-8. The chevron band treatment is a recognised technique of the Hellenistic Greeks, particularly in Provence: J-C. Bessac and N. Lambert, 'La pierre à Glanum', *Doss. Arch.* (n. 33 above), 8-13, esp. 10.

44. Priene: D.S. Robertson, *Handbook of Greek and Roman Architecture* (Cambridge, 1964), 190, fig. 85. Agora: so identified by A. Roth Congès (*et al.*), *Doss. Arch.* (n. 33 above), 18. She also identifies nearby buildings with traditional Greek names (*bouleuterion*, *prytaneion*), but this, like the agora, seems to be conjectural, and if unfounded could be misleading. Salviat (n. 34 above), 29, simply marks the *bouleuterion* on his plan as a 'salle d'assemblée' (which, given its internal layout, it certainly is). This seems to me to be a lot safer, particularly if the site really is a non-Greek one.

45. Marc Bouison, 'Architecture et décor des maisons', *Doss. Arch.* (n. 33 above), 52-8.

46. 'Rien n'indique à ce jour que des Grecs aient vécu en permanence à *Glanon*' – A. Roth Congès (n. 33 above), 354. In her n. 12 she stresses that in the field of monumental (i.e. non-domestic) architecture several 'gallo-grec' structures offer links between the two cultures. The trouble is that though the principle of Gallic adaptations of Greek models is a common one in many areas (sculpture, coinage, etc.) it is usually quite clear that what we are dealing with is an adaptation (with varying degrees of fidelity), while the Glanum Delian houses are closer to faithful reproductions. Subjective judgements are seldom to be relied on implicitly, but I find it hard to look at these houses and not see them as having been built by Greeks.

47. Three of them are in the Musée de l'Hôtel de Sade at St. Remy (inv. nos.

4245, 6976, 7020). Similar statues have been uncovered at the Celtic *oppida* of Roquepertuse, Entremont, and Constantine (Musée Granet, Aix, and Musée Borely, Marseille). For the typically Gallic pose, see Strabo 4, 4, 3.

48. Pierced skulls of this type have been found in Celtic sites at La Cloche, Entremont, and Roquepertuse, masonry hollowed out to receive them at Entremont, Roquepertuse, Cadenet, and Saint Blaise. François Salviat, n. 34 above, 122; *id.*, 'Les gaulois et l'exposition des têtes humaines', *Doss. Arch.* (n. 33 above), 23. Strabo 4, 4, 5; Diod. 5, 29. H. Rolland, 'Sculptures héllenistiques découvertes à Glanum', *CRAI* 1968, 94-114, esp. 103, fig. 5.

49. 'L'art salyen au faîte de sa maîtrise' – A. Roth Congès *et al.*, *Doss. Arch.* (n. 30 above), 20: photographs, 21, attributed by Roth to Salviat *EM* 3, (n. 33 above), 367; see also *id.*, 360. The definitive publication is H. Rolland, 'Sculptures à figures découvertes à Glanum', *CRAI* 1967, 111-19, and Rolland (n. 48, above); *id.*, *Gallia* 28 (1970), 435-42. See also F. Salviat, 'Un image de l'Afrique sur un chapiteau à figures de *Glanum*', *RAN* 5, 1972, 21-30. Note: the reference in Roth (n. 33 above), 360, to *RAN* 1978, is incorrect. Carthaginian 'merlons', Tréziny (n. 37 above): Roth, *EM* 3 (n. 33 above), 360, n. 46.

50. Pierre Gros and Pierre Varène, 'Le forum et la basilique de Glanum: problèmes de chronologie et de restitution', *Gallia* 42 (1984), 21-52.

51. Skymnos 208; Mela 5, 3, 2; Ptolemy 2.

52. Its name, said Ternaux (94) in one of those off-the-cuff assertions that never seem to inspire quite the same confidence in the reader as in the author, 'quite certainly' (*sine dubio*) commemorated a victory over the Volci or Iberi at the 'Arauris'. I suspect that it may do no more than reflect a kind of general hopeful optimism on the part of traders or colonists far from home, something like 'Gold Nugget City' – it has a kind of Alaska Gold Rush ring to it. See p. 167 above, Hemeroskopeion ('Fort Look-out').

53. *Gallia* 36 (1978), 438; *RAN* 1976, 45-62; André Nickels, 'Agde grecque: les recherches recentes', *P del P* 104-7 (1982), *I Focei dall'Anatolia all'Oceano* (published Transactions of Conference (1982) on 'Velia et les Phocéens: un bilan dix ans après'; publ. at Naples, 1982, ISSN 0031-2555), pp. 269-79. See also 'Recherches stratigraphiques ponctuelles à proximité des remparts antiques d'Agde', *RAN* 9 (1976), A. Nickels and G. Marchand, pp. 45-62.

54. Bromwich (n. 2 above), 52. For Béziers and its surroundings, see Monique Clavel, *Béziers et son territoire dans l'antiquité* (Paris, 1970).

55. Caesar, *BC* 1, 36; 2, 5. Avienus, *Or. Mar.* 689-91. Skymnos, (n. 2 above), 208. J-M. Roquette and C. Sintes, *Arles antique* (Guides Archéologiques de la France, 17; Paris, 1989).

56. 'The first Phokaian settlement was destroyed by the Ligurians in 535 BC' – R. Amy, *PECS*, 87.

57. 'Arles est très certainement un centre mixte' – Pierre Rouillard, *EM* 3, 183. 'Arles – et ceci est une hypothèse à vérifier – a dû fonctionner comme un centre de redistribution alimenté par Marseille dès milieu du VIe s.; mais Arles a pu fonctionner aussi comme un *emporion* à la tête du delta du Rhône, selon un schéma que l'on a plus l'habitude de trouver sur les côtes' – *ibid.*

58. There is some question whether the Apt road crossed at Arles or at Tarascon. It probably did the latter. But the point is that, irrespective of the route taken by the official Roman road, Arles, once it was built, offered a convenient crossing and must have carried an extensive traffic. The pontoon bridge (probably so built to accommodate flood levels on the river) is sketchily illustrated in a black-and-white mosaic floor preserved at the office of the Arles Shipping Agency in the Square of the Corporations at Ostia. A convenient illustration is in R. Chevallier, *Roman Roads* (London, 1976), 94. The position of the bridge in Arles is marked in the plan printed by Rivet, 192, fig. 22, and minor remains of the approaches are visible on the site (*PECS* 87); ref. in Ausonius, *Ordo Urbium Nobilium* 10 (= Rivet, 208).

59. Near Arles, and sometimes to be considered an outlying part of it, the remarkable Roman-date water-mills of Barbegal are sufficiently unusual to merit a digressive mention in passing. See R.H.J. Sellin, 'The large roman watermill at Barbegal', *Hist. of Technology* 8, (1983), 91-109; A. Trevor Hodge, 'A Roman Factory', *Scientif. Amer.*, November 1990, 58-64.

60. Pliny, *NH* 3, 36; P. Mela 2, 5, 57; Steph. Byz. *s.v.* Auenion. The best account is in Rivet, 265-71, whom I here follow. In *PECS*, surprisingly, it is not listed.

61. Rivet, 268.

62. Steph. Byz. s. v. Cabellio. Pliny, *NH*, 3, 36, lists it as a city with Latin rights. Rivet, 262, apparently assumes that Cabellio formed part of the *chora* of Massalia, for 'Massalia was surely deprived of the town in 49 BC', which means it must previously have possessed it.

63. Durance crossing: Strabo 4, 1, 11. Coins, inscriptions: *PECS* 179, Rivet, 262, and 263 n. 1 (biblio.). The best concise account is that of Rivet. Cavaillon is today famous for its melons, and those interested in pursuing their possibly ancient origins are referred to Rivet's fascinating n. 16, p. 264. A rough summary of his verdict is that nobody can tell for sure.

64. Strabo 4, 1, 3-6; Pliny, *NH* 3, 22; Ptol., 2, 10, 2; Avienus, *Or. Mar.*, 559.

65. G. Barruol, *PECS*, 733; J. Jannory, *RE* 22, 1, 411-18.

66. Strabo 14, 2, 10 (First Olympiad); Strabo 3, 4, 8. Skymnos 196 (anc. tradition). Rhode 'is undoubtedly the oldest Greek city in the West and antedates the foundation of Cumae in Italy by Greeks from Chalkis' – J. Maluquer de Motes, *PECS* 754. 'Rhodian character', *PECS, loc. cit.*

67. Not much has been published on Rhode and this account is based largely on the *PECS* entry. Its coins, dated to around 250 BC, were struck to a drachm-weight of 70-78 grains with types of (ob.) Persephone and (rev.) a rose. The rose (Gk. *rhodos*) was a punning type referring to the founding city, Rhodes, which also struck coins carrying roses: B.V. Head, *Historia Numorum* (London, 1963 (repr.)), 2.

68. Full discussion of the evidence and various conclusions therefrom in J-P. Morel, 'Les Phocéens en occident', *P del P* 1966, 392 n. 52.

69. Scylax 3; Skymnos 202-4. Other references are in Avienus, *Or. Mar.*, 527-9, Livy 34, 9, Strabo 3, 4, 8, Polyb. 1, 82, 6, and Steph. Byz. Mela 5, 2; 5, 3, 2 (for form of name); Pliny, *NH* 3, 4.

70. A common appellation in the Greek colonial world, as in an initial 'New' in British place-names ('Newcastle', 'Newport', 'Newton'). The best-known Neapolis is the one now known as Napoli, Naples.

71. See p. 252 n. 2 above. 'No love lost', P. MacKendrick, *The Iberian Stones Speak* (New York, 1969), 47. Patriotic Spaniards *ibid.*, Cohabitation, Clerc, 1, 151. following Strabo 3, 4, 8. On 1, 276, he adopts a less optimistic perspective – the Greeks in Emporion lived 'une vie assurément fort austère' and lived in 'une ville forte bloquée' not far removed from a ghetto, 'enfermés dans leurs murs, sans banlieue'. A contrary view is maintained by Maluquer de Motes in *PECS* 303: 'Because it was frankly a mart the Greek settlement grew rapidly.' Rushes, linen: Strabo 3, 4, 9.

72. See Pierre Rouilland, 'Les colonies grecques du sud-est de la péninsule ibérique', in 1982 conference on 'Velia et les Phocéens: un bilan dix ans après', the transactions being printed as a special issue of *P del P*, Fasc. 204-7 (1982), entitled 'I Focei dall'Anatolia all'Oceano' (publ. Naples, ISSN-0031-235). The Rouillard article is pp. 417-30 (biblio. 417-19 nn. 1-5; map of find-spots of Greek ceramics,

420). He locates Hemeroskopeion at Denia or Peñon de Ifach (Calpe), Akra Leuké at Alicante or thereabouts, and Alonis at Santa Pola or Benidorm. See also Rhys Carpenter, *The Greeks in Spain* (Bryn Mawr, 1975), 54-5 (now somewhat out-dated). We may also note, in the same *P del P* volume, Martin Almalgo-Gorba, 'La Colonizacion focense en la Peninsula Ibérica: Estado actual de la cuestíon', 432-44 (biblio. 432-3 nn. 1-10); it is based largely on ceramics. It is worth noting that this entire volume is full of valuable material, apart from the articles I have actually quoted.

73. Hemeroskopeion: Strabo 3, 4, 6; Avienus, *Or. Mar.* 476-78; site plan (?), Clerc, 1, 267. Mainake: Avienus 425-31. Full bibliography and discussion, J.P. Morel (n. 68 above), 391 n. 45. *RE* 14, 1, 575 (Schulten); Denia, see Cic. *In Verr.* 1, 34; 5, 56. Strabo gives the Denia-Hemeroskopeion identification, adding that it had a famous temple of the Artemis of Ephesos (presumably a Phocaean import), and offering this as the source of its Latin name Dianium (from Diana), whence, of course, Denia. Paul MacKendrick, *The Iberian Stones Speak* (New York, 1969), 43 records that 'Cean-Bermudez, writing in 1832, remarks that the antiquities from the temple are the playthings of the children of the town, in their barbarism and ignorance'. In 1989 we read in *Frommer's Spain and Morocco on $40 a Day* (by Darwin Porter; New York, 1967 ed., repr. 1989), 253, that at Denia 'in the town hall ... there are remains of the temple'. I have not seen them myself and would normally hesitate to quote a 'Dollar-a-Day' tourist guidebook as a scholarly author-ity, but the author adds that the name Denia comes from the cult of Diana, which goes straight back to Strabo. It would be churlish to deny that a 'Dollar-a-Day' guidebook basing itself on Strabo does inspire a certain confidence that one would normally withold from the genre.

74. Identifications: François Lasserre, *Strabon, Geographie* t.2 (Budé ed.; Paris, 196), 65, n. 2.

75. Stesichorus is quoted in Strabo 3, 2, 11. It is a fragment of his lost poem extolling the exploit of Heracles in rustling the cattle of Geryon; his local knowl-edge of the area may be derived from the exploratory (though involuntary) voyage to Tartessos of Colaios of Samos around 660 BC (Herod. 4, 152); so Lasserre (n. 74 above), 191. Cadiz: Avienus, *Or. Mar.*, 269-70; Pliny, *NH* 4, 120; 7 156; Val. Max. 8, 13, 4; Sall. *Hist.* 1, 100. Islands: see *PECS* 884 and Pliny (*loc. cit.*). Modern scholars have located the city in various places – Jerez, Huelva, Carteia (near Algeciras), even Seville; the best easily accessible account is in MacKendrick (n. 73 above), 23-32. See also Paus. 6, 19, 3; Steph. Byz. *s.v.* Tartessos; Skymnos, 162; Strabo, *loc. cit.* The general region was also known as Turdetania and corresponds, more or less, to the modern Andalusia.

76. Hdt. 4, 152; Paus. 6, 19, 2; MacKendrick (n. 73 above), 24-8.

77. I have some doubts about this – A. Trevor Hodge, 'Massalia, meteorology, and navigation', *Anc. World* 7 (1983, 81 n. 26). See also p. 29 above.

78. Disputed by Aubet (235 n. 39 above), 177-9 (full discussion).

79. Hdt. 1, 163; Anacr. Frag. 8 (Bergk) *ap.* Strabo 3, 2, 14 (see D.L. Page, *Poetae Melici Graeci* (Oxford, 1962), 184n. for biblio. and ancient sources for Argan-thonios); Val. Max. 8, 13, 4. Macrob. *Sat.* 1, 20, 12 (Theron); Justin 44, 4, 11 (Habis); *PECS* 884 (on the *Res Gestae* of Habis). There is also a King Gargoris.

80. These two Labours form part of the canonical list of twelve, but on his journey to and from the Straits of Gibraltar local legend credited Heracles with a stopover at practically every Greek settlement that was even vaguely on the route, often (as in the Crau, p. 238 n. 15 above) performing some notable exploit before passing on. In this Heracles was quite untypical of the Olympian gods from whom he was descended, and who, apart from occasional regular trips to the Hyperbore-ans and Ethiopians, seem to have been stay-at-homes who never travelled any further outside of Greece than Troy. Heracles was also to be identified with the Phoenician deity Melkart.

81. MacKendrick, *op. cit.* (n. 73 above), 29.

10. The Greeks on the Côte d'Azur

1. A useful collection of the ancient references to places along this coast will be found in the *Notes Complementaires* of A. Silverman, *Pomponius Mela: Chorographie* (Budé ed.; Paris, 1988), 213-16. For modern directions, see James Bromwich (p. 269 n. 2 above).

2. Tutela Charsitana: Jean-Paul Clébert, *Provence antique 2* (Paris, 1970), 125; Lenthéric, 57-9. He quotes the inscriptions on Cassis stone from the *Répertoire des travaux de la Société de statistique de Marseille*, 1857, vol. 20. 'Port Miou' is apparently a corruption of *Portus Melior*. In 1377, Pope Gregory XI refers to it as the *Portus Milonis*.

3. Clébert (n. 2 above), 124; Lenthéric, 60-7. Before we place too much store on his castigation of La Ciotat, we should remember that this is the same author who (*op. cit.*, 322) complains that nobody can get a decent view of Marseille because it is perpetually enshrouded in a murky smog coming from the breath of its inhabitants. Ancient sources for the name Citharista (and not much else about the place) are Mela 2, 77; Pliny, *NH* 3, 34; Ptolemy 2, 10, 5, 9; G. Denizot, *REL* 23 (1957), 43; Clerc, 1, 262, speculates that the harbour town, i.e. La Ciotat, was the real Greek colony and Citharista a Celtic *oppidum*; in this case Citharista (otherwise a very odd name for a city – how many towns are called 'guitar-player'?) would be a *rhabillage*, turning an original Ligurian name into something resembling a Greek word, however implausible.

4. Strabo 4, 1, 9; Ptolemy 2, 10, 8; Scymnos 5, 215; St. of Byz. (ed. Cougny, 1, p. 372); Mela 2, 5, 3, 77; Caes. *BC* 2, 4.

5. *PECS* 493 (C. Goudineau). Some of the variant identifications are listed, with comments, by F. Benoit, *HMG* 104, and at rather greater length, by Clerc, 1, 249-54 ('La situation de Tauroentum a fait couler en Provence des flots d'encre, depuis le fin du XVIIIe siècle'). Lenthéric (1895), who maintains that extensive remains of the city had been found at the Les Lecques (i.e., St. Cyr) site, quotes one of his Provençal predecessors, Joseph Méry, who, going there to see the antiquities found that they had all disappeared, though that did not inhibit the local customs officers who acted as guides: 'At the present day we are introduced at Tauroentum to three absent temples, two absent baths, two non-existing promenades, such as Martial delighted in, an undiscoverable circus, the barrier of which was adorned with obelisks, and a vanished praetorian camp. The visitor to the spot opens his eyes wide, and sees two officers of the customs sitting on twelve acres of petrified nothing' (original text in Clerc, 1, 250 n. 4). Lenthéric's judgement (116) that 'Méry had more sense of fun than altogether becomes a grave archaeologist' may be echoed by some of my readers, if not by myself. Full account, Lenthéric 71-124. The account of some of the earliest excavations, V. Marin, *Mémoire sur l'ancienne ville de Tauroentum* (Marseille, 1781) has been reprinted (Aubagne, 1973). Denizot (n. 3 above), 38, describes the Les Lecques location as 'une fantasie d'érudition, de ce qu'on a appelé la méthode du calembour'. See also J. Mouquet, *RA* 1925, 128 (La Ciotat); A. Berthelot, *REA* 1936, 419 (St. Mandrier). In *Gallia* 33 (1975), 563, Goudineau describes 'sondages' carried out in 'La grande villa gallo-romaine dite (à tort) de Tauroentum'. 'A tort' or not – I do not seriously question the Le Brusc identification – the Les Lecques museum has a lot of interesting material in it. Clerc, 1, 253, locates Tauroention at Sanary. See also

Clébert (n. 2 above), 123-4; Fr. Brien, 'A Tauroentum (Le Brusc) des recherches ... vaines', *Doss. Arch.* 57 (Oct. 1981), 31.

6. Names: *HMG* 104. Mosaics: *PECS*, 493.

7. *HMG* 103.

8. *HMG* 105; Mela 2, 6, 93; Spanish Alonis, see p. 277 n. 72 above. J. Brunel, 'Etienne de Byzance et le domaine Marseillais', *REA* 1945, 122.

9. Sil. Ital. 14, 443, gives 'Telo Neptunicola' (Telo of the Seashore) as the name of a Roman fighter in the Second Punic War; *HMG* 104; Clébert, 118-21; Lenthéric, 204. Large harbour: with a hard Mistral blowing, I have stood and watched a heavy chop already building up at the beaches of the Mourillon, not more than 1 km SE from the calm water of the sheltered waterfront.

10. For the other two Olbias see *PECS* 642-3. The Sardinian one (Ptol. 3, 3, 4), originally attributed to the Phocaeans, is now thought to have been a Carthaginian foundation.

11. Strabo 4, 1, 8. He lists four 'Massaliot cities' on this coast – Tauroentum, Olbia, Antipolis and Nikaia. Other references in Skymnos 216; Mela 2, 77 (cf. Athen. 6, 233, for Olbia as a former name of the Alps); Steph. Byz. *s.v.* J. Coupry, *CRAI* 1964, 'Les fouilles d'Olbia'. Rivet, 200. It is possible, but uncertain, that it was the Pomponia mentioned by Pliny, *NH* 3, 35. The entrance to the excavation site is on the coastal road D559.

12. 'Olbia n'était sans doute, en quelque façon, qu'un quartier de Marseille' – J. Coupry, *Doss. Arch.* 57 (1981) 30. Population, *ibid.*

13. Photograph and speculations, Coupry, *ibid.* (n. 12 above). An altar found close by and dedicated to an anonymous 'Hero', leads him to reflect upon a 'couple Aphrodite-Héraclès? et non sans rapport, en cet Occident, avec Astarté-Melkart?'

14. Coupry, *ibid.* (n. 12 above). The 1:5 relationship between blocks and streets is pointed out by Goudineau, *PECS*, 643.

15. Roman camp layout is prescribed (from a much later date) in Hyginus, *De metatione castrorum* (ed. A. Grillone; Leipzig, 1977 (Teubner)); development of city plan from camp, M. Wheeler, *Roman Art and Architecture* (London, 1964), 42-3; J. Bradford, *Ancient Landscapes* (London, 1957), 256-63. The chief argument against any Roman influence on the design of Olbia is the date. At 350 BC, it is really too early for any such cross-contact, perhaps too early even for the Romans to have developed the standard square camp from which Olbia would have to have been copied. On the other hand, the plan itself shows so close a resemblance that it is very tempting to see a connection, even in spite of chronology. Dates, after all, can sometimes be wrong.

16. Coupry, *op. cit.* (n. 12 above), 29. Strabo 4, 1, 10. As noted (p. 59 above) the Stoechades also produced coral. See also Jean-Pierre Brun, 'Le village massaliote de La Galère à Porquerolles (Var), et la Géographie des Stoechades, au Ier s. av. J-C.', *EM* 3, 279-88 (with extensive biblio.). There is also the consideration that, as Strabo says, the Massaliots may have had to occupy the Stoechades simply to prevent them being used by pirates. The ancient names of the islands, from west to east, were Prote, Mese, and Hypaia. For Aristaios, mythically the offspring of Apollo and Cyrene, see Virgil, *Georg.* 4, 282ff.

17. Coupry, *op. cit.* (n. 12 above), 33-4. 225 names have been identified, under great difficulties: excavation produced a total of 35,000 sherds, sometimes very tiny, representing a total of 500-600 vases, which had evidently been smashed on the spot.

18. Clébert (n. 2 above), 115-16, quoting Benoit, however, thinks otherwise, for the Roman period at least. See also *HMG* 106.

19. *HMG* 19, 97. Lenthéric, 236-7. Clébert, 115.

20. So G. Denizot, 'Le rivage de Provence et de Languedoc au temps des Ligures', *REL* 23 (1957), 33. Iron, *HMG* 107.

21. Pliny, *NH* 3, 4, 5; Mela, 2, 5, 77; Varro, *De lingua latina* 8, 18, 35.

22. 'Commentators have placed Athenopolis here or there, according to their fancy; some at Toulon, others at Agay, at Saint-Tropez, at Grimaud, and even at Marseilles' – Lenthéric, 240. Al. N. Oikonomides, 'Athenopolis Massiliensium and Saint Tropez', *Anc. World* 1, 1 (March 1978), 33-44. Rivet, 13, 232. Clébert, 114.

23. *HMG* 107 n. 115. One is reminded of the scarcely more probable story, how Les Saintes-Maries-de-la-Mer, in the Camargue, was founded by a boatload of biblical figures, including notably Lazarus and Mary Magdalene. An alternative origin for Saint-Tropez has been sought in an Italian saint, San Trovato. A sub-variant of this legend appears in the anonymous *Guide de la Provence myster-ieuse* (ed. Tchou Princesse, Paris, 1979), 477, and its distinctive flavour can only be preserved by quoting it in full: 'Une dernière légende, nettement "païenne" celle-là, prétend que San Trovato ne serait qu'une statue d'Hermès fortement sexuée, christianisée d'un coup de hache. A ce prix, le dieu païen devint patron de la ville chrétienne. Une chanson provençale, populaire dans la région, reprend cette légende.' After that it comes as something of a let-down to find that Benoit, resolutely philological in his approach as always, declares that 'En fait, Tropez n'est que la déformation du provençal *Troupet* ou *Estropi* = Eutrope' (*HMG* 97 n. 67). Others have attempted to derive the name from some form of 'tripod'.

24. Rivet, 13, 34, 18 n. 32; *HMG* 107; Clébert, 104. Sheltered harbour: 'Still more important must this excellent anchorage have been in former days to the timid sailors of those times, and especially in this part of the Ligurian coast, where a south-easterly storm could very easily wreck vessels and drive them ashore before they could make the gulf of Cannes, or that of Fréjus. It was then that the little harbour of Agay would be welcomed as a real harbour of refuge' (Lenthéric, 318). His patronising scorn for 'the timid sailors' (ancient insurance rates and the large number of known wrecks suggest that they had plenty to be timid about) does not invalidate his main point, the importance of Agay. The wildness of this rugged coast seems to have been matched, until the nineteenth century, by that of its inhabitants (colourful description in Lenthéric, 313-15).

25. Polyb. 33, 8-10; Rivet, 32-5 (with translated text of Polyb.). F.W. Walbank, *A Historical Commentary on Polybius*, 3 (Oxford, 1979), 549. *HMG* 100, 108. Strabo 4, 1, 10. On the whole question see N. Lamboglia, 'Questioni de topografia antica nelle Alpi marittime', *REL* 10 (1944), 26; and J.-E. Dugand, *De l'Aegitna de Polybe au trophée de la Brague*, Publ. Fac. des lettres et sciences humaines de Nice (Paris, 1970).

26. Clébert, 103. The name Cannes is apparently Latin, from the *cannae*, rushes, of a local marsh.

27. *Ad Horrea*: so in the Antonine Itinerary and on the Peutinger Table (= Mougins? La Napoule? – Clébert, *ibid.*). Lenthéric, 338, 351. Resort area: Pliny, *NH*, 53, 4. The modern city owes its origin to the accident that the English statesman Lord Brougham, on his way to Nice and Italy, was stopped at the border by the Sardinian police who were enforcing a quarantine aimed at protecting Italy from cholera. During his protracted and involuntary sojurn in the Hotel de la Poste-aux-Chevaux at Cannes, then a minor fishing port, he was so captivated by the place that he not only built a villa there but spread the word among his friends in London society, who hastened to do likewise.

28. Strabo 4, 1,10; Pliny, *NH* 3, 2; Ptolemy 2, 9, 21 (but see Rivet, 242 n. 10).

29. Strabo 10, 5, 12-13; Pliny, *NH*, 4, 25, 5; 5, 36, 2. Clébert, I, 207.

30. Rivet, 240; *Gallia* 5 (1947), 146-55; 31 (1973), 564-5; 35 (1977), 505-7; 37 (1979), 564-7; 39 (1981), 541-3; *Doss. Arch.* 57 (Oct. 1981), 62-6. (NB – not the Nov.

issue, as in Rivet). Pliny, *NH* 3, 79, records the previous existence on the island of a town called Berconum, and a full account of the Lérins and their later history will be found in Lenthéric, 352-68. The chief feature of Sainte-Marguérite is the fort built by Richelieu and rebuilt by Vauban in which Louis XIV incarcerated 'The Man in the Iron Mask'. On Saint-Honorat, the other and smaller island, there was founded in 375 a monastery which from the seventh to the eleventh centuries achieved great celebrity as 'a real nursery of doctors, scholars, saints and martyrs' (Lenthéric, 361), housing no less than 8,000 monks. Thereafter going into a decline, it was closed only in 1788, after over a millennium of service.

31. Easily the best concise account of ancient Antibes is that of Rivet, 239-42, with copious bibliography. Fuller accounts, with emphasis on the Roman period, are Pierre Cosson, *Civitas Antipolitana* (Serre Editeur, Nice, 1995: ISBN 2-86410-219-6), and Maurice Morena and Dominique Counord, *Antipolis, municipe romain* (Catalogue of an Exhibition presented by the Musée d'Histoire et d'Archéologie, Antibes), (Antibes, 1994; no ISBN).

32. Strabo 4, 1, 5; 9; his other three cities (*poleis*) are Tauroentum, Olbia, and Nice. Pottery, *PECS* 64. Mela 5, 3, 2. Ps. Skymnos 5, 216; Livy, *Epit.* 47. Polyb. 33, 8 (quoted in full and in English translation by Rivet, 33). In Scylax, *Peripl.* 4, it is apparently confused with Antion, 'ville extrème de la Ligurie cisalpine, confinant avec les Étrusques (Anzo, près de Framura)' (*HMG* 108). See also Pliny, *NH* 3, 35; Mela 2, 5, 75.

33. Tac. *Hist.* 2, 15.

34. See p. 28 above.

35. For philological discussion of the name, see *HMG* 108. 'Facing Nice' – a common interpretation, often repeated as established fact: so Paul MacKendrick, *Roman France* (London, 1971), 12. 'Rhabillage': so Rivet, 239.

36. Rivet, 239-40. The sea-wall blocks are shown in Rivet, 49, and the cathedral foundations in Jacques H. Clergues, *Antibes: la ville grecque du IVe siècle avant J.-C. et l'habitat protohistorique* (Antibes, 1969), Planche II. See also P.-A. Février, 'Plans antiques de Fréjus et d'Antibes', *Gallia* 17 (1959), 207-13; A. Rousselle, A. Olivier and G. Rogers, 'Le monument romain de Vaugrenier', *RAN* 11 (1978), 143-94. A good survey is Raymond V. Schroder, S. J., 'Ancient Antipolis in southern France', *Anc. World* (1983), 89-98 (with biblio., 98).

37. Abundant inscriptions: 'The area has yielded more and longer Greek inscriptions than anywhere else in S. France' – *PECS* 64. 'Le galet d'Antibes': *IG* 14, 2424; see also *id.*, 2425-30. Clerc, 1, 255-7. The inscription is in an Eastern Greek alphabet, datable to the late fifth century, and was presumably set up in the earliest days of the settlement: the stone (diorite) is not locally found, and Clerc speculates that we may be dealing with an import: 'Et justement le surnom de Cypris, attribué à la déesse, est assez étrange pour une déesse qui serait venue là de Marseille.' Full discussion in E. Muterse and H. Ménêtrier, *Antibes: introduction historique* (1939; repr. Chicago, 1975: ISBN 0-8905-080-5), appendice I, 'le galet d'Antibes', 71-6; with plate 7, clear photograph of the inscription, illustrated also in H. Roehl, *Imagines Inscriptionum Graecarum Antiquissimarum* (Berlin, 1907), p. 31 (no. 52). For a lead tablet inscribed with a curse, see *Gallia* 18 (1960), 320, fig. 48; *HMG* 23.

38. *Doss. Arch.* 57 (Oct. 1981), 31 (very clear photo on p. 30).

39. *HMG* 109 (identification of type as 'tête de Vénus'). Muterse (n. 37 above), xvi; illustrations (from 1765), viii.

40. Tunny: Martial 13, 103; Pliny *HN* 31, 94. *Viviers*: F. Benoit, *REL* (1952) 290-7; figs. 53-8. They were usually circular pools of around 4 m diameter, communicating directly with the sea. Of particular interest among the maritime exhibits in the museum is a set of two lengths of lead piping designed to carry pumped-out bilge water across the deck and over the side into the sea. The pump being amidships, two pipes were provided, one on each side; at any given time only one would be in use, the one running downhill to the leeward (i.e. lower) scuppers, depending on which tack the ship was on. So far as I know, this device is unique.

41. *HMG* 110-11.

42. Clerc, 257-8: 'Il paraît bien que c'est pour commémorer une victoire navale remportée sur les Etrusques que les Marseillais donnèrent à leur colonie ce nom glorieux.' The name was not uncommon in the Greek world, and Clerc records Nikaia as existing in Bithynia, Thrace, Locris, Illyria, and India (founded by Alexander), and, closer to home, Diodorus (5, 13, 3-4) maintains that there was in Corsica a Nikaia, founded by the Etruscans. 'Nikaia' not being an Etruscan name, this is probably wrong (unless it is yet another *rhabillage* or a later re-naming, such as 'New Amsterdam' = 'New York'; this, however, happens only rarely). *HMG* 42 n. 29; 110.

43. *HMG* 110; Rivet, 12, agrees.

44. Pliny, *NH* 3, 7; Strabo 4, 1, 9; 4, 6, 3 (Ligurian piracy); Mela 2, 77; Rivet, 32-3, 68.

45. Rivet, 222; *Gallia* 12 (1954), 441-2; M. Bordes (ed.), *Histoire de Nice et du pays niçois* (Toulouse, 1976), ch. 2 (J. Ducat and B.C. Farnoux), 15-19. Strabo 4, 1, 5. Pottery: *HMG* 102.

46. *PECS* 211; Rivet, 341. Maurice Bordes (ed.) (n. 45 above) (good plan of Cemenelum, pp. 38-9). Also to be noted is the out of date but still sometimes interesting E. Tisserand, *Histoire civile et réligieuse de la cité de Nice et du département des Alpes-Maritimes* (Nice, 1862; repr. Marseille, 1973). Danièle Mouchot, 'Les fouilles de Cimiez', *Doss. Arch.* 57 (Oct. 1981), 55-61; *Gallia* 22 (1964), 608; 29 (1971, 463-4; 33 (1975), 508; 35 (1977), 508; 37 (1979), 568; *id.*, *Nice-Cimiez, Le Musée d'Archéologie* (Nice, 1989).

47. Hecataios ap. Steph. Byz. (fr. A 65 (57); exhaustive discussion in Reymond and Dugand (below), 28-41); Strabo 4, 6, 2-3; Virgil, *Aen.* 6, 824-61; Sil. Ital. 5, 568. Ptolemy 3, 2 lists it as a port. For a full modern account, see the very full G. Reymond and J.-E. Dugand, *Monaco antique* (Publications de la Faculté des lettres et sciences humaines de Nice (Paris, Les Belles Lettres) 1970).

48. If indeed it is not yet another *rhabillage*, with no Greek origin at all. Full philological discussion in *HMG* 96-7. The 64 Heracles sites are individually listed and briefly described, with source references, by J.-E. Dugand (n. 47 above), 126-32.

49. Monegasque poverty is summed up by the traditional rhyme (which 'everybody knows' – Lenthéric, 448):

Son Monaco sopra scoglio,
Non semino e non racoglio,
E pur mangiar voglio

'Monaco am I, high on a rock; I neither plant crops nor harvest – and, just the same, I want to eat.' Lenthéric's caustic verdict, 'Monaco is faithful to its motto and eats very well. This miniature people ... lives entirely on the money of the stranger, to whom in return it gives absolutely nothing' dates from a later age, when 'The ancient kingdom of Hercules has become an opulent gaming house. The lion's skin and the club of the son of Jupiter have been replaced by the black coat and the rake of the croupier'. La Turbie (*PECS* 936-7) was the highest point of the Via Julia on its way from Italy to Cemelenum (Nice) and in the Antonine Itinerary is listed as 'Alpis summa'. With a total height of 49 m Augustus' monument was almost exactly as high as the Pont du Gard, or something like a 10-12 storey modern building. It was built in the 'wedding cake' style of architecture, with successive storeys set back, and may have superficially resembled the Mausoleum of Halicarnassos (if one may compare a pair of largely hypothetical restorations). On the base it carried an inscription listing all the tribes of Gaul that lay ahead of the traveller. The implication, since this was a trophy – Tropaeum Augusti – was that he could thank the Emperor for his safe and peaceful journey, and the listing of the tribes recalled the manifold imperial achievements that made this possible. An intriguing parallel from the Victorian age is the conceit of inscribing prominently outside large railway termini the names of the romantically far-flung destinations that could be reached from within. We may adduce the example the inscribed piers still visible outside Euston Station, London; and a long frieze running round the booking hall at Union Station, Toronto, enumerates practically every city in Canada as being accessible from it. Such are the later, if unwitting, inheritors of Augustus' legacy at La Turbie. Cynics may also wonder whether the Antonine Itinerary's laconic verdict on the place, 'Huc usque Italia abhinc Gallia', 'Up to here, Italy; from here on, Gaul', might not reflect, if not actually trigger, an involuntary gut reaction from traditionally-minded Italian patriots akin to that of later Englishmen, that 'The wogs begin at Calais'. The Roman world doesn't generally seem to have thought this way, but I can't be sure. For the monument, see J. Formigé, *Le trophée des Alpes, La Turbie* (*Gallia* suppl. 6 (1949)).

50. *HMG* 75-6: coins, *ibid.* and n. 9. Full description of coins in Reymond and Dugand (n. 47 above), 53-4, pl. VIII (Carthaginian); 55-6 (Greek).

51. The prize for ingenuity goes to E. Desjardins, *Géographie politique et administrative de la Gaule romaine* (Paris, 1978-93) 2, 2, 4, who points out that, Phoenician script being retrograde, Herakles is really just Melkarth spelled backwards, M being a sideways-written sigma. Lenthéric, 441.

52. Attempts have been made to compensate for this historical lacuna by the exercise of a colourful imagination: 'Is it then to give too loose reign to one's imagination if one pictures to oneself all the promontories of this favoured shore, covered with their little sacred woods, where half-clad Maenads carried away by Bacchic phrenzy, gave themselves up in the mysterious night to the intoxication of their voluptuous dances, and trembling and convulsed with excitement, surrendered themselves to their sacred orgies?' – Lethéric, 444. So much for the 'Hellénisation du Midi de la Gaule'! One can see why Lenthéric laments the supersession of such traditions by the black coat and rake of the croupier (n. 49 above). Lenthéric is outdated, valuable on antiquarian matters, seldom to be relied on uncritically, and always a pleasure to read.

53. Reymond and Dugand (n. 47 above), do their best to provide an account of the Greek history of Monaco but, though their work is to be honoured as sound and careful scholarship, they are faced with making bricks with a minimum of straw. The chief sections relevant to our topic are pp. 59-71 (ch. 4, 'Du VIe au IIIe siècle'; 67 (Massaliot coins found at Monaco; they are rare); 167-188 (ch. IX, 'L'archéologie romaine à Monaco'); 181-6 (Roman inscriptions).

11. The Celtic Neighbours

1. J-P. Clébert, *Provence Antique* (Paris, 1966), 1, 210f.

2. 'La Barbarie Ligure' – Benoit, *REL* 1962, 117-24: on 117 the whole of Liguria is 'une zone repulsive' that everybody tries to avoid, even armies. In level of culture, Papon – writing be it noted, in 1777 – equates the Ligurians to the Americans: on the arrival of the Greeks at Massalia, 'ils étoient à-peu-près dans le même état où sont aujourd'hui quelques peuples de l'Amérique' (Papon, n. 19 below, 503). For their shocking habits, see nn. 19, 30, 35 below. Clébert, 1, 138-42. The spelling of the name varies: sometimes they are 'the Ligyes', and it has even been suggested that the Gulf of Lions, off Marseille, owes its name to the corruption of Ligyes. The real origin of the name is uncertain.

3. Full account of these 'Eastern Gauls' in Rankin (n. 6 below), 188-207.

4. Even 'indigenous' is a questionable term, for the tribes surrounding the Greeks were not autochthonous, having themselves arrived in the region from elsewhere. Just the same, it is in widespread use.

5. In Latin, the word is normally translated 'town' (so Lewis and Short), not necessarily Gaulish or barbarian. So in English the two words are usually equated, and at Eton College 'oppidans' is the traditional term for those living outside the college, in the town, without necessarily any implication that Eton town is a barbaric encampment; and the Shorter Oxford English Dictionary derives the word 'oppidan' from the Latin '*oppidanus*, belonging to a town (other than Roman)', Rome being the *urbs*. It was, of course, also applicable in Latin literature to Gallic settlements such as we are here considering, and, naturally, was frequently so used by Caesar.

6. For general accounts of this civilisation, see Clébert, 222-56; *Doss. Arch.* 35 (juin 1979), esp. 67-75, Jean-Luc Fiches, 'Habitat et fortifications: la civilisation des oppida'; also n. 18 below. F.R. Hodson and R.M. Rowlett, 'From 600 BC to the Roman Conquest', in Stuart Piggott, Glyn Daniel, and Charles McBurney (ed.), *France Before the Romans* (London, 1973), 157-91, has good illustrations but concentrates more on small finds (pottery, bronzes) than is strictly relevant to this present study. H.D. Rankin, *Celts and the Classical World* (London, 1987) tends to the readably anecdotal; T.G.E. Powell, *The Celts* (London/New York, 1958), and M. Dillan and N. Chadwick, *The Celtic Realms* (New York, 1967) have material relevant to our field but are devoted to the Celts in general, especially in Ireland.

7. Especially impressive is the photograph of a veritable mountain of sling-stones heaped against the rampart of Nages, in *Doss. Arch.* 99 (Nov. 1985), 85.

8. F. Benoit, 'Resultats historiques des fouilles d'Entremont', *Gallia* 26 (1968), 1-31. There is a fine air photo of the central area in *Doss. Arch.* 154 (Nov. 90), 59 (article by Patrice Arcelin, 'L'environment indigène de Marseille grecque', pp. 58-69. See also P. Arcelin, *L'habitat d'Entremont: urbanisme et modes architecturaux*, in *Archéologie d'Entremont au Musée Granet* (Aix-en-Provence, Musée Granet, 1987), 56-98; P. Arcelin, 'Société indigène et propositions culturelles massaliotes', in *EM* 3, 305-36, esp. 327. Clébert, 238-41. Bromwich (ch. 9, n. 2; p. 269 above), 130-4.

9. The actual difference in level between the Upper and Lower Towns is very small, no more than a metre or so, and to a cursory glance the whole site looks more or less flat. On seeing the term 'Upper Town' the reader must not imagine it as some sort of precipitous acropolis.

10. Full discussion by Henri Tréziny, 'Sur quelques problèmes d'architecture et d'urbanisme en Gaule méridionale' *EM* 3, 338-42 (with biblio., 348-9): also Patrice Arcelin, 'Société indigène et propositions culturelles massaliotes', *ibid.*, 326-30 (biblio., 332-6).

11. The architectural remains are 'fairly poor' (H. Gallet de Santerre, *PECS* 303. 'They did not adopt Roman comforts; their houses were unheated' – Paul MacKendrick, *Roman France* (London, 1971), 18. For a general account, see H. Gallet de Santerre, 'Ensérune, an oppidum in southern France', *Archaeology* 15 (1962), 163-71; *id.*, 'Fouilles dans le quartier ouest d'Ensérune', *RAN* 1 (1968), 39-83; J. Jannoray, *Ensérune, Contribution à l'étude des civilisations préromaines de la Gaule méridionale* (Paris, 1955). *Gallia* 6 (1948), 112-15; 8 (1950), 112-15; 11 (1953), 96-9; 12 (1954), 417-22; 16 (1956), 210-15; 22 (1964), 495; 24 (1966), 470; 27 (1969), 397; 31 (1973), 496; 33 (1975), 508; 37 (1979), 532.

12. Illustrated in A. Trevor Hodge, *Roman Aqueducts and Water Supply* (London, 1992), 61.

13. Also a few contracts and commercial documents written on lead sheets: M. Bats, 'Marseille, les colonies et les relais indigènes', *EM* 3, 273.

14. The reader may appreciate the summary verdict of MacKendrick (n. 11 above), 18: 'In sum, what the excavations at Ensérune have unearthed is six centuries of the history of a native people rooted in prehistory, but independent, though open to cultural influences from abroad, as the French have been ever since.'

15. Publications: *Gallia* 20 (1962), 631-2; 22 (1964), 500-2; 27 (1969), 406; 29 (1971), 393-4; 31 (1973), 503-6; 33 (1975), 517-21; 36 (1978), 452-4; 37 (1979), 540-3; 39 (1981), 518-21. F. and M. Py, in *RAN* 2 (1969) 97-121; *PECS* 604-5 (by M. Py). The site is reached by taking the highway D40 from Nîmes, then the D14 to Langlade, and thence the D737.

16. M. Py, *PECS* 604.

17. Publications: J.-L. Fiches, 'Ambrussum et la voie Domitienne', *Riv. di Stud. Liguri* 46 (1980), 132-57; *Gallia* 27 (1967), 401; 29 (1971), 388-9; 31 (1973), 498-91; 33 (1975), 510-12; 36 (1978), 445; 37 (1979), 535-6; 39 (1981), 511-13; 41 (1983), 524-6; 43 (1985), 411-13. J.-L. Fiches, *Les maisons gallo-romaines d'Ambrussum* (Paris, 1986).

18. Le Baou-Roux: Philippe Boissinot, 'Le Baou-Roux et le problème du territoire de Marseille', in *EM* 1 (Université de Provence, Aix-en-Provence, 1986; Actes de la Table-Ronde, 16 Mars 1985, ed. M. Bats and H. Tréziny), 117-18; J.-P. Tenevin, *Le Baou-Roux, oppidum celto-ligure* (Aix, 1972). For a general overview of the Celtic *oppida* see the extensive and important article by Patrice Arcelin, 'Le territoire de Marseille grecque dans son contexte indigène', *EM* 1, 43-104. The bibliography, exhaustive up to the date of publication, covers all possible aspects of the topic, listing no less than 192 references.

19. Diod. 5, 39,1 (stony and wretched character of the land); *id*. 24-32 for a wild collection of stories and anecdotes (e.g. 32-7 – they are raving homosexuals; *ibid*.: all Irishmen are cannibals). Sil. Ital. 15, 169-72 (Massalia surrounded by dreadful barbarians with shocking rites). For a general account of these ancient views see Benoit, *REL* 1962, 117-24 (e.g. armies avoiding Liguria, p. 117; Benoit makes the sensible point that the real reason was that often the inland passes offered an easier and shorter route). Papon, *Histoire de Provence* (Paris, 1777), 503, and n. 2 above. For the Ligurians in general, Clerc, 1, 31-43.

20. e.g. Cic. *Pro Flac*. 63: 'cum in ultimis terris cincta Gallorum gentibus barbariae fluctibus [Massilia] adluatur ...', and Cato, *ap*. Serv. *ad* Verg. *A*, 11, 715: 'Ligures omnes fallaces.' They come out of it rather better in Plato, *Phaedr*. 237A, where they are praised as great music-lovers, but the passage is a mock-serious invocation and poor evidence for reality – rather as if a famous concert violinist were quoted as speaking admiringly of the harmonious qualities of the bagpipes.

21. Justin 43, 4-5: 'magna illis cum Liguribus, magna cum Gallis fuere bella'. Also Livy 49, 18 (piracy). Lenthéric, 312-15, has a full and highly coloured description of the eighteenth- and nineteenth-century brigands ('they yell like tigers, they behave like madmen') of the Esterel, who were their latter-day descendants.

22. Diod. 5, 39, 5 (troglodytes). Clerc (138) comments that this probably refers more to the mountain-dwellers of the Alpes Maritimes rather than Ligurians in general. He also notes that in Provence 'si la pierre abonde, le bois de construction a toujours certainement été rare' (38 n. 1); but Diodorus (5, 39, 1) specifically says that logging is one of the Ligurians' main industries. Baby delivery on the job: Strabo 3, 4, 17. The same story is also told of Thrace (Arist. *De mirab. ascult.* 91).

23. For the Gallic character in general, see Strabo 4, 4, 2.

24. Strabo 4, 4, 4. Caesar, *BG* 6, 13-16 (Druids), DS 5, 31, 2. On the *vates*, discussion in François Lasserre, *Strabon, Géographie 3 et 4* (Budé ed., Paris, 1966), 2, 215 n. 2.

25. MC-L, 193.

26. Springs seem at all periods to have been particularly venerated in Gaul. At the springs of the Seine the goddess Sequana was not only worshipped but gave the river its Latin name (if not *vice versa*). The springs, located some 30 km NW of Dijon, just off the N71 highway, were architecturally decorated with a peristyle, terrace, pool, and temple in Roman days, and were 'embellished – if that is the word – in 1867 with an artificial grotto and an equally artificial nymph, both now much dilapidated' – Paul MacKendrick, *Roman France* (London, 1971), 178, which also see for Gallic springs (176-83); also A. Grenier, *Manuel d'archéologie gallo-romaine* 4, 1 (Paris, 1960), 'Les monuments des eaux', 477-516. General account of Celtic religion, Patrice Arcelin, 'Croyances et vie religieuse', *Doss. Arch.* 35 (juin, 1979), 99-107. Greek religious influence: Strabo 4, 1, 5 maintains that there was such influence upon the Iberians.

27. Strabo 4, 4, 5. In Spain, the Lusitanians did the same thing (3, 3, 6).

28. Strabo 4, 4, 5; DS 5, 29, 5.

29. Strabo 4, 4, 5. La Cloche skulls: *Doss. Arch.* 35 (1979), 102 (with photo); see also p. 157 above, Glanum).

30. Roquepertuse: illustrations in *Doss. Arch.* (n. 29 above), 99; *Musée d'Histoire de Marseille* (p. 245 n. 11 above), 23; Doc. A. Mérid. 14 (1991), 7-88 (as quoted in *EM* 3, 325; H. de Gérin Ricard, 'Le sanctuaire pré-romain de Roquepertuse', *Centennaire de la Societé d'histoire, de statistique et d'archéologie de Marseille, 1927*; brief mention in MacKendrick (n. 26 above), 28.

31. Illustrations in *Doss. Arch.* (n. 29 above), 44-5, 111. The entire article, 'La sculpture préromaine en Provence', by François Salviat (*op. cit.*, 31-51) is a good introduction of the topic in general.

32. Polyb. 2, 19, 4; 11, 3,1; Livy 5, 33, 3, and 44, 6 ; Diod. Sic. 5, 26, 3; Dion. Hal. 14, 8, 12; Plut. *Camill.* 15, 2; App. *Celt.* 7; Polyainos 8, 25, 1; Amm. Marc. 15, 12, 4 (references are reprinted from Tschernia (n. 34, p. 260 above), 88, n. 142).

33. DS, 5, 28,3, tells us that the long moustaches so notoriously favoured by the Gauls were highly functional. They drank their beer through them, so as to strain off the froth. Unfortunately when it came to eating, their moustaches often got tangled up with their food and they ended up chewing them. One is glad that the ancient world never invented spaghetti.

34. Unmixed wine: Poseidonios, *ap.* Athen. 4, 36 (=152C). MC-L, 52. The best general study of the topic, though now somewhat dated, is Roger Dion, *Histoire de la vigne et du vin en France* (Paris, 1959). An up-to-date bibliography may be found in *EM* 3, 408-10, compiled by Michael Dietler and running to 86 titles; it is particularly strong on the anthropological approach and parallels from other primitive societies. A much shorter but more readily accessible bibliography will be found in *Doss. Arch.* 154 (Nov. 1990), 96 ('Le vin de Marseille'), while the largest bibliography of all, though dealing with all Roman wines, not just at Massalia or in Gaul, is in A. Tschernia, *Le vin de l'Italie romaine* (École française de Rome, Rome, 1986), 361-74.

35. DS 5, 26, 3. His depiction of the Celts reminds one of the stereotype of an Irish pub on a Saturday night, but he may not be at all reliable. Drunkenness was so rare among the Greeks and Romans (as indeed it still is) that perhaps it would not have taken too much to impress them; and for the reliability of Diodorus on the Irish, see n. 19 above. Nervii, Caes. *BG* 2, 15,4.

36. Dion (n. 19 above), 88: 'on l'honorait d'une présentation magnifique.'

37. R. Joffroy, 'Le trésor de Vix', *Mon. Piot* 48 (1954), 1-68; *id.*, *Vix et ses Trésors* (Paris, 1979). The krater is conveniently illustrated in Paul MacKendrick (n. 11 above), 15, and also in *Doss. Arch.* 109 (Oct. 1986), 9-11. Routes by which it could have been transported to Vix (Rhône, Adriatic, Danube): Villard, 127, 141.

38. The figures are from Joffroy, *op. cit.* (n. 37 above), 6, 22. It also had a lid (in place when excavated) weighing 13.8 kg (*id.*, 19). The krater is dated to the late sixth century BC, and the tomb in which it was found to 500 BC, which means it was probably in use for over a hundred years. The extreme thinness, and hence fragility, of the sides of the krater is surprising – how did they ever transport such a thing from wherever it was made in the Mediterranean, without damage (even allowing for the fact that it came apart and could then be re-assembled on delivery)? As a matter of interest, I approached a colleague in engineering to ask whether a vessel of such thin sides could even contain so heavy a load of wine without bursting. The relevant calculations were made, and the answer was, yes, it could. I still think it must have been a close thing, though.

39. *HMG* 191. The prestige of wine suggests another reason for the burial. The Celts were strong believers in a life after death and buried the corpse with an array and offerings they thought it would need or like. The krater was accompanied in the tomb by two cups and a serving-jug (*oinochoe*), all the apparatus of a party. There is nothing quite so depressing as arriving at a party and finding everything else there but the drink has run out, and I doubt if the royal house of Vix would have risked it happening to the princess they were burying. The obvious suggestion is that the krater was put in the tomb filled with wine – the princess was given a proper send-off with a two or three years' supply to get her off to a good start in the next world and ensure her welcome there (and if the reader suspects me of an indulgence in frivolous triviality, who is to say how the minds of the Celtic mourners worked?).

40. One is tempted to add a fifth point. If the Celts went in for what, I suppose, we may call ceremonial binge drinking, one of the occasions when it would be appropriate would presumably be in the preparations for war or major battle. May this then help to explain their undisciplined ferocity in the field, which so impressed the Romans? It has been noted that in more recent times drinking, often officially organised, has formed a vital element in preparing troops for battle. At Agincourt many of the troops went 'into the mêlée less than sober, if not indeed fighting drunk'; at Waterloo many of the British soldiers drank gin while fighting, and a cartload of spirits was forwarded by their high command into the middle of one of their defensive squares; while at the Somme J.F.C. Fuller concluded that 'many of the men in the front line must have been drunk well before zero hour' (John Keegan, *The Face of Battle* (London, 1976), 114; 183; 245; 333). The possible Massaliot contribution to the well-known Celtic bellicosity has never, I think, been explored. The Romans themselves never seem to have been drunk in battle (or at least one never hears of it), though no doubt any subsequent plundering would tell a different story. Tschernia (n. 34, above), 87 notes that while Gallic consumption of wine was enormous, relatively little of it went to the Roman army, and on the Rhine frontier 'Quand une occupation militaire a succédé à un site indigène, comme sur le Munster hügel de Bâle, on note une chute de l'arrivée des amphores de vin' (88). But there was a good deal of variation in this and troops in a permanent garrison, and not campaigning, seem to have drunk much more (18-19). Caesar's opinion, contradicting what I have suggested above, was that wine made the Gauls soft and lacking in disciplined courage (*BG* 1, 1, 3; see also 2, 15, 4 (Nervii) and 4, 2,1 (Suevi).

41. F. Benoit, *Recherches sur l'héllenisation du Midi de la Gaule* (Publications des Annales de la Faculté des lettres, Aix-en-Provence, 1965; repr. Lafitte,

Marseille, 1980) (abbrev. *HMG*). R. Busquet, 'Marseille: a-t-elle ou n'a-t-elle pas civilisé la Gaule?', *Rev. Historique* 211 (1954), 1-10. Monique Clavel-Lévêque makes it clear where her sympathies lie, referring to the Greek influence as the 'processus dits d'acculturation qui ont contaminé les sociétés gauloises' (MC-L, 192). Good summary in Ch. Goudineau, 'Marseille et la Gaule: en guise de conclusion générale ...', in *EM* 3, 451-6 (esp. 451).

42. See the account in Benoit (n. 41 above), 20-4 ('Le mythe linguistique ou le "faux grec" '). See also my p. 269 n. 4 (above) for *rhabillages*. The non-Greek origin of most place-names is supported by Ch. Rostaign, *Essai sur la toponymie de la Provence* (Paris, 1950); but see also J.-J. Hatt 'Répartition des mots d'origine hellénique en France', *RAE* 6 (1955), 147-50 (accepted by Clavel-Lévêque: MC-L, 21). Full account with discussion and biblio., J.-P. Morel, 'Les Phocéens en Occident', *P del P* 1966, 414 n. 113. Clerc, 1, 48f., on the name Massalia.

43. In the seventh century BC the Iberians of North Spain introduced Phoenician, developing a semi-syllabaric script, while at the East the Ligurians sometimes adopted the Etruscan alphabet. Between these two frontier zones, Ionian Greek, from Phocaea via Massalia, was the rule (Michel Bats, 'La logique de l'écriture d'une société à l'autre en Gaule méridionale protohistorique', *RAN* 21 (1988), 121-48 (esp. 129-3). See also Vittorio Vertold, 'Contatti e conflitti di lingue nel antico Mediterraneo', *P del P* fasc. 33 (1953), 407-48.

44. Strabo 4, 1, 5. Full discussion by Pierre-Yves Lambert, 'La diffusion de l'écriture gallo-grecque en milieu indigène', in *EM* 3, 289-94; esp. 291 for *hellenisti* possibly meaning 'à la manière grecque'. The texts of the inscriptions are collected in P.M. Duval, *Recueil des inscriptions gauloises*, I (éd. du C.N.R.S., Paris, 1985) (suppl. à *Gallia* XLV).

45. Letter to Q. Cicero: Caesar, *BG* 5, 48; Helvetii: 1, 29; druids: 6, 14; Diviciacus: 1, 19. The above references are collected by *HMG* 22, where (n. 28) we learn that Tacitus believed in the existence of Greek tomb inscriptions on the borders of Germany and Rhaetia. For Greek inscriptions on lead tablets found in Spain, see P. Bosch-Gimpera, 'The Phokaians in the far west', *CQ* 38 (1994), 53-9, esp. 57 n. 7. I have myself seen a lead tablet inscribed in Greek on exhibition in the museum of Cáceres (an improbable find-spot, for Cáceres is in West Spain, near the Portuguese border and just north of Mérida, but since it appeared to be a set of regulations for a market it is not the sort of thing one would expect to be carried off as booty); if local, it would again show the extent of the Greek linguistic diaspora.

46. Varro, *ap.* Jerome, Commentary on St. Paul, Second Epistle to the Galatians, 425; Isidore of Seville, *Origines* 15, 1,63.

47. Locations of Philippeioi-hoards, see C. Seltman, *Greek Coins* (Methuen, London, 1933; repr. Spink, London, 1977), 201. The various stages in the degeneration of the types to a state unrecognisable as a picture at all are well illustrated in his pl. XLVII. Seltman (215) thinks that the Philippeioi were brought to Gaul by the Romans, but his work is by now somewhat outdated, and Clavel-Lévêque, with much more probability, assumes that 'Il est évident que Marseille a assumé le rôle fondemental dans la transmission de ces prototypes' (MC-L, 173 and 180 n. 30). The Arverni (the Celtic tribe inhabiting the modern Auvergne) were particularly prominent in producing these native imitations, and so were the Belgae, though they modelled their products rather on the coinage of Tarentum.

48. MC-L, 176-7.

49. Aphrodite Pyrénaia: MC-L, 192; Strabo 4, 1,3. It is not, apparently, entirely clear whether this means 'the cult of Aphrodite located at the Pyrenees', or 'the Pyrenean Aphrodite'; the second interpretation would imply a much closer local involvement and integration. The adjective *Pyrenaia* is not present in Strabo's text, but there is no doubt about the existence of the sanctuary. It was near Port-Vendres, which presumably derived its name from it (Portus Veneris). General discussion 'Les formes d'acculturation', MC-L, 192-5.

50. Some examples: Ephoros, *ap.* Strabo 4, 4, 6, (who strongly disbelieves him) maintains that the Celts are philhellenes. Ps. Scymnos (third-century), 183-7, has the Celts learning Greek customs and becoming familiar with Greece from offering hospitality to Greek travellers. Justin (43, 4), summarising Pompeius Trogus, asserts that instead of the Greeks having emigrated to Gaul, you'd swear the whole of Gaul had been transported into the middle of Greece. And Strabo, no doubt unconsciously plagiarising Pericles' famous remark on Athens and Greece, asserts that Massalia was a school for 'the barbarians' (4, 1, 5). For Massalia viewed through Roman eyes, see pp. 253 n. 17 above.

12. Conclusion

1. Or, of course, as the statisticians would put it, 'both of the above'. Broken reed, see pp. 105-6 above. Livy 40, 18, tells us that following the second Punic War, the Massaliots actually complained of being attacked at sea by, of all people, the Ligurians ('Massilienses de Ligurum navibus querebantur').

2. p. 36 above. In the Second Punic War, Massalia did also render general assistance to the Romans: Livy 21, 20; 25-6; 26, 19.

3. Claudius, travelling north from Ostia by sea on the first stage of a journey that was to culminate in his invasion of Britain was twice almost wrecked by the Mistral in the Gulf of Lions. He settled the matter by getting off at Massalia and going on to Boulogne by land. Suet. *Claud.* 17, 2.

4. T.J. Dubabin, *The Western Greeks* (Oxford, 1948), 348.

5. The best estimate of the modern equivalent of ancient drachmae (a notoriously difficult subject) is that of David C. Young, *The Myth of Greek Amateur Athletics* (Chicago, 1985), 124 n. 15, where one drachma is somewhere around 100 (1985) US dollars. A tetradrachm would thus be worth something of the order of $500 (p. 127 above).

6. Strabo 4, 1, 5; Caesar, *BG* 1, 29 (Helvetii); 6, 14 (druids), MC-L, 196-9, 'L'extension d'une culture écrite'.

7. 'Hellenisation' – *HMG*, MC-L, *passim*. The whole volume of *EM* 3 is devoted to 'Marseille grecque et la Gaule', with (451-6) a good summary by Christian Goudineau. On shifting data he remarks that 'nous nous sommes aperçu que cette vaste question demandait à être "périodisée" ... Au début, face à un monde peu organisé, c'est l'affirmation de Marseille, son développement, ses initiatives. Puis, des pouvoirs se constituent qui vont devenir des interlocuteurs, voire des opposants. Le poids de l'Italie ne cesse de croître. Le monde change, en Gaule intérieure, et partout ailleurs. Les conduites se transforment, l'économie monétaire se crée et se développe. Les schémas simples doivent évoluer' (456).

8. In *EM* 3 (n. 7 above), 452, he stresses that in the Greek world, Massalia had a tremendous reputation, that 'Massalia est grande, l'une des très grandes', but the only evidence he quotes for it is the existence of the Massaliot treasury at Delphi. Personally, I should like to see this viewpoint supported by evidence somewhat wider and more general in scope.

9. Sextus Julius Africanus, *Olympioricarum Fasti*, ed. I. Rutgers (1862) is most readily available in the Chicago (1980) reprint (ISBN 0-89005-351-0). Several other lists existed in antiquity (e.g. Eratosthenes: see Rutgers, III n. 2; also I n. 4, quoting esp. Paus. 5, 8, 6.). Africanus (fl. under Elagabalus, 218-22 AD) evidently wrote in the 249th Olympiad (217 AD), and his text later survived embedded in the work of Eusebios.

10. Even on the much shorter and easier trip between Puteoli and Alexandria it was not easy to fit in an extra run in the same summer. St. Paul got wrecked on Malta by a captain who tried it: Lionel Casson, *Ships and Seamanship in the Ancient World* (Princeton, 1971), 272 n. 5.

11. Oregon trail: e.g. women's dress. 'Sometimes there was a conflict between mothers and daughters as the overland journey led young girls into "loose" behaviour. Mothers tried to impose Victorian proprieties, and ... . Frontier woman resisted any form of dress that would accommodate their daily life and work. No change that might seem to bring women closer to the dress of men or of Indian women was tolerated. The word "squaw" appears occasionally in diaries, always as an epithet of utmost disgust' [compare Massaliot attitudes to living among the Celtic 'barbarians'] – Lillian Schlissel, *Women's Diaries of the Westward Journey* (Schocken, New York, 1982; ISBN 0-8052-3774-4), 84-5. Dawson City: Pierre Berton, *I Married the Klondike* (Toronto, 1961).

Bibliography

Since this book was intended not just for professional academics but also the interested general reader, a few introductory notes may perhaps be helpful to those unfamiliar with this specialised field.

1. None of the books listed below can be bought in an ordinary bookstore. All are too specialised and most are out of print. They are available through any good university library, possibly through inter-library loan.

2. For any further study of the subject, some knowledge of French is essential, and preferably Italian also.

3. Outside France, the most readily available source is the semi-professional journal *Les dossiers d'archéologie* (*Doss. Arch.*). The most important issues are nos. 35, June 1979 ('Au temps des Gaulois en Gaule méridionale'); 57, October 1981 ('La Côte d'Azur'); 59, December 1981/January 1982 ('La société gallo-romaine'); 99, November 1985 ('Recentes découvertes en Languedoc Roussillon'); 154, November 1990 ('Marseille dans le monde antique' – strongly recommended); 140, July/August 1989 ('Glanum, cité grecque et romaine de Provence').

4. For an individual site the first place to turn to is the *Princeton Encyclopedia of Classical Sites* (*PECS*).

5. Perhaps the three most basic studies in the field are the articles by Lepore, Morel, and Nenci (§§6 & 8 below); each has footnotes giving a very extensive bibliography for further study.

6. The most relevant periodicals are *Gallia*, a record of current French archaeological activity; critical studies and discussions appear in *Revue archéologique de la Narbonnaise* (*RAN*) and in the *Revue des études ligures* (*REL*).

7. Current French researches into ancient Massalia are now published in *Études massaliètes* (*EM*); at the time of writing three volumes are in print.

Contents

Abbreviations

In the text and notes all usual abbreviations are employed, as listed in *L'Année Philologique*, and in addition the following:

24. Lerin Islands
25. Antibes
26. Nice
27. La Turbie
28. Others

Celtic civilisation and sites
29. Celtic civilisation and culture
30. Ambrussum
31. Ensérune
32. Entremont
33. Nages

Clerc: Michel Clerc, *Massalia* (2 vols.) (Marseille, 1927-9; reprint Lafitte, Marseille, 1971)
EM 1, 2, 3: *Études massiliètes* (pub. A.D.A.M. éditions, Lattes/Univ. de Provence, Aix-en-Provence)
Vol. 1, 'Le territoire de Marseille grecque' (1978)
Vol. 2, 'Les amphores de Marseille grecque', ed. Michel Bats (1990)
Vol. 3, 'Marseille grecque et la Gaule' (1992)
HMG: Fernand Benoit, *Recherches sur l'hellénisation du midi de la Gaule* (Aix-en-Provence, 1965; repr. Lafitte, Marseille, 1980)
Lenthéric: Charles Lenthéric, *The Riviera: ancient and modern*, tr. Charles West (London, 1895, repr. Ares, Chicago, 1976)
MC-L: Monique Clavel-Lévêque, *Marseille grecque: la dynamique d'un impérialisme marchand* (Lafitte, Marseille, 1977)
PECS: *Princeton Encyclopedia of Classical Sites*, ed. Richard Stillwell (Princeton, 1976).
Rivet: A.L.F. Rivet, *Gallia Narbonensis* (London, 1988)
Ternaux: Henricus Ternaux, *Historia Republicae Massiliensium* (Goettingen, 1826; repr. Ares, Chicago, 1974)
Villard: François Villard, *La céramique grecque de Marseille* (Paris, 1960).

The accepted abbreviations for the academic journals most commonly referred to are:
REL – Revue des études ligures
RAN – Revue archéologique de Narbonnaise
P del P – La Parola del Passato
Doss. Arch. – Les dossiers d'archéologie

1. General reference

Bloch, R., *The Etruscans* (London, 1958)
Boardman, J., *The Greeks Overseas* (Harmondsworth, 1964)
Bradford, J., *Ancient Landscapes* (London, 1957) [interpreting air photography]
Bradley, K., *Slaves and Masters in the Roman Empire* (Brussels, 1984)
Cary, M., *The Geographic Background of Greek and Roman History* (Oxford, 1949)
Dennis, G., *Cities and Cemeteries of Etruria* (2 vols., London, 1848; repr. Everyman, London, 1907)
Dunbabin, T.J., *The Western Greeks* (Oxford, 1948)
Farrington, B., *Greek Science* (Penguin, Harmondsworth, 1961)
Forbes, R.J., *Studies in Ancient Technology* (9 vols., Brill, Leiden, 1964)
Grant, M., *The Ancient Mediterranean* (Penguin/Meridian, London, 1969)
Grenier, A., *Manuel d'archéologie gallo-romaine*, vols I-IV (Paris, 1931-60)
Hasebroek, J., *Trade and Politics in Ancient Greece* (New York, 1965)
Hodge, A.T., *Roman Aqueducts and Water Supply* (London, 1992)
Hodges, H., *Technology in the Ancient World* (Penguin, Harmondsworth, 1970)
Hodson, F.R. and Rowlett, R.M. 'From 600 BC to the Roman Conquest' in *France before the Romans*, S. Piggott, G. Daniel and C. McBurney (ed.) (London, 1973)
Inscriptiones Graecae XIV suppl. (Berlin, 1890; repr. Ares, Chicago, 1978)
Keay, S.J., *Roman Spain* (Berkeley, 1988)
King, A., *Roman Gaul and Germany* (Berkeley, 1990)
MacKendrick, P., *The Iberian Stones Speak* (New York, 1969)
MacKendrick, P., *Roman France* (London, 1971)
Ormerod, H.A., *Piracy in the Ancient World* (Liverpool, 1924; repr. 1978)
Pauly, A. Wissowa, G. and Kroll, W. (ed.), *Real-Encyklopädie der classischen Altertumswissenschaft* (1893 onwards) [abbrev. *RE*]
Richardson, E., *The Etruscans* (Chicago, 1964)

Bibliography

Rostovtzeff, M., *Social and Economic History of the Roman Empire* (2 vols., Oxford, 1957)

Smith, N.A.F., 'Roman canals' in *Trans. Newcomen Soc.* (1977-8) 49: 75-80

Spivey, N. and Stoddart, S., *Etruscan Italy* (London, 1990)

Stillwell, R. (ed.), *Princeton Encyclopedia of Classical Sites* (Princeton, 1976) [abbrev. *PECS*]

von Cles-Reden, S., *The Buried People* (London, 1955) [Etruscans]

Wheeler, M., *Roman Art and Architecture* (London, 1964)

White, K.D., *Greek and Roman Technology* (London, 1984)

Wycherley, R.E., *How the Greeks Built Cities* (London, 1962)

2. Provence in general, and Spain

Bats, M., 'La Provence protohistorique' in *La Provence des origines à l'an mil. Histoire et archéologie*, P.-A. Février (ed.) (Rennes, 1989), 169-256

Bosch-Gimpera, P., 'The Phokaians in the far West', *Classical Outlook* (1994) 38: 53-9

Busquet, R. and Bourilly, V.L., *Histoire de la Provence* (Paris, 1957)

Chevallier, R., *Bibliographie de la Narbonnaise* (*Bulletin de l'Institut d'études latines*, Orléans-Tours, 1971)

Clébert, J.-P., *Provence antique,* vol. I: *Des origines à la conquête romaine* (Paris, 1966)

Clébert, J.-P., *Provence antique,* vol. II: *L'époque gallo-romaine* (Paris, 1970)

Courtin, J., 'Le néolithique de la Provence', *Memoires de la Société préhistorique française* (1974)

Denizot, G., 'Le rivage de Provence et Languedoc au temps des Ligures (1) La côte rocheuse provençale', *REL* (1957), 23: 5-50

Denizot, G., 'Le rivage de Provence et Languedoc au temps des Ligures (2) Les bouches du Rhône et la côte Languedocienne', *REL* (1959), 25: 23-86

Dirkzwager, A., *Strabo über Gallia Narbonensis* (Leiden, 1975)

Ebel, C., *Transalpine Gaul: the emergence of a Roman province* (Leiden, 1976)

Février, P.A., 'La ville antique' in *L'histoire de la France urbaine* I (Paris, 1980)

Février, P.-A., *Le développement urbain en Provence de l'époque romaine à la fin du XIVe siècle* (Boccard, Paris, 1964)

García y Bellido, A., *Hispania Graeca* (3 vols., Barcelona, 1948)

Lamboglia, N., 'Prata Liguriae', *Rivista di Studi Liguri* (1959), 25: 5-22

Lamboglia, N., 'Questioni de topografia antica nelle Alpi maritime', *REL* (1944), 10: 26ff

Lenthéric, C., *The Riviera: ancient and modern* (London, 1895; repr. Chicago, 1976) [abbrev. Lenthéric]

Lenthéric, C., *Les villes mortes du Golfe de Lyon,* (Paris, 3rd edn., 1879)

Lenthéric, C., *La Grèce et l'orient en Provence,* (Paris, 1878)

Lenthéric, C., *La region du Bas Rhône* (Paris, 1881)

Mistral, F., *Trésor du félibrige* (1878) [Provence folklore and sourcebook for Oc (Provençal) language]

Papon, *Histoire de Provence*, vol. IV (Paris, 1777)

Pelletier, A., *Histoire et archéologie de la France ancienne Rhône-Alpes* (Le Coteau-Roanne, 1989)

Rivet, A.L.F., *Gallia Narbonensis* (London, 1988) [abbrev. Rivet]

3. Ancient sources and commentaries

Athenaeus, *The Deipnosophists*, C.B. Gulick (ed.) (6 vols., Loeb edn., London, 1927)

Avienus, *Ora Maritima*, J.P. Murphy (tr.) (Ares Press, Chicago, 1977)

Barruol, G., 'La Gaule méridionale préromaine: points de vue des auteurs anciens', *Doss. Arch.* (1979), 35: 12-20

Berthelot, A., *Festus Avienus, Ora Maritima* (Paris, 1934)

Diodorus Siculus, C.H. Oldfather (ed.) (12 vols., Loeb edn., London, 1968)

Euzennat, M. Salviat, F. and Veyne, P., 'Les scholies bernoises de Lucain, César, et Marseille antique', *Études classiques* (1968-70), 3: 13-24

Müller, K. (ed.), *Geographi Graeci Minores* (3 vols., Paris, 1855; repr. Hildesheim, 1965) [including Scylax, Skymnos, Hanno]

Oikonomides, Al.N. (ed.), *Hanno the Carthaginian: Periplus* (Ares, Chicago, 1977)

Bibliography

Pettorelli, E., *Fonti per la Storia della Colonizzazione Greca nel Mediterraneo Occidentale* (Casa Patron, Bologna, 1962)

Pliny, *Naturalis Historia*, J. André (ed.) (Budé edn., Paris, 1958)

Pliny, *Naturalis Historia*, H. Rackham et al. (ed.) (Loeb edn., London, 1938-43)

Plutarch, *Moralia*, F.C. Babbitt (ed.) (Loeb edn., Cambridge, Mass./London, 1961)

Pomponius Mela, *Chorographie* (Budé edn., Paris, 1988)

Ramin, J., *Le Périple d'Hanno – The Periplus of Hanno* (British Archaeological Reports, suppl. ser. 3, Oxford, 1976)

Rougemont, C. and R., 'Marseille grecque: les textes antiques' in *Marseille grecque: Marseille et la Gaule* (Préactes d'un colloque international d'histoire et d'archéologie; Marseille, 1990)

Rutgers, I. (ed.), *Sextus Julius Africanus, Olympionicorum Fasti*, (1862; repr. Chicago, 1980)

Schulten, A., *Avieno – Ora Maritima* (Barcelona, 2nd edn., 1955)

Stephanus of Byzantium, *Ethnika* (Berlin, 1849; repr. Graz, 1958)

Strabo, *Géographie 3 et 4*, Lasserre, François (ed.) (Budé, Paris, 1966)

Strabo, *Geography 3-4*, H.L. Jones (ed.) (Loeb edn., London, 1922; repr. 1969)

Ugolini, D. and Olive, C., 'Béziers et les côtes languedociennes dans l'*Ora Maritima* d'Avienus', *RAN* (1987), 20: 143-54

Walbank, F.W., *A Historical Commentary to Polybius* (Oxford, 1972-79)

4. Phocaia and Ionia

Akurgal, E., *Ancient Civilizations and Ruins of Turkey* (Istanbul, 6th edn., 1985)

Akurgal, E., 'La Grèce de l'Est' in *Phocée et la fondation de Marseille* (Marseille, 1995)

Keil, J., 'Phokaia', *Real-Encyclopädie der classischen Altertumswissenschaft* (1941), 20,1: 443-8

Langoltz, E., 'Beobachtungen in Phokaia', *Archäologischer Anzeiger* (1969) 84: 377-85

Sartiaux, F., 'Recherches sur le site de l'ancienne Phocie', *Comptes rendus des séances de l'Académie des inscriptions et belles lettres* (1914), January: 6-18

Sartiaux, F., 'Nouvelle recherches sur le site de Phocie', *Comptes rendus des séances de l'Académie des inscriptions et belles lettres* (1921), April: 119-29

de Vita-Evrard, G., 'Vilia et les Phociens au Centre Jean Birard', *P del P* (1970), 290-300

5. Carthage

Asheri, D., 'Carthaginians and Greeks', *Cambridge Ancient History* (Cambridge, 1988), 4: 739-90

Aubet, M.E., *The Phoenicians and the West* (Cambridge, 1993) [tr. from Spanish *Tiro y las Colonias Fenicas de Occidente*, ed. Bellaterra, 1987]

Frèzouls, E., 'Une nouvelle hypothèse sur la fondation de Carthage', *Bulletin de correspondance hellénique* (1955), 79: 153-76

Lancel, S., 'Fouilles françaises à Carthage. La Colline de Byrsa et l'occupation punique VII siècle – 146 av. JC', *Comptes rendus des séances de l'Académie des inscriptions et belles lettres* (1981), 156-93

Moscati, S., *I fenici e Cartagine* (Turin, 1972)

Neimeyer, H.G., *Das frühe Karthago und die phönizische Expansion in Mittelmeerraum* (Göttingen, 1989)

Neimeyer, H.G. (ed.), *Phönizier im Westen* (Mainz, 1982)

Picard, C., 'Les navigations de Carthage vers l'Ouest' in *Phönizier im Westen*, 166-73

Rakob, F., 'Deutsche Ausgrabungen in Karthago. Die punische Befunde', *Römische Mitteilungen* (1984) 91: 1-22

Rakob, F., *Karthago. Die deutschen Ausgrabungen in Karthago*, vol. 1 (Mainz, 1990)

Strager, L.E., 'Excavations at Carthage. The Punic Project: first interim report', *Annual of the American School of Oriental Research* (1978), 43: 151-90

Bibliography

6. Greek colonisation

Almalgo-Gorba, M., 'La colonizacion focense en la péninsula Ibirica: estado actual de la cuestíon' in *I Focei dall'Anatolia all'Oceano* (*P del P*, Transactions of 1982 conference: Velia et les Phocéens: un bilan dix ans après, Naples, 1982)

Benoit, F., *Recherches sur l'hellénisation du Midi de la Gaule* (Publications des annales de la faculté des lettres, Aix-en-Provence, 1965; repr. Lafitte, Marseille, 1980)

Bérard, J., *La colonisation grecque de l'Italie méridionale et de la Sicile dans l'antiquité, l'histoire et la légende* (Paris, 2nd edn., 1957)

Bérard, J., 'L'hellénisation de la Grande Grèce', *Revue Archéologique* (1950) 35: 182-8

Bertoldi, V., 'Antiche correnti di cultura Graeca nel mediterraneo occidentale', *P del P* (1946), 64

Camps, G., 'Navigations et relations interméditerranéennes préhistoriques et protohistoriques', *IX Congrès de Union internationale des sciences préhistoriques et protohistoriques* (1976), colloque II: 168-79

Carpenter, R., *The Greeks in Spain* (Bryn Mawr, 1975)

Langoltz, E., *Die Hellenisierung der Küsten des Mittelmeers durch die Stadt Phokaia* (Cologne, 1966)

Lepore, E., 'Strutture della colonizzazione focea in occidente', *P del P* (1970), 25: 41-54

Morel, J.-P., 'Les Phocéens en occident, certitudes et hypothèses', *P del P* (1966), 21: 378-420, 1008-1100

Morel, J.-P., 'Phocée et ses colonies d'occident' in *Phocée et la fondation de Marseille* (Musées de Marseille, Marseille, 1995)

Morel, J.-P., 'Marseille dans la colonisation phocéenne' in *EM* 3 (1992), 15-25

Morel, J.-P., 'Les Phocéens d'occident: nouvelles données, nouvelles approches' in *I Focei dall'Anatolia all'Oceano* (*P del P*, 1982), 204-7: 479-500

Morel, J.-P., 'L'expansion phocéenne en occident, dix années de recherches', *BCH* (1975) 99: 853-96

Nickels, André, *I Focei dall'Anatolia all'Oceano* (*P del P*, 1982)

Roebuck, C., *Ionian Trade and Colonization* (New York, 1959; repr. Chicago, 1983)

Rouillard, P., 'Les colonies grecques du sud-est de la péninsule Ibérique' in *I Focei dall'Anatolia all'Oceano* (*P del P*, 1982), 417-30

Vallet, G., *Rhégion et Zancle. Histoire, commerce et civilisation des cités chalcidiennes du détroit de Messine* (Paris, 1958), 225-34

7. Navigation

Blackman, D.J., 'Ancient harbours in the Mediterranean', *International Journal of Nautical Archaeology* (1982), 11: 79-104, 185-211

Bourdeaux, C., *Guide du yachtsman en Méditerranée: Marseille-St. Raphael* (Paris, 'École' edn., 1963)

Casson, L., *Ships and Seamanship in the Ancient World* (Princeton, 1971)

Casson, L., 'The feeding of trireme crews', *Transactions of the American Philological Association* (1995), 125: 261-9

Casson, L., 'The *Isis* and her voyage', *Transactions of the American Philological Association* (1950), 81: 43-56

Casson, L., *The Ancient Mariners* (New York, 1959)

Denham, H.M., *The Tyrrhenian Sea: a sea guide to its coasts and islands* (London, 2nd edn., 1978)

Gagé, J., 'Gadès. L'Inde et les navigations atlantiques dans l'antiquité', *Revue historique* (1951) 205: 189-216

Hodge, A.T., 'Massalia, meteorology and navigation', *The Ancient World* (1983), 7: 67-88

Kemp, P. (ed.), *The Oxford Companion to Ships and the Sea* (Oxford, 1976)

Instructions nautiques (Service hydrographique – État-major général de la Marine, Paris, 1913)

Lefebvre des Noettes, R., *De la marine antique à la marine moderne* (Paris, 1935)

Lehman-Harleben, K., *Die antiken Hafenanlagen des Mittelmeers* (Kilio, Beiheft 14, Leipzig, 1923)

Bibliography

Morrison, J.S. and Coates, J.F., *The Athenian Trireme* (Cambridge, 1986)

Morrison, J.S. and Williams, R.T., *Greek Oared Ships* (Cambridge, 1968)

Oleson, J.P., 'The technology of Roman harbours', *International Journal of Nautical Archaeology* (1988), 17: no.2: 147-57

Ponisch, M., 'La navigation antique dans le détroit de Gibraltar' in *Mélanges offerts à Roger Dion*, R. Chevallier (ed.) (Picard, Paris, 1974), 257-73

Rougé, J., 'Routes et ports de la Méditerranée antique', *Rivista di Studi Liguri* (1987), 53: 151-70

Rougé, J., *Ships and Fleets of the Ancient Mediterranean* (tr. S. Frazer from *La marine dans l'antiquité*, Paris, 1975) (Wesleyan Univ. Press, Middletown, Conn., 1981)

Vallet, G. and Villard, F., 'Les Phocéens en Méditerranée occidentale à l'époque archaïque et la fondation d'Hyele' (= Velia), *P del P*, fasc. 108-10 (1966), 166-90

Weather in the Mediterranean (British Meteorological Office, HMSO, London, 1962)

8. Economics, trade and industry

Amouretti, M.-Cl., 'La viticulture antique: contraintes et choix techniques', *Revue des études anciennes* (1988), 90: 5-17

André, J., *L'alimentation et la cuisine à Rome* (Paris, 1981)

Bedon, R., *Les carrières et les carriers de la Gaule romaine* (Paris, 1984)

Benoit, F., 'L'économie du littoral de la Narbonnaise à l'époque antique: le commerce du sel et les pêcheries', *Rivisti di Studi Liguri* (1959), 25: 87-110

Benoit, F., 'L'économie de la Provence – Le grenat des Marseilles et les mines des Maures', *REL* (1960), 26: 221-32

Brun, J.-P., *L'oléiculture antique en Provence* (Paris, 1986)

Chevallier, R., 'Pour un inventaire des carrières antiques de Gaule', *Caesarodunum* (1974), 9: 184-205

Chevallier, R., 'Mines et carrières dans le monde romain', *Caesarodunum* (1979), suppl. 14 (1979)

Davies, O., *Roman Mines in Europe* (Oxford, 1935; repr. Arno, New York, 1979)

Finley, M.I., *The Ancient Economy* (Berkeley, 1973)

Frank, Tenney, *An Economic Survey of Ancient Rome* (4 vols., Baltimore, 1933; repr. Paterson, New York, 1959)

Goudineau, Chr., 'Marseille, Rome and Gaul from the third century to the first century BC' in *Trade in the Ancient Economy*, P. Garnsey, K. Hopkins and C.R. Whittaker (ed.) (1983), 76-86

Grenier, A., 'Roman Gaul' in *An Economic Survey of Ancient Rome* (Baltimore, 1933), 3: 379-644

Grimal, P. and Monod, Th., 'Sur la véritable nature du "garum" ', *Revue des études anciennes* (1952) 54: 27-38

Hodge, A.T., 'A Roman factory', *Scientific American* (1990), 262: 58-64

Labrousse, M., 'Amphores rhodiennes trouvées à Toulouse et Vieille-Toulouse', *RAN* (1971), 4: 35-46

Nenci, G., 'L'allume di Focea', pp. 183-8 in Almalgo-Gorba, 1982: see section 6 above

Nenquin, J., *Salt: a study in economic prehistory* (Bruges, De Temple edn., 1961)

Ponisch, M. and Tarrandell, M., *Garum et industries antiques de salaison dans la Méditerranée occidentale* (Paris, 1965)

Scarborough, J., *Roman Medicine* (London, 1969)

Sellin, R.H.J., 'The large Roman watermill at Barbegal', *History of Technology* (1983), 8: 91-109

Snodgrass, A.M., 'Heavy freight in Archaic Greece' in *Trade in the Ancient Economy*, Garnsey, Peter et al. (ed.) (London, 1983)

9. Wine

André, J., 'La vigne et le vin en Provence dans l'antiquité', *Mélanges E. Bénévent* (1954), 361-8

Billiard, R., *La vigne dans l'antiquité* (Lyons, 1913)

Bouloumié, B., 'Le vin étrusque et la première hellénisation du midi de la Gaule', *Revue des études anciennes* (1981), 32: 75-81

Curtel, G., *La vigne et le vin chez les romains* (Paris, 1903)

Dietler, M., 'Commerce du vin et contacts culturels en Gaule au premier âge du fer', *EM* 3 (1992), 401-10

Dietler, M., 'Driven by drink: the role of drinking in the political economy and the case of Early Iron Age France', *Journal of Anthropology and Archaeology* (1990), 9: 352-406

Dion, R., *Histoire de la vigne et du vin en France* (Paris, 1959)

Heurgon, J., 'Les Lassii Pompéiens et l'importation des vins italiens en Gaule', *P del P* (1952), 7: 113-18

Isnard, H., *La vigne en Algérie*, vol. 2 (Gap, 1955)

Jeanmarie, H., *Dionysos* (Paris, 1951)

Laubenheimer, F., 'Le vin gaulois', *Revue des études anciennes* (1989), 91, 3-4: 5-22

'Le vin de Marseille', *Doss. Arch.* (1990), 154: 96 [bibliography]

Tchernia, A., *Le vin de l'Italie romaine: essai d'histoire économique d'après les amphores* (École française de Rome, Rome, 1986)

Tchernia, A., 'Italian wine in Gaul', *Trade and the Ancient Economy*, P. Garnsey, K. Hopkins and C.R. Whitttaker (ed.) (London, 1983), 87-104

Thévenot, E., 'Les importations vinaires en pays bourguignons avant le développement de la viticulture', *Revue archéologique de l'est et du centre-est consacrée aux antiquités nationales* (1953), 234-9

Villard, P., *Recherches sur l'ivresse dans le monde grec* (Thèse d'état, Université de Provence, Aix-en-Provence, 1988)

10. Tin

Amandry, P., 'Vix et la route d'étain' in *Hommage à J. Carcopino* (Paris, 1977), 13-19

Dayton, J.E., 'The problem of tin in the ancient world', *World Archaeology* (1971), 3: 49-70

Dion, R., 'Le problème des Cassitérides', *Latomus* (1952), 11: 306-14

Earl, B., 'Experimental tin smelting', *HMS News – Journal of the Historical Metallurgical Society* (1922), 22

Mulhy, J.D., *Copper and Tin* (New Haven, 1973)

Mulhy, J.D., 'Sources of tin and the beginnings of bronze metallurgy', *American Journal of Archaeology* (1985), 89.2: 275-91

Penhalurick, R.D., *Tin in Antiquity* (Institute of Metal, London, 1987)

Ramin, J., *Le problème des Cassitérides et les sources de l'étain occidental depuis les temps protohistoriques jusqu'au début de notre ère* (Picard, Paris, 1965)

Willies, Ll., 'Kestel tin: Early Bronze Age mining in Turkey', *HMS News – Journal of the Historical Metallurgical Society* (1922), 22: 3

Yener, K., Aslihan Özbal, H., Kaptan, E. et al., 'Kestel: an Early Bronze Age source of tin ore in the Taurus mountain, Turkey', *Science* (1989), 244: 200-3

11. Underwater archaeology

Benoit, F., *L'épave du grand Congloué à Marseille* (suppl. XIV to *Gallia*, Paris, 1961)

Dioli, P., *Promenades d'archéologie sous-marine* (Paris, 1952)

Hesnard, A., 'Nouvelles recherches sur les épaves préromaines en baie de Marseille', *EM* 3 (1992), 233-43

Lamboglia, N., 'Il relevamento totale della nave romana di Albegna', *Rivista di Studi Liguri* (1961), 27: 213-20

Liou, B., 'Recherches sous-marines', *Gallia* (1973), 31: 579-89

Liou, B., 'Recherches sous-marines', *Gallia* (1975), 33: 578-84

Liou, B. and Gassend, J.-M., 'L'épave Saint Gervais 3 à Fos-sur-mer (milieu du Ie siècle ap. J.-C. Inscriptions peintes sur amphores de Bétique. Vestiges de la coque', *Archaeonautica* (1990), 10: 157ff

Long, Luc et al, 'Les épaves archaïques de la Pointe Lequin (Porquerolles, Hyères, Var)', *EM* 3 (1992), 199-234

Tchernia, A., 'Directions des recherches archéologiques sous-marines', *Gallia* (1969), 27: 465-99

Weiss, I., 'Fossae', *Real-Encyclopädie der classischen Altertumswissenschaft* 7.1: 74-6

12. Linguistics

Bats, M., 'La logique de l'écriture d'une société à l'autre en Gaule Méridionale protohistorique', *RAN* (1988), 21: 121-48

Bertoldi, V., *Colonizzazioni dell'antico Mediterraneo occidentale alla luce degli aspetti linguistici* (Naples, 1950)

Dauzat, A., *Les noms de lieux* (Paris, 1937)

Duval, P.M., *Recueil des inscriptions Gauloises* (suppl. XLV to *Gallia*, Paris, CNRS edn., 1985)

Hatt, J.J., 'Répartition des mots d'origine hellénique en France', *Revue archéologique de l'est et du centre-est consacrée aux antiquités nationales* (1955), 6: 147-50

Lambert, P.-Y., 'La diffusion de l'écriture gallo-grecque en milieu indigène', *EM* 3 (1992), 289-94

Laubenheimer, F., 'De l'usage populaire de l'écriture grecque dans la Gaule du centre-est', *Revue des études anciennes* (1987), 38: 163-7

Lejeune, M. 'Textes gallo-grecs' in *Recueil des inscriptions gauloises* 1, P.M. Duval (ed.) (suppl. XLV to *Gallia*, Paris, CNRS edn., 1985)

Rostaign, C., *Essai sur la toponymie de la Provence* (Paris, 1950)

Vertold, V., 'Contatti e conflitti di lingue del antico Mediterraneo', *P del P* (1953), 33: 407-48

von Wartburg, W., *Évolution et structure de la langue française* (Paris, 1934)

13. Coinage

Brenot, C., 'Le monnayage de Marseille au Ve s. av. J.-C.', *EM* 3 (1992), 245-53

Brenot, C., 'La monnaie de Marseille', *Doss. Arch.* (1990), 154: 88-93

Colbert de Beaulieu, J-B., *Traité de numismatique celtique* I (Paris, 1973)

Duval, P.M., 'A propos de la signification des images monétaires gaulois', *Comptes rendus de l'Académie des inscriptions et belles lettres* (1975), 241-55

Furtwangler, A.E., *Monnaies grecques en Gaule. Le trésor d'Auriol et le monnayage de Massalia 525/520-460 av. J.-C.* (Office du livre, Fribourg, 1978)

Head, B.V., *Historia Numorum* (Oxford, 1911; repr. Spink, London, 1963)

Richard, J.-C., 'La diffusion des monnayages massaliètes au delà du territoire de Marseille' in *EM* 3 (1992), 255-60

Rolland, H., *Monnaies gallo-grecques* (Congresso internazionale di numismatica, Roma, 1961)

Seltman, C., *Greek Coins* (Methuen, London, 1933; repr. Spink, London, 1977)

Massalia
14.1. Archaeology

Arcelin, P., 'Les amphores de Marseille grecque: chronologie et diffusion (VI-I s. av. J.-C.)', *EM* 2 (1990), 191-2

Bats, M. and Triziny, H. (ed.), *EM* 2 (Travaux de centre Camille Jullian, Université de Provence, Aix-en-Provence, 1990)

Bats, M., *Les amphores de Marseille grecque: chronologie et diffusion (VIe-Ier siècles avant J.-C.: confrontation chronologique* (Actes de la table ronde de Valbonne, 11-13 novembre 1986, Paris, CNRS edn, 1990)

Benoit, F., 'Roman "docks" ', *Gallia* (1948), 6: 208

Benoit, F., 'Roman "docks" ', *Gallia* (1960), 18: 286-8

Benoit, F., 'Le chapiteau ionique de Marseille', *Revue archéologique* (1954), 1: 17-43

Bertucchi, G. et al., 'Les fouilles de la bourse à Marseille (1975-76)', *RAN* (1977), 10: 235-46

Bertucchi, G. and Salviat, F., 'Un monument méconnu de Massalia: les caves de "Saint Sauveur", citernes-fontaines de la cité antique', *Archéologie du midi méditerranéen* (1981), 3: 8-17

Bibliography

Demians d'Archimbaud, G., 'Les fouilles de Saint-Victor', *Comptes rendus des séances de l'Académie des inscriptions et belles lettres* (1971), 87-117

Euzennat, M. and Salviat, F., *Les découvertes archéologiques de la bourse à Marseille* (Marseille, 1969)

Euzennat, M., 'Ancient Marseille in the light of recent excavations', *American Journal of Archaeology* (1980), 84: 133-40

Gantès, L.-F., 'Massalia retrouvée', *Doss. Arch.* (1990), 154: 14-21

Grosson, J-B., *Recueil des antiquités et monuments marseillais qui peuvent intéresser l'histoire et les arts* (Marseille, 1773)

Guery, R., 'Le port antique de Marseille', *EM* 3 (1992), 110-21

Le musée d'histoire de Marseille: l'antiquité (Marseille, 1988) [catalogue]

Martin, R., 'Chapiteau ionique d'Halicarnasse', *Revue des études archéologiques* (1959), 61: 65-76

Moliner, M., 'La plus ancienne adduction d'eau de Marseille grecque', *Doss. Arch.* (1990), 154: 42-3

Py, M., 'La diffusion des amphores massaliètes sur le littoral du Languedoc oriental', *EM* 2 (1992), 73-86

Rolland, H., 'Fouilles à Marseille dans le quartier du Vieux-Port', *Gallia* (1947), 5: 155-60

Sciallano, M. and Sibella, P., *Amphores: comment les identifier?* (Edisud, Aix-en-Provence, 2nd edn., 1994)

Tréziny, H., 'Les fortifications grecques', *Doss. Arch.* (1990), 154: 22-5

Tréziny, H., 'Cité et territoire: quelques problèmes', *EM* 1 (Université de Provence, Aix-en-Provence, 1985), 7-15

Tréziny, H., 'Les fortifications de Marseille grecque', *EM* 3 (1992), 89-107

Tréziny, H., 'Métrologie, architecture et urbanisme dans le monde Massaliète', *RAN* (1989), 22: 1-46

Trousset, P., 'L'eau à Marseille dans l'antiquité', *Doss. Arch.* (1990), 154: 34-5

Villard, P., *La céramique grecque de Marseille (VIe-IVe siècle)* (Bibliothèque des écoles d'Athènes et de Rome, Paris, 1960) [p. 143 – corpus of ancient texts on tin; abbrev. Villard]

Villard, P., 'La céramique archaïque de Marseille', *EM* 3 (1992), 164-70

14.2 Territory and topography

Arcelin, P., 'Le territoire de Marseille grecque dans son contexte indigène', *EM* 1 (1985) 43-104

Barroul, G., 'Le territoire des Albiques', *REL* (1958), 24: 228-56

Bats, M., 'Marseille, les colonies et les relais indigènes', *EM* 3 (1992), 263-78

Bats, M., 'Le territoire de Marseille grecque: réflexions et problèmes', *EM* 1 (1985), 17-42

Bellet, M., *Guide archéologique des rives de l'Étang de Berre* (Aix-en-Provence, Edisud edn., 1979)

Benoit, F., 'L'evolution topographique de Marseille', *Latomus* (1972) 31: 54-70

Benoit, F., 'Topographie antique de Marseille: le théâtre et le mur de Crinias', *Gallia* (1966), 24: 1-22

Brunel, J., 'Étienne de Byzance et le domaine Marseillais', *Revue des études anciennes* (1945), 122-33

Euzennat, M. and Salviat, F., 'Sur un passage de César et la topographie de Marseille pré-romaine', *BC* II 1, Ann. Fac. Lettres d'Aix-en-Provence (1967), 179-83

Gantès, L.-F., 'La topographie de Marseille grecque: bilan de recherches (1829-1991)', *EM* 3 (1992), 71-88

Guery, R., Pirazzoli, P. and Trousset, P., 'Les variations du niveau de la mer depuis l'antiquité à Marseille et à la Couronne', Doss. Arch. (1981), 154: 8-27

Hesnard, A., 'Marseille et la mer', *Doss. Arch.* (1990), 154: 50-7

Jullian, C., 'Le port du Lacydon et le ruisseau sacré de Marseille', *Provincia* (1921), 1: 1-6

Liou, B. 'Les découvertes archéologiques du Golfe de Fos et les traces du littoral antique', *Déplacements des lignes de rivage en Méditerranée* (Colloques de CNRS, Aix-en-Provence, 1985, Paris, 1987)

Morel, J.-P., 'Le "domaine" de Marseille', *P del P* (1966), 30: 114, n. 99

Morel, J.-P., 'A la recherche d'un territoire: le cas de Marseille', *EM* 1 (1985), 161-78

Bibliography

14.3 Foundation and history

Brunel, J., 'Marseille et les fugitifs de Phocée', *Revue des études anciennes* (1948), 50: 2-26

Busquet, R., *Histoire de Marseille* (Paris, 1945)

Clavel-Lévêque, M., *Marseille grecque* (Marseille, 1977) [expanded from article in *Hellenische Poleis* (Berlin 1974); abbrev. MC-L]

Clerc, M., *Massilia: histoire de Marseille dans l'antiquité* (2 vols., Marseille, 1927) [abbrev. Clerc]

d'Arnaud, B., *Evocation de vieux Marseille* (Paris, 1959)

Escalon de Fonton, M. et al., *Naissance d'une ville: Marseille* (Aix-en-Provence, 1979)

Goudineau, Chr., 'Marseille, Rome and Gaul from the third century to the first century BC' in *Trade in the Ancient Economy*, P. Garnsey, K. Hopkins and C.R. Whittaker (ed.) (London, 1983)

Gras, M., 'A propos de la "bataille" d'Alalia', *Latomus* (1972), 31: 698-716

Jacob, J.-P. and Morel, J.-P. et al., 'Marseille dans le monde antique', *Doss. Arch.* (1990), 154: 2-96

Jehasse, J., 'La "Victoire à la Cadméenne" d'Hérodote et la Corse', *Revue des études anciennes* (1962), 64: 241-86

Morel-Deledalle, M., *Naissance d'une ville: Marseille grecque* (Editions Edisud, Aix-en-Provence, 1979)

Nenci, G., 'Le relazioni con Marsiglia nella politica estera Romana', *REL* (1958), 24: 25-47

Ruffi, A. de, *Histoire de la ville de Marseille* (2 vols., Marseille, 1996)

Salviat, F., 'Marseille grecque' in *Histoire de Marseille*, E. Baratier (ed.) (Toulouse, 1973)

Ternaux, H., *Historia Reipublicae Massiliensium* (Goettingen, 1826; repr. Chicago, 1974) [abbrev. Ternaux]

Vasseur, G., *L'origine de Marseille* (Annales du Musée de l'histoire naturelle de Marseille, 1914)

14.4. Culture and exploration

Bommelaer, J.F., *Guides de Delphes* (École française d'Athènes, Paris, 1991) [for Massaliot treasury at Delphi]

Daux, G., 'Notes de lecture', *Bulletin de correspondance hellénique* (1958), LXXXII: 360-4 [identification and date of the Treasury of Massalia at Delphi]

Davin, E., 'Euthymènes le Massaliote', *Bulletin de l'Association G. Budé* (1955), 2: 17-32

Gisinger, F., 'Pytheas von Massalia', *Real-Encyclopädie der classischen Altertumswissenschaft* (1963), 24: 314-66

Hawkes, C.F.C., *Pytheas: Europe and the Greek Explorers* (The Eighth J.L. Myers Memorial Lecture, Oxford, 1975)

Lallemand, F., *Le journal de bord de Pythias* (Paris, France-Empire edn., 1974)

Mette, H.J., *Pytheas von Massalia* (Berlin, 1952)

Roseman, Christina Horst, *Pytheas of Massalia* (Ares, Chicago, 1994)

Salviat, F., 'Sur la réligion de Marseille grecque' *EM* 3, (1992), 142-50

Scolardi, P., *Marseille la grecque* (Marseille, 1975)

Stichtenhoth, D., *Pytheas von Marseille über das weltmeer* (Weimar, 1959)

14.5. Trade and industry

Bats, M., 'Commerce et politique massiliètes au IV et III siècles avant Jésus Christ' in *I Focei dall'Anatolia all'Oceano* (*P del P*, Transactions of 1982 conference: Velia et les Phocéens: un bilan dix ans après, Naples, 1982)

Bertucchi, G., 'Les amphores et le vin de Marseille, VI s. av. J.-C. - II s. ap. J.C.', *RAN* (1992), suppl. 25

Busquet, R., *Histoire du commerce de Marseille* (Paris, 1949)

Fabre, P., 'Les Massaliotes et l'Atlantique' in *107th Congrès national de sociétés savantes d'archéologie* (Brest, 1982)

Gantès, L.-F., 'L'apport des fouilles récentes à l'étude quantitative de l'économie Massaliète', *EM* 3 (1992), 171-8

Bibliography

Levy, M., 'Le grenat de Marseilles', *Revue des études anciennes* (1907), 287ff

Liou, B. and Morel, M., 'L'Orge des Cavares: une amphorette à inscription peinte trouvée dans le port antique de Marseille', *RAN* (1977), 10: 189-97

Pomy, P. and Long, L., 'Les prémiers échanges maritimes du midi de la Gaule du VIe au IIe s. av. J.-C.', *EM* 3 (1992), 189-98

Rouillard, P., 'La place de Marseille dans le commerce des vases attiques à figures rouges en Méditerranée occidentale (Ve-IVe s. av. J.-C.)', *EM* 3 (1992), 179-87

14.6. Relations with the Celts

Arcelin, P., 'L'environment indigène de Marseille grecque', *Doss. Arch.* (1990), 154: 58-69

Arcelin, P., 'Société indigène et propositions culturelles Massaliotes en basse Provence occidentale', *EM* 3 (1992), 305-36

Benoit, F., 'Les relations de Marseille grecque avec le monde occidental', *Rivista di Studi Liguri* (1956), 22: 5-32

Brun, P., 'L'influence grecque sur la société celtique non-méditerranéenne', *EM* 3 (1992), 389-99

Busquet, R., 'Marseille: a-t-elle ou n'a-t-elle pas civilisé la Gaule?', *Revue historique* (1954), 211: 1-10

Cunliffe, B., *Greeks, Romans and Barbarians* (London, 1988)

Gantès, L.-F., in *Marseille grecque: Marseille et la Gaule: Préactes d'un colloque international d'histoire et d'archéologie*, A. Guilcher and M. Pagni (ed.) (Marseille, 1990)

Goudineau, Chr., 'Marseille et la Gaule: en guise de conclusion générale', *EM* 3 (1992), 451-6

Gros, P., 'Nature et signification de l'hellénisme glanique', *EM* 3 (1992), 373-4

Leveque, P., 'Les populations indigènes de la Gaule et les Grecs', *EM* 3 (1992), 383-8

Nickels, A., 'Les Grecs en Gaule: l'exemple du Languedoc' in *Actes du colloque de Cortone* (24-30 May 1981; Coll. Ec. Franç. de Rome 67, 1983), 404-28

15. Agde

Jully, J. et al., *Agde antique* (Pézenas, 1978)

Nickels, A., 'Agde grecque: les recherches recentes', *P del P* (1982), 104-7: 269-79

Nickels, A. and Marchand, G., 'Recherches stratigraphiques ponctuelles à proximité des remparts antiques d'Agde', *RAN* (1976), 9: 45-62

16. Ampurias

Maluquer de Motes, J., 'Emporion [Ampurias]' in *PECS*, R. Stillwell (ed.) (Princeton, 1976), 303

Perilló, E.R., *Ampurias* (Barcelona, 6th edn., 1979)

Sanmartí-Grego, E., 'Les influences méditerranéennes au nord-est de la Catalogne à l'époque archaïque et la réponse indigène' in *I Focei dall'Anatolia all'Oceano* (*P del P*, Naples, 1982), 204-7: 281-98

Sanmartí-Grego, E., 'Massalia at Emporion', *EM* 3 (1992), 27-41

17. Arles

Amy, R., 'Arelate' in *PECS*, R. Stillwell (ed.) (Princeton, 1976), 87

Benoit, F., 'Le sanctuaire d'Auguste et les cryptoportiques d'Arles', *Revue archéologique* (1952), 39: 31-67

Constans, L.A., *Arles antique* (Boccard, Paris, 1921)

Gauthier, M., 'Arles (esplanade site)', *Gallia* (1986), 44: 388-402

Roquette, M. and Sintes, C., *Arles antique* (Guides archéologiques de la France, no. 17, Paris, 1989)

Bibliography

18. Glanum

Bessac, J.-C. and Lambert, N., 'La pierre à Glanum', *Doss. Arch.* (1989), 140: 8-15

Bouison, M., 'Architecture et décor des maisons', *Doss. Arch.* (1989), 140: 52-8

Brenot, C., 'La "drachme" de Glanum', *Doss. Arch.* (1989), 140: 75ff

Gros, P. and V., 'Le forum et la basilique de Glanum: problèmes de chronologie et de restitution', *Gallia* (1984), 42: 21-52

Rolland, H., 'Fouilles de Glanum', *Gallia* (1946)

Rolland, H., 'Fouilles de Glanum (1947-56)', *Gallia* (1958)

Rolland, H., 'Fouilles de Glanum', *Gallia* (1967), 25: 407

Rolland, H., 'Fouilles de Glanum', *RAN* (1968), 1: 93-9

Rolland, H., 'Fouilles de Glanum', *Gallia* (1969)

Rolland, H., 'Le mausolée de Glanum', *Gallia* (1969)

Rolland, H., 'Sculptures héllenistiques découvertes à Glanum', *Comptes rendus de l'Académie des inscriptions et belles lettres* (1968), 94-114

Rolland, H., 'Sculptures à figures découvertes à Glanum', *Comptes rendus de l'Académie des inscriptions et belles lettres* (1968), 111-19

Roth Congès, A., 'Le centre monumental de Glanon', *EM* 3 (1992), 351-67; 473

Salviat, F., *Glanum et les antiques* (Guides archéologiques de la France, no. 19, Paris, 1990)

Salviat, F., 'Un image de l'Afrique sur un chapiteau à figures de Glanum', *RAN* (1972), 5: 21-30

19. Lattes

Arnal, J., Majurel, R. and Prades, H., *Le Port de Lattera* (Bordighera/Montpellier, 1974)

Py, M. and Garcia, D., 'Bilan des recherches archéologiques sur la ville portuaire de Lattara (Lattes, Mirault)', *Gallia* (1993), 50: 1-93 [summary in English]

Py, M. (ed.), *Lattara* (Association pour la recherche archéologique en Languedoc oriental, route de Pérols, F34970, Lattes; series of volumes, five up to 1992)

20. St Blaise

Bouloumié, B., *Guide archéologique de St Blaise* (Rognes-Marseille, 1980)

Bouloumié, B., 'Un oppidum Gauloise à St Blaise en Provence/ Saint Blaise: oppidum du sel', *Doss. Arch.* (1984), 84: 5-96

Bouloumié, B., *St Blaise* (Marseille, Provence edn., 1980)

Bouloumié, B., *Saint Blaise: L'habitat protohistorique; les céramiques grecques* (Travaux du Centre Camille Jullian 13 – Université de Provence, Aix-en-Provence, 1992)

Bouloumié, B., 'Saint-Blaise: note sommaire sur cinq années de fouilles et de recherches (1974-1978)', *Gallia* (1979), 37: 229-36

Rolland, H., *Fouilles de St.-Blaise* (Martigues, 1967)

Rolland, H., 'Fouilles de St.-Blaise', *Gallia* (1951), suppl. 2

Rolland, H., 'Fouilles de St.-Blaise', *Gallia* (1956), suppl. 7

Treziny, H., 'Rémarques sur la fonction du rempart hellénistique de Saint-Blaise', *EM* 1 (1985), 145-51

21. Corsica

Battesti, M.J., 'Étude biométrique de colonies d'abeilles Corses', *Bulletin de la Société des sciences historiques et naturelles de la Corse* (1983), fasc. 644, 73-98

Jehasse, J., 'Les fouilles d'Aléria', *Gallia* (1963), 21: 77-109

Jehasse, J. and L., *Aléria antique* (Les Amis d'Aléria, Lyon, 2nd edn., 1991) [local guidebook – first edition printed in 1982]

Jehasse, J., *Corsica Classica* (ed. La Marge, Ajaccio, 1986)

Simi, P., *Précis de géographie de la Corse* (Bastia, 1981)

Bibliography

22. Tauroentum

Brien, Fr., 'A Tauroentum (Le Brusc) des recherches ... vaines', *Doss. Arch.* (1981), 57: 31
[short note]
Duprat, E., *Tauroentum* (Marseille, 1935)
Marin, V., *Mémoire sur l'ancienne ville de Tauroentum* (Marseille, 1781; repr. Aubagne, 1973)

23. Olbia

Coupry, J., 'Les fouilles d'Olbia', *Doss. Arch.* (1981), 57: 29-31
Coupry, J., 'Fouilles à Olbia', *Gallia* (1954), 12: 3-33
Coupry, J., 'Les fouilles d'Olbia', *Comptes rendus de l'Académie des inscriptions et belles lettres* (1964), 313-21

24. Lerin Islands

Vindry, G., 'L'Acropole de Lero à l'Ile Sainte Marguerite', *Doss. Arch.* (1981), 57: 62-6

25. Antibes

Clergues, J.H., *Antibes: la ville grecque du IV siècle avant J.-C. et l'habitat protohistorique* (Antibes, 1969)
Cosson, P., *Civitas Antipolitana* (Serre Editeur, Nice, 1995)
Février, P.-A., 'Plans antiques de Fréjus et d'Antibes', *Gallia* (1959), 17: 207-13
Morena, M. and Counord, D., *Antipolis Municipe Romain* (Musée d'histoire et d'archéologie, Antibes, 1994)
Muterse, E. and Ménêtrier, *Antibes: introduction historique* (1939; repr. Chicago, 1975)
Raymond, V. and Schroder, S.J., 'Ancient Antipolis in Southern France', *Ancient World* (1983), 89-98
Rouselle, A., Rogers, G. and Olivier, A., 'Le monument romain de Vaugrenier', *RAN* (1978), 11: 143-94
Violino, J.-P., 'Antibes', *Archéologie du midi méditerranéen* (1983), 8: 9-88
Violino, J.-P., 'Antibes et sa vocation maritime à l'époque romaine', *L'exploitation de la mer de l'antiquité à nos jours* (Vième rencontres internationales d'archéologie et d'histoire d'Antibes, Juan-les-Pins, 1986)

26. Nice

Benoit, F., *Le Cimiez antique* (Paris, 1977)
Bordes, M. (ed.), *Histoire de Nice et du pays niçois* (Toulouse, 1976)
Mouchot, D., *Nice-Cimiez, Le Musée d'archéologie* (Nice, 1989)
Mouchot, D., 'Les fouilles de Cimiez', *Doss. Arch.* (1981), 57: 55-61
Tisserand, E., *Histoire civile et réligieuse de la cité de Nice et du département des Alpes-Maritimes* (Nice, 1862; repr. Marseille 1973)

27. La Turbie

Formigé, J., *La Trophie des Alpes* (*Gallia*, suppl. 11, Paris, 1949)

28. Others

Aubenas, J.A., *Histoire de Fréjus* (Fréjus, 1886)
Brun, J.-P., 'Le village Massaliote de La Galère à Porquerolles (Var), et la géographie des Stoechades, an Ier s. av. J.-C.', *EM* 3 (1992), 279-88
Clavel, M., *Béziers et son territoire dans l'antiquité* (Paris, 1970)
Donnadieu, A., *La Pompeii de la Provence: Fréjus* (Paris, 1927)

303

Dugand, J.-E., *De l'Aegitna de Polybe au trophée de la Brague* (Faculté des lettres et sciences humaines de Nice, Paris, 1970)

Maluquer de Motes, J., 'Rhode' in *PECS*, R. Stillwell (ed.) (Princeton, 1976) 754

Mouquet, J., 'Les Stoechades sont-elles nos îles d'Hyères?', *Revue archéologique* (1925), 22: 95-104

Oikonomides, Al. N., 'Athenopolis Massiliensium and Saint Tropez', *Ancient World* (1978), 1.1: 33-44

Reymond, G. and Dugand, J.-E., *Monaco antique* (Publications de la faculté des lettres et sciences humaines de Nice, Paris, 1970)

29. Celtic civilisation and culture

Arcelin, P., 'Croyances et vie religieuse', *Doss. Arch.* (1979), 35: 99-107

Barroul, G., *Les peuples préromains du sud-est de la Gaule: étude de géographie historique* (Paris, 1969)

Benoit, F., *Arts et dieux de la Gaule* (Paris, 1969)

Benoit, F., 'La Barbarie Ligure' *REL* (1962), 28: 117-24

Benoit, F., 'Autour du cratère Vix. La voie du Rhône Rhodania', *Revue archéologique* (1956), 31: 15-18

Chevallier, R., *Les Ligures* (suppl. 34 to *Caesarodunum*, Tours, 1980)

Dillan, M. and Chadwick, N., *The Celtic Realms* (New York, 1967)

Dinsmoor, W.B., *The Architecture of Ancient Greece*, vol. 3 (London, 1950)

Dupuich, J.J., 'De Giens à Vix: une antique voie commerciale', *Caesarodunum* (1977), 1: 129-31

Duval, P.M., *Les dieux de la Gaule* (Paris, 2nd edn., 1976)

Fiches, J.-L., 'Habitat et fortifications: la civilisation des oppida', *Doss. Arch.* (1979), 35: 67-75

Gruel, K., *La monnaie chez les Gaulois* (Paris, Errance edn., 1989)

Guilaine, J., 'Les débuts de la métallurgie dans le Midi de la France et en Italie du Nord', *IX Congrès de l'Union internationale des sciences préhistoriques et protohistoriques* (1976), 46-79

Hatt, J.J., *Mythes et dieux de la Gaule* (Paris, 1989)

Jullian, C., *Histoire de la Gaule* (Paris, 1908)

Lumley-Woodyear, H. de, *Le paléolithique inférieur et moyen du Midi méditerranéen dans son cadre géologique* (2 vols., CNRS, Paris, 1969)

Powell, T.G.E., *The Celts* (London/New York, 1958)

Ramin, J., 'L'éspace économique en Gaule: les documents concernant les mines', *Mélanges offerts à Roger Dion* (Picard, Place, 1974), 417-37

Rankin, H.D., *Celts and the Classical World* (London, 1987)

Salviat, F., 'La sculpture préromaine en Provence', *Doss. Arch.* (1979), 35: 31-51

Tréziny, H., 'Sur quelques problèmes d'architecture et d'urbanisme en Gaule méridionale', *EM* 3 (1992), 337-49

[various authors], 'Les Ibères', *Doss. Arch.* (1997) 228 [esp. Rouillard, P., 'Les Ibères et leurs partenaires méditerranéens', pp. 14-21]

30. Ambrussum

Fiches, J.-L., 'Ambrussum et la voie Domitienne', *Rivista di Studi Liguri* (1980), 46: 132-57

Fiches, J.-L., *Les maisons gallo-romaines d'Ambrussum* (Paris, 1986)

Fiches, J.-L. (ed.), *L'oppidum d'Ambrussum et son territoire* (Monographie du CNRS no. 2, Paris, 1989)

31. Ensérune

Gallet de Santerre, H., 'Ensérune', *Archaeology* (1962) 15: 163-71

Gallet de Santerre, H., *Ensérune: les silos de la terrace est* (Paris, 1980)

Gallet de Santerre, H., 'Ensérune, an oppidum in Southern France', *Archaeology* (1962), 15: 163-71

Bibliography

Gallet de Santerre, H., 'Fouilles dans le quartier ouest d'Ensérune', *RAN* (1968), 1: 39-83

Jannoray, J., 'Ensérune', *Bibliothèque des Ecoles Françaises d'Athènes et de Rome* (2 vols., 1955)

Jannoray, J., *Ensérune. Contribution à l'étude des civilisations préromaines de la Gaule méridionale* (Paris, 1955)

32. Entremont

Arcelin, P., 'L'habitat d'Entremont: urbanisme et modes architecturaux', *Archéologie d'Entremont au Musée Granet* (Aix-en-Provence, 1987), 56-98

Benoit, F., *Entremont – Capitale celto-ligure des Salyens de Provence* (Aix-en-Provence, 1957)

Benoit, F., *Entremont, capitale celto-ligure des Salyens de Provence* (Gap, 1965)

Coutagne, D., *Archéologie d'Entremont au Musée Granet* (Aix-en-Provence, 1987)

Salviat, F., *Entremont antique* (Aix-en-Provence, 1973)

33. Nages

Py, F. and Py, M., 'Contribution à l'étude des remparts de Nages, Gard', *RAN* (1969), 2: 97-121

Py, M., 'Nages' in *PECS* (1976), 604-5

Py, M., *L'oppidum des Castels à Nages* (suppl. 35 to *Gallia*, 1978)

34. Other Celtic sites

Boissinot, Ph., 'Le Baou-Roux et le problème du territoire de Marseille', *EM* 1, M. Bats and H. Triziny (ed.) (Actes de la Table Ronde, 16 March 1985, Université de Provence, Aix-en-Provence, 1986)

de Gérin-Richard, H., 'Le sanctuaire préromain de Roquepertuse', *Centenaire de la Société d'histoire, de statistique et d'archéologie de Marseille* (Marseille, 1927)

Goudineau, Chr., 'Une enceinte protohistorique: l'oppidum du Fort à Taradeau (Var)', *IX Congrès de l'Union internationale des sciences préhistoriques et protohistoriques* (Nice, 1976), 7-32

Joffroy, R., 'Le trésor de Vix', *Monuments Piot* (1954), 48: 1-68

Joffroy, R., *Vix et ses trésors* (Paris, 1979)

Lantier, R., 'Le sanctuaire de Roquepertuse', *Archäologische Anzeiger* (1929), 281-92

Nickels, A., 'Les maisons à abside d'époque grecque archaïque de la Monédière, à Bessan (Hérault)', *Gallia* (1976), 34: 95-128

Salviat, F. and Barroul, G. (ed.), *Provence et Languedoc Méditerranéen: sites protohistoriques et gallo-romains* (USIPP Livret-Guides C3, Nice, 1976)

Tenevin, J.-P., *Le Baou-Roux, oppidum celto-ligure* (Aix-en-Provence, 1972)

35. Roman Gaul

Barroul, G. and Martel, P., 'La voie romaine de Cavaillon à Sisteron', *REL* (1962), 28: 125-202

Benoit, F., 'L'usine de meunerie hydrolique de Barbégal (Arles)', *Revue archéologique* (1940), 15: 42-80

Berthelot, A.,'Questions hannibaliques: les éléphants d'Hannibal au Mont Cenis', *Revue des études anciennes* (1936), 35-8

Brogan, O., *Roman Gaul* (London, 1953)

Bromwich, J., *The Roman Remains of Southern France* (Routledge, London/New York, 1993) [see section 2 above]

Chevallier, R., *Roman Roads* (London, 1976)

Clemente, G., *I Romani nella Gallia meridionale* (Il mondo antico II, Bologna, 1974)

Clerc, M., *Aquae Sextiae* (Aix-en-Provence, 1916)

Constans, L.A., *Guide illustré des campagnes de César en Gaule* (Paris, 1929)

Desjardins, E., *Géographie politique et administrative de la Gaule romaine* (Paris, 1978-93)

Drinkwater, J.F., *Roman Gaul* (London/Canberra, 1983)

Euzennat, M., 'L'époque romaine', *Histoire de Marseille*, Privat, Toulouse, 1973)

Bibliography

Grenier, A., *La France gallo-romaine* (Paris, 1991)

Hall, W.H., *The Romans on the Riviera and the Rhône* (London, 1898; repr. Chicago, 1974)

Heurgon, J., *Rome et la Méditerranée occidentale jusqu'aux guerres puniques* (Paris, 1969)

Lerat, L., *La Gaule romaine* (Paris, 2nd edn., 1986)

MacKendrick, P., *Roman France* (London, 1971)

Williams-Thorpe, O., 'Provenance and archaeology of Roman millstones from the Mediterranean area', *Journal of Archaeological Science* (1988), 15: 253-305

306

Index

Principal references are given in bold type, e.g. **123**.

307